Whom Shal

Pushing the Politics of Change

Ewart F. Brown, M.D.

Premier of Bermuda 2006-2010

Rivertowns
BOOKS

Printed in the United States of America · February 2022 · I

ISBN-13: 978-0-9790080-2-3
LCCN Imprint Name: Rivertowns Books

Rivertowns Books are available from Amazon, B&N.com, and other online merchants, as well as from bookstores and other retailers. Requests for information and other correspondence may be addressed to:

Rivertowns Books
240 Locust Lane
Irvington NY 10533
Email: info@rivertownsbooks.com

To my parents, D. A. and Helene Brown

THE LORD IS MY LIGHT AND MY SALVATION; whom shall I fear? The Lord is the strength of my life; of whom shall I be afraid?

When the wicked, even mine enemies and foes, came upon me to eat up my flesh, they stumbled and fell.

Though an host should encamp against me, my heart shall not fear; though war should rise against me, in this will I be confident.

One thing have I desired of the Lord, that will I seek after; that I may dwell in the house of the Lord all the days of my life . . .

Psalms 27:1-4 (KJV)

Contents

Part Four: The Battle Continues

Preface to the Paperback Edition

THIS BOOK'S ORIGINAL HARDCOVER EDITION was published at the end of 2019, on the eve of the COVID-19 pandemic. As my publisher brings out this paperback edition, Bermuda, like the rest of the world, continues to experience the pandemic's impact, and my first thoughts are for all those, especially fellow Bermudians, whose lives have been damaged or cut short by the pandemic and their families. I am thankful that most Bermudians over 65 have been vaccinated, but too many younger Bermudians have not.

The pandemic has taken a heavy toll on Bermuda economically, undermining efforts to renew our tourism sector. Competitive destinations are doing better than we are at bringing travelers back. One very salient issue in this context is that there is still no casino gaming in Bermuda. I tabled the first Parliamentary paper on gaming, to enable it on cruise ships in port, in 2009, and a more substantive paper supporting onshore gaming in 2010, evoking fierce criticism from my political opponents, as you'll read in the book. The One Bermuda Alliance (OBA) Government of 2012-2017 passed the necessary legislation for gaming in 2014, but failed to get it started. Likewise, the Progressive Labour Party (PLP) Government, elected in July 2017 and returned with a 30-6 majority in a snap election in October 2020, has not yet been able to make gaming a reality. It all speaks to the difficulty of substantive change.

A serious new problem also looms for Bermuda's financial services sector. In the past year, a global corporate minimum tax regime has begun to take shape. What this will mean for Bermuda remains to be seen, but the consequences for domiciling subsidiaries of American and other foreign companies will likely be major. Bermuda's public and private sector leaders should be game-planning scenarios to prepare the country to adapt as resiliently as possible.

Meeting these challenges and others this book considers will require much creativity, energy, and determination. A small country like Bermuda, where a legacy of racism and colonialism still forces many of our best and brightest young people to make their careers abroad, never suffers from an overabundance of talent and experience. But I believe we have the ability to adapt, if we can find the will to change. Without the drive to shake things up when it is necessary, however, the end result will be stagnation. The PLP and Bermuda's trade unions remain the most effective incubators of positive change for the country, and I hope they will show sufficient vision and courage in the years ahead.

At the end of 2020, Bermuda saw history being made when Britain's Rena Lalgie, a U.K. Treasury official, was sworn in as the country's first woman and first Black Governor. It was indeed important that these firsts occurred. But they do not change the underlying dynamic of Bermuda's colonial status and its mainly white financial power structure.

Our fellow Caricom member Barbados, fully independent since November 30, 1966, walked a different path when it shifted from being a constitutional monarchy, with Queen Elizabeth II as head of state, to a republic on November 30, 2021. The shift occurred with the Queen's blessing and with Prince Charles in attendance, and Barbados remains a member of the Commonwealth of Nations. In the long run, this must also be Bermuda's path in order to shed the last vestiges of an obsolete British colonial system.

MY PERSONAL CONFLICT with the Combined Opposition, the standard bearer of that colonial system, continues. It persists in trying to convict me on baseless charges of corruption, to punish me for granting asylum to innocent Uighurs released from the American prison in Guantanamo, Cuba, and for my other efforts to advance racial equality and socioeconomic justice, as this book relates, during my time as a PLP MP from 1993 to 2010 and as Premier of Bermuda from 2006 to 2010.

Although the *Royal Gazette* seems to be maintaining its membership in the Combined Opposition with regard to the PLP and me, I have to note an exception in news editor Tim Smith's November 15, 2019 review of this book. Under the headline "Confrontational, dismissive, vengeful, compelling," the review said in part, "Through 416 forcefully articulated pages . . . Dr. Brown . . . argues convincingly that Bermuda's racist structures are so deeply rooted that they will not be fixed by shrinking violets." Describing my account of my political journey as that of "the rebellious child who grew up to be one of his country's most significant political leaders in a time of racial and political change," the review also said, "That story is well told and has the power to capture the imagination of readers who might never even have heard of Bermuda." The review concluded, "[L]ove him or loathe him, his views always make compulsive reading." Any author would be proud of such a review.

In January 2021, Bermuda's Director of Public Prosecutions (DPP), who is appointed by the Governor, filed thirteen charges of corruption against me. Five of the charges relate to a 2001-2010 contract I had with the Lahey Clinic in Massachusetts as a practicing physician and owner of a Bermuda medical business, and the other eight charges relate to my fundraising for the PLP and the Bermuda Health Foundation. As the book explains, my contract with the Lahey Clinic never affected my public duties or the public purse, and the fundraising was all above board and in keeping with normal political and philanthropic practice in Bermuda. Yet the decades-long vendetta against me had to be pursued, it seems, in a desperate effort to justify a politically motivated investigation that has cost Bermuda's taxpayers in excess of $10 million.

The wheels of justice often grind slowly. They are grinding even slower in Bermuda now, owing to a pandemic-related backlog in our court system. If there is a trial, it is unlikely to begin before sometime in 2023. In the meantime, my legal team has offered what we feel are compelling reasons for the Supreme Court justice presiding over the case to recuse herself and for the charges to be thrown out on constitutional grounds. The justice is the daughter of a physician with whom two other physicians and I had an acrimonious business dispute, when she was a teenager. In judicial matters, it is not necessary to prove bias but merely to show that there is an apparent cause for bias in the eyes of reasonable, disinterested observers. My lawyers and I believe this past history falls well within that scope of apparent bias.

The constitutional issue is clear-cut. The lengthy investigation of me was driven by a joint investigation and prosecution team (JIPT) that was not only unprecedented for Bermuda, but that also brought the Deputy Governor and the DPP together for regular meetings and discussions. According to the Bermuda Constitution, the DPP is supposed to act with complete insulation from the Governor and Deputy Governor in all decisions about investigations and both civil and criminal charges. The separation of powers and executive function required by the Constitution was flouted throughout the activity of the JIPT, which was plainly used as a political weapon against me.

If my lawyers eventually have to argue the merits of my case during a trial, I am confident we will prevail and my innocence will be confirmed. But the questions of judicial bias and political meddling with the DPP's constitutional role should bring the matter to the same end more quickly—and at less additional exorbitant cost to Bermuda's taxpayers.

THE PASSAGE OF TIME brings losses and gains to every family. My extended family experienced one important loss when my cousin Walton Brown died on October 8, 2019, aged 59; a second when my older cousin and primary school teacher Calvin Smith died on August 21, 2020, aged 87; and a third when my cousin and childhood playmate, LaVerne Furbert, died on January 31, 2021, aged 74. They were all wonderful people, stalwart members of the PLP, and great defenders of me against unfair attacks and accusations. They each did enormous good in Bermuda, and my wife, Wanda, and I miss them dearly.

On the plus side, my sons, Kevin, Maurice, Trey, and Donovan—you'll meet them in the book—are all doing well. Kevin and Maurice have both put their difficult pasts behind them. Trey and Donovan are making strides as entrepreneurs. And I gained a fourth grandchild (joining Kevin's son, Caleb, and his daughter, Kira, and Maurice's daughter, Kesi) on December 28, 2021, with the birth of Trey's son, Nolan.

Above all, my beloved wife, Wanda, and I continue to enjoy a marriage that I can only feel was truly made in heaven.

As I write these words, a new year is beginning, fraught with problems for the world and for Bermuda and bringing unpredictable challenges for each of us as human beings. But with faith in God and our best efforts for justice and progress, whom shall we fear?

Ewart F. Brown, M.D.
January, 2022

Prologue: The Politics of Change

T HE MORE YOU PUSH FOR PROGRESSIVE CHANGE, the more entrenched power pushes back. This fact has formed the context of my life in politics from my Bermudian childhood in a politically engaged family through my leadership of Bermuda's Progressive Labour Party (PLP) and service as Premier of Bermuda to a continuing campaign by my opponents to smear my integrity and besmirch my record in office.

I encountered the same dynamic as a student activist at Howard University in the 1960s and as an inner-city physician in Los Angeles, California, in the 1970s and 1980s before returning home to enter electoral politics. Indeed, this is the situation of would-be change agents everywhere, not least of all in the Black diaspora throughout the Americas.

In that regard, despite their vast difference in size, Bermuda and the United States mirror each other in countless ways. The progress of each holds important lessons for the progress of the other, especially as both countries seek growth and renewal in the twenty-first century.

An increasingly technological economy, driven by the financial services industry; a labor market troubled by issues of immigration and citizenship and scarred by ongoing racism; a multicultural society whose most extreme injustice remains separate and unequal treatment of Black people—these characteristics of the United States define Bermuda, too. And in the microcosm of Bermuda, we can see them all the clearer.

My experience in political office reflects the experience of Bermuda as a whole in relation to its racist history and White establishment. Still wealthy and powerful, the White establishment clings to its old ways behind a facade of change. It exemplifies the regressive forces Frederick Douglass described when he said, "If there is no struggle, there is no progress. . . . Power concedes nothing without a demand. It never did and it never will."

Progressive change continually risks being co-opted and undermined. Nevertheless, progress is possible. If I have been demonized beyond any leader in Bermuda's history, it is because of the often painful strides toward a stronger, more racially just society that the country made while I was Premier.

It is no coincidence that this went hand in hand with significant achievements in Bermudianization (putting Bermudians, Black and White, into positions formerly reserved for White expatriates), infrastructure, stewardship of the economy, and the equitable provision of social services such as FutureCare, Bermuda's first comprehensive health insurance program for senior citizens.

Much remains to be done to make Bermuda a just society. That includes what I believe is an inevitable, if long delayed, move to status as an independent country rather than remaining a dependent overseas territory of Great Britain.

Some in Bermuda claim that racial equality and independence are not inherently linked. I believe they are, because political independence is a natural consequence of mature political growth and development.

The reverse is also true. Bermuda's status as a dependent overseas territory has often been used to halt and slow racial progress. The local White power structure has been adept at managing relations with London and frustrating substantive change.

We can achieve a better future if Bermuda knows and appreciates its history, including the recent history of the PLP versus the party of the White establishment, formerly the United Bermuda Party (UBP) and now, unchanged except in name, the One Bermuda Alliance (OBA). "United Bermuda," "One Bermuda"—these phrases ironically mask the White establishment's divide-and-conquer methods.

I have written this book to address the lies about my administration and me not solely on my personal behalf, but for all those in Bermuda, White as well as Black, who understand that unity can only come with full racial equality. In these pages I aim not only to set the record straight about my integrity in office, but also to show what good government committed to a progressive agenda can achieve—against the odds.

This book is not a comprehensive autobiography despite its length. It tries to present simply and directly the experiences that most shaped and affected me as a person, a physician, and a politician committed to countering racism. Much of the story as concerns both the PLP and me is not widely known, or has only been told from the point of view of our political opponents.

The false charges of corruption and other lies about my administration and me gained traction largely because of the White establishment's control of most of the country's news media, especially the *Royal Gazette* newspaper, the virtual Fox News of Bermuda. In what follows, you will soon see why I called the newspaper and the UBP/OBA partners in the Combined Opposition.

Like most other educated Bermudians, I commonly mix British and American spellings. Because this book has an American publisher, it uses American spellings except, of course, when quoting published sources that use British spellings or in such cases as the "labour" in the Progressive Labour Party's name. In keeping with usage on the Island—our main shorthand term for Bermuda although we are actually a small archipelago—I refer to titles in the Bermudian context, such as Premier, Governor, Cabinet Minister, and Shadow Minister, and various public and private organizations in upper rather than lower case and by their customary acronyms (see List of Terms, Abbreviations, and Acronyms).

Like an increasing number of Black writers, I also refer to Black and White in upper rather than lower case. This gives the terms the importance they deserve. I only use "white" and "black" to refer to colors.

Finally, I have tried to tell my political story as I lived it, and the narrative of my time in office often moves as abruptly from issue to issue as I had to do at the time. The result may not be as graceful as it could be, but it is faithful to the events I relate. My sources are my personal records and recollections, communications from colleagues, and the online archives of Bermuda's two leading news outlets, Bernews.com and the *Royal Gazette*. I am, of course, solely responsible for the opinions I express based on the facts as I know and understand them.

MY POLITICAL JOURNEY BEGINS WITH A FORTUNATE BOYHOOD in the Flatts area of Bermuda during the late 1940s and early 1950s. It was there and then that my two great ambitions in life, to become a doctor and to help lead Bermuda to a better future, took root in my mind. My parents and extended family planted the seeds of both ambitions with daily examples of hard work and success in several walks of life, including business, education, medicine, and politics.

From Flatts Village to the highest public office in Bermuda, to begin to show how I traveled that path, I have to tell you about the Darrells of Flatts Village and the great expectations they had of me and of Bermuda.

Part One: Finding My Way

1. Great Expectations

P OLITICS WAS PREDOMINANT IN MY PARENTS' HOUSE. You could talk about politics at any hour of the day or night. That had a lot to do both with who my parents were and with the time and place. For Black people in Bermuda in the 1940s and 1950s, politics was both the greatest frustration and the greatest hope. The manipulation of politics by the White minority limited the Black majority's access to education, entrepreneurship, professional development, and political participation. White political and economic power was traditionally headquartered on Front Street in Hamilton, Bermuda's capital, and its most important holders were known as the Forty Thieves, the descendants of twelve White families who originally amassed power and wealth as pirates, shipwreckers, slavers, and smugglers.

But politics was also the only viable means of achieving racial, economic, and social justice in Bermuda. Every striving Black family was concerned about politics in Bermuda as a matter of survival and a medium for social progress. Some of my earliest memories are of hearing grownups talk about how a mortgage or business loan was called in because the borrower was disturbing the White power structure. Or how others had kowtowed to Henry Tucker, the chief power broker among the Forty Thieves and the architect of modern Bermuda's economy, to assure him they were not radicals and keep their credit in good standing at the Bank of Bermuda (a private commercial enterprise like Bank of America, not a public institution like the Bank of England in the United Kingdom or the Federal Reserve Bank in the United States).

The first election I can remember is the general election of 1953. I was seven years old and my sister, Emelita, was five. (Our birthdays were almost exactly twenty-five months apart, on May 17, 1946, and June 18, 1948, respectively.) Our mother, Helene Darrell Brown, was driving us home from somewhere when we passed a polling station at a local church. A worried tone came into my mother's voice as she told us, "Scrunch down tight, you two, and don't let that policeman see you."

Emelita dutifully curled into a little ball on the floor between the front and back seats. She always says she learned to be obedient by watching me get spanked day after day. I was a strong-willed, energetic, curious child, who wanted to know how everything worked and debated and questioned everything.

I scrunched down a little, but barely pulled my head below the level of the side window before lifting it back up to peek at the White policeman standing in front of the polling station. Catching sight of me in the rear view mirror my mother said, "Ewart, what did I tell you? Are you disappointed because you haven't had your licks yet today?" My mother loved us to the full, but she had a sarcastic streak. And the tone of her voice said she wasn't playing. The chances of my getting a spanking had just gone up considerably.

"We're already past, and he didn't notice us," I said, in for a penny in for a pound. "Why do we have to hide from him anyway? We're not doing anything wrong."

My mother began to explain, a process that continued at home around the dinner table with my father, Ewart Alstead "D. A." Brown, and his older brother George, who was at our house a lot in those days. No one now alive is quite sure why my father's nickname was D. A.; it may have stemmed from childish slips of the tongue for "E. A." by him or one of his five sisters and two brothers. In any case, the fact that we were talking about politics, and my mother's edginess about the election, had fortunately driven any thought of spanking me out of her mind.

I learned that my mother was concerned because in that election many Black voters were "plumping" rather than splitting their votes as normal. At the time, every constituency elected two representatives to the House of Assembly, Bermuda's main parliamentary body, and so every ballot had spaces for entering two candidates' names. Plumping was entering only one candidate's name to improve the odds of that candidate's being elected. A police presence at polling stations is normal enough in any democracy, but the Black community sensed that Bermuda authorities were monitoring the 1953 election with extra fervor, a show of force to make Blacks less likely to plump their votes for Black candidates.

The White establishment certainly didn't want more Black Members of Parliament, and the electoral system was heavily stacked against Black candidates. Although Black people made up most of Bermuda's population, voting was tied to ownership of property and only a minority of the Black majority owned enough to qualify. In contrast, many White voters cast ballots in multiple constituencies wherever they owned sufficient property. Voting in general elections commonly went on for three consecutive days so that prosperous White voters could get around the Island to cast all their votes.

Women, Black or White, had been allowed to vote only since 1944, if they owned sufficient property. In the previous general election, in 1948, two White Bermudians, Helen Aitken and Edna Watson, had become the first women in the House of Assembly.

Race relations were not often openly violent in Bermuda, and my mother was no shrinking violet. So her reaction at the polling station during the 1953 election—I never saw her act the slightest bit nervous or furtive around a policeman before or after that—made an enormous impression on me. I was all ears as my parents and Uncle George hashed over the election and the situation of Blacks in Bermuda.

Uncle George was a radical compared to my mother, with my father somewhere in between their two positions. They all agreed that Bermuda needed a lot more Black people in Parliament, including "Black women, too," as my mother said. But Uncle George was skeptical about how much would change without direct action in the form of strikes and other protests led by the Bermuda Workers Association (BWA), later the Bermuda Industrial Union (BIU), and its firebrand president, Black physician Dr. Edgar Fitzgerald Gordon.

My mother had been raised to distrust labor unions, and she put her faith in gradual change through the House of Assembly. She said, "In Bermuda we have one of the most venerable parliaments in the world, and that's where we have to initiate and legitimate change." Uncle George snickered and said, "Did you say venerable or despicable?" That drew a flashing look of disdain from my mother and a grin of agreement from my father.

My mother and Uncle George were both right. In continuous operation since 1620, the House of Assembly was certainly venerable and was the ultimate medium for any substantive change in Bermuda's segregationist politics and laws. But for more than three hundred years, until 1968, Bermuda's Parliament was not run according to the Westminster system. The power of government was vested in a president and executive council rather than a premier or prime minister and a formal cabinet. The president and executive council functioned primarily as a board of directors running Bermuda as a profit-making enterprise for its leading White families.

My parents, Uncle George, and the rest of our extended family hoped for the day when Bermuda would have a truly representative number of Black people in Parliament and when Black as well as White Bermudians could reach the country's highest public office and serve as head of Government. They also weren't shy about encouraging me to think that I might be one of those leaders if I followed the family example of hard work and achievement. "From those who have received much, much is expected," my parents and extended family often told me.

It's impossible to know whether plumping votes made the difference, but the 1953 election increased the number of Black Members of Parliament to nine. The most prominent of them was Dr. Gordon. Another was my great-uncle Russell Levi Pearman, my mother's uncle on her mother's side of the family. When the new Parliament convened, Russell Levi Pearman immediately called for an interracial committee, the first in Bermuda's history, to consider issues of segregation and discrimination. This resulted in a nine-member committee, chaired by Henry Tucker, with four Black members including Dr. Gordon.

The committee was a regular topic of conversation in our house. My mother stressed what a big shift it was to have such a committee in Parliament. Uncle George, on his frequent visits, countered with the inevitability that the Black committee members would be outvoted. As it happened, no substantive change came from the committee's work. But in hindsight I see that, once again, my mother and uncle were both right. Politics is about substance and symbolism, and the connection between the two. The challenge is to get them in sync with each other.

Over the next two years Dr. Gordon's name and his political positions and rhetoric came up in innumerable conversations and debates between my parents and extended family members and friends. Born in Trinidad, Dr. Gordon settled in Bermuda in 1924 and soon became an active writer of letters to the *Royal Gazette* on issues such as the Bermuda Welfare Society's refusal to employ Black nurses. In 1944 he became President of the Bermuda Workers Association, and his fiery speeches attracted many new members to its ranks. In 1946 he won a seat in the House of Assembly in a by-election. He lost the seat in the 1948 general election, before reentering Parliament with a victory in the 1953 election. From his first published letter to the editor of the *Royal Gazette,* he brought a new substance and style to politics in Bermuda with his willingness to challenge the White establishment openly and often on issues of racial injustice. In the process his rapier wit and dapper persona endeared him to many Black Bermudians, as did his competence as a physician.

He thought Black Bermudians were far too accepting of their lot, and he gave the country a much-needed role model in forming and sustaining a credible political opposition to the White power structure. He was indispensable in getting the labor movement going strong in Bermuda and an enduring inspiration for the Progressive Labour Party (PLP), which was founded after his death. (Given Dr. Gordon's unyielding attacks on Bermuda's White establishment, it is ironic that when his daughters, Pamela and Patricia, entered politics in the 1970s, they went the other way and joined the United Bermuda Party [UBP]. Pamela Gordon, now Dame Pamela, became Bermuda's first female Premier as a member of the UBP in 1997. Patricia Gordon-Pamplin was Deputy Leader of the UBP in 2006–2007, and she became a Cabinet Minister in the first Government led by the One Bermuda Alliance [OBA], the successor to the UBP.)

Although my mother never really warmed up to labor unions, she admired Dr. Gordon, although somewhat less enthusiastically than my father and Uncle George did. A recurring theme in discussions of Dr. Gordon was the political value of his medical profession. The House of Assembly meets around fifty days a year and is not a full-time job for Members of Parliament. And the presidency of the BWA/BIU did not pay much then either. As a Black physician with an all-Black patient roster, however, Dr. Gordon was not dependent on White people for his income.

My dad often told the story of asking Dr. Gordon whether I should study medicine or law. "Medicine is a safer profession in Bermuda," Dr. Gordon said. "They can easily reverse him legally, but it's more difficult for them to reverse him medically."

As soon as I grew out of the "I want to be a cowboy" stage, I was drawn to the idea of becoming a doctor. That had nothing to do with Dr. Gordon. It was because of my maternal uncle Bert. (I also had a paternal uncle Bertie, the middle brother between Uncle George and my father.) My mother had two younger sisters, Gloria and Winifred, and Uncle Bert—George Bertram McPhee, M.D.—was Aunt Gloria's husband.

Uncle Bert made an indelible impression on me as a boy. For one thing I had never seen my father, whom I worshipped, so pleased and happy to spend time with anyone outside our immediate family as he was with Uncle Bert. The two of them seemed almost more like brothers than my father and Uncle George did. Both my father and Uncle Bert were handsome, charming men with wonderful senses of humor. And I felt the same kind of inner strength radiating from Uncle Bert as from my dad.

As Darrells of Flatts Village, my mother and her sisters were members of one of Bermuda's leading Black families. Aunt Gloria was even more politically inclined than my mother and one day aimed to become active in Bermuda politics. The Darrell legacy would be valuable in that regard. When Aunt Gloria died in 2007, a *Royal Gazette* opinion article celebrating her life and political career referred to the Darrells of Flatts Village and other such families as Bermuda's "coloured royalty." I am proud to be a member of the Darrell family, but "coloured royalty"? In 2007? That description says more about Bermuda's White power structure than it does about my family legacy.

That legacy, so far as my generation knows it, began with my mother's grandfather, Clarence Orrister Darrell. Born in 1859, Clarence was the out-of-wedlock son of a White man, Richard Darrell, CMG (Companion of the Order of St. Michael and St. George), who was the son of John Harvey Darrell, CMG, Bermuda's Chief Justice from 1856 to 1870. Richard Darrell served as Bermuda's Solicitor General during the latter part of the nineteenth century.

The first member of their family to settle in Bermuda was John Darrell of Kent, England, a cousin of Sir Nathaniel Rich, a key stockholder in the Virginia Company and its Bermuda offshoot, the Somers Island Company. (Bermuda, named for its 1505 Spanish discoverer, Juan de Bermudez, was settled in 1609 when the *Sea Venture*, commanded by Sir George Somers and bound for Jamestown, Virginia, with much needed supplies, was shipwrecked off the island, which for a time was known as Somers Island.) On his arrival in Bermuda in 1645, John Darrell and his wife, Sarah, immediately became leading figures among the White population.

Clarence Darrell's mother was Sarah Catherine Kiel, born a slave in 1831. A photograph of her with her son and only child shows a beautiful, impeccably dressed, dark-skinned woman of Native American and African heritage. Both Native Americans and Africans were enslaved on Bermuda before the British abolished slavery in most of their empire in 1834; the exceptions were India, Ceylon, and Saint Helena, where slavery continued until 1843.

Sarah declared her hopes for her son to rise in the world in his baptismal name, Aristo Gilbert Kiel. At some point he traded this aspirational name for that of Clarence Orrister Darrell, although there would be more than one Gilbert among his descendants. According to family lore, Clarence used a small financial start in life from his father to set up a provisions business. A lifelong entrepreneur, he became one of the most successful Black businessmen and one of the most important Black civic leaders in Bermuda. He was one of the first three Black businessmen to own property on Front Street in the stronghold of the Forty Thieves. He bought an extensive piece of land in Flatts Village, on the eastern outskirts of Hamilton Parish, where he built our homestead, named Signal View, and developed a community of Black homeowners by selling lots cheaply to his employees. On his death in 1922, the *Mid-Ocean News* reported the flags in Hamilton flew at half-mast and "the funeral . . . was witnessed by hundreds of people from all over the Island including many of Bermuda's leading businessmen as well as other well-known citizens."

Far though Clarence Orrister Darrell had risen compared to most Black people in Bermuda, there was an arbitrary limit on his achievements. The White elite of Bermuda were part of a regional aristocracy that linked entrepreneurs, plantation farmers, shipowners, bankers, and commercial traders on the Island with their counterparts in the Carolinas and Virginia and investors in New York and London. They were all links in the trans-Atlantic economy whose explosive growth from the early seventeenth century depended so heavily, and literally, on the sweat and blood of non-Whites.

In a racist, post-slavery society, family lines form both vital connections and rigid boundaries. Clarence Orrister Darrell could never sit down as a social or business equal with his father's White children. He could never buy property in Tucker's Town, which during his last years was being developed as a White residential and resort enclave, the Black residents having been displaced from their land against their will and at bargain prices. The Mid Ocean Club, Bermuda's most exclusive golf club, opened in Tucker's Town in 1921, and it did not have a Black member until 1973 when Uncle Bert was invited to join.

In 1883 Clarence married Henrietta Almeria Stowe, and they had seven children—four daughters and three sons—who all got higher education outside Bermuda. Their daughters Amy and Gladys were the first Bermudian women, White or Black, to qualify respectively in dentistry and pharmacy, earning their degrees at Howard University. My great-aunt Amy was licensed as a dentist in Bermuda and had a practice serving Black patients. There was apparently White opposition to registering my great-aunt Gladys as a pharmacist, but it was her preference to join the family dry goods business instead. She always avoided confrontation. Although Amy and Gladys both married, neither had children.

Their brother Hilgrove Charles was my maternal grandfather. He married Dorothy Bernice Pearman, who gave our family a second mixed strand of Native American and African heritage. Through the Pearmans, another prosperous Black family, we are connected to Jacob Minors, a legendary Bermuda harbor pilot who died in 1875. In addition to his African slave heritage, Jacob Minors was descended from Native Americans of several tribes in colonial Massachusetts. Jacob's Native American ancestors were sold into slavery in Bermuda in 1678 after their tribes were defeated in the three-year conflict known as King Philip's War, for the English name of the Wampanoag leader Metacom.

Emelita and I were taught to be proud of all our Darrell-Pearman ancestry, but never to be stuck up about it. Even at the age of nine, however, I found it much easier to understand why I should be proud of my non-White ancestors for making their way against the odds than of the White ones who were part of stacking the odds against them.

The poison of judging people by gradations of color got into my head for a time when I was a child. I felt Emelita was receiving too much attention because her skin was lighter than mine. (My father's maternal grandfather was Scottish, and there was also someone relatively light-skinned among the children of each of his five sisters and two brothers.) I teased Emelita mercilessly and frequently reduced her to tears, saying she received everything she wanted because she was so pale. One of the first words she learned how to spell was "ignore." When she complained about my teasing her, our mother said, "I-G-N-O-R-E, Emelita. Tune him out."

Our parents told me plainly that my teasing was ridiculous and wrong. But they also felt that given the nature of sibling rivalry, Emelita had to get thicker skinned, so to speak, and I had to grow out of my behavior. Eventually both things happened, but I'll always regret how hurtful I was to Emelita.

There's no denying I could be quite a handful to manage as a child, and I knew it. Witness my letter to Santa Claus, printed by the *Royal Gazette* just before Christmas 1951 as a winning entry in their holiday promotion and toy giveaway.

Signal View
Flatts

Dear Santa,

I am trying to be a good boy, but it is kind of hard. I am onny five years old and I am writing this letter all by myself.

If you can make it will you please bring me a few toys. What I would like most of all is a pair of cowboy pans, and a gun.

Mary Christmas, your mate,

Ewart Brown

P.S. don't forget to bring my sister a doll.

The *Royal Gazette* faithfully reproduced my spelling, a standard of accuracy I came to miss in its frequently outlandish, innuendo-filled coverage of my political career and government leadership. During my adult life Bermuda's primary news source has also rarely given me credit for trying to be good.

One of the key differences of political opinion in the family developed at this time. After Dr. Gordon died, Henry Tucker was the only White Member of Parliament to address the House of Assembly in praise of him and the only one to attend his funeral. My mother and Aunt Gloria thought this was wonderful and showed that Tucker was someone Black politicians could work with and trust. Uncle George said it was only lip service on Tucker's part.

As with most things, I looked to my father for the truth of the matter. He told me that Henry Tucker was a very smart man who was doing some excellent things for Bermuda. Tucker's avowed goal from before World War II was to make Bermuda the "Switzerland of the Atlantic." In very simple terms, my father explained that this goal appealed to a lot of successful companies and wealthy individuals who wanted to "park their money" in Bermuda to avoid taxes elsewhere. It was because Tucker was such a smart man, my father went on, that he was willing to cooperate in a limited way with Black politicians like Dr. Gordon. Tucker recognized that Bermuda had to change, but he was going to try to make that change as small and gradual as possible. "He's keeping control," my father summed up.

Much later I heard it was Henry Tucker who first famously said, "In Bermuda, if you don't have a conflict, you don't have any interest." This was when he ran the Government, the Bank of Bermuda, the Bermuda Broadcasting Corporation, Belco (the Island's electric utility), and many other important enterprises. During the Bermuda Constitutional Convention in London in 1966, a Labour MP in Westminster questioned how Bermuda could achieve any progress in social justice and democratic politics given Tucker's virtual dictatorship and crony capitalism.

At the age of nine I only got the gist of what my father was saying. But he had a knack for seeing and setting things straight. His way of explaining things made me think nothing was really complicated, that with enough hard work and common sense you could solve any problem.

I mentioned that my father's maternal grandfather was Scottish. My father's father, Charles Joseph "C. J." Brown, had come to Bermuda from Cuba by way of Jamaica, where he married Alice Petgrave. The young couple then moved to Bermuda, where my father and his brothers and sisters were all born and grew up. My father started his working life as a waiter, performed professionally as a tap dancer, and shot up to the point where he became the owner of a popular nightclub. He also went into the vending machine business, leasing out coin-operated pool tables, jukeboxes, and pinball machines. He became the guy in Bermuda for those things.

I tagged along with my father everywhere I could, soaking up how he did things. He approached life with a glint in his eye, and he never let a problem fester. If a vending machine was broken or there was a misunderstanding or disagreement with a merchant leasing the machine, he immediately took a first step to clearing up any confusion and resolving the issue, even if it was only to note what the problem was or to initiate a discussion with the other party. And then he followed through, step by step, until the matter was settled. He was the same way at home with a chore that needed doing or disputes between neighbors. It's because of my father's daily example that I can't see a crooked picture without wanting to straighten it.

I marveled at how relatives, friends, neighbors, employees, and strangers lit up when my father came on the scene. I saw that they not only delighted in his good-humored jokes and repartee, but that they also turned to him for advice on matters big and small, and that they genuinely liked and admired him. The way other people responded to my father strengthened my instinctive sense that he was someone I could always trust and rely on to be there for my mother, my sister, and me.

In hindsight I think the experience that really sealed that in my mind was how he dealt with his brother George. Both my father's older brothers, George and Bertie, shared his entrepreneurial streak. Uncle Bertie had a travel agency, Brown Cotton Tours, which over the years brought many Black Americans to Bermuda, including a number of beauty pageant winners. As for Uncle George, in the 1930s he began setting up a small network of fruit-and-vegetable stands and shops in Bermuda, importing produce from relatives and other connections in the Caribbean. He built up the business to the point where he had about twenty different retail outlets around the Island and was threatening the business of White merchants. The Forty Thieves decided to call in the note on his loan, and because he was putting every penny into running and expanding the business, he was immediately bankrupted. And so he left Bermuda, leaving his wife and children behind to make their way as best they could with the help of my father, Uncle Bertie, and other relatives.

Uncle George went to Saint Lucia and after a few years got himself elected to the island's Legislative Council. However, his Bermuda creditors tracked him there. Because he had not divulged his past financial troubles, the government of Saint Lucia charged him with filing false papers as an electoral candidate and threw him in jail.

That could have been more or less the end for Uncle George. But as my father often said, "You don't run away because it's raining." Before Uncle George had served his term in full, my father somehow got him released from jail and brought him back to Bermuda. Because of all the stories I had heard about Uncle George, he was a giant in my mind. When we picked him up at the harbor, I was shocked to see a smallish man who had front teeth missing and cardboard in the bottom of his shoes. But he wasn't a broken man, even if he looked like one, and within a couple of years he was a prominent union organizer, working to advance the BWA.

When he first returned to Bermuda, Uncle George ate dinner at our house practically every night. He had an opinion on everything, and it was usually contrary to my mother's. I remember asking her once, "Is Uncle George coming to dinner?"

She said, "Oh, do you mean It's-Not-Red-It's-Scarlet?"

I enjoyed Uncle George's spirit of resistance, and what he said about the situation of Blacks in Bermuda always made sense to me. Aunt Gloria and my mother strongly espoused the ideal of a color-blind Bermuda. To which Uncle George said, "Color blind is still blind," arguing that the past might be forgiven but must never be forgotten, a principle I came to share and have always tried to act on as an adult.

As I've also already noted, my parents agreed with him on race relations, even if they frequently differed with him on the strategies and tactics for improving them. What I loved most of all, however, was how my father had rescued Uncle George and helped him get a new start in life.

The bond between my father and me was so close that it triggered my mother's sarcasm and after her, Emelita's. Whenever my father came in the house and heard my mother say, "Let me tell you what that son of yours did," a frequent occurrence, he said, "Well, I have to talk to Ewart first." He took me aside to discuss the situation, giving me a chance to tell my side of the story and then reasoning with me about what I needed to do, or not do, in the future. That pattern was so habitual that when my father said, "I have to talk to Ewart first," my mother replied, "Sorry, can't talk about your Jesus." Before long "Sorry, can't talk about your Jesus," or some slight variation, was Emelita's refrain as well.

MY EARLY BOYHOOD INTEREST IN POLITICS WAS PRECOCIOUS, no doubt about it, but mostly I was just a boy doing boy things. If there was a choice between discussing politics and playing sports, the latter usually won. Of course, sports and politics aren't always separate.

One of the biggest occasions of the year in Bermuda is Cup Match weekend. Cup Match began in the 1830s with freed slaves celebrating the abolition of slavery with picnics and cricket games. Cup Match was formalized in 1902, and in 1947 the two days of the event, held on the Thursday and Friday closest to August 1, became official national holidays. During the PLP's first Government, from 1998 to 2003, the Thursday became Emancipation Day, commemorating the end of slavery, and the Friday became Somers Day, commemorating the colonization of Bermuda for the British by Sir George Somers. The tension between freedom and exploitation that is implicit in the naming of the holidays is not only historical by any means; among other things, it evidenced the compromising character of the first PLP Government.

In 1954, when I was eight, I dressed and got a ride to the cricket field early on the Thursday morning of Cup Match. When I reached the field I noticed a group of men talking politics. I had no business being part of the discussion, but I was so curious to hear what they were saying that I stuck my head right in the middle of them. A man was gesturing with his arm as he spoke, and his elbow knocked out one of my remaining baby teeth.

I was a skinny kid, but tall for my age, and I often played with older boys. At any time of the year that meant lots of cricket and football. (I mean real football, soccer, not American football.) In summer, we played cricket and football in the evenings and spent our days in and around the water. We jumped off the Flatts dock, dove from the bridge, and rode the tidal currents on an improvised surfboard. Boys who were thirteen or so were the top of the play pyramid, and the younger boys like me tried to impress them and hang around with them. I treated any competitive situation with great seriousness, and eventually I became one of the better divers. Years later, when we were both grown up, Emelita spotted a Bermuda travel postcard for sale in a Hamilton shop with a color photograph of me, age ten or eleven, jumping off the dock in Flatts.

One of my best friends at this time was Morris Wainwright, who was ten months younger. Morris, his sister, Muriel, and his parents were my parents' tenants and lived in the ground floor apartment of our house. Morris and Muriel's father, Mr. Billy Wainwright, was a carpenter who was busy with projects around Bermuda as people kept up and added to their houses or began to build new ones. A house might be only two rooms to start with, and ten years later have eight rooms, all of good, solid construction.

Roaming around Flatts Village, Morris, Muriel, my cousin LaVerne Furbert, and I, as well as other children, often stopped at Mr. Wainwright's job sites to see what he was doing. He took a kindly interest in us youngsters and often asked what we wanted to be when we grew up. With Uncle Bert back in Bermuda, I was forming a firm ambition to become a doctor, and Mr. Wainwright told me, "You want to be a doctor, Ewart? Well, be the best." That was his characteristic injunction no matter what a kid wanted to be in life: "Be the best."

Morris had an older brother, Dennis, who lived with his uncle about a hundred and fifty yards away and often worked with his father. Dennis became a hero of mine because of his sporting prowess. He was just then beginning to represent Bermuda internationally in both football, as a goalie, and in cricket, as a wicket keeper. When I saw Dennis working out, running laps or sprints on the cricket or football pitch, I literally followed in his footsteps, running my lungs out to try to catch and keep up with him. Gibby Wainwright, Morris and Dennis's older brother, was also a nice guy and great athlete and someone I admired.

Mr. Wainwright once told me, smiling, "I always know when you're around, Ewart. If I don't see you coming, I hear you because you've always got an opinion to share. The way you argue, you should be in Parliament one day."

I said earlier that I had a fortunate boyhood in Flatts, and a big part of what made it fortunate was that the influences on me were all so positive and consistent with one another. At home I learned that given our extended family's history, we had a right and a responsibility to contribute to Bermuda's progress as a country, especially with regard to racial equality and justice, and that a good life meant service to others as well as personal success. My parents and my aunts, uncles, and cousins gave me strong role models, both male and female, to emulate, and they were reinforced by other good role models in the Black community, especially in the segregated school system.

My parents naturally put a heavy emphasis on education. After kindergarten at a local church, taught by a kindly woman named Miss Hill, I attended

Harrington Sound School for first grade, or first standard as it was called then. The first standard teacher was Calvin Smith, my mother's first cousin and my first cousin once removed. My mother, who was eight years older than Calvin, was his colleague at Harrington Sound, where she taught second standard. My mother never had to ask me what I had done in school because Calvin had already told her. Fortunately, that very rarely led to a spanking because I enjoyed school and had too much fun learning to cause trouble there.

To keep me out of my mother's class, I was transferred to the Elliott School for second standard. Another cousin, Lorraine Darrell Fubler, taught there, which in due course triggered another transfer, this time to the Central School, as it was then called, the biggest and best primary school in Bermuda.

Central's principal, Victor Scott, was renowned for his dedication. He worked relentlessly for the school—so much so that I once saw him spit up blood from a stomach ulcer in the boys' washroom. His spirit of excellence made Central a winner in academics and sports. I loved that school, and I thrived in its classrooms and on its sports teams. There was a sense at Central that everyone there could and would succeed. Mr. Scott regularly told students, "Anyone with half a brain could learn this. Do you have a whole brain? Then you can learn this!" And learn we did.

Mr. Scott's wife, Edna Mae, was a teacher at Central. Mrs. Scott regularly singled me out by trusting me to get money from her purse for beef pies from a shop about a hundred yards down the street. It was quite an honor, and I was conscious of it as such.

My favorite subject was math. Early on Saturday mornings I rode my bike to Mr. and Mrs. Scott's house and did a hundred math problems at a large table in the living room. I was one of a number of boys and girls who went there for extra study and tutoring in different subjects. After I finished my hundred math problems, I was free to go to the movies with my friends. But I didn't see Saturday morning math as a chore. Riding my bike around Flatts, I added and subtracted and then multiplied and divided license plate numbers in my head.

As I reached the end of primary school, the question was where I would go to school next. At that time, public secondary education in Bermuda was not free, and the better the school the higher the fees were. At eleven I scored well enough on a competitive exam to win a government scholarship to Bermuda's best government secondary school, the Berkeley Institute. Berkeley followed the British model of combining middle school and high school for students ages twelve to seventeen or eighteen.

My parents could have paid the fees at the Berkeley Institute, but winning the scholarship was very important to me. Everyone told me I was bright, and I knew I tended to catch on to things faster than other kids. But this wasn't just my parents or relatives or family friends telling me I was smart. This was a totally objective third party. It made me think of myself and my future in a different way, and I couldn't wait to start my first year at Berkeley.

Everything seemed to be right in my young world. But although I wasn't conscious of it, I began to be affected by a tension between my parents. The first hints of it came with the news of my scholarship. My mother told my father, "You see what those Darrell genes are worth now, don't you?" She made this sort of comment several times, and on each occasion I could see my father biting his tongue, which to say the least was unusual for him. Both my parents came straight out with whatever was on their minds.

I didn't understand the edginess that flashed between my parents in these moments, but for the most part I put it out of my mind, exercising a penchant for compartmentalizing that has been far more beneficial to me than otherwise. I remained secure in my parents' great expectations of a good future for Bermuda, our family, and me.

2. Almost Hopeless

I N MY YOUTH IT WAS THE CUSTOM for kids in Bermuda to have a little book with multicolored blank pages where parents, relatives, friends of the family, teachers, and other adults wrote messages of congratulation, encouragement, and motivation on birthdays, holidays, and special occasions. My mother always wrote, "To thine own self be true, / And it must follow, as the night the day, / Thou canst not then be false to any man." She also often recited these lines from Shakespeare's *Hamlet*, in which Polonius counsels his son, Laertes. Yet I can't say I dwelt on the words much as a boy or pondered why my mother felt they were so important for me to know as I would later in life.

In the summer of 1957, having just turned eleven and looking ahead to my first year at the Berkeley Institute, I got my first job. I was hired as a tool cleaner and mechanic's helper in a boat and car engine repair shop run by Mr. George Dowling, a friend of my father's. The shop was in St. George's on the eastern end of the Island, and I'll never forget taking the bus by myself, carrying my little lunchbox, to report for my first day of work. I wound up working there all that summer and the next, as well as many weekends and holidays, and I really enjoyed it.

I couldn't wait to get my first wages. As I've said, work was hallowed in our family, and I was excited to be old enough to have a part-time job. But there was a more immediate reason. The trigger for my getting a job at such a young age had been a recent exchange with my mother at the dinner table. I said I didn't want to eat the liver and onions we were having for dinner.

My mom said, "Let me tell you something. When you have a job, you can ask for what you want."

At the end of my first week at the auto marine shop I brought home my pay, put it on the kitchen table, and told my mom, "I'll have a steak."

She laughed and said, "That won't buy half of one."

I didn't get steak when I wanted, but I was proud to be earning money by doing a job well. From that time forward I usually had a part-time job of some kind. It did me a world of good to build a practical understanding of work while I was so young, and I always felt it gave me a leg up on my peers. I was the only one of my friends who was likely to have any money in his pocket, and the fact that I had earned the money myself made it all the sweeter.

At the end of the summer I started at the Berkeley Institute, and to my great surprise I didn't like it there. Without realizing it, I had entered a situation in which I struggled to be true to myself. I couldn't put my finger on what was wrong. The Berkeley Institute was and is a fine school with a great tradition of excellence. But it struck me as rigid and lifeless, and I couldn't help feeling that it was not the right place for me.

The problem in hindsight appears to have been the simple, but for me profoundly important, fact that the Berkeley Institute had a dismissive attitude to sports in comparison to academic achievement. It only gave lip service to the second part of *mens sana in corpore sano,* "a sound mind in a sound body," and the mind set of the teachers and administration seemed to be that smart kids shouldn't want to excel in sports. That disturbed me because I loved sports and I was athletic. I enjoyed the competition, I knew I could excel, and I liked the attention that came with winning. Central School had celebrated all student successes with great enthusiasm, while giving pride of place to academic achievement, and that was perfect for me. I exerted myself to shine both in the classroom and on the sports teams. To be at a school where sports activities were looked down on made me uneasy in my own skin.

After having been a star student at Central, in addition to scoring so well on the government scholarship test, I went into immediate—and to me and everyone else at the time, inexplicable—academic decline. I say inexplicable, but I was also very much aware of saying to myself, "I'm not going to do well here." I made a conscious decision to fail. The only subjects I did well in were French and Latin, which happened to be taught by the two prettiest women teachers, Mrs. Eloise Furbert and Miss Helen Somersall.

I became an antsy disciplinary problem, and by the middle of the fall I was a regular in detention. After classes ended every afternoon, I asked the teacher in charge if I was on the detention list, even if there were no particular cause for it that day. I was basically thumbing my nose at everyone, trying to show that I didn't care if I was in detention or not.

At home things were also turbulent. My mother's temper was getting shorter and shorter where I was concerned, and my spankings were harder and more frequent. That kind of discipline was becoming more problematic as I grew older and bigger. A chronic battle of wills with my mother developed, and Emelita recalls me often clenching my jaw and muttering, "I'm not gonna cry, I'm not gonna cry, I'm not gonna cry," as my mother administered discipline with a harness strap repurposed from the horses her father and one of her uncles kept in a barn on our property.

I thought my mother was picking on me, and at times I detested her. During my first term at Berkeley I realized that I was also pushing her buttons. I often deliberately provoked her in order to see her get bent out of shape at me. It was the only way I had to fight back at her. Looking back I see, too, that these episodes were threatening to become the dominant way we related to each other.

My father tried to counsel me through things in his usual no-nonsense, reasonable manner. Uncharacteristically for me, what he said went in one ear and out the other.

Every once in a while an exchange between my parents indicated that they were still very much at odds about something. But the open tumult in the family centered around me. Only as an adult did it occur to me that my mother was taking out anger on me that she really wanted to take out on my father, and that I had become the focal point for a conflict in their relationship. At eleven, going on twelve, years old, I had no conscious thought of that. Instead I felt that maybe my troubles at Berkeley were to blame, that maybe I wasn't good enough to fulfill any great expectations.

I was certainly acting as if I wanted to prove I was a bad kid. One day at Berkeley I went to the detention room and cheekily asked, as had become my habit, "Am I in today?" I was, and the teacher running detention that afternoon was Mrs. Juanita Furbert Guishard. She taught religion and was one of the few teachers at Berkeley I related to well. She was also a nurse and had recently become the first Black psychiatric nurse at King Edward VII Memorial Hospital. (Barbara "Lovie" Wade was its first Black nurse.) This was big news in Bermuda, and my respect for Mrs. Guishard was amplified by what Uncle Bert told me about her breaking the color bar on the hospital nursing staff. Finally, Mrs. Guishard was such a positive person—if it was raining cats and dogs, she said, "You know, we need this rain"—that she got through the shell I was hiding inside and had a calming influence on me.

Mrs. Guishard took the detention roll and said that we should each write two pages on what we wanted to be in life. If it had been anyone but Mrs. Guishard, I would have made a travesty of the assignment right from the start. But because of her I wrote the truth: I wanted to be a doctor and help people who were sick.

She was going around the detention class looking over shoulders to see what everyone was writing. When she saw what I was writing, she picked the paper off my desk and said, "Children, I want you to listen to what Ewart has written."

While she was reading aloud what I had put down about wanting to be a doctor, I was thinking, "Oh, no. She's blowing my cover."

When she handed my paper back to me, I immediately crossed everything out and began writing that I wanted to be a gangster and rob banks and shoot anyone who got in my way. Mrs. Guishard saw that—and right there in the middle of the detention class she began to cry. That memory still hurts.

After the Christmas–New Year holidays, things went from bad to worse. Teachers repeatedly complained to my parents about my behavior, and several times the school's highly respected headmaster, F. S. "Freddie" Furbert, called me in and asked what was wrong. Mr. Furbert knew I could do the work. I had no answer except to say, "I don't know what's wrong, sir. But I don't want to be here."

My parents saw me barreling toward a crash, and in early spring of 1958 they arranged for me to be transferred to the Bermuda Technical Institute (BTI), a vocational secondary school where students did basic studies like geography, math, and English, but mainly concentrated on learning trades like woodworking, metal work, technical drawing, and so on. I got there and my immediate reaction was, "Oh, no, what have I done? This is not the place for me either."

Shortly after my school transfer, my father came home one day full of high spirits. It was a year since I had won the scholarship to Berkeley. He went into the kitchen where my mother was preparing dinner, and said, "Guess who won a scholarship to Berkeley this time? And guess what? No Darrell genes!" My father's tone of voice was triumphant. There was no answer from my mother, which was odd. She was a quick-witted woman and gave as good as she got, whether in a political debate with Uncle George or a disagreement, joking or serious, with my father. Over the next days I heard my father make a few similar comments while my mother bit her tongue. I didn't understand this, but it was obvious that neither of my parents wanted to talk to me about what was going on between them.

Soon it was summer and I gave my energy—and thanks to my ability to compartmentalize my conscious attention—to running around with my buddies: swimming and diving off the bridge in the heat of the day and playing football and cricket in the cool of the evening. I also went back to work as a mechanic's helper at Mr. Dowling's auto marine shop, which contributed a lot to my improved state of mind compared to the school year. It was a good summer, all things considered.

In the fall it was back to BTI, however, and a grinding year of getting into escalating amounts of trouble and being punished for it. Bit by bit I was sinking into despair and becoming hope-less, by which I mean that I hoped less for myself than I did for others. I was losing the sense that my own future could be interesting and worthwhile.

Although my own issues turned out to have causes that could arise in any family of any race or ethnicity, all too many young disadvantaged Black people, especially boys, experience feeling hopeless. I'll have more to say about this later from my perspectives as an inner-city physician, a father, and an elected official.

I don't want to give the impression that BTI was a bad school or that it was in any way responsible for my downward spiral at the ages of eleven and twelve. To the contrary, BTI was an excellent school, which produced many of Bermuda's entrepreneurs. It was so successful that in 1980 the UBP Government led by Premier David Gibbons shut it down. Although ostensibly it was folded into the newly created Bermuda College, the Island's first and only two-year community college, the pipeline of successful, entrepreneurial Black tradesmen BTI had produced quickly dwindled away. Apparently too many young Black men were graduating from BTI and going on to set up successful repair and construction businesses. If that trend were allowed to continue, the UBP saw, before long the small business class of Bermuda would be majority Black rather than majority White. So BTI was closed and its remaining operations were marginalized with predictable rotten consequences for the country's young Black men.

My parents knew that BTI was not the ideal place for me and that I should be studying a challenging academic curriculum. The options for my schooling were limited, however. My parents couldn't send me to a White school in our segregated society, and they didn't want to send me away from home to school somewhere else.

They probably hoped that my time at BTI would calm me down to the point where I could make a fresh start at Berkeley or a less prestigious Black high school in Bermuda. If that didn't happen, maybe I would become interested in learning a trade that could be the basis of a successful business. There were a number of prosperous tradesmen in the Darrell-Pearman clan.

My state of mind at BTI was such, however, that I gravitated toward the tough guys among the older boys, the small minority of the mostly Black student body who were hardening into thuggishness. At home I was insolent and uncommunicative. My extended family, as well as my parents and teachers, did their best to discipline me and correct my course. I was so angry and confused, however, that it had little effect. One day my maternal aunt Winnie, who was only ten years older than I was, became so exasperated by my conduct, and I guess so frightened, that she beat me with a wooden coat hanger and broke it over my arm as I was advancing toward her. Hurt and enraged, I went into the kitchen to look for a knife to try to defend myself, until I fortunately thought better of it.

In the spring of 1959 I was hanging around with some of the older more trouble-prone students at BTI, and we were all teasing one guy. He got upset, and he fixed on me as the easiest target for revenge. I was tall for my age, but I was skinny and nowhere near as strong as any of the others. The guy who was being teased grabbed me by the arms and slammed me up against a wall.

I had an open penknife in my hand because I was sharpening a pencil. I managed to wrest that arm free, and I cut his cheek.

I was suspended for a month. As my father was driving me home, he said, "You know, in case you're thinking that I'm going to punish you physically, don't worry about that. That's not going to happen. But I want you to understand that you are moving in two opposite directions at the same time."

Jaw clamped shut, I wondered what the hell he was talking about.

Dad went on, "I know deep down you want to be a doctor. But the kind of behavior you're exhibiting now is going in the opposite direction. They don't make doctors in prison."

That got to me. Uncle Bert had recently given me a part-time job cleaning up his office. I liked dusting off bits of medical apparatus and wondering exactly how they were used to examine patients. The longer I attended BTI, however, the less of this I did. It was painful to feel my dream of becoming a doctor receding out of reach.

One day shortly after I'd served my month's suspension, I was sitting in the metalwork shop at BTI. We had been making paint scrapers, and I had stayed behind after everyone left to put some finishing touches on mine. I looked up from the workbench at the sunlight streaming in the window and thought, "I am on the wrong path. How am I going to become a doctor if I keep on like this?"

I never voiced my fear for my future to my parents or anyone else. Fortunately, my parents were not going to sit by and watch me become a juvenile delinquent. With my thirteenth birthday approaching and the school year at BTI coming to a close, my mother asked, "Would you like to spend the summer with your cousin John in Jamaica?"

John's mother, Alma Brown Jones, was the third oldest of my father's five sisters, in the middle between older sisters Adelle and Grace and younger sisters Cynthia and Eileen. A change of scenery sounded good to me, so I said I would like to go. That prospect steadied me through the last month of school.

My best friend, Murray, had also gone off-track after leaving Central Primary School. About six months earlier, his parents had sent him to school in Jamaica in hopes of straightening him out. It didn't occur to me that this might be a model for my parents, and I was disappointed that Murray was spending the summer in Bermuda and returning to Jamaica just as I was coming back home. We might not see each other until Murray was home for Christmas.

On the Sunday in June when I was to leave Bermuda, however, I looked in my closet in my bedroom and was startled to see that all my clothes, not just my summer ones, were gone. I said, "Mama, why is my closet empty?"

Dismay and embarrassment came into her face. She always had a quick answer for everything, but not that time. Finally she said, "Your father and I thought you might get down there and want to stay through the school year."

I thought to myself, "Oh, man, are things this bad? They are sending me away. They are sending me away."

At the airport in those days, the airplane crew mingled with passengers and people seeing them off in the same waiting area before flights departed. I was booked on a British Overseas Airways Corporation (BOAC) flight to the Bahamas. Aunt Cynthia was a schoolteacher in Nassau, and I was to stay with her for two weeks before continuing on to Jamaica. But I wasn't going without a fight. I marched up to the BOAC pilot and co-pilot and told them, "The plane can't take off. There's a bomb on it."

A minor hullabaloo ensued as my parents told me in no uncertain terms to stop my nonsense and explained to the BOAC plane crew and airport staff that I was upset about leaving home. Reminiscing about the incident with me years later when we were adults, Emelita told me, "I thought you were going to get a whipping right then and there in front of everyone."

In due course the plane took off with me in my assigned seat. I wished I wasn't on it. I wished I wasn't being banished. I cried all the way to Nassau.

3. Back on Track?

A LTHOUGH PART OF ME FELT BANISHED BY MY PARENTS, I knew they were trying to help me out of an unhealthy state of mind. Wanting to make the best of it buoyed me through the summer despite the harsher aspects of my transition to life in Jamaica. I was convinced that this was my last shot to become the person I really wanted to be.

I certainly wasn't being cast down and out socially. Aunt Alma's husband, my uncle Basil, was the Reverend Canon Basil C. Jones. Uncle Basil was canon of St. James Cathedral in Spanish Town, fifteen miles or so from Kingston. The cathedral of the Jamaican diocese of the Church of England, St. James was also known as St. Jago, pronounced "Jay-go," because the original name of Spanish Town was Santiago (or Saint Jago de la Vega, "St. James on the plain") and the Anglican church stood on the site of a Spanish Roman Catholic cathedral that was destroyed by a hurricane in 1712.

As residentiary canon, occupying the cathedral rectory with his family, Uncle Basil was the third man in the cathedral hierarchy after the bishop of Jamaica and the dean. This gave Uncle Basil and Aunt Alma a significant social position. Yet their household had a straitened, penny-pinching atmosphere. There was a lock on the refrigerator and even the cold water pitcher was accessible only on Aunt Alma's say-so. If you were going to have hot chocolate, she'd put a half teaspoon of cocoa in your mug before she added hot water, not milk. After the abundance of good food at home in Bermuda, this was definitely a tough change, especially since my parents were sending money for my room and board.

Fortunately, the rectory grounds, about half a mile from the cathedral, held many mango trees of different varieties and as the Jamaican saying goes, "In mango season, you wash the pot and turn it down." If mangoes were ripening, which depending on the variety could be anytime from April to October, there was no need to cook and no one need go hungry. That's an exaggeration because mangoes are not that rich in nutrients, but they've been an important food in Jamaica since the 1780s. When I took up residence in the rectory in mid-June 1959, I made myself sick eating mangoes nonstop. But I was soon eating them again, albeit not so many at once. The beefy mangoes— beefy, or beef, mango is one of many local Jamaican names for different mango varieties—particularly tempted me. They were not all that sweet, but if you got a big red one, it was delightful.

Aunt Alma's doling out food so sparingly reflected the strict control Uncle Basil exercised in his household. My cousin John, six months older than I, and his sister, Dorothy, around the same age as Emelita, had grown up in this environment. Their stolid acceptance of the grim regime reinforced my innate tendency to stoicism in response to any physical hardship.

My will to rebel against what I saw as unreasonable authority hardly vanished, however, and it didn't take long for me to get into trouble in minor ways. Within the first days of arriving in Spanish Town I threw myself into football and cricket with John and other boys who lived near the rectory. One evening near the end of June, I kept playing when John left to be home in time for our curfew. I was planning to catch up with John on the way, but wound up getting back an hour late because I was having so much fun. As punishment, Uncle Basil decreed that I could not climb any of the mango trees for a week.

A couple of days into the one-week ban, Uncle Basil and the rest of the family went out and left me alone in the rectory. I couldn't resist climbing the beef mango tree. I was about fifteen feet up the tree, reaching for the biggest and reddest of the mangoes with one hand, when I lost my hold on the tree with the other hand. Fortunately a wire fence broke my fall, and I escaped injury with no one the wiser. Although I still wanted that mango, I decided discretion was in order and didn't break the tree-climbing ban again until the next time there was no one around to see me.

Different as the rectory and home were, they also had a lot in common. In both there was a heavy emphasis on education and striving for excellence. One Saturday morning early in the summer, Aunt Alma said, "Listen, you're not doing anything. Why don't you come with me? I'm going to help supervise the Jamaica high school entrance exam."

I went along, and while I was there one of the other teachers, no doubt at the behest of my aunt, said, "Why don't you take the test, too?" I took the test, and two weeks later a notice came saying I had won a government scholarship to high school.

I was euphoric. I kept saying to myself *Oh, man, I'm back on track!* Two weeks later another notice came, canceling the scholarship because I was not a Jamaican citizen. That didn't matter. I knew my parents could afford to pay the school fees. What did matter was that an impartial third party had said I was smart. That gave my confidence an enormous boost.

At summer's end I jumped right into classes at St. Jago High School, determined to make up for lost time. Like the Berkeley Institute, St. Jago was organized on the lines of elite British schools with six forms over six or seven years. It was the equivalent of sixth through twelfth grades in the American high school system.

At thirteen years of age I belonged in third form. Balancing my excellent score on the Jamaica scholarship exam against my academic decline in the first form at Berkeley, plus my missing a whole year of rigorous academic study while attending the Bermuda Technical Institute, St. Jago placed me in second form with boys and girls six months to a year younger than I was. However, I'd been such a precocious student at Central School that even with all the missed time I was ahead of the St. Jago second formers. At night I found myself helping John with his third form homework.

"This isn't fair," I thought. I asked my aunt to talk to St. Jago's headmaster about letting me move up a year. She didn't feel that was the right thing to do. One morning I went to school half an hour early. I pulled my desk out of my classroom, dragged it down the hallway to John's classroom, and put it beside his desk. I was sitting there when Mr. Johnson, the math teacher, came in.

He said, "Son, what are you doing here?"

I said, "I'm old enough for third form, and I'm doing my cousin John's homework every night. If I can do his homework, I should be in his classes."

Mr. Johnson said, "Hmmm. I'm going to give a test right now. If you do well on it, you can stay as far as I'm concerned. But I can't speak for any of the other teachers."

"That's fine with me, sir," I said. "Thank you."

When he checked my test paper, Mr. Johnson told me I had done well enough to stay in the class, but he repeated that he could not speak for the other teachers.

Most of the faculty were Black men and women. But there were several White teachers, and one of them, Mr. Rapp, who was from New Zealand, taught the next class, which was French. Mr. Rapp was known throughout the school as a strict disciplinarian. He was also a sharp dresser with a rather limited wardrobe. By that I mean he wore the same clothes all the time, but he was always neat as a pin. He was not an imposing figure physically, only five feet eight inches or so, and he had virtually no lips. But he had a scathing wit.

As soon as he walked into the classroom, Mr. Rapp said, "Brown, you don't belong in this class. What do you think you're doing here, my lad?" Every male student was "my lad" to Mr. Rapp, and every female student was "my lass."

I gave him the answer I had given the math teacher, and he said, "No, no, no, my lad. That's not the way it goes. Let's see what Mr. Bell thinks of this."

Mr. Bell was the headmaster. Mr. Rapp hooked his finger inside my shirt collar and escorted me to Mr. Bell, whose first response was to reprimand me for moving my desk without permission. But he wound up saying that he would let me stay in third form contingent on my good performance.

That was one of the two biggest differences I found in Jamaica compared to Bermuda. Jamaicans love to argue, and if you can offer good grounds for your position, you can win. That's why Rastafarians say, "Let's reason." In Bermuda, and especially at the Berkeley Institute, I didn't have a right to my own reasons.

Mr. Rapp's nose was a little out of joint about Mr. Bell's decision. But he quickly accepted me in the higher class, although he showed it mainly by the zeal with which he remarked on my failings. We students all knew that his bark was worse than his bite and that he wanted the best for us.

I joined the cadet corps to go camping and learn to fire a rifle, read maps, and so on. Mr. Rapp was the commanding officer. There were thirty of us lined up in our uniforms when Mr. Rapp came down the line for inspections. He used to eye me very carefully without saying a word and then move on to the next boy and say something like, "When you have a moment, teach Lance Corporal Brown how to shine his boots." He'd move farther down the line and then say, "Lance Corporal Brown, did you hear what I said about your boots?"

"Yes, sir."

"Take it to heart."

Whenever a teacher entered a classroom at St. Jago, the class stood and greeted him or her by name. There were five boys in my class who were particularly mischievous: the Knott brothers, my cousin John Jones, Lenox Miller, and me. One of Mr. Rapp's signatures was that he always jingled the loose change in his pocket, playing "pocket billiards," as we called it. So one morning when he entered the room and the rest of the class stood up and said, "Good morning, Mr. Rapp," my four co-conspirators and I stood with our mouths pressed tightly together so that it looked like we had no lips, just like Mr. Rapp, and played pocket billiards.

Mr. Rapp was livid. In his clipped British accent, he barked, "Brown, Jones, the Knotts, and Miller, you're all going to the headmaster." Mr. Bell gave each us of us "three of the best," as they say, on the backside with his cane.

I'm afraid Mr. Rapp sent us to the headmaster for a caning quite often. And it was always the same refrain: "All right, my lads. Brown, Jones, the Knotts, and Miller, off you go to Mr. Bell."

Every year the graduating class put on skits in front of the teachers, and the skits could be about them. When my friends and I graduated a few years later, Lenox Miller and I did a skit where he was chomping on some gum. I came in, thin-lipped and playing pocket billiards, and said, "Are you chewing gum, my lad?"

Lenox, who was known to stutter, replied, "N-n-n-n-no, sir. I am not Chewing Gum. I am Miller."

The audience, teachers and students alike, howled with laughter. Mr. Rapp turned cherry red, but he took it like a champ. So there was discipline at St. Jago, but there was also give and take and a spirit of fun.

At Christmas 1959 I went home to Bermuda and had a joyful reunion with my parents and Emelita. It was great to be with my mother and father and have no battles over my behavior. And despite my history of teasing Emelita, the two of us were extremely close and we had missed each other a lot.

Among other activities over that Christmas–New Year's school break at home, I had my first experience of going to an unsegregated movie theatre in Bermuda. A theatre boycott had taken place in the summer, just after I left for Jamaica, and quickly succeeded in ending decades of segregated seating. Under pressure to end practices that might begin to limit tourism by disturbing progressive-minded American and British visitors, segregation also ended in restaurants and hotels. It would be more than a decade before Bermuda officially ended school segregation with the Education Act of 1971, and of course de facto segregation lingered everywhere.

Everyone in our family and circle of friends was happy with the desegregation of theatres, restaurants, and hotels, but no one talked about them much. In hindsight, I think Black Bermudians, at least, were ashamed that this minimal progress had taken so long to achieve.

Delighted with my academic rebound and positive attitude and seeing how happy Emelita and I were to be together, my parents decided she should go back to Jamaica with me. That was quite a shock for Emelita. She had barely a week to adjust to the idea and say good-bye to all her friends. I didn't realize how traumatic the move was for her, however, until we spoke about it as adults.

Emelita told me, "I was a sheltered girl. I was devastated to be torn away from Mommy and Daddy and sent to a foreign country at age eleven. I missed my friends. And life in the rectory was horrible. John and Dorothy were alright, but their parents were so cold and unemotional. And the way Aunt Alma was so stingy mean about food—for pity's sake, a lock on the refrigerator? With all the money our parents were sending for room and board? We went to church every Sunday in Bermuda, but in Spanish Town it was two long services on Sunday and another long one on Wednesday evening. On top of that I became another church servant along with Dorothy, having to clean all the altar vessels and polish the candlesticks. You and John got out of that because you were boys. But I could never understand how you tolerated it there, especially given how brutal Uncle Basil was to you."

I might not have had to polish the candlesticks with Emelita and Dorothy, but I did have to clean the chalices as an altar boy. And at that point I probably would not have called Uncle Basil brutal. He was certainly quick to discipline me for any infraction of his rules, including corporal punishment with a belt when he was especially displeased. But it was only later that this became really problematic for me.

In the early part of my time in Spanish Town, my punishment for bad behavior was more likely to be church service every morning for a week. At communion one day I was serving Uncle Basil as altar boy, which included pouring wine for him to consecrate. I was angry at him for punishing me over something, and when he brought the chalice to where I was kneeling at the side of the altar and nodded for me to pour the wine, I only dribbled in a few drops. He nodded again, and I dribbled in a few more drops. And then he glared at me, and I poured in the full measure. That brought me a week's worth of church attendance early every morning.

Unaware of how miserable Emelita was in Jamaica, I was glad to have her company. Emelita at least did not have a difficult transition scholastically. She was in first form back in Bermuda, and she joined Dorothy in the first form at St. Hugh's, an all-girls school in Kingston, run by the Church of England, with both boarding and day students. She did well as a student there. When the school year ended, Emelita and I went home to Bermuda for the summer.

The summer passed without any notable incident until August. Early that month my father took me aside and said, "I want to talk to you about Philip Butterfield."

Huh? I couldn't imagine what my father had to tell me about Philip Butterfield, who was one year behind me at Central and had just finished his second year at Berkeley. Philip and I knew each other, but we rarely crossed paths.

My father said, "I am Philip's father. He's your and Emelita's brother. Don't tell Emelita because your mother doesn't want her to know yet. However, your mother agrees that since you're already fourteen, you should know about Philip. Bermuda is a small place, and we don't want the two of you to stumble into any conflict, not knowing that you are brothers."

This explained a lot. It was Philip my father was referring to when he came home that day to crow to my mother about the boy who won a scholarship to Berkeley with "no Darrell genes!"

Where before I was angry at my mother for picking on me, now I was angry at my father for betraying and hurting her. In that same conversation, and a follow-up talk before Emelita and I left for Jamaica, my father said in his no-drama, let's-face-the-facts manner, "You can be mad at me all you want, Ewart. But you should accept Philip as your brother and treat him accordingly." He also made it clear that he was going to fulfill his responsibilities as Philip's father as he always had and that this situation in no way affected my position as his son.

Back in Jamaica my mind was a jumble of conflicting thoughts and feelings about my father and about what it would be like whenever I happened to meet Philip in Bermuda. It's probably not surprising that I misbehaved a bit more at school and was sent to the headmaster more often by Mr. Rapp and other teachers. But I didn't go off the rails academically, and I kept myself in reasonably good standing at St. Jago.

The real target for my discontent was Uncle Basil and what I saw as his martinet ways. I flouted my curfew and I was insolent, among other misdeeds. He responded by beating me more, although to my great surprise he once stopped on the verge of a beating.

That occurred when he drove his car into the rectory parking lot and saw me playing football with Jerry, a sixteen-year-old boy from Spanish Town who did the rectory yard work. Uncle Basil got out of his car, red-faced with anger. He stood six feet six inches tall and weighed over two hundred pounds. Striding toward me and reaching for his belt, he yelled, "You should know better than to be gallivanting with the yard boy!" Jerry wisely took off. I instinctively reached for a rock to defend myself. Seeing that, Uncle Basil stopped unbuckling his belt and with a bit more verbal scolding went into the rectory.

There were many things I didn't understand about Uncle Basil, especially the contrast between his Christianity and his stinginess and class snobbery. To shun playing with a nice guy like Jerry because he was of a lower social class never occurred to me.

The incident did not dispose me to treat Uncle Basil and his ideas of proper social behavior with greater respect. One evening in early November I was supposed to go to St. Jago to perform in a play put on by the fourth and fifth formers. At the last minute I was punished for insolence and ordered to stay home while Aunt Alma and Uncle Basil went to the play with John.

Emelita and Dorothy, then both twelve-year-old second formers at St. Hugh's, were also staying home. Before she went to bed, Emelita looked at me sorrowfully and said, "Ewart, don't do anything to make things worse for yourself."

"I won't, Sis."

As soon as she was gone, however, I got a couple of sheets of paper and tore them up into little slips. With slight variations here and there, I continued my adolescent rebellion and wrote notes on the slips that I knew would anger Uncle Basil. I put my little slips of paper all around the floor of the rectory and then went to my room to await the return of Uncle Basil, Aunt Alma, and John. In due course they came home, and my desire to enrage Uncle Basil was fulfilled beyond my expectations.

Until then I had never given Uncle Basil the satisfaction of crying out in pain when he beat me. That night he whipped the screams right out of my lungs. The combined noise of his thrashing me and my howls of pain woke Emelita. She was badly shaken by the sight of my back, red with blood from overlapping welts.

Emelita's presence no doubt helped end the beating. A couple of weeks passed, during which Uncle Basil only disciplined me verbally. To my great surprise, my mother showed up in Spanish Town, brought by a letter from Emelita describing what had happened and pleading for a rescue from the rectory for her and me. Emelita did leave the rectory, going to board at St. Hugh's. She was a lot happier living there, especially when several other girls we knew from Bermuda also became students at St. Hugh's, but she never took to Jamaica as I did.

I don't know what conversations my mother had about me with Aunt Alma and Uncle Basil, but she satisfied herself there was not going to be a second beating of an extreme nature, and I told her I was willing to continue living in the rectory. I was happy at St. Jago, and I didn't want to change schools.

At the same time, something in my attitude toward my mother shifted. Although I didn't dwell on it or how it made me feel, the fact was that my mother had come all the way from Bermuda to Jamaica to make sure I was okay. From then on there was never any great conflict between us, and our relationship got better and better in the succeeding years.

A big part of my wanting to continue going to school in Jamaica was St. Jago's attitude toward sports. Like Central School in Bermuda, St. Jago celebrated both academics and athletics. That was exactly what I needed. One without the other would not have satisfied me.

High school sports were and are extremely important in Jamaica, much more so than in Bermuda. High school football, cricket, and track in Jamaica are like high school (American) football in Texas and high school basketball in Indiana. A Jamaican high school track meet is like *Friday Night Lights* with thousands of people in the stands. Champs, the all-Jamaica high school competition in track, draws tens of thousands of spectators and its results are national news.

I played whatever sport was in season and went out for St. Jago's teams in cricket, football, and track. I wasn't a star my first couple of years, but I was good enough to make the teams and compete against other schools.

That gave me opportunities to see Murray Brown, who was attending Knox College, a Presbyterian secondary school in the middle of the Jamaican countryside. Murray competed for Knox in football and track. We fought hard to defeat each other during the game or meet, but outside the lines we remained the best of friends.

Track was the sport where I did best, competing in the 220- and 440-yard (quarter-mile) dashes and relays. But the first two years I ran at the high school championships, I didn't have the confidence to beat the guys from Kingston College, a powerhouse on the Jamaican high school sports scene. Kingston had such a big sports reputation, especially in track, that I assumed their sprinters had to be superior athletes. You can't beat someone you believe is better than you.

My breakthrough in track came at St. Jago's sports day near the close of fifth form, when I had just turned sixteen. St. Jago students were sorted into houses that competed against each other inside and outside the classroom. I belonged to Smith House, and I won my races that sports day by quite a margin.

Not long afterward Howard "Fudge" Aris came by to see me at track practice. Fudge, the name most people knew him by, had grown up in Spanish Town and been a star track athlete at Kingston College in the early 1950s before becoming a coach. In the 1970s and 1980s he became one of the leaders, and eventually the president, of the Jamaican Amateur Athletic Association (now the Jamaican Athletics Administrative Association), where he played a prominent role in the development of many Jamaican athletes, including multiple gold medal winner Usain Bolt. His death in late 2011 at age seventy-five was a sad day for Jamaica and the world of track. Even in 1962, the athletics community in Jamaica referred to Fudge with respect bordering on awe.

I was stunned that Fudge wanted to talk to me. (Although I thought of him as Fudge and he was only ten years older, twenty-six to my sixteen, I addressed him as Mr. Aris.) When he said, "You don't know how good you can be; there's no telling how far you can go," it was music to my ears. Fudge suggested a workout routine, and I immediately started to follow it. Within a year I was one of the fastest schoolboy quarter-milers in Jamaica.

As part of improving at track I moved from the rectory in Spanish Town to live with a family in Kingston, the Munroes, in order to be close to the national training facilities there. It was all arranged through Aunt Alma, and I still went to school at St. Jago every day. Sometimes I took a bus, but more often I caught a ride in either direction with one of the many St. Jago faculty who lived in Kingston.

In my final year at St. Jago, Herb McKenley, the national track coach for Jamaica, picked me for the all-high-school team that was going to compete against a visiting all-high-school team from Trinidad. In his own athletic career, Coach McKenley set a world record in the 400 meters in 1948 and competed for Jamaica at the 1948 London Olympics and the 1952 Helsinki Olympics, winning a gold medal in the 4×400 relay and three silver medals in the 100- and 400-meter dashes. Yet his decision to pick me did not go unquestioned. One high school coach went on the radio to say I had no right to be on the team because I was not a Jamaican citizen. Coach McKenley said, "Ewart

Brown has no right to represent Jamaica. But he is not representing the country. He is representing the high schools. So he stays on the team." That was a great experience for me.

I earned first team all-Jamaican-high-school honors in cricket as well as track and second team honors in football. I enjoyed all of it tremendously, but I can't write about my high school sports career in Jamaica without mentioning St. Jago's cricket coach, George Moodie. The first word that comes to mind when I think of Mr. Moodie is cantankerous. Oh my, he could be miserable to deal with. Yet I loved playing for him. He had played for the West Indies in international test matches, and he knew cricket inside and out: the history, the techniques of bowling, batting, and fielding, and match strategy and tactics. He had high standards for his cricket team in every way. If you came to practice with your shirt outside your pants, he said, "You didn't come to practice with *my* team, did you? If you can't dress properly, how can you play cricket properly?" Because of Mr. Moodie, St. Jago's cricket team was considered the equal of any in Jamaica.

In my second to last year at St. Jago, we were playing Kingston College in Kingston. We had batted first and only scored 80-odd runs. In the afternoon Kingston came to bat with 5 wickets in hand and needed only 40 or so runs to beat us. Yet there was an unspoken agreement on our team that we could beat these guys. We turned on our A game and fought to get their batsmen out and hold them to as few runs as possible. The last hour of the game was so intense, it felt like a full day's play in itself.

Balls that would normally get past our fielders and reach the boundary for 4 runs just didn't. Our bowlers—I was one of them—were bowling aggressive lines and giving the Kingston batsmen fits. In the end we won by 1 or 2 runs, the slimmest of margins in cricket. It was only possible, in my view, because of the spirit of excellence that Mr. Moodie engendered in us.

What a glorious victory! We sang the St. Jago song all the way back to Spanish Town: "Born in the shade of Ancient Santiago/Old Mother Church our School still lives and toils . . . " Not a chart-topping melody and lyrics, perhaps, but a song I'll always be happy to sing. Likewise St. Jago's Latin motto, *Labor Omnia Vincit* ("Work conquers all"), will always be important to me as an expression of St. Jago's, my parents', and my own deepest values.

I haven't said anything about social life during my high school days. There wasn't much partying to speak of. Even when I moved out of the rectory at the cathedral and went to live with the Munroe family in Kingston, I was too busy with studying and sports to get into serious trouble.

Then as now, music was a big part of Jamaican culture. Ska, the precursor to reggae, was in its heyday, and I became a fan of artists like Prince Buster,

Toots and the Maytals, and Millie Small. If I were compiling a soundtrack album of my St. Jago years, the first song would probably be Millie Small's "My Boy Lollipop," with its bouncy melody and sassy lyrics.

My favorite band, however, was Byron Lee and the Dragonaires, who had their own hits and also backed all the biggest stars who toured Jamaica, such as Harry Belafonte. My father's youngest sister, my aunt Eileen, had a stepson, Billy Vernon, who played guitar in the Dragonaires. My love of ska segued into a love of reggae, when it came along a few years later.

Don't get the wrong idea from my mention of ska and reggae. In my St. Jago days there was nothing like the availability of alcohol and other drugs among so many of today's high schoolers. I had one experience with marijuana in Jamaica. During the middle of my time at St. Jago I was leaving school after track practice, when a guy in the neighborhood who was two or three years older stopped me and said, "Why don't you come down by the river and see how the rastas deal with the chillum pipe?"

He probably took it as a challenge to tempt Canon Jones's nephew from the straight and narrow way. Curious about marijuana I said, "Okay."

We went down by the Rio Cobre River, right behind St. Jago High, and I hit that chillum pipe. The next thing I knew I fell asleep and woke up a couple of hours later. I thought to myself, "Man! Is that what the fuss is all about?" So I stayed away from marijuana for the rest of high school.

My first romantic experience was happier. Visiting Emelita at St. Hugh's, I met her schoolmate Rosemarie Halliburton, who was also a boarding student there, and I was smitten.

My cousin Dorothy continued to be a day student at St. Hugh's, living at home in Spanish Town. Every day when I went to school at St. Jago, I stopped by the rectory to give Dorothy a note to take to Rosemarie. And every day Rosemarie gave Dorothy a note for me, which I picked up on my way back to Kingston from St. Jago. This went on for two years, with me splashing Old Spice on my notes and Rosemarie putting a few drops of cologne on hers. Emelita teased me that the only reason I came to visit her was to see Rosemarie.

Things with Rosemarie never progressed beyond puppy love: dates to the movies, well-chaperoned school dances, and such. And the relationship didn't survive my graduating from St. Jago and going to college in the United States. But I'll always be grateful that Emelita went to St. Hugh's.

Likewise I'll always be grateful for my five years at St. Jago High in Spanish Town. Life in the rectory may have had its challenges, but I knew my aunt and uncle were fundamentally good people who wanted me to grow up well. In hindsight I see a lot to admire in their service to others through the church. Going to stay with them stopped me from careening down a very bad path and opened up a vast horizon of positives for me in my academic and athletic development. If I had it to do over, I wouldn't change a thing.

4. Campus Radical

I N THE SPRING OF 1964 THE MAIN QUESTION for me was where I was going to earn a bachelor's degree before going on to medical school. My parents wanted me to attend what was then Sir George Williams University in Montreal (now Concordia University as a result of a 1974 merger with Loyola College of Montreal). Uncle Bert had finished his undergraduate degree at Sir George Williams, and the thinking was that this would position me to follow him in earning a medical degree at Montreal's McGill University.

The prospect of Quebec winters chilled me to the bone. For a little while I thought I had an alternative at the University of Illinois's flagship campus in Urbana-Champaign, when Herb McKenley, who had gone there on a track scholarship, secured scholarships for half-miler George Walker and me. Before I had a chance to discuss this with my parents, however, I saw a picture in *Ebony* magazine of Illinois in January with snow completely covering parked cars. That was no improvement on Montreal in my mind, and the next day I phoned Coach McKenley in Jamaica and explained that my parents wanted me to go to Sir George Williams. I decided not to say anything to my parents about the scholarship for the time being.

George Walker wasn't so worried about the cold. He went to the University of Illinois, did very well there, and eventually became a dentist in Chicago. We see each other every spring at Champs, the high school track championships in Jamaica.

Although I was hoping some other possibility would arise, I was resigning myself to going to university in Montreal. But late in the spring there was a dormitory fire at Sir George Williams—fortunately there were no casualties—and thus no residence for the next class of freshman students.

I've already mentioned that several members of the Darrell family attended Howard University. That was where Aunt Gloria and Uncle Bert had met. Aunt Gloria suggested that as the family's most recent Howard graduate she should use her contacts there to try to get me in for a semester, and after that I could transfer to Sir George Williams.

I rushed to send in an application before Howard's final deadline. When I told Murray Brown about this, he decided he was also going to Howard. Although he had the grades to get in, Murray just missed the final application deadline. Fortunately for him, however, Howard's director of international students, Dr. Ernest Wilson, was a friend of his family's. Dr. Wilson said there were always accepted students who didn't enroll or who changed their minds on arrival and immediately withdrew. He advised Murray to come to Howard at the start of the academic year, so that he could be ready to take one of these places as soon as it became available.

Murray did that, tagging along with me wherever I went. I let him sleep in my dorm room, and he persuaded the cafeteria staff to sell him meal tickets without a student identification card by claiming his admission was pending. Near the end of September he finally heard from Dr. Wilson that a spot had opened up, and he became a bona fide member of the Howard University Class of 1968.

It didn't take a month for me to recognize that I never wanted to transfer to Sir George Williams. One day on the Howard campus told me that. The atmosphere was electric. In my first call home to my parents, I said I wanted to stay at Howard. "Are the girls that pretty?" my father asked.

They were. But that was the icing on the big multilayered chocolate cake that was Howard. Its extraordinarily distinguished faculty and its student body, mostly American but with many students from Africa and throughout the Black diaspora in the Western Hemisphere, had long made it a world center of Black cultural, intellectual, and political activity. That was becoming even more the case as the Black civil rights movement in America reached its peak. I thanked my lucky stars that I had ended up exactly where I felt I should be.

One day in October I walked into the cafeteria, picked up a tray, and got in line behind two tall guys in military fatigues and boots. Their hair was fairly closely cropped by today's standards, but it was both longer than was then usual and completely natural, a harbinger of the big Afros to come. They both turned toward me as I approached. The slightly taller of the two said, "Young brother, how are you doing? Let us introduce ourselves. We're from the Student Nonviolent Coordinating Committee. We're going to be working in Lowndes Country, Alabama, for the freedom of Black people, and we're here trying to recruit some students to join us."

I said, "Well, can you tell me some more about what you're doing?"

We sat down, and they began to describe going door to door in little farming communities in the South helping Black people register to vote. Over the next hour and a half our conversation attracted Murray and other students, all of whom I invited to join us. A few of the newcomers drifted off after a few minutes, but most stayed for quite a while. As for me, I was riveted.

The slightly taller guy was Stokely Carmichael, and the other was Cleveland "Cleve" Sellers. Wow! I had been reading and hearing about these guys, and they were right across from me. There was nothing boastful or arrogant about them. They radiated a quiet confidence and competence—and unmistakable commitment to justice for Black people. I already admired them for the activism I'd seen reported in *Ebony*, *Jet,* and the *Washington Afro-American*, including Stokely's participating in the Freedom Rides to integrate southern interstate buses and trains in the summer of 1961—not to mention his fifty-three days of solitary confinement at Parchman State Prison Farm in Sunflower County, Mississippi, for breaking local laws segregating buses and trains. With many others from the Student Nonviolent Coordinating Committee (SNCC, pronounced "snick"), the Congress of Racial Equality (CORE), the National Association for the Advancement of Colored People (NAACP), and the Southern Christian Leadership Conference (SCLC), as well as thousands of Black Mississippians, Stokely and Cleve had participated in the Freedom Summer that had just taken place in Mississippi. News accounts were fresh in my mind, especially the murders of civil rights workers James Chaney, Andrew Goodman, and Michael Schwerner, and of three Black Mississippians who were standing up for their civil rights.

The voter registration drive in Lowndes County, Alabama, was the next big thing they were tackling. Stokely, who hailed from Trinidad by way of New York City, had graduated from Howard with the class of 1964 just before Mississippi Freedom Summer started. But Cleve, an entering member of the class of 1966 whose activism began with lunch counter sit-ins in his native South Carolina, had put his studies on hold after his sophomore year so that he could do civil rights work. When Stokely and Cleve got up to leave the cafeteria, I went straight to the dorm and called home.

My mother answered the phone. All fired up, I said, "I have to go to Alabama!"

"To where?"

"Alabama!"

"For what?"

"To register Black people to vote! The Freedom Riders and the people who were working for civil rights in Mississippi this summer are all involved, and I want to join them."

My mother said, "Listen, we sent you to the university so you could be educated and get your degree, not so you could go to Alabama. If you wish to go, you will have to find the means."

"I don't have any money."

My mother knew that. Although I had summer job earnings for books and spending money, I didn't have enough to support myself during several months of field volunteer work. There were no stipends for civil rights workers that I could apply for. So I put that idea on hold and went on with freshman year. As time passed I realized that there was plenty for me to do on the Howard campus, which was a key stopping point for anyone speaking and working for civil rights. Throughout my undergraduate years I was probably on campus eighty to ninety percent of the time, whether it was for my studies, sports, student government, activism of one kind or another, or social life.

I threw myself wholeheartedly into curricular and extracurricular activities in my freshman year. Not quite realizing the enormous time commitment involved, but with qualifying for medical school in mind, I immediately declared a major in chemistry and a minor in math. I played freshman soccer and ran the 440-yard dash and the relays with the varsity track team. I wrote sports stories for Howard's daily student newspaper, the *Hilltop*, which Zora Neale Hurston co-founded in 1924. My editor was Rayton Gerald, who was a couple of years ahead of me and who later became very successful on Wall Street.

The president of the Howard University Student Association (HUSA) that year was Togo West, who would cap a distinguished legal and U.S. federal government career by serving as secretary of the army from 1993 to 1997 and secretary of veterans affairs from 1998 to 2000. I'm sure I would have become involved in student government anyway, but the impression Togo made on me contributed to my running at the end of freshman year to be one of two sophomore representatives on HUSA—my first political campaign and my first electoral success. In his way Togo West was as much a role model for me as Stokely Carmichael and Cleve Sellers. Even as a freshman undergraduate I could see the fiber of the man. Togo West, who passed away in 2018, had the penetrating intellect, the moral seriousness, and the weight of purpose that the word *gravitas* is meant to evoke.

In the fall of 1965, when he was a first-year student at the Howard University School of Law, West made the sponsoring speech when I pledged the service fraternity Alpha Phi Omega. He ended by saying, "If you wish to join this organization, come high or stay at home." Two or three years later he probably would have used a slightly different idiom as recreational use of drugs besides alcohol became more common on American campuses, although I doubt he would ever have been a partaker himself. Other members of Alpha Phi Omega who mentored me in different respects were Norman Powell, later a dean at Nova University in Florida; Bill Keene, later associate dean of students at Howard; Cleve Christophe, who had a very successful business career and became an outstanding investment banker; Marshall Morrison, a gifted vocalist; and Guy Draper, a legendary character at Howard who wound up being an agent for several NFL players.

The toughest part of freshman year was learning to manage my money. But after a few weekends in which I found myself short of funds to do things with my friends, I got practical and never let that happen again. My father's advice about having fun and following your passions—"Always cover your breakfast first"—really sank in at this time, and it has stood me in good stead ever since. Nowadays I often find myself repeating my father's words to my own sons.

In freshman year I was really only beginning to learn about different varieties of Black and pan-African ideology and social analysis. One of the landmarks in my education about these matters was the tragic assassination of Malcolm X on Sunday, February 21, 1965. Guy Draper was driving the two of us to a restaurant in the late afternoon when the news came on the car radio. That made me curious to learn more about who Malcolm X was and why he was so threatening to elements of the Nation of Islam and others. The more I read of what he did, wrote, spoke, and stood for, the more excited I became about countering racism and the more Malcolm X became a hero of mine.

Over the next couple of years my understanding of racism against Black people as a global phenomenon, and of its particular impacts in the Western Hemisphere, deepened thanks to a number of inspiring younger faculty members at Howard, especially English professor Andress Taylor, who was from North Carolina; economist Acklyn Lynch, who was from Trinidad; sociologist Nathan Hare, who was born on a sharecropping farm in Oklahoma; Linda Blumenthal, who also taught sociology; and William Augustus Banner, who was professor of philosophy. In my junior and senior years at Howard, when other politically active students and I needed an intermediary between the administration and us, we turned to these faculty members.

Unfortunately, Howard's administration did not look kindly on the young assistant professors who were most in tune with students on issues like the Vietnam War and a greater focus on Black history, culture, and community. Despite the solid academic achievements of Taylor, Lynch, Hare, and Blumenthal, Howard denied them tenure or contract renewals. They all lost their positions between 1966 and 1968.

An important influence in a different but still ultimately positive way was Dr. Moddie Daniel Taylor, who was professor of chemistry. Born in Alabama in 1912, Dr. Taylor had worked on the Manhattan Project during World War II, and in many ways he typified the conservative core of Howard's tenured faculty. I thought I had earned an A in one of his courses, only to find that he had marked me all the way down to a B for missing a quiz while I was competing for Howard at a track meet in New York. When I showed him the official form releasing me from classes for the track meet, he was unmoved. "That's not my business," he told me. "That was your choice."

Dr. Taylor's refusal to make any allowances struck me as unfair, but I respected his scientific achievements and his rigor as a teacher and I recognized that he was within his rights to grade as he saw fit. Although I still think my running in the track meet was a positive choice for Howard as well as myself, Dr. Taylor gave me a valuable lesson in not expecting others to share your priorities and applaud your behavior, no matter how reasonable or well intentioned it may be. You've got to operate by your own inner compass and accept the consequences.

At the end of freshman year I had a B-plus average, and I decided that I would throttle back to a B average in order to allow more time for extracurricular activities and social life. In truth I was going to become a weekend party animal during the school year, but I managed to maintain the B average.

I went home for the summer of 1965, needing to earn as much as possible for my education. I worked for my father, cleaning up his nightclub, the Clayhouse Inn, and doing the rounds to service the vending machines he had in various establishments around the Island. The Clayhouse Inn was on the ocean side of North Shore Road, with a beautiful view of the water. My father leased the club premises from James Browne, the father of lawyer Lois Browne-Evans. It was the hottest club in Bermuda, the last place in the history of the Island, down to the present day, that drew both Black and White patrons in large numbers.

The club's success stemmed in part from my father's savvy in paying taxi drivers to bring tourists there from the hotels. He also brought in the best Black acts from America. He had a great relationship with Ruth Bowen, whose Queen Booking Corporation in New York City was the first booking agency owned by a Black woman. She had started off booking her first husband, Wallace "Billy" Bowen, one of the original Ink Spots, and then become Dinah Washington's booking agent. From the 1950s on, the Clayhouse Inn showcased many of her artists—among others, jazz great Louis Jordan, Jerry Butler, Nipsey Russell, and Sarah Vaughan, as well as Dinah Washington—often before White American tourists from outside major U.S. cities commonly saw them at home.

I enjoyed working with my dad, but there was a shadow on the summer because two people I knew and liked were in prison. Bermuda was going through its own civil rights upheavals, and in January of that year Black workers at the Bermuda Electric Light Company (Belco) had struck in protest of unequal working conditions. White workers had a five-day work week, paid public holidays, paid vacation time, and a pension scheme, but Black workers had a six-day work week and none of the benefits.

The BIU called the strike on behalf of the workers on January 16, 1965, after Belco refused to allow a secret ballot to determine whether workers wanted to form a union. The strike proceeded with nothing more than peaceful picketing for sixteen days. But on February 2, the authorities had the assembled members of the Bermuda Police Service (hereafter also the Police or the BPS) and militia attempt to break the strike by force, first firing tear gas into the picket line and then advancing with truncheons. The unarmed strikers defended themselves with sticks and rocks and their own bare hands. Among the severely injured, mostly strikers, was one White policeman.

In the *Royal Gazette*'s version of history, the events of February 2, 1965, are known as the "Belco Riots" as if they occurred over multiple days. To call what happened that day a riot is itself a distortion that requires a modifier, the Belco Police Riot, to provide a more accurate label for the violent disruption of a peaceful labor strike.

Bermuda's 1964 Trade Union and Trade Disputes Act decreed illegal any "picketing deemed to be intimidating." With such vague language, the authorities had free rein to prosecute picketers. They arrested nine people and sent four to prison for several months. One of them was a cousin of mine, Kerwin Ratteray, and another was a friend, Kenneth Paul, who later earned renown as one of Bermuda's best cricketers for his left-arm, medium-pace bowling. (Much later, he became my patient.)

Nothing better illustrates the attitude of Bermuda's UBP Government and its other White authorities toward even peaceful race-related protest at this time than its treatment of Dr. Barbara Ball, who was the first female doctor to practice on the Island, an outspoken member of the PLP, and the BIU's first White official (she became BIU general secretary in 1962). Ball, a judo expert who taught the martial art to members of the BPS, used its techniques to defend herself against Police violence during the 1965 Belco strike. The year before, King Edward VII Memorial Hospital (KEMH) had suspended her admitting privileges for attempting to organize an employees union under the BIU umbrella.

The brutality of depriving a physician in good standing of the right to aid patients who require hospitalization is remarkable, isn't it? It was a barbaric act by the White establishment, heedless of any pain, suffering, or death that might result. And it was profoundly racist. Dr. Ball was White, but as a physician committed to social justice in Bermuda she served patients who were almost all Black.

Another shadow on the summer of 1965 fell over the United States as a series of riots took place in the Watts neighborhood of southern Los Angeles from August 11 to 17. I saw events in Bermuda and the United States as part of one pan-African drive for justice and equality. I was eager to get back to Howard to join the social and political activism going on there and prepare myself to contribute in a bigger way in the future.

AT THE START OF THE 1965–1966 ACADEMIC YEAR I took up my role as one of two sophomore class representatives in the Howard University Student Association, focusing on all the normal campus issues like improving the food in the cafeteria. Encouraged to do so by Sanford Cloud, who was then HUSA president, I also became student representative on an athletics advisory committee. With a perspective much like that of Togo West, Sanford Cloud taught me a great deal about leadership including the value of *Robert's Rules of Order* for ensuring fairness in meetings—good grounding for my time in Bermuda's Parliament.

Howard did not then have any athletic scholarships, whereas all the schools we competed against did. Howard's only provision for athletes was meal tickets. So I organized Students Negotiating for Athletic Progress, or SNAP. I ordered five hundred buttons from a company in Minnesota, and I began talking up SNAP and athletic scholarships wherever and whenever I could. The administration thought all this was harmless and probably figured I'd lose steam after a while. But I kept at it. In my junior year Howard decided to grant athletic scholarships, and in my senior year I received one myself. SNAP proved to be a good trial run for other activism and campaigning.

To go back to my sophomore year, at the beginning of the second semester I also went to volunteer at the recently opened local SNCC office—it had the easiest possible address to remember, 1234 U Street NW. My first assignment as a volunteer was in late January when I was sent to 15th Street and L Street NW, to assist Marion Barry, who had been SNCC's first chairman in 1960–1961 and who had set up the local SNCC office at the request of the organization's executive secretary, James Forman. Marion was leading a boycott of the DC Transit bus company which was privately owned and had announced a fare increase from twenty to twenty-five cents. At the time an additional five cents was a severe prospective hardship for low-income people, which in Washington, D.C., mostly meant Black people.

In the first few minutes of talking with me, Marion Barry found out that I was a chemistry major and shared the fact that he had a master's in chemistry from Fisk University in Nashville, Tennessee. (He had earned his undergraduate degree at another historically Black school, LeMoyne-Owen College, in his native Memphis.) He explained that our goal was to build up the bus boycott over the next few days and have a major impact on the following Monday, when the Washington Metropolitan Area Transit Authority was meeting to review the prospective fare increase. Our job was to persuade as many people as possible not to take the bus by walking to work or school, driving their own cars, or forming neighborhood car pools, taking taxis, and riding the SNCC Freedom Buses, which were not actual buses but volunteers' personal automobiles. Marion emphasized that we could not ask people to boycott the bus without offering them a reasonable alternative.

Hearing this, I went to a pay phone on the corner and called two friends at Howard with cars. They agreed to come help ferry people around. After I spent the day talking to people about not taking the bus, Marion said, "I want you to keep working with me." The boycott quickly gathered support and produced a big decrease in bus ridership on Monday, January 24, 1966, which kept the fare increase from going through as planned and also persuaded D.C. Transit to improve its night schedule. It was a victory for SNCC, and I personally felt as if I had just successfully completed Community Organizing 101. Throughout the spring I continued to volunteer for SNCC activities, and Marion Barry and I developed a friendship that would last almost fifty years until his death in 2014.

Around the same time there was big news from home about Calvin Smith, my first cousin once removed and my teacher in first standard at Harrington Sound Primary School. As was typical in the United Kingdom and the British Commonwealth generally, Calvin had become a primary school teacher straight out of secondary school, in his case after finishing the upper sixth form as a scholarship student at the Berkeley Institute. Teaching school was more or less the only way that a Black Bermudian who could not afford the cost of higher education abroad would have any chance of further study. Thanks to his teaching career, Calvin won a Bermuda government scholarship to go to Queen's University in Kingston, Ontario, where he studied economics. He then went to work for the Canadian government statistics agency, where he did so well that by 1965 he was managing a staff of thirty people and likely headed toward a senior management job. But then Bermuda came calling.

To a great extent that was because the Belco strike had succeeded in the end. In December 1965, the working conditions and pay of Black workers at Belco were finally put on the same basis as that of White workers. In addition the strike gave great impetus to a push by Bermuda's British Governor at the time, Lord Martonmere, to integrate the Island's civil service. When Lord Martonmere found out that a Black Bermudian was such a well-qualified statistician, he personally went to Canada in the fall of 1965 to recruit Calvin to return home and set up Bermuda's first Government Statistics Department. Calvin's appointment as Bermuda's first statistician and one of the very first Black people to hold a senior position in the country's civil service was big news all over the Island, as well as cause for celebration within our extended family.

On the social front, my first serious girlfriend at Howard was Candy James, who was also a sophomore member of the class of 1968. Candy had a great sense of humor and was a talented singer. She belonged to the Howard chapter of Gamma Sigma Theta, a service sorority that was the counterpart to

Alpha Phi Omega, and one of her big sisters in the sorority was Jessye Norman, the future opera and recital star. Candy and I dated for much of sophomore year, and then we grew apart while still remaining on friendly terms.

The spring semester of 1966 brought me to my high point in Howard athletics achievement. In the Penn Relays, which always take place the last week of April, my Howard teammates and I won a gold medal in the 4×440 yard relay.

The other big extracurricular win for me that spring was being elected as the incoming vice president of the student association. That summer I stayed in Washington, D.C., until mid-July to work for Upward Bound on learning and recreation activities for young teenaged boys. Until then I knew about street kids, so to speak, only in theory. Working everyday with boys who didn't know who their fathers were or lived in households that never sat down together for a meal, among many other problems, really opened my eyes to the devastation of Black families in America's inner cities. A number of kids who would never have gone on to college did so as a result of that program.

In late July I returned home to compete in trials for Bermuda's team for the 1966 Commonwealth Games. Although I hadn't worked out much since the Penn Relays, I thought I had a good chance to make the team. I came first in the 440-yard dash and second in the 220-yard dash, qualifying for both the individual sprints and the 4×110 and 4×440 relays.

At that time the events were still called the British Empire and Commonwealth Games. The games had begun in Canada in 1930 and since then had been held there and in the United Kingdom, Australia, and New Zealand. The 1966 games, slated for the first two weeks of August in Kingston, Jamaica, were the first to take place outside the "White dominions" of Britain's empire and Commonwealth, the first since independence for countries like Jamaica (1962) and Kenya (1963). It was enormously exciting to be part of Bermuda's team on that account.

Shortly before we were to leave for Jamaica, however, Coach D. J. (Donald James) Williams announced that he was naming as captain the long jumper John Morbey, a teacher and one of three White athletes on the team. The others were Tony Harper, a policeman, and Colin Davey, also a teacher. They were all British expatriates working in Bermuda on temporary contracts.

I had no objection to their being on the team. But putting a resident Englishman forward as the chief representative of Bermuda did not seem right, and so I said to Coach Williams, "We should have a Bermudian as captain."

Coach Williams said, "I didn't ask you who was going to be captain, I told you."

I said, "In that case, I'm not running. I'll stay home."

Coach Williams, a White man, plainly thought I was being uppity. In 1935 he had won a Rhodes Scholarship from Bermuda to Oxford University, where he did a bachelor's degree in history and a diploma in economics. After serving as a lieutenant in the Bermuda Volunteer Rifle Corps from 1939 to 1946, he had trained as a physical education teacher and made a career in the Bermuda school system. In 1966 he was Bermuda's Director of Education. A Black Bermudian with a background in physical education would never have been offered that post.

I figured I was off the team. But a day or so later, Coach Williams said that he was naming native Bermudian high jumper Randy Benjamin as co-captain. That was fine with me, a good win-win compromise, and I gladly competed for Bermuda in Jamaica. It was an especially happy experience because I was able to see all my friends in Spanish Town and Kingston. The only disappointment was that I didn't advance past the second round of the 440.

Now and then I've thought back to Fudge Aris's telling me in Spanish Town, "You don't know how good you can be. There's no telling how far you can go." I've wondered if I could have gone a lot farther if I had devoted myself single-mindedly to track. But by temperament and inclination I really was a classic all-rounder. I wanted to experience lots of different endeavors. Academics, athletics, politics, and social life were all important to my being true to myself.

After the Commonwealth Games I spent a week or so in Bermuda before returning to Howard. During that time I helped Uncle Bert cut down some spruce trees on land where he and Aunt Gloria were going to build a new house. I complained about how tough my chemistry major and math minor were and how long it would take to become a doctor. Uncle Bert stopped cutting. He looked me in the eye and said, "Let me tell you something. If it's worth achieving, it's worth working for." That was a bingo moment for me, and I returned to Howard determined that no subject in the pre-med curriculum would stop me.

MY JUNIOR YEAR AT HOWARD, 1966–1967, was memorable among other reasons for sharing an apartment in Washington, D.C., with my mother. Like Calvin Smith, she had become a primary school teacher without a bachelor's degree, but she was determined to earn one, even though it would make no difference at that point to her teaching career or salary. She had begun the process by taking classes in Bermuda at the University of Maryland Extension, which existed primarily to serve military personnel and their families at U.S. bases on the Island. Now she was going to finish up her degree at the University of Maryland's flagship campus in College Park.

Sharing an apartment with my mother didn't cramp my style. We got along well, each of us mainly focusing on our respective studies. We didn't always go our separate ways, though. My mother often accompanied me to talks on the Howard campus by visiting civil rights activists and politicians. From time to time we did social things together, and in general it was a big plus for me to have my mother there for mutual support. My father, Emelita, our whole extended family, and I were very proud when she graduated at the end of the 1966–1967 academic year.

In my junior year I began gravitating toward a steady relationship with Beverly Johnson, a microbiology major from Tulsa, Oklahoma. My mother and Beverly got along very well, and my father got to know and like her when he came to visit my mother. I also met and liked Beverly's parents. Her father was a lieutenant colonel in the army and her mother was a schoolteacher.

Beverly and I were both in the class of 1968 and had met at the beginning of freshman year. We didn't date until after Candy James and I had broken up, however. The way that came about was that Beverly had a girlfriend, Jo Helen Alexander, who used to eat in the cafeteria around the same time every day. A couple of times a week I ate dinner in the cafeteria at the same time, sitting beside Jo Helen and asking her about Beverly. Eventually that paid off when Beverly and I had our first date.

As with most college students, our dates often involved campus events or parties with our friends. It was the heyday of Motown, and the nearby Howard Theatre (not a part of the university) hosted all the biggest stars. For $5 you could see Smokey Robinson, Gladys Knight, or another headliner, plus a second-billed musical act and a comedian.

Two highly symbolic and politically significant events—one on and one off the Howard campus—occurred in the fall of my junior year. On campus, a developing Black consciousness penetrated even the most traditional of social events, homecoming.

As at most colleges and universities, Howard's student body voted to elect a homecoming king and queen from candidates nominated by campus organizations, especially the fraternities and sororities. In 1966 a group of politically active students asked Robin Gregory to run for homecoming queen. Robin was a wonderful choice for more than her beauty: she was already a seasoned activist who had helped organize the 1962 March on Washington for Jobs and Freedom, and as a SNCC liaison she had contributed to the 1964 Mississippi Freedom Summer. At the 1964 Democratic National Convention in Atlantic City, she had participated in the unsuccessful effort to seat members of the Mississippi Freedom Democratic Party as the state's rightful delegates. State Democratic Party officials had denied Black Mississippians the right to vote for the official delegates in defiance of the national Democratic Party's rules.

It was at the convention, Robin recalled for *Eyes on the Prize*, the book and PBS series, that she saw Black women from Mississippi "wearing their hair natural." She soon began wearing her hair that way. In the early twenty-first century it is easy to miss how important this was, how dramatically it announced, "I am not going subject myself to White ideas of beauty and value."

The Howard administration was aghast at Robin's candidacy and even tried to exclude her on the grounds that she was not being nominated by a university-recognized-and-approved student group. The candidates from the sororities all had money for their campaigns, and Robin and her supporters campaigned on the proverbial shoestring. On October 19, 1966, the winner would receive her crown.

I was there that night, and it was as dramatic an event as I've witnessed. To describe it, I quote the distinguished African-American historian Paula Giddings, a friend of mine at Howard who graduated a year later.

She told *Eyes on the Prize*, "I remember very much the evening when the homecoming queen was crowned. The lights went down, the candidates went back. Then you heard the curtains open, and you heard the crank of the revolving stage begin. And as the stage revolved and turned around toward the audience, the lights began to come up at the same time. Well, before you saw Robin, you saw the way the lights cast a silhouette of her Afro before you saw her. Well, the auditorium exploded and everybody exploded. It was a wonderful moment. People started jumping up and screaming and some were raising their fists.

"Then spontaneously, a chant began. The chant was *umgawa*, black power, *umgawa*, black power. And a [human] chain was created, people began to march to it, to the rhythm of *umgawa*, black power. And there was a line and it went all the way around the auditorium and more, and finally out the door and into the streets of Washington, D.C., past the campus and still chanting, *umgawa*, black power. And that was really the launching of that movement at Howard."

To punish Robin for her temerity in winning the election, the Howard dean of women students, patron of the candidates with straightened hair, canceled the usual reception for a newly crowned homecoming queen. If you wonder why Howard administrators were so conservative, consider that since its foundation by the U.S. Congress in 1867, the university has relied on federal funds to operate.

On October 29, 1966, on the other side of the country, Stokely Carmichael gave his famous Black Power speech to a packed auditorium at the University of California, Berkeley. The phrase "Black Power" deservedly captured media attention and people's imaginations. It's only a shame that more people didn't look closely at exactly what Stokely was saying about Black Power and being a Black person. He was a philosophy major at Howard, and he made the speech a Socratic and existentialist questioning of attitudes about Blackness on the part of both Black and White people. Stokely's analysis was brilliant, leavened with his characteristic humor about conventional liberal attitudes toward racial integration. For example: "Now, you're all a college university crowd. You've taken your basic logic course. So people have been telling me anything all Black is bad. Let's make that our major premise. Major premise: Anything all Black is bad. Minor premise or particular premise: I am all Black. Therefore . . . I'm never going to be put in that trick bag . . . " a zinger that broke the audience up in laughter.

It didn't take long for a Black Power Committee to form at Howard. On February 22, 1967, the Black Power Committee held a press conference on the Howard campus together that included Professor Nathan Hare, whose teaching greatly influenced Stokely Carmichael. Professor Hare read "The Black University Manifesto," calling on Black people to join in "the overthrow of the Negro college with white innards . . . and to raise in its place a Black university, relevant to the Black community and its needs."

That speech followed a host of other disturbing actions by Professor Hare insofar as the Howard administration was concerned. Among the most notable was a scathing letter, printed in the *Hilltop* the previous September, blasting Howard's president, James M. Nabrit, Jr., for telling the *Washington Post* he wanted to make the university's student body 60 percent White by 1970. At the time, White students already formed a majority in Howard's dental school.

A month later, on the evening of March 21, 1967, Lieutenant General Lewis B. Hershey, the head of the U.S. Selective Service System, spoke at Howard in defense of the military service draft. Opposition to both the Vietnam War and the draft's disproportionate effect on young Black men was building to the boiling point. Protestors went on stage to interrupt General Hershey, chanting "America is the Black man's battleground," and prevented him from continuing his remarks.

A month after that, on April 18, there was a Black Power rally on campus. In the course of the rally, the participants burned effigies of General Hershey, President Nabrit, and Howard Dean of Liberal Arts Frank Snowden. Dean Snowden was the administrator most involved in disciplinary proceedings for undergraduate students, and he had earned a lot of antagonism by pushing for the expulsion of politically active students.

Four days later, on April 22, Muhammad Ali came to campus to speak at the invitation of Nathan Hare. The university would not let Ali speak in a campus auditorium, so he addressed a huge crowd from the steps of Frederick Douglass Hall. It was Ali's "Black Is Best" speech, and in closing he serenaded the audience with a rendition of "A White Man's Heaven Is a Black Man's Hell," which Louis Farrakhan recorded in 1955, including the lyrics "Raping, robbing, and murdering everything in his path / The whole black world has tasted of the white man's wrath / So, my friend, it's not hard to tell / A white man's heaven is a black man's hell."

Bringing Muhammad Ali on campus was the last straw for the Howard administration as far as employing Nathan Hare was concerned, and he was fired at the end of the semester. One of his parting shots was to dub Howard "the Ebony Tower" for its conservative administration and lack of connection to the Black community during those years. I'll also always recall sitting in his sociology class when he said of the Easter Bunny, "Who ever heard of a rabbit that lays eggs?" It instantly conveyed that in human culture, logic does not always rule.

Hare then took a post at San Francisco State University (SFSU), where he helped student activist Jimmy Garrett found the academic world's first Black studies department and served as its first chair. The installation of conservative academic S. I. Hayakawa as SFSU's president soon put Hare out of a job again, but he continued his activism and eventually transitioned to a new career in clinical psychotherapy with an emphasis on supporting and strengthening Black families. I was fortunate to take classes with him and other brilliant young faculty at Howard.

During the spring semester 1967 there were two more very significant events for me. The university administration drafted a letter decrying the disruption of General Hershey's speech and exhorting the student body to stop protesting and quiet down. President Nabrit was going to sign the letter on behalf of the administration, and he wanted me to sign it in my capacity as the incoming president of the student association. My refusal marked the first time that anyone in the traditional student government had ever identified with the radical student movement. The administration tried to persuade me to sign, but I wouldn't budge.

At more or less the same time I also became the new sports editor of the *Hilltop*. In that capacity I organized a meeting to discuss the *Washington Post*'s coverage of Howard and of the current scene in general with the paper's managing editor, Howard Simons, and the sports editor, Marty Zad. At one point Marty Zad said, "If you have so much to tell us about how to improve, why don't you come down and show us?"

I said, "When do you want me to start?"

He turned red because he wasn't expecting that. After an uncomfortable few seconds, during which he exchanged glances with Howard Simons, Marty said, "Tomorrow."

I said, "I'll be there."

They probably figured I'd fade away when they asked me to do the usual low-man-on-the-totem-pole stuff like go for coffee and sandwiches. But I remembered what Aunt Alma told me when I criticized the St. Jago teachers after my first classes there: "You've come to drink the milk, not count the cows." So I just asked Marty and the others how they wanted their coffee and went to get it.

Before long they gave me reporting assignments in and around Washington, D.C. One of the most memorable was covering an NCAA Division II basketball playoff game featuring the previous year's champions, North Carolina's historically Black Winston-Salem State University and its star player and future NBA great, Earl "The Pearl" Monroe. Winston-Salem lost that night, and Earl Monroe was disconsolate afterward, but we laughed about it together years later when we met socially in New York City.

Toward the end of July I went home to Bermuda for a month. But I wasn't just relaxing on the beach. On the strength of my sports articles for the *Hilltop* and the *Post,* I got a 9-to-5 job as a sports reporter for the weekly *Bermuda Sun.* At lunchtime I read the news on ZFB Radio. And in the evenings I worked as a wine steward at the Bermudiana Hotel. After all that I went to meet my friends at the clubs. But then around 1 a.m. I'd leave my friends to go back to ZFB, pull the U.S. Armed Forces Radio news feed off the teletype, and prepare and edit a version to be read on the early morning news.

THE FALL SEMESTER OF MY FOURTH YEAR AT HOWARD, 1967–1968, was fairly calm politically. That quiet time was helpful as I finished up required courses for my chemistry major and math minor and applied to medical schools.

That fall I also began to think more and more seriously about asking Beverly to marry me. I saw beginning medical school as the right time for me to settle down and start a family. When our relationship had started getting serious during junior year, Beverly had insisted that I stop dating other people. I resisted that decision for a while, but it was clear to both Beverly and me that we were a great match. By the beginning of spring semester it was agreed: Beverly and I would marry right after graduation and we would then stay in Washington, D.C., or move to another city, depending on my medical school acceptances.

I was looking forward to getting married and going to medical school. However, the climate was such that some other student leaders in the class of 1968 stepped back from campus politics for fear of endangering their graduations and prospective offers of jobs or admission to graduate degree programs. I respected those decisions, but I didn't feel it was the right path for me. Occupying a middle ground between the radical and conservative elements on

campus, I felt I could contribute to moving the university in a progressive direction without its being torn apart. The events of the spring semester increasingly challenged that goal, however.

Cleve Sellers was then in South Carolina, and on February 5 and 6, 1968
he led a protest to integrate a bowling alley in Orangeburg. The protestors
were mainly students from two historically Black schools in the area: private
Claflin University and public South Carolina State University. During the second day of the protest, seven students and a police officer were injured. The
police arrested fifteen students, and Governor Robert McNair declared a state
of emergency and called out the National Guard. On February 7, state police
sealed off the South Carolina State campus. The next day a student protestor
threw a piece of lumber and knocked down one of the state troopers. Testify-
ing later that they thought they were being shot at, the state troopers opened
fire without warning. Their bullets killed three Black students and wounded
thirty-four others, including Cleve, who was also arrested, and later served
seven months in prison for inciting a riot.

Later that month there was a protest rally on the Howard campus in support of the students in Orangeburg. In what became known as the "Orangeburg Ultimatum," the protestors demanded that Howard President James
Nabrit, his top vice president, and Frank Snowden resign within three weeks,
that faculty members who had lost their jobs because of politics be reinstated,
and that a new student judiciary committee be formed to handle the cases of
activist students threatened with expulsion.

Howard commemorates its founding on March 2, 1867 during the first
week of March every year, beginning with a Charter Day Convocation and
ending the next evening with a Charter Day Dinner. On March 1, 1968, protesting students took over the Charter Day Convocation stage in Cramton Auditorium. When all the hullabaloo was over, the university ordered thirty-
nine students to appear before a disciplinary board on Tuesday, March 19.

As president of the student association, I met with other student leaders
to organize a rally that day in support of the students who were being disciplined. We also wanted to protest Howard's firing of untenured professors
for their activism against the Vietnam War, demand an end to compulsory
ROTC for male U.S. students, and add our voices to calls for a more Black-
focused undergraduate curriculum.

By the time the first of us spoke at the rally, there were more than a thousand students in Howard's main quadrangle. I was the last to speak. Quoting
Fannie Lou Hamer's "I am sick and tired of being sick and tired," I told the
crowd, "If you really want change, follow us into the administration building."

I expected that only a few would follow us into the building and that
campus security would soon put us out. But the students kept coming in, and
within fifteen minutes the whole first floor was full. There were four floors in

the building, and we filled it up floor by floor. There were about five hundred students in the building and a thousand outside in the quadrangle. The entire administration had slipped out the back door along with all of the staff except for a custodian. The custodian, who had a large ring of keys jangling on his belt, obviously felt conflicted about leaving his post and he accompanied me silently as I surveyed the situation throughout the building. In those few minutes I think he saw that we were going to treat the building and its various offices with respect. As the two of us were coming down in the elevator alone together, I stuck out my hand, palm up, and he put his keys there without either of us saying a word. At that point I asked which was the key to the president's office, and he pointed to it.

After the custodian left the building, a few other students and I went to the president's office and gave ourselves the pleasure of sitting behind the desk for a few minutes. And then I placed the president's office off-limits and we locked the door. We set a strict rule not to damage anything inside the building. We organized study sessions so students could keep up with their course work. And we redirected food trucks from the cafeteria and fed everyone in shifts. There was a tremendous spirit of camaraderie throughout the sit-in. And it had an effect on everyone. There were some who walked into the administration building with processed hair, but they came out with Afros.

The second day of the sit-in, March 20, the university administration suspended classes and told everyone to go home. Around fifteen hundred students refused to do so and instead conducted a sit-in in their own dorm rooms, including barricading the entrances to their dormitories and taking turns standing guard. Over fifty neighborhood establishments donated food and utensils so the students could cook for themselves.

I led a steering committee which also included Adrienne Manns and Tony Gittens, respectively the editor and features editor of the *Hilltop*. Although Adrienne, Tony, and I each had individual points of view on the protest and what it might accomplish, we had excellent rapport and quickly established a consensus whenever we had to make an important decision.

During the sit-in we held a number of press conferences. There were usually several reporters on hand at any time as well as students from other colleges and universities, some of whom filed stories with their school newspapers. We also gave special access to two young African-American journalists who were then making names for themselves, Charlayne Hunter-Gault and Max Robinson.

In response to remarks I made about Black higher education at one of our press conferences, a reporter asked, "Do you consider Howard a Black university?" I said it wasn't, but it could and should be. I explained, "We want to make Howard University a university which is quite relevant to the Black community. We want Howard not shut off from Georgia Avenue and 14th

Street. We want Howard University to stand as a pinnacle of Black America as far as education is concerned."

The following days were a tense time because there was every chance the university would ask the local and federal governments to send in riot police and the National Guard to remove us forcibly. Death threats were being made against the other student leaders and me, which was certainly uncomfortable. But I learned important things about myself during the sit-in that I don't think I could have learned any other way.

I learned that thanks to my ability to compartmentalize my thoughts and feelings, I could remain calm in the midst of crisis. I also found that I had the ability to guide others through a collaborative decision-making process and provide the inspirational energy and direction for the group to follow through on those decisions. It was the making of me as a leader.

On Wednesday evening, about thirty-six hours into the sit-in, Stokely Carmichael came to the administration building and spoke to the protesting students. It was typical of Stokely that he asked us to keep the big picture in mind. He said, "This protest is not just a matter of students and academic freedom. It is a case of Black students at a Black school fighting against an anti-Black education."

The next afternoon, Adrienne, Tony, and I had a three-hour meeting with representatives of the university administration. We presented four demands for ending the sit-in: the resignation of President Nabrit: an emphasis on Black history and culture in the Howard curriculum and an initiative to improve relations between the university and the surrounding Black community, amnesty for the students involved in the Charter Day protest and those occupying the administration building and refusing to leave their dormitories, and a new university judiciary system with student involvement in all decisions on discipline.

The administration flatly rejected all four demands. However, another negotiating meeting was scheduled for 7 p.m. that evening. In advance of that, the other members of the steering committee and I chaired a meeting with our fellow students in the administration building. One of our discussion items was that no one had seen President Nabrit on campus since the sit-in began three days earlier. There were rumors that he was in Puerto Rico and was communicating with the rest of the administration by phone. For that reason we decided that the steering committee would not attend the 7 p.m. meeting, and that other students would go in our place. I told reporters, "If the administration won't send their first team, we won't send ours."

Meanwhile the university was seeking an injunction requiring all students to leave campus, and it ordered the students in the dormitories to "clear out" by midnight Friday. The student bar association of Howard's law school sought a counter-injunction requiring the university to reopen and continue with the rest of the spring semester.

As the occupation of the administration building continued, the Board of Trustees held an emergency meeting. Some trustees wanted to use force to expel us. Knowing that, I told my fellow students that if the university got its injunction we would be "up against the full might of the federal government." Adrienne and Tony agreed with me that it was important to acknowledge that fact clearly on behalf of the group, so that everyone there could make an informed decision about continuing the protest. We knew from the media and other contacts that Walter Washington, who had been appointed mayor-commissioner of Washington, D.C., by President Lyndon B. Johnson, was under pressure to end the sit-in from southern politicians in Congress, particularly Senator Robert Byrd of West Virginia and Senator Strom Thurmond of South Carolina. Every time we heard a siren, we thought the riot police and the National Guard might be coming to break our heads.

Other trustees, including psychologist Kenneth B. Clark, whose research with Black children was a foundation point for *Brown v. Board of Education,* the U.S. Supreme Court decision declaring public school segregation unconstitutional, and Percy Julian, a chemist who was then almost seventy and only the second African-American to be inducted into the National Academy of Sciences, recommended patience and warned against using force to end the sit-in. Dr. Julian became the university's chief negotiator with us. He told his fellow trustees and the administration, "These are our children," and he asked for time to work things out with us.

When we brought Dr. Julian inside the administration building on Friday, March 22, he said, "Things look cleaner here than they were before you occupied it." Dr. Clark came and spoke to us on Friday evening, saying that the trustees would not endorse our definition of a Black university but that they would bring students into decisions on curriculum.

Both Dr. Clark and Dr. Julian were able to humanize our side of things when they went back to their fellow trustees and the administration. One thing the trustees let us know was that President Nabrit was going to retire in another year, and so we dropped his resignation from our list of demands. After much discussion among the students, we submitted a new list of demands we wanted met before we left the building. We didn't get everything we wanted by any means, but the university agreed to remove a vice president who had taken a punitive stance against student activism, end compulsory ROTC, and give students a role in deciding the outcome of student disciplinary proceedings. These were all major concessions by the administration. We then held a vote of the protesting students and agreed to end the sit-in on its fifth day, Saturday, March 23.

At Howard as at other campuses that saw upheaval and protest during the 1960s, the generation gap became a yawning chasm. But at Howard the generation gap was particularly poignant. People like Kenneth Clark, Percy Julian, and James Nabrit, Jr., had fought against racism their whole lives. On behalf of themselves and others they had broken through many unjust barriers.

In addition to making pivotal advances in synthesizing human hormones from plant substances for medical treatment, Dr. Julian had set up a thriving chemical laboratory that employed both African-American scientists and Jewish refugee scientists he had come to know while doing his Ph.D. at the University of Vienna in the 1930s. For his part, James Nabrit had offered the first civil rights law course in the United States when he began teaching law at Howard in the 1930s. Yet the older generation at Howard did not fully appreciate that their progressive energy had subsided into incrementalism and that a new time called for new action.

Eleven days later, on April 4, 1968, Martin Luther King, Jr., was shot dead in Memphis by James Earl Ray. I remember being on campus when I heard about it, and wondering if continued nonviolent resistance could be viable. It made me think of Malcolm X's saying that no matter what your level of resistance, the White power structure would trample on you. I spent a quiet, contemplative evening, which was jarred by the news of rioting breaking out in Washington, D.C.

The reports of Dr. King's murder brought a large crowd out at the intersection of 14th and U Streets, NW, the center of one of the city's most densely populated Black neighborhoods. Stokely Carmichael and other SNCC members went door to door urging local businesses to close out of respect for Dr. King. Addressing the crowd, Stokely advised them to "go home and get your guns."

Over the course of the night, multiple instances of arson occurred and looting became widespread. The next day Stokely insisted that there was "no alternative to retribution." He stated, "Black people have to survive, and the only way they will survive is by getting guns." Although I've always opted for the strategy of nonviolence for pragmatic reasons, it wasn't hard at the time to understand why Stokely spoke as he did. He articulated the desperate rage that the assassination of Dr. King triggered in countless Black people.

Calm was not restored until April 7 after President Lyndon B. Johnson deployed federal troops. Thirteen people were killed by fires, the police, or rioters. According to a fiftieth anniversary assessment in the *Washington Post*, property damage totaled $175 million in 2018 dollars. Some burned-down blocks remained derelict for more than thirty years.

As president of the Howard University Student Association I had a pass that allowed me to go through the National Guard and police checkpoints, and

I used it to get to my part-time job at the *Washington Post*. As was typical of that time, most of the editors and reporters lived not in Washington, D.C., but in White enclaves in the suburbs. A number of them drove by Howard every day on their way to and from the *Post*. But during the previous two years none of them had ever offered me a lift. Suddenly I had my choice of drivers eager to have a Black person sitting beside them in the front passenger seat. I took the rides without commenting on the discrepancy. If their consciences didn't already bother them, nothing I said was going to make them see themselves any clearer.

Meanwhile, my dream of becoming a doctor was in jeopardy. Among the medical schools I had applied to were the ones at Howard and the University of Chicago. Earlier in the spring I had received a preliminary acceptance from Chicago, pending letters of recommendation and final grades. I was looking forward to going there despite the harsh winters. But after I led the occupation of the administration building, the letters of recommendation from my pre-med professors and my final grades were caught in limbo.

At that crucial moment for my future, President Nabrit demonstrated great generosity and kindness. A few days before my birthday in May the two of us met to discuss the issues that the occupying students and the administration had agreed to work on together. When we finished with that, he asked, "What are you doing next year? Are you going to medical school?"

I said, "Well, I applied here at Howard, the University Chicago, and a couple of other places, and I thought I was going to Chicago. But from what I understand, one of your vice presidents has been sitting on my paperwork and I haven't heard anything more from Chicago."

President Nabrit said, "Really? Well, would you go to medical school here at Howard if you were accepted?"

I said I would be very happy to study medicine at Howard. When I opened my mailbox on my birthday, May 17, there was a letter of acceptance.

ALL-ROUNDER AT HEART THAT I WAS, I wasn't ready to give up on competing in track. After the sit-in at the administration building, I joined my Howard teammates Bill Ritchie, Tyrone Malloy, and Ron Lassiter to win the 4×440 yard relay at the NCAA Mid-Atlantic Regionals at Mount St. Mary's University in Maryland. Unfortunately, I couldn't run in the NCAA Championships in June because it conflicted with getting married to Beverly. The wedding was set for the day after commencement. My mother was recovering from a heart attack and couldn't be there, but my father, Emelita, and Aunt Gloria and Uncle Bert were all going to attend along with Beverly's family and our Howard friends.

The day before commencement, Robert F. Kennedy was shot to death in Los Angeles by Sirhan Sirhan. The disjunction between the tragic events of that spring and the positive developments in my own life was acute. But on balance I felt hopeful for the future both for society as a whole and for Beverly and me. I was eager to see what I could contribute to achieving a better future on both counts.

5. Becoming a Physician: Sufficiently Counter-Racist?

M Y ACCEPTANCE AT HOWARD UNIVERSITY COLLEGE OF MEDICINE was contingent on my completing a summer biology course. But after my mother's heart attack, which frightened the whole family, I felt I had to spend some time with her in Bermuda. Fortunately the medical school agreed that this was appropriate and told me they'd see me in the fall, when they expected me to put my nose to the grindstone.

In Bermuda (Beverly came with me, and we had our honeymoon there) I was relieved to find my mother recovering well. In fact she had many more years to live, but the time we spent together in the summer of 1968 was good for both of us. Among other things, it grounded me once again in my immediate and extended family in Bermuda—and its then dramatically changing politics.

As small a country as Bermuda is, and as different as it is from the United States in many respects, it was the parallels between the two that struck me then. In both countries there was the same deeply entrenched resistance to racial equality with here and there beacons of progressive change and reform. Two events in Bermuda in the spring of 1968, the so-called Floral Pageant Riots on April 25 to 27 and the general election on May 22, had exemplified that observation.

Like the Belco Riots, a nonviolent labor strike until the Police used force to disrupt it, the Floral Pageant Riots have been misnamed in the White establishment's version of history. Those disturbances should really be called the Fair For All mess.

On Thursday, April 25, Hamilton hosted three major public gatherings: the annual Floral Pageant Parade, the opening of the annual Fair For All charity event to raise money for handicapped children, and a PLP rally to announce the Party's platform and candidates for the May 22 election. The Floral Pageant Parade occurred without incident as it progressed from Bernard Park south down Cedar Avenue and Burnaby Street to Front Street and then east

along Front Street to the corner of Court Street between a dignitaries reviewing stand at the Cabinet Building (then called the Secretariat), on the north
side of Front Street, and Hamilton Hall, on the south side. According to the
1969 report of a Government Commission of Inquiry, the Wooding Commission, the parade concluded shortly before 4 p.m.

Planned to begin after the parade, the PLP rally was half a mile away at
the old Transport Control Board location at the other end of Court Street. Because of an intervening hill, there is not a line of sight to and from the Front
Street end of Court Street. The rally did not begin until around 5:15 p.m., and
it ended around 8:40 p.m. After the fact, the UBP laid great stress on the fiery
nature of the speeches at the rally and claimed they incited the public to violence. In truth the speeches were no more fiery than was to be expected in
any election of those years in Bermuda or the United States or any time since
for that matter. The rally was still going on when the disturbances falsely
called the Floral Pageant Riots began at the Fair For All.

The fair usually ran in Hamilton Hall on Friday and Saturday after the
parade on Thursday. Because of disappointing results in 1967, the fair organizers had decided to open on Thursday to capitalize on the parade crowd. Another change to boost attendance was to make each day's tickets, which
formerly allowed one-time entry to Hamilton Hall, good for reentering at any
time during the day shown on them. Each numbered ticket also represented a
chance to win a door prize.

The fair organizers were well intentioned and were working for a good
cause. But they seriously misjudged the crowd control issues their innovations
created. Entrance had to be halted because the hall was jammed with so many
people.

The result was that many young Black Bermudians were kept waiting to
enter the fair all through the late afternoon and early evening. Meanwhile they
saw many White teenagers, some but not all of them fair volunteers, ushered
into Hamilton Hall. Individuals in the crowd called out to ask why "we chocolate kids cannot [go in]" and so on, but nothing else untoward happened until
closing time approached and people became upset that their tickets, good only
for that day, were about to become useless. Some people, mostly children,
were trying to gain admittance with wadded up tickets discarded by people
leaving the fair, but there is no dispute that the majority of the crowd had valid
tickets they had purchased.

Only one policeman was on duty at Hamilton Hall. When a young Black
man in the crowd cursed at him, the policeman arrested him. The young man
struggled to get out of the policeman's grasp, the two fell, and the young man
escaped, abetted by others in the crowd who got in the way. One of these
other young men threw a bottle against the wall, "occasioning slight injury to

a male [fair volunteer] who was near at hand," to quote the Wooding Commission Report.

Things quieted down, and other policemen arrived on the scene. One of them was a Black Bermudian, a minority on the mostly White BPS, which included many officers recruited from other parts of the British Commonwealth. The Black police officer let a childhood friend, also Black, enter the fair when the friend said that he had just left to go to the toilet and had lost his ticket for reentry. As soon as this man entered the hall, a White former policeman, an Englishman who had served on the Bermuda police force and was there with his wife, a fair volunteer, ordered him to leave and allowed no discussion. The White former policeman grabbed the Black man, who resisted and swore at him. The Black policeman then moved in to arrest the Black man. According to the Wooding Commission, "A struggle ensued in the course of which [the White former policeman] punched [the Black man] in the face."

The crowd protested what it saw happening to a Black Bermudian who had been admitted to the fair by a Black policeman, only to have a White former policeman violently exercise the putative authority of his Whiteness. Tear gas was used to move the crowd away from Hamilton Hall on Front Street and into Back o' Town, the poorest area of the city. Friday and Saturday saw considerable unrest, including arson, and several people were injured, although fortunately no one was killed. Early Saturday morning Bermuda's resident British Governor declared a state of emergency and a curfew, and at his request the British government sent a company of the Royal Inniskilling Fusiliers and HMS *Leopard* to Bermuda. By the time the soldiers arrived by air and the ship docked, the disturbances were over.

In the aftermath, White fingers pointed at the PLP rally's "incendiary" speeches. The Wooding Commission Report gave a measure of credence to the idea that these speeches contributed to the unrest in some degree, although it emphasized that PLP leaders played an important role in ending the crisis through their appeals for calm. The report stated plainly that the real cause of the violence was Bermuda's past and present racism, including "stop and frisk" anti-drug policing that succeeded only in antagonizing much of the Black community, unfairness in hiring and housing, school segregation, the banning of literature about the Black Muslims and the Nation of Islam from 1963 to 1968, and countless other forms of public and private discrimination against Black Bermudians. The continuing racism was plain enough in 1968 to anyone with eyes to see it, but White Bermuda refused to acknowledge its extent or its brutality.

I've gone into detail because White Bermuda remains in denial about the events of late April 1968. For example, the compendium "Bermuda's History from 1952 to 1999," created by Bermuda-online.org, has a lengthy entry beginning "1968. April 25 and 26. Floral Pageant Riot. A State of Emergency was called. Black Beret Cadre–led waves on [sic] insurrection and rioting followed, that lasted until 1972." As I will discuss, the Black Beret Cadre began in 1969, and although there were other widely separated incidents of violent racial unrest to come in Bermuda, there were no waves of insurrection and rioting led by anyone from 1968 to 1972. "Waves of insurrection and rioting" describes a Bermuda that has always existed only in certain imaginations, not reality.

Despite the facts established by the Wooding Commission and confirmed by the 1978 report of the Pitt Commission (see the next chapter), the history of the April 1968 disturbances continues to be distorted by calling them the Floral Pageant Riots, laying blame on the PLP's 1968 electoral campaign, and omitting or slighting mention of the racist actions at the Fair For All and its poor planning and management. Hindsight is 20/20, to be sure, but think how much trouble might have been averted if the fair organizers had simply announced that Thursday tickets would be honored on Friday. Continue that thought experiment by asking if the fair organizers would have dealt differently with a crowd of young White, rather than Black, people. Consider, too, that the White former policeman was a civilian citizen, just like the Black man, and should have been arrested for assault.

The unfair blame cast on the PLP undoubtedly lost it many potential votes when the election took place on May 22. Of 40 available seats, the PLP won 10 and the UBP 30. It was the first election in Bermuda without a property qualification for voting or extra "plus" votes for those owning a certain amount of land, the first with universal suffrage for all adult Bermudians age twenty-one and over, and the first with office-seekers campaigning as members of opposing political parties. In addition, at the beginning of June Bermuda's first written constitution came into force.

Landmarks of progress, no doubt about it. But this was 1968, not 1868, much less 1834 when Black Bermudians' emancipation was declared the law of the land. So Black Bermudians were not exactly bubbling over with talk about the voting reforms. There was general satisfaction that changes had come at last, but also a sense of relief, of shame lessened, that Bermuda no longer stood out like a sore thumb among the other countries of the New World.

There was no escaping how hard won the changes were. They had only come about because of unrelenting efforts by the BIU, the PLP, and a third organization, the Committee for Universal Adult Suffrage (CUAS).

Dr. Roosevelt Brown (no relation; he later changed his name to Pauulu Karamakafego), who earned his Ph.D. in engineering at the California Institute of Technology in 1959 before returning to his native Bermuda, had set up CUAS in 1960. It was thanks to the BIU and CUAS that the Parliamentary Elec-

tion Act 1963 legalized political parties and introduced universal adult suffrage for Bermudians ages twenty-five and older. The minimum voting age
was twenty-five rather than twenty-one (then the legal age for buying alcohol) or eighteen at the insistence of White politicians led by Henry Tucker.
They wanted to limit the extent to which universal adult suffrage would increase the number of Black voters in proportion to White voters, and there
were a lot more Black than White Bermudians in that age demographic and
younger, the leading edge of Bermuda's baby boom generation.

The law further diluted the impact of making more Black people eligible
to vote by confirming electoral districts along the lines of Bermuda's original
nine Church of England parishes. This first form of gerrymandering had created electoral districts along racial lines with very unequal numbers of voters,
making White voters more powerful than Black voters in terms of electing
their favored candidates. The new electoral law solidified this arrangement by
dividing the nine parishes into double-seat constituencies, giving less populous White majority parishes even more disproportionate voting power.

That wasn't all. The law's Watlington Amendment preserved a property-
based vote by giving a second, or "plus," vote to those who owned more than
two thousand square feet of land.

Last but not least, the 1963 law gave a vote to non-Bermudian British
subjects resident in Bermuda for three years or longer.

Thus the odds were as stacked as they could be against politicians who
sought racial equality in Bermuda. However, the PLP formed in early 1963
and ran nine candidates in the May 16, 1963, general election. Bermuda's first
political party won 6 seats, and the winners of the other 30 seats were all nom-
inally independent. The next year Henry Tucker put an end to that charade
by forming the UBP along with twenty-three others elected in 1963. The remaining six members of the House of Assembly were indeed independent of
Henry Tucker's regime, in that they were even more conservative and resistant to racial equality. (Later a third party formed, the Bermuda Democratic
Party, but it never succeeded in electing any candidates and soon disbanded.)

Henry Tucker and other members of the newly formed UBP were already acting as the executive council of the House of Assembly and thus in
effect as the Government, although much decision-making authority remained in the hands of the Governor. Because Tucker and his leadership team
hadn't been elected on a UBP platform, however, the PLP petitioned the Governor for a new election. The PLP had a winning argument in terms of constitutional law, I believe, but the Governor simply confirmed Tucker and his
fellow UBP politicians as Government Leader and Executive Council. This
cozy relationship between Government House, the Governor's residence, and
any White-dominated Bermuda Government has never wavered.

The BIU, the PLP, and CUAS kept their shoulders to the wheel and won more progress with the Parliamentary Election Act 1966. This revision of Bermuda's election law ended the "plus" vote and lowered the voting age to twenty-one (it finally went to eighteen in 1990). But it continued the vote for non-Bermudian British subjects who had lived on the Island for three years or more (eventually legislation eliminated this vote for anyone taking up residence after May 1, 1976), and it split Pembroke Parish into four double-seat constituencies, raising the number of seats in Parliament from 36 to 40.

That year a Bermuda Constitutional Conference convened in London with eight UBP representatives, three PLP representatives, three Members of Parliament's appointed upper house, the Legislative Council, and four Independent members of the House of Assembly. The resulting draft constitution enshrined all the provisions of the Parliamentary Election Act 1966, and it renamed the Legislative Council the Senate. It also formally transferred most government authority, with the notable exceptions of the Police and the Bermuda Regiment, from the Governor to the House of Assembly.

The PLP representatives submitted a minority report pointing out that the gerrymandering of electoral districts made it impossible to achieve true racial equality in voting and arguing for districts with as near as possible equal numbers of voters. At the same time two of the Independents, Sir John Cox CBE and H. T. Watlington, submitted their own minority report calling for a return of the property-based vote.

In 1967 the British Parliament passed the Bermuda Constitution Act, ratifying the draft constitution without any changes. The UBP then quickly passed the Parliamentary Election Act 1968, adding a few extra difficulties to voter registration.

All the changes going back to 1960 and earlier formed the deeper context of the 1968 general election alongside the more immediate context of the Fair For All mess and the UBP's efforts to blame the PLP for it. I've gone into detail because this deeper history has also been distorted and ignored. Bermuda likes to celebrate the continuous operation of the House of Assembly since 1620, but it wasn't until after World War II that Bermuda really began to aim at being a democratic society whose electoral system respects and facilitates the will of the people. Our failure to be clear about this makes it difficult to see who the real founders of Bermuda as a democratic society were—they include members of both the UBP and PLP in addition to earlier figures such as E. F. Gordon—and to appreciate their respective contributions.

AUNT GLORIA WAS ONE OF SEVERAL NONWHITE POLITICIANS who won election to the House of Assembly as a member of the UBP in 1968. Henry Tucker was her political mentor, and in announcing her candidacy he called her the UBP's "secret weapon" with Black voters. She was not Bermuda's first Black woman Member of Parliament, an honor that belonged to the PLP's Lois Browne-Evans. But when the new Parliament convened in June, Aunt Gloria became the country's first woman Cabinet Minister, Black or White, as Minister of Health and Human Services in the country's first Cabinet (the terms then still in use were Government Leader and Executive Council; they changed to Premier and Cabinet in 1973). Lois Browne-Evans got another first, however. Aunt Gloria's defeat of PLP Leader Walter N. H. Robinson in the Hamilton West constituency made Browne-Evans, then the PLP's Deputy Leader, the first woman Opposition Leader in the British Commonwealth.

Thanks to my family background there was talk in Bermuda of a political future for me even before I entered Howard as a freshman undergraduate. And thanks to the media attention I received for my campus activism, the political movers and shakers in Bermuda also knew that I was frankly ambitious to become leader of Bermuda's Government one day. Most people thought that both the PLP and the UBP could use me in their fold.

In the summer of 1968 my mother and aunt exerted themselves to persuade me that I should work for progressive change in Bermuda from within the ruling system as a member of the UBP. I exerted myself just as vigorously to persuade them that the UBP's apparent embrace of Black people like them was part of the establishment's unrelenting effort to co-opt, divert, and frustrate the energies of those seeking fundamental change. Although I was happy for Aunt Gloria and knew she would do a lot of good in office, I saw the PLP as the best hope for progressive politics in Bermuda. The argument with my mother and my aunt went on for several years.

WHEN BEVERLY AND I GOT BACK TO WASHINGTON, D.C., in mid-July, I picked up my part-time job in the *Post*'s sports department. I was at work on the evening of July 23, when a shootout occurred between the police and members of the Black Nationalists of New Libya in the Glenville district of Cleveland. Around 9:30 p.m., news came that four African-Americans, three members of the New Libya group, and a bystander had been killed by police bullets.

There was a big blackboard in the sports department where we kept track of scores in different games. Riffing on the NFL's Cleveland Browns, Marty Zad went to the scoreboard and wrote, "Cleveland Whites 4—Cleveland Blacks 0." Marty was well known for being sarcastic, and his notation elicited quite a few laughs. A little later, the news came in that three White police officers had also been killed. Although I thought I would probably get fired, I went up to the scoreboard and changed it to read, "Cleveland Whites 4—Cleveland Blacks 3." The room got quiet, there were a couple of forced laughs, and then someone changed the subject. The next day, the score line was gone.

The Glenville Riots, triggered by the shootout, included a considerable amount of police brutality and the deaths of two innocent African-Americans. If the score line hadn't been erased, probably by Marty Zad himself, I would have had to update it again.

Before I matriculated as a Howard medical student I made one more brief trip. The Ford Foundation-sponsored Center for the Study of Democratic Institutions brought me to its small jewel of a campus in Santa Barbara, California, for a conference on racism in America. Stan Miles of SNCC was also an invited guest, subbing for H. Rap Brown, who was then incarcerated. The Center for the Study of Democratic Institutions was a hotbed of elite liberal thinking and its leading figure was Bishop James Pike, the Episcopal bishop of California (a little over a year later it was headline news when Bishop Pike died wandering in the California desert after his car broke down). Other members of the center I recall from the conference include Alvin Toffler, the author of *Future Shock*, and scientist Linus Pauling, winner of the 1954 Nobel Prize in Chemistry and the 1962 Nobel Peace Prize.

That trip was memorable on several counts. I was astonished at the level of technological resources and physical amenities at the center, located on a hilltop overlooking the Pacific Ocean. I also immediately fell in love with Southern California's climate and topography and began to think about living there when I finished medical school. But most important was the opportunity to interact with members of the liberal wing of the U.S. social, political, and academic elite.

Early in the conference Stan Miles and I had quite a confrontation with Bishop Pike over the role of White people in what he termed Black people's "salvation from oppression." Our point was that White people could contribute to the movement for Black empowerment, but could not lead it. Without Black leaders any movement for Black people's progress would inevitably lapse into a continuation of White patriarchy—and Black oppression—by other means. But Bishop Pike's good intentions ran neck and neck with his inability to imagine anything but a leading role for himself in any enterprise he chose to join. We went round and round on this issue, with Bishop Pike continually repeating and varying his expressions of personal Christian commitment to the political salvation of Black people.

I was well used to White people's unconscious presumption of, and confidence in, their superiority. But I had never seen it in the guise of Bishop Pike's expansive noblesse oblige. The experience constituted a good lesson in the foibles of the human ego and the limits of good intentions as well as the politics of race relations. By the end of the conference Stan Miles and I had the satisfaction of hearing Bishop Pike repeat a number of our arguments about the importance of Black leadership as if he'd always held them. There was no mistaking his stubborn conviction that he himself was an exception when it came to White people's ability to help lead Black people to the promised land, but I didn't zing him on that account.

BACK AT HOWARD, I PLUNGED INTO MY MEDICAL STUDIES while continuing to remain politically active, although in a quieter way than during the takeover of the administration building a few months before in the spring. Beverly meanwhile began an interesting research job in a lab at the National Institutes of Health. Thanks to her job we were able to furnish our first apartment on credit, and together we paid everything off in a timely way. We experienced all the normal difficulties that young married couples encounter, but it was a happy, productive time for both of us. We had many good times together while also being thoroughly engaged in our respective activities, and we had a great circle of friends in common.

In those days campus activism and study kept colliding, which was soon the case for me in medical school. The signature course of the early part of medical school is anatomy, and for Howard medical students from the 1930s through the 1960s that meant the lectures of W. Montague Cobb, M.D., Ph.D. By the late 1960s Dr. Cobb was a grand old man in both style and substance.

To take the substance first, after earning his undergraduate degree at Amherst College and his medical degree at Howard, in 1932 Dr. Cobb became the first African-American to earn a Ph.D. in anthropology (the second did not come until the mid-1950s) and helped to pioneer the field of physical anthropology. Cobb used anthropological and anatomical data to debunk any claim of mental or physical superiority based on race. Through his tireless activity as a leading member of the National Medical Association (NMA), founded when Black medical professionals could not gain admission to the American Medical Association (AMA), he embodied the institutional memory of African-Americans in medicine. Starting in the mid-1950s he organized annual Imhotep Conferences, named for the ancient Egyptian physician Imhotep, to spur racial integration of American hospitals.

Despite the radicalism implicit in all this, including the Afrocentrism behind his self-identification with Imhotep, Dr. Cobb took a dim view of recent campus activism. This was not something I was inclined to make any fuss about. And Dr. Cobb had no personal animosity toward me. He once took me into his inner office to show me how he debunked the Nazi German myth that Jesse Owens won gold medals at the 1936 Olympics in Berlin because Black people's ankles were constructed differently from White people's. Dr. Cobb had the ankle skeletons with which he demonstrated that there was no such difference.

I was prepared to give my full attention to learning anatomy from Dr. Cobb. However, that's where his grand personal style came into play. He frequently interrupted his anatomy lectures for half an hour or more to play snatches of Bach on the violin or discourse on Shakespeare or Imhotep. He constantly wanted to demonstrate that the world of the late 1960s might be full of new knowledge, but that it contained no new wisdom. In quite a confrontational way, he challenged students to offer an example of contemporary wisdom that he could not trace to an ancient antecedent. He had always done these things in his lectures, but now he was doing them more than ever before because of his open disdain for "revolutionary" talk and activism.

My classmates and I implored him to concentrate on anatomy because our exams were not going to feature questions about Bach, Shakespeare, or Imhotep. But he refused to listen to us, much less discuss the matter or alter his approach substantively. In the aftermath of the recent demonstrations at Howard and other campuses, not listening to students was the one unforgivable sin for an academic administrator or instructor.

The last straw was when we asked Dr. Cobb and the rest of the anatomy faculty to meet us formally. Only two junior members of the faculty attended the meeting. Dr. Cobb came to the door of the meeting room and said, "We're ten minutes late for the anatomy lecture; let's get started," and then turned on his heel and left.

In response I organized a boycott of Dr. Cobb's anatomy lectures. My classmates and I studied anatomy on our own, and we got older students to teach and quiz us.

The situation was typical of the generational divide on campuses in those days, but it was regrettable just the same. There was no denying Dr. Cobb's brilliance and the significance of his efforts to integrate hospitals and achieve equality of respect for both Black medical professionals and Black patients. However there was also no denying that the gulf between him and the students had become unbridgeable.

Without my realizing it fully at the time, the conflict with Dr. Cobb undermined my commitment to medical school, which seemed divorced both from the tumult in society and from the needs of patients. The reason I wanted to be a physician was to help patients, especially minority patients in disadvantaged circumstances, and I often asked my professors why their courses couldn't include some patient contact. One day a biochemistry professor was discussing a serious vitamin deficiency solely in terms of carbon atoms. I asked, "What do Black people who don't have enough of this vitamin look like?" My classmates laughed, but the professor didn't like the question and didn't answer it. I was really just trying to say, "Can you show us what it means for a sick person?"

Nowadays, medical schools give students patient contact as early as the first year. But patient contact was then nonexistent in the first two years of study.

Although I'd handled the academic load well, toward the end of my first year I began to wonder if I should remain in medical school or find another way to contribute to the struggle for racial and social justice. This was the spirit in which I participated in a May 1969 Playboy Panel Discussion, a recurring feature of *Playboy* magazine in those years. The topic of discussion was student revolt, and the other student activist participants included Tom Hayden, Harry Edwards, and Linda Morse. Representing various strands of more or less rigid conservatism were Phillip Abbott Luce of Young Americans for Freedom, S. I. Hayakawa, and Buell Gallagher.

Political events in both Bermuda and the United States contributed to my feeling that I needed to do something more dramatically counter-racist than earning a medical degree. At the end of the year I emptied my medical school locker intending not to return in the fall. As I was walking out the door, however, I encountered Dr. Frances Cress Welsing, a young member of the psychiatry faculty.

She picked up on my emotional state and asked me, "Are you okay?"

I said, "Yeah, I'm all right. But I'm getting out of here."

"What do you mean?"

"I'm leaving. I don't want to do this anymore. Society is at a crossroads, people are dying because of racism and oppression, and I'm not doing enough."

She said, "Well, listen—before you make any rash decisions, there's a meeting at my house every week that you might find interesting. We discuss racism in all its aspects, and where each of us fits in combating it. There is one person in particular I'd like you to listen to before you decide whether or not to finish medical school."

The one person in particular was Neely Fuller, Jr., a self-educated thinker who earned his living as a security guard at the United States Bureau of Engraving and Printing, which made and safeguarded the printing plates for America's paper currency and Treasury bills, and at that time for postage stamps as well. Neely Fuller was then finishing writing *The United Independent Compensatory Code/System/Concept: A Textbook/Workbook for Thought, Speech, and/or Action for Victims of Racism (White Supremacy)*. For her part, Frances Cress Welsing was the author of *The Isis Papers: The Keys to the Colors*.

Both Fuller and Welsing wanted to delineate a functional definition of racism and how to counter it. I responded positively to their emphasis on self-reliance and common sense, as well as solidarity among Black people, in navigating one's way through a racist society. For example, Fuller counseled that solidarity with other Black people meant lending them only as much money as one could afford to lose and sending them to the banks for anything beyond that. I had been burned a few times by folks who asked for loans based on our shared identity as Black people, and Fuller's words rang in my ears in harmony with the dedication to work and striving for excellence that my parents always espoused. Talking with Fuller, Welsing, and others attending their meetings did more than my first-year medical school experiences to convince me that becoming a doctor was not selfish or irrelevant to the struggle of Black people at that moment in time. It was up to me to see that my medical career was sufficiently counter-racist.

Frances Cress Welsing died January 2, 2016, at the age of 80. Without her intervention and the inspiration she and Neely Fuller provided during my time in medical school, I might never have become a physician.

In the spring and early summer of 1969 I worked for Marion Barry at Pride, Inc. After leaving SNCC in 1967, reportedly in protest of H. Rap Brown's being named chairman from May 1967 to June 1968, Marion had founded Pride with activist Mary Treadwell. I edited the organization's weekly newspaper, *Harambee*, which took its title from the Swahili word meaning "pull together." Among other activities Pride had a government contract for job training, which took the form of a rat eradication program with young men in Washington's Black community being trained in pest control. On the front page of every edition of *Harambee* we had a box with the number of rats killed in the previous week. That number always had some guesswork in it, but the program won a lot of support in the community because it was having a visible positive effect.

In the middle of the summer I went home to Bermuda to assist in preparation for the Regional Conference on Black Power that was being held there. Pauulu Karamakafego had a lot to do with the conference being held in Bermuda, and I was glad to get to know him in the days leading up to it. The conference took place at various Black workmen's clubs around Bermuda, including the Devonshire Recreation Club in Lois Browne-Evans's constituency and the Warwick Workmen's Club.

Conspicuously absent, because they had been denied entry to Bermuda at the last minute, were Stokely Carmichael, Rap Brown, Maulana Karenga (a.k.a. Ron Karenga, who created the holiday of Kwanzaa), and other activists from the United States. But there were at least a hundred attendees from abroad, including C. L. R. James, the great Trinidadian historian, social theorist, and writer on cricket. Around five hundred people from Bermuda also took part. I will always cherish the memory of sitting on the bleachers at Pembroke Hamilton Club's football field talking politics with C. L. R. James and Pauulu Karamakafego.

A less happy memory is being part of a group of sixty conference attendees who went to observe proceedings in the House of Assembly. The UBP had us ejected for heckling, although we were doing nothing of the kind, and the PLP's representatives, including Lois Browne-Evans and her protégé, L. Frederick "Freddie" Wade, walked out after us in protest. The real problem with our presence in the visitors gallery was that many in the group were wearing dashikis. The dashiki "shouted" revolution in the eyes of the UBP, and that silent visual disturbance counted as heckling as far as they were concerned.

The start of my second year in medical school coincided with the appearance in *Playboy*'s September 1969 issue of "Playboy Panel: Student Revolt," an edited version of what Tom Hayden, Harry Edwards, the other participants, and I had said in the spring. At the time, events in Bermuda were also occupying part of my attention, when I wasn't focusing intently on the new term's courses.

I mentioned that Lois Browne-Evans became Bermuda's first Black female Member of Parliament as a Leader of the PLP. She and the PLP's other guiding light, Freddie Wade, were already looking forward to Bermuda's next general election, which by law had to occur within five years of the 1968 election (it took place in May of 1972). During a conversation with my father at the Clayhouse Inn, Lois Browne-Evans said, "Ewart's talking about revolution in America. He should forget about medical school and come help us win the revolution in Bermuda. We need him here."

Browne-Evans was an attorney, and my father said, "You finished your law degree, so you always had that to fall back on. Let Ewart finish his medical degree."

She was very dissatisfied with this answer. I believe it was the seed, or one of the seeds, of a seesaw relationship for Lois Browne-Evans and me when I eventually came home to enter Bermuda politics, as I'll describe later.

There was no political tumult in the rest of my medical school career at least in comparison to the boycott of Dr. Cobb's anatomy lectures during my first year. The faculty members who had the strongest influence on me were Dr. Tazewell Banks, a brilliant young cardiologist whose course in physical diagnosis gave me a first taste of applying medical knowledge to patients' real needs; Dr. Walter Booker of the pharmacology department, who was always kind and supportive; Dr. Wharton Young, who taught a memorable course in neuroanatomy; and the two jewels in the crown of Howard's excellent surgery department, Dr. Jack White and Dr. LaSalle Leffall, Jr.

I heard from other faculty members that Drs. White and Leffall stood up for me on a few occasions during my first two years in medical school, rebutting those who said I didn't belong there because I was really just an activist. Both men achieved extraordinary careers. Dr. White broke the color bar as Memorial Sloan Kettering Cancer Center's first Black surgical oncology trainee and was elected to the Institute of Medicine in the National Academy of Sciences, Engineering, and Medicine. He mentored Dr. Leffall, who became the first Black president of the American Cancer Society and the American College of Surgeons. Dr. Leffall was renowned among Howard medical students for pithy expressions such as "The mark of a great surgeon is equanimity under duress."

During the spring semester of my second year in medical school, I went to look for a summer job at the National Urban Coalition, now defunct but then a vital organization. I was referred to George A. Silver, M.D., who had just joined Yale University's faculty as a professor of public health after a stint as deputy assistant secretary for health and scientific affairs at the U.S. Department of Health, Education, and Welfare (HEW), forerunner of the Department of Health and Human Services (HHS). He split his time between Yale and running the National Urban Coalition's health programs.

Dr. Silver and I had a great talk, although he didn't have a job for me. Not long afterward, however, he called and asked me to come see him when he was next in Washington. At this second meeting he offered me what amounted to a good full-time position.

The job, as Dr. Silver outlined it, entailed traveling all over the United States to talk to two groups. One group comprised admissions offices and committees at medical schools, which needed to be persuaded, pushed, and prodded to recruit and accept qualified minority students. The second group comprised high-achieving minority students, whether at historically Black colleges and universities or other schools, who had an interest in medicine. Like most medical schools of the day, most undergraduate programs were still looking at minority students through the lens of implicit racism, which decreed that minority students were not physician material. These students needed to hear that if they had good grades and an interest in medicine, they should consider going to medical school instead of traveling the career paths their guidance counselors and academic advisors were recommending.

The job excited me in prospect. However, I didn't see how I could take it on and keep up with my own medical studies. So I asked Dr. Silver if he could increase the budget a bit and let me enlist a few other minority medical students to do the work as a team.

Dr. Silver liked this plan, and I soon got my Howard undergraduate friend and protégé Reed Tuckson, who became an executive vice president and chief of medical affairs at UnitedHealth Group, to sign on. Reed was in medical school at Georgetown. Lou Simpson, another Howard undergraduate friend who was at the Howard University College of Medicine with me and later became an outstanding psychiatrist in Los Angeles, joined the team. I also recruited two other Howard medical students, Aaron Long and Marshall Nickerson, who had earned their undergraduate degrees elsewhere.

The five of us got together over a map of the United States and divided up responsibility for visiting the different states. I used my prerogative as team leader to choose some warm states—Florida, Texas, Arizona, and California—for my trips. Our field reports in the summer of 1970 became the core of a guideline document that HEW followed over the next decade as it sought to encourage and support members of minority groups to become physicians and physician-scientists. For the rest of my time in medical school I continued to visit both medical schools and undergraduate programs during the summer breaks. As a result I got to know practically every minority medical student in the country during the early to mid-1970s.

Early in May 1970, I visited Bishop College, a historically Black college in Dallas, Texas. One of the students I met there was a young lady, Georgia Long, who would become the mother of my first son, Kevin.

DURING THE FALL OF MY THIRD YEAR in medical school, Bermuda celebrated the 350th anniversary of the House of Assembly. Britain's Prince Charles was coming to Bermuda to open the 350th session of the House on October 21, 1970, in St. Peter's Church in St. George's, the site of the first session in 1620. In advance of the Prince's arrival there was racial unrest in Bermuda, and the Black Beret Cadre was implicated. Bobby "Dion" Bassett, an acquaintance of mine in my preteen years, had started the Black Beret Cadre late in 1969, inspired by the Black Panthers in the United States. The Bermuda authorities cast their net wide, however, and arrested PLP MP Freddie Wade on a charge of inciting unrest. Actually Freddie had been trying to end the crisis, not inflame it, but he was jailed for five days, and he had to take his case to Bermuda's Supreme Court before he was finally exonerated. In the meantime, the PLP boycotted Prince Charles's visit.

I got a direct taste of tensions in Bermuda when I made a brief visit over Christmas and New Year while Beverly went to visit her parents. On New Year's Eve the Black Beret Cadre held a rally on the steps of the Hamilton City Hall on Church Street, and Bobby Bassett asked me to speak. During my remarks BPS officers started moving through the crowd, apparently hoping to provoke something. I said, "Do not hit the police on the head. Do not kick them. Do not stab them. Do not spit on them." The next few moments were nervous ones, but the Police were called back out of the crowd, and the rally proceeded without any incidents.

That night I went to the Castle Harbour Hotel in the eastern part of the Island to meet friends at the nightclub there. When I arrived there was a message to call Aunt Gloria. When I got her on the phone, she told me that there was trouble brewing in Hamilton, that the authorities would probably blame my speech earlier in the day, and that I should go there and see if I could do anything to calm things down.

I drove straight to Hamilton. In front of City Hall there was a crowd of two hundred or more young Black men, mostly teenagers, and on the other side of the street a large group of Police officers. I walked up to the front of the group of Black kids and spoke to them for a while, trying to gauge their mood and form a connection with them

Before long the Police Commissioner, Mr. George Duckett, drove up. He was a White man who had been recruited to the BPS after serving as police commissioner in Jamaica. It was clear right away that he wasn't getting out of his car because he was drunk.

By now it was close to midnight. Mr. Duckett called me over to his car. Just as I was stepping toward the car, I heard one of the kids say, "I'm right behind you, and I have some copper wire. If they do anything to you, I have at least one cop in sight and I'll put the wire around his neck."

I asked him to remain calm and went over to speak to Mr. Duckett. He went into a long ramble, describing the young men repeatedly as "thugs" and asking why I would associate with people like that. And then he asked me to send them home.

I responded that the young men were not under my command and were not going to obey any orders from me. I pointed out that the Police were under his command and said that if he ordered the officers to leave the scene I was sure the young men would also leave and the situation would be over.

To my great relief, Mr. Duckett agreed. He sent the Police away, and the crowd of young men quickly dispersed.

Not long after I got back to medical school, Georgia Long called. On February 1, 1971, she had given birth to a son, whom she named Kevin Antario Long. A few months later, while I was on another recruiting trip, I met Georgia at the airport in Little Rock. She had little Kevin with her, and as soon as I saw him I felt love and a fatherly connection. I began to send some financial support, and thanks to my work getting minority students into the medical profession I was able to send Georgia the money she and the baby needed in addition to the help she was getting from her family. While her parents took care of the baby, Georgia finished her bachelor's degree at Bishop College. On her return to Arkansas she trained as a nurse. She subsequently worked for the Veterans Administration in Missouri, eventually finishing her career there as a physician assistant and nurse practitioner. That didn't surprise me at all; she was a very bright lady.

Except for a few months when Georgia was married and her husband insisted that I not do so, I continued to send financial support, in increasing amounts, while Kevin was growing up. But I was not involved in raising him and saw him only a few times until he became an adolescent. Until then I also kept his existence a secret from Beverly and everyone else I knew—another example of my compartmentalization. It always seemed to me that feeling too much about things would drive me crazy, and I had to keep moving forward. So I avoided dwelling on my emotions by putting various matters into little mental boxes and tucking them away in my mind.

In the summer of 1971 the Medical Student Section of the American Medical Association was meeting at the Chase Park Plaza Hotel in St. Louis, and on a whim I decided to attend. By the middle of the first day there was a groundswell of people telling me I should run for president of the Student AMA, and by the next day it was a flood tide. I threw my hat into the ring and wound up losing by a handful of votes to a fellow named Bruce Fagel. He had been angling to be president for a while and he was very upset to have a serious challenger appear out of nowhere. But as soon as the election was over he made me an ally by appointing me to chair the Student AMA's committee on minority group affairs, a job I was happy to do.

In that capacity I soon received a letter of congratulation from Dr. Joseph F. Boyle, a prominent internist in Los Angeles and a leading figure in the AMA who would later serve as its president. Dr. Boyle wrote that he was impressed both by my putting myself up for election and the way I had handled my "campaign" over the course of the weekend-long meeting. He urged me to be in touch if there were ever anything he could do for me.

Not long afterward the Student National Medical Association met in Nashville. On that occasion I found myself alone in an elevator with Dr. Cobb, who said, "Brown, I presume."

"Yes, Dr. Cobb," I said.

"It's good to know that you're in the land of the living," he said. And then he stuck his pipe in his mouth and walked off the elevator. Dr. Cobb was still on the Howard faculty and in 1970 he had become Howard's first Distinguished University Professor, but he was not much in evidence around the medical school by then and in 1973 he retired from teaching.

I was running for president of the Student NMA, and I won the election handily, despite the fact that I did not receive strong support from the Howard delegation. A medical school classmate of mine, Jim Tate, had had enough of my leadership and had recruited Howard delegates who would support his candidacy. To amass a winning total, I had to split the votes of the delegations from Howard and from Meharry Medical College in Nashville, and garner votes in ones and twos from other schools' delegations.

However, the leadership of the NMA—with or without the involvement of Dr. Cobb, who remained one of its most influential figures—nullified the election and disbanded the Student NMA for more than a year rather than see a "firebrand" like me at the head of it. That made me feel I should take a break from political organizations of any kind, because I had won the post fair and square. I was angry about what happened. But it also built up my confidence to know that these guys were so worried about me, in the sense that they thought I was such a strong leader that they couldn't control where I might take the Student NMA and perhaps after that the NMA as a whole.

The energy I might have given to the Student NMA got drafted for something worthwhile, however. Jimmy Garrett was now in Washington, D.C., and he enlisted me to help set up a Black studies department at Federal City College, a two-year community college that is now part of the University of the District of Columbia. I also taught in the fledgling department.

AT THE END OF THE 1971–1972 ACADEMIC YEAR I graduated from medical school. The question for Beverly and me was where I was going to do my hospital internship. Internships are assigned on a national basis; medical students identify six they consider desirable and hope that they will get their first or second choice. I picked one hospital in Florida, one in Arizona, and four in Southern California. No more snow for me!

California, and specifically Los Angeles, was where Beverly and I wanted to be. Her parents had recently moved there from Oklahoma after her dad had retired from the army as a lieutenant colonel, but her mom was still working. She was teaching school in Watts and preparing to embark on a second career as a real estate agent. Beverly wanted to be close to them, which was fine with me. We all got along extremely well. And Beverly and I were both eager to try life in Los Angeles.

In due course I visited all the hospitals, or nearly all. The hospital in Miami looked so bleak that I didn't get out of the cab. The hospital in Arizona seemed like a good fit, but the temperature was 110 degrees Fahrenheit when I was there. Each step outside sank perceptibly into the asphalt. I wasn't sure I was ready to live in the desert.

Three of the Southern California hospitals were in the Los Angeles metropolitan area, but the fourth was way out in San Bernardino. My number-one choice, the number-one choice for countless fresh medical school graduates, was UCLA Harbor General Hospital. The hospital was just north of Long

Beach, mainly White and middle class, and near both Compton and Watts, almost all Black and working poor. The connection with UCLA's medical school and the diversity of the patient population attracted me to the place even before I saw it. The expertise and energy of everyone I met there sealed the deal, as far as I was concerned. UCLA Harbor General's team was definitely the one I wanted to join.

Given how desirable the few available internships there were, I'm convinced it was only politics that won me a spot, especially since I hadn't endeared myself to UCLA's medical school in my work to increase the number of minority medical students. Early in 1969 I had gone to a meeting with the medical school's admissions committee together with community activists including a member of the Black Panthers. UCLA had by that point in time graduated fewer than half a dozen Black physicians.

The director of admissions made a speech in which he said, "We've combed the country north to south and east to west, and we simply cannot find qualified Black students."

I jumped up and said, "Then you should be fired, and they should replace you with John Wooden, the basketball coach, because he knows how to find qualified Black students." Of course, John Wooden was recruiting basketball players, but his teams' graduation rates show that he didn't ignore their academic abilities.

In any case, although it was three years later and the internship decision was made by the hospital, not the medical school, I felt I needed support to get one of UCLA Harbor General's internships. As soon as I finished my tour of the hospital, I went to a pay phone and called Dr. Joseph Boyle, who was then president of the Los Angeles County Medical Association and an associate clinical professor at the University of Southern California School of Medicine. Dr. Boyle put in a good word for me with his friends at UCLA Harbor General; Dr. Columbus McAlpin, a Howard grad who was a resident at the hospital, spoke for me from the inside; and the result was that I got an internship there.

My parents, Emelita, and my extended family all sent congratulations. I sent congratulations back to Aunt Gloria, who had just been reelected to Parliament in the Bermuda general election of June 1972, and my mother, who had also won a seat as a UBP candidate. Of 40 available seats in the House of Assembly, the UBP had won 30 and the PLP 10. Although I told my mother and aunt they were on the wrong side of the aisle and should be in the PLP, I was very happy about their victories.

They were the first two sisters to serve together in a parliament anywhere in the British Commonwealth. An Associated Press story about them ran in newspapers all across North America, and it reported that my mother was inspired to run for office after meeting Congresswoman Shirley

Chisholm. That made me smile, because that meeting took place on the Howard campus when my mother and I were sharing an apartment.

I remained ambitious to run for office in Bermuda myself, but I was in no hurry, not while I had a chance to live and work in L.A.

6. Private Practice and Public Policy

ON JULY 1, 1972, I BEGAN MY ONE-YEAR INTERNSHIP in family practice medicine at UCLA Harbor General Hospital. Beverly and I had each been to Los Angeles several times before. I had been there on half a dozen recruiting trips, and Beverly had visited her parents, who were living in the Baldwin Hills area. But we were both still bowled over by the California lifestyle and how well it suited us.

We found a great two-bedroom apartment in Redondo Beach for $265 a month. There was space for each of us to work and study, it was only a ten- or fifteen-minute drive to UCLA Harbor General, and it was also convenient for Beverly.

After four years working at the NIH, while I got through medical school, Beverly was eager to continue her education and try new things. She got into the Masters of Public Health (MPH) program at UCLA, and she found a job on the task force responsible for the emergency services infrastructure at the brand new soon-to-open Martin Luther King, Jr. Community Hospital in the Willowbrook area of South Central, between Watts and Compton.

I hadn't yet told Beverly about Kevin. I justified my silence to myself on the grounds that Kevin was an infant and didn't need anything from me right now except financial support, which I was glad to be providing. And I reckoned that the most opportune time to tell Beverly that I had fathered a child with another woman was after she became pregnant and the two of us knew we had a child of our own on the way. So I just kept it in a separate compartment in my mind.

Another compartment in my mind held everything to do with Bermuda politics. There was a big event to file away in that compartment when the news came that George Duckett, Bermuda's Police Commissioner, had been shot dead on the night of September 9, 1972. The authorities looked in the direction of the Black Beret Cadre, but no suspects were identified. Living almost 4,000 miles away in California, I could only wonder what else was in store for Bermuda. The Wooding Commission Report in 1969 had warned that relations between Black and White Bermudians needed immediate and sustained action by the UBP Government if the situation was not to worsen dangerously. But that warning had been ignored. The opposition PLP had continued to press for change, but the parliamentary system gave it no opportunity to initiate substantive action of any kind.

Poor race relations had largely continued to fester rather than progress, although Bermuda had gained its first Black Government Leader on December 29, 1971, when Edward Richards succeeded Henry Tucker at the helm of the UBP. (It was during Edward Richards's tenure that the Government Leader and Executive Council in Parliament became formally known as Premier and Cabinet.) Aunt Gloria and my mother assured me that Edward Richards had the best intentions and fervently wanted to see racial equality in Bermuda. But the speed of events was accelerating, while the White Bermudians who dominated the UBP behind the scenes, and still controlled all the levers of political and economic power in the country, were dragging their feet. Nothing on the UBP agenda promised to dismantle Bermuda's version of apartheid, no matter how personally devoted to that goal Richards was.

However, my immediate concern was getting through the internship year in one piece. Internship is an inherently grueling experience, but it was much more so then before there were any serious limits on the length of time an intern had to be on call without a break. The record for me was fifty-two hours straight, except for perhaps three hours' worth of five- to ten-minute naps.

I wasn't in competitive track shape anymore, but my high fitness level helped me cope with all the physical demands of the year. On the doctoring side of things, I found I was a bit ahead of my fellow family practice interns in some ways and a bit behind in others. I was ahead in actual patient contact. For example, I had caught my first babies as a fourth-year medical student at Howard, whereas a number of the other interns had not yet had that experience. I was behind a little in biochemistry. But by the end of the internship year in June 1973, I was well prepared and capable in every area of the field.

That spring had seen new troubles arise in Bermuda. On the night of March 10, 1973, the new Governor, Richard Sharples, was shot dead outside Government House along with his Great Dane, Horsa, and his aide-de-camp, Captain Hugh Sayers. Not quite a month later, on April 6, two more White men, Victor Rego and Mark Doe, respectively the owner and bookkeeper of the Shopping Centre supermarket in Hamilton, were found shot dead. Scotland Yard was called in to manage the investigations into these killings, and ballistics evidence tied them to the killing of George Duckett.

In the last weeks of my internship, a well-informed person in Bermuda called and said the Police were wondering if I knew anything about the shootings, based on my tangential acquaintance with some members of the Black Beret Cadre. I didn't, and no one in authority ever contacted me. But the call indicated how wide a net the BPS and Scotland Yard were casting to try to find those responsible.

In reasonable fear of being railroaded by Bermuda's criminal justice system, Black Beret Cadre founder Bobby Bassett left the country. So did two other Black Beret Cadre leaders, Ottiwell Simmons, Jr., and Charles De Shields, who flew to Toronto in the company of Larry Tacklyn, who had a criminal record. Tacklyn was detained at the Toronto airport and returned to Bermuda.

Meanwhile I was focused on finishing my internship and realizing my dream of going into practice as a family physician like my childhood idol Uncle Bert. I confidently registered for the next offering, scheduled for the fall, of the U.S. national board exam in medicine, the last step for American-trained physicians before securing a license to practice in a particular state.

Until I took and passed the test, I could only work as a physician under the supervision of a licensed physician or in a continuing residency program. I lined up a job working in the South Central office of Dr. Gil Faustina, a general practitioner and surgeon. Dr. Faustina, a very light-skinned Louisiana Creole, had two offices: the one in South Central, where he passed as Black, and another in a White community, where he passed as White. Talk about double consciousness and the need to compartmentalize mentally and emotionally—Dr. Faustina faced that every day. I detested the need for him to present himself as anything other than who and what he was.

Before I started that job, however, I went home to take the Bermuda medical licensing exam. Although Beverly and I were planning to live in California for some time, the long-term plan was that we would move to Bermuda where I would practice as a physician and run for a seat in Parliament. There was no rush to take the Bermuda exam. But having just finished my internship year in fine form, I knew I was at the top of my game and it seemed like the perfect time to get the exam out of the way.

The test went as smoothly as I expected. In a few places I had to remind myself to use British rather than American medical jargon, but I knew I had done well. To my astonishment the Bermuda Medical Council (BMC) informed me in due course that I "did not perform satisfactorily" and denied me a license to practice medicine in Bermuda. I asked for my numerical score on the exam, but they said no without explaining that the scoring was pass/fail. In most jurisdictions at that time, those who failed a medical license exam were told where they were deficient to enable them to improve their chances on retaking the test.

My political ambitions were no secret in Bermuda, and both parties had an interest in whether I came back to live there sooner or later. The PLP was eager to have me return as soon as possible. Politically minded friends told me that the UBP Government was just as eager to keep me away as long as possible because my entering Bermuda politics would increase the pressure for progress in race relations. It was obvious that my obtaining or not obtaining a medical license had significant political implications. Although I made a public plea to the BMC for a more transparent response, they stuck to repeating I "did not perform satisfactorily" and refused to provide any more information. I knew I would not be allowed to practice medicine in Bermuda anytime soon.

In October, Erskine "Buck" Burrows was arrested for robbing a branch of the Bank of Bermuda the previous month and then charged with the murder of George Duckett and linked to Larry Tacklyn in the murders of Richard Sharples, Hugh Sayers, Victor Rego, and Mark Doe. By then I had returned to Los Angeles and gone to work for Dr. Faustina. We had an understanding that I would be leaving to set up my own practice in South Central as soon as I could. I took the national board exam in the fall, and right after the holidays I got the news that I had passed with room to spare in my score. I felt bittersweet elation, happy that I could practice medicine anywhere in the United States, but disappointed, though not surprised, that my native land had deemed me unsatisfactory.

A few weeks later I was driving through the intersection of Vermont Avenue and Century Boulevard when I saw a For Sale sign on the medical office at the corner. I immediately changed directions and went to see my friend Marvin Johnson, who was a loan officer at Security Pacific Bank. Beverly and I had met Marvin at a club on Wilshire Boulevard called the New York Experience, which was popular with young Black professionals in Los Angeles.

Beverly's mother had wanted to take out the mortgage on the building, but I felt I had to do this on my own. She understood fortunately, and there were no hard feelings. With a loan from the bank to buy the building and spruce it up, I dove into the adventure of setting up my medical practice.

It generally takes a couple of years for a medical practice to build up a viable patient roster and cash flow. But when I opened the door of the Vermont-Century Medical Clinic to patients in March 1974, it was like opening a well in the desert. From the start we had twenty-five to thirty patients a day across the whole spectrum of South Central, from ministers and their families to real and wanna-be gangsters to striving working-class people to the terribly disadvantaged.

I made a lot of rookie business mistakes in the early days and months of my practice, especially in hiring. At the end of the practice's first year, I discovered that $100,000 in medical insurance claims had never been processed, and that it was too late to submit them for payment. It hurt to take such a big loss, and I had to replace my office manager. But it was tremendously exciting to grow the practice with satisfied patients, whose health was visibly improving. Even with the lost billings we were also basically on a sound financial footing, and the economics of the practice improved from there.

LATE IN THE SUMMER OF 1974 BEVERLY AND I managed to take a much-needed week's vacation in Bermuda. Beverly had also been working hard in her MPH program and her job at Martin Luther King, Jr. Community Hospital, and we both just wanted to relax. To avoid any attention from the press about my political ambitions, we stayed in a small private guesthouse rather than one of the big hotels. But on our second morning Uncle George tracked us down and knocked repeatedly at the door.

"I must speak to you urgently, Ewart," Uncle George said, when I finally came to the door. Everything was always urgent for Uncle George, and I tried to put him off. But I wound up sitting on the porch of the little bungalow with him for the next three hours as he exhorted me to abandon my fledgling medical practice and return to Bermuda to prepare to run for the PLP in the next general election, which would occur no later than 1977 (as it happened, the next election came sooner, in May 1976).

"It may seem far away, Ewart, but it's not. You've got to get positioned within the PLP to run in the right district. You've got a lot of advance work to do."

As always with Uncle George, much of what he said was sensible and much was hyperbole. Returning to Bermuda to be a political candidate was indeed going to take a lot of advance work. But now was not my last best chance to run for electoral office. I envisioned coming back to Bermuda as a seasoned person in every way, with professional and leadership experiences that would enhance my potential to be a progressive change agent. Among other things I was determined that I would only come back to Bermuda as a practicing physician with a Bermuda medical license. And for the immediately foreseeable future, it did not look as if the Forty Thieves—the White power elite who continued to dominate life in Bermuda—were willing to give me a fair opportunity to qualify for that license.

So I continued to bide my time, while devoting most of my energy to building up my practice. I learned the hard lessons from my initial business mistakes, and step by step got things running well. Over time I was able to add diagnostic services, such as ultrasound, x-ray, and EKG machines and a lab for blood work and other basic testing. This was especially helpful in terms of both cost effectiveness and patient outcomes to the large number of my patients who were dependent on public transportation. In a city as geographically spread out as Los Angeles, those without cars could spend hours waiting for and riding buses from one part of town to another; that factor alone often derailed needed care. After a few years I was also able to hire first one and then a second associate physician to work with me. Although the term was not then in use, I strove to make my practice an early example of what is now called a medical home: both a place for me and my staff to deliver care and a center for organizing and coordinating any specialist treatment my patients needed. It was a comprehensive one-stop shop for family medical care.

The quick yet sustained growth of my practice attracted various kinds of attention—wanted and unwanted. On the favorable side it kept bringing new patients in the door. On the unfavorable side was an overture from a wanna-be kingpin from Memphis named Eddie, a skinny little fellow who couldn't have weighed more than 120 pounds. In his bell-bottom pants, shirts with huge lapels, and big-brimmed hats, he was the picture of mid-1970s style, a matchstick version of the crime bosses and drug dealers in the era's blaxploitation movies. Eddie had himself driven around South Central in a Buick Electra 225 with a vinyl roof, and his main source of income was being a small-time loan shark. One day he came to see me, and I assumed he was there as a patient. No, he wanted to tell me how easy it would be to make "grand theft dough" with fraudulent billing, using Medicaid cards he had collected from people who couldn't repay the money he loaned them at very high interest.

I said, "Eddie, how much are you going to pay me when I lose my license?" Without waiting for an answer I turned him down flat.

He urged me to reconsider, repeating, "Doc, this is grand theft dough on a weekly basis. We'll get rich quick."

I told him no again, and he went away unhappy. A couple of months later I heard he died choking on a chicken bone.

Of course, there were physicians and other caregivers of varied ethnicities who were running Medi-Cal mills, sending fraudulent bills to the California agency that administered the state's Medicaid funds. The success of my practice was a red flag to those who found it hard to imagine that a Black physician in South Central was prospering on the up and up. In the early years of the practice in particular, state investigators periodically came calling, convinced that they were going to find little more than a façade with few or no real patients, a pill mill. My staff and I always enjoyed their shock at seeing the waiting room crowded with patients through the day. It never took long for the investigators to recognize that we were billing for a high volume of actual treatment and walk back out the door.

The fact of the matter was that I was working my tail off. Adding staff, including associate physicians, did not change that situation throughout my years in Los Angeles. Not that I'm complaining about the workload. I loved what I was doing.

Nevertheless, a couple of weekends a month Beverly and I drove somewhere in Southern California like San Diego or Palm Springs, or we hopped a plane to places like San Francisco, Las Vegas, or New Orleans. One day outside the delivery room of the West Adams Community Hospital maternity ward, a Black doctor my age gave me grief about taking so many pleasure trips out of town. Dr. Leroy Weekes, at that time the unofficial dean of the Black doctors in Los Angeles was passing by. Dr. Weekes stopped in his tracks, turned to me, and said, "Keep doing that. I'm almost sixty years old, and I have hell getting away for a weekend. You go ahead and take your breaks. You and your patients will both benefit."

Beverly and I were enjoying our life together, but a nagging disappointment for both of us was our inability to conceive a child. There was no apparent medical problem, so we kept trying. Meanwhile it was in both our personalities to accentuate the positive, and there were so many positives to be grateful for and celebrate.

In addition to our frequent travels, we had a busy social life in Los Angeles. Cars are of great importance in the California scene, and I was able to buy Beverly a Mercedes-Benz 450SL, which she loved. Our friends used to tease me about my only driving a Datsun 240Z, and later one of the successor 260Zs. But I loved those little Datsun sports cars. Driving on the freeway with the top down and my favorite music on the eight-track tape player always put a smile on my face. One tape I practically wore out from playing it so much was Harold Melvin and the Blue Notes' 1975 album, *Wake Up Everybody*, the last album the group made before Teddy Pendergrass went out on his own as a solo artist.

Beverly and I shared another characteristic: we both immersed ourselves in our work. In the fall of 1976 Beverly entered the dental school at UCLA, and I enrolled in the MPH program at UCLA that she had recently completed. Dr. Paul Torrens mentored me in the MPH program as he had Beverly. Aunt Gloria steered me to another mentor, Dr. Derrick Jelliffe, who chaired UCLA's program on population control and international health. The two of them had met when Aunt Gloria was Bermuda's Minister of Health and Human Services from 1968 to 1972. Dr. Jelliffe in turn steered me to a United Nations fellowship for doctors working in underserved communities, and the stipend helped compensate for the time I had to take away from my practice.

It was tough being a student with classes three days a week while still keeping the practice humming. Some of the faculty complained about my beeper always going off because of a patient in labor or some other emergency, even though UCLA's official policy was to encourage practicing physicians to enroll. But I didn't want to delay doing the MPH in part because I reckoned that sooner or later Beverly would get pregnant and I'd have even

less time available. In any case it was all worth it for my professional development as a physician in the inner city. It also gave me a perspective that would
be valuable when I returned to Bermuda to campaign for a seat in Parliament.
The health disparities between Bermuda's White and Black populations represented one of the most important issues I ultimately wanted to address as
an elected official. It was with exactly that ambition of mine in mind, Aunt
Gloria said, that she urged me to study under Dr. Jelliffe.

In 1977, along with work on my MPH, I rounded off my professional
qualifications as a specialist in family practice by passing the specialty board
exam and thus becoming a Diplomate of the American Board of Family Practice. No sooner had I become board-certified, as the saying goes, than I got a
call from David Satcher, who in 1998 would become the sixteenth U.S. Surgeon General. David was then a research professor at UCLA School of Medicine and Public Health, and he had just agreed to become interim dean of
Charles Drew Postgraduate Medical School in Los Angeles.

The Martin Luther King, Jr. Community Hospital was formalizing a relationship with Drew as the King-Drew Medical Center, and David was starting
and chairing the King-Drew Sickle Cell Research Center and the King-Drew
Department of Family Medicine. He invited me to become an adjunct professor in the new department of family medicine, and I was happy to accept.
Working with David to build up the department was a highlight of my time in
Los Angeles, and I continued to teach there after David left to become chair
of the department of community medicine and family practice at Morehouse
School of Medicine.

On top of all that, I was ambitious to open a second practice a fifteen-
minute drive away at the intersection of Crenshaw Boulevard and Imperial
Highway. I opened the Crenshaw-Imperial Medical Clinic in 1977, and for
several years I divided my time between it and Vermont-Century.

Looking back I have to be grateful for my strong constitution and a great
staff, especially my sister, Emelita. From the minute I started Vermont-
Century Medical Clinic I wanted Emelita to move to Los Angeles and run the
office for me. For the past ten years she'd been working at Bermuda's only
hospital, King Edward VII Memorial Hospital (KEMH). But she was finding it
less and less comfortable to work there because of the hospital's hostile
response to the changing times. I kept asking her to come work for me, and
finally she said yes. She and her then husband, Derek Robinson, decided they
were ready for a change, and in 1977 they moved to Los Angeles with my
wonderful niece, Kimberly, who was four years old.

I had a solid staff then as well as an excellent medical practice consultant,
Kelley McKinney, who taught Emelita the complex procedures Medi-Cal and
Medicare imposed on billing. Emelita meshed beautifully with Kelley and the

rest of the staff, and then she raised everybody's game as she brought her organizational talents and people skills to bear on the office.

With Emelita there, I never had a moment's concern about missing problems that might come up in the normal course of things and need my attention. That allowed me to focus my energy on treating patients, teaching at King-Drew, and from 1978 on some new challenges as well.

TONY JOHNSON, A JAMAICAN URBAN PLANNER who worked for Mayor Tom Bradley in the second of his five consecutive four-year terms, was a friend of mine in Los Angeles. Tony came to our house one day and said, "You know, I want to go back to Jamaica, but I want to go back bringing the world's largest reggae festival." In my den he came up with the name for it: Reggae Sunsplash.

In the last week of June 1978, Tony and four Jamaican partners—Don Green, Ronnie Burke, John Wakeling, and Ed Barclay—put on the first Reggae Sunsplash. I got to know the partners because I was the festival's inaugural medical director and served in that capacity every year until 1993. I brought other doctors and nurses with me from Los Angeles, with everyone working as volunteers, expenses only paid.

The festival was an immediate sensation and a transformative event for summer tourism in Jamaica as well as for the world of reggae. Bob Marley refused to participate the first year because he and Tony Johnson were pursuing the same beauty queen. By the second year, however, that rivalry was over, everything was patched up, and Bob performed at the festival.

One of my housemates the first year at Reggae Sunsplash was Ellie Bank from Trinidad. He kept me up night after night, saying he thought he could persuade Bob to perform for the first time ever in Trinidad, if I could find the investors. We talked and talked, and in the end I found the investors and Bob agreed to perform in Trinidad at the end of the year in two "December to Remember" concerts.

A lot of oil money was flowing through Trinidad then, and we were confident we would do well. Everything looked rosy until the other investors and I got to Trinidad. That's when the situation turned gray.

It turned out that the two concerts on December 9 and 10 at PSA Auditorium were not only going to be Bob Marley's first performances in Trinidad, they were also going to be Ellie Bank's first promotion anywhere. By the time I arrived on December 9, he had gotten on the wrong side of the local politicians and civil servants by refusing to give them the usual complimentary tickets and not doing the rest of the glad-handing that promoters generally do everywhere.

Long story short, the airport customs wouldn't release Bob's equipment, and Ellie Bank had to put up his mother's house as collateral to guarantee payment of customs duties. Partly for that reason, Bob went onstage very late the first night. There were around 8,000 people in the arena, and others waiting to get in, but the police weren't assisting with crowd control. Police officers backstage whispered to me that my fellow investors and I had already gotten our return on our money and taken it out of the country. That was ridiculous. I said nothing and just smiled, so as not to antagonize the police any further.

The next day we found out someone had told the media Bob was canceling the second night's show. We hustled him onto television and radio where he said, "Ah be there tonight."

We knew the sabotage attempt was serious, and there was an eerie feeling over the arena that evening. Bob went onstage on time at about 9 p.m. He was performing his third or fourth song, "No Woman, No Cry," when something hit the backdrop over his head—"Pow!"

People dropped. They didn't know what it was. From the wings I could see someone had thrown an empty Coke bottle at the stage.

Bob kept playing "No Woman, No Cry," but he edged over toward me. When he got close enough he said, "Doc, Ah gone." That concert was the last time I saw him.

Tony Johnson, Ronnie Burke, and I left the arena in the same car—or tried to. Right in the middle of the entrance gate, the crowd blocked the way and would not let us move, thinking Bob might be inside. Over a thousand people swarmed over the top of the car. Inside we were silent, breath bated, hoping the crowd would let us move before they crushed the car roof. *Crack!* The plastic molding of the interior light over the back seat dropped down to the floor of the car. We all gave a nervous laugh, but no one said a word.

After we finally got out of there I went straight to my hotel. I kept a cab waiting while I packed my bag and paid my bill, then asked the driver to take me to the airport.

The driver said, "Sir, that's dangerous at this time of night. You don't want to do that."

"Yes, I do," I said. I thought the police were going to try to stop us from leaving the country, and I figured I'd take my chances at the airport. I persuaded the driver to take me there and had him drop me off in front of Eastern Airlines. I lay down in front of the door and went to sleep with my head on my folded garment bag.

A female employee of Eastern Airlines woke me in the morning and asked, "Sir, are you all right?"

"Yes, I'm fine. I just need to get out of here. What's your first flight?"

"Our first flight is going to Barbados."

"That's fine with me," I said, and I went inside and bought a ticket. My fellow investors and I lost our money, and I didn't return to Trinidad for about ten years.

DURING THOSE YEARS I AVIDLY FOLLOWED MUHAMMAD ALI'S FIGHTS. I had met Ali a few times at Howard, and on one occasion I managed to arrange for him to make an impromptu address to my medical school class. I admired his moral and political courage as well as his extraordinary performances in the ring.

Unfortunately I was not in Las Vegas to see him lose a split decision to Leon Spinks on February 15, 1978. When a rematch was announced for September 15 at the Superdome in New Orleans, I immediately made plans to go. The day of the fight, my friend Earl Johnson and I were checking into our hotel rooms in New Orleans when I picked up a message that West Adams Community Hospital in Los Angeles had been locked shut and put into receivership for its debts.

Concern about the future of the hospital had been percolating for a while in the surrounding community and among the doctors who had admitting privileges and patients there. It galled me to risk missing the Ali-Spinks rematch, but I immediately turned around and went back to the airport to fly home to Los Angeles. My fellow West Adams physicians and I had a heavyweight fight of our own to wage.

Before I left, Earl Johnson said, "Give me your ticket in case you don't get back in time, and I'll make sure it isn't wasted."

I said, "I'll let you hold the ticket for me. But I will be back in time. No matter what, don't you dare give it to someone else until the bell rings for the first round."

Back in Los Angeles, I addressed a late afternoon press conference at the Century Plaza Hotel in Los Angeles as a spokesperson for West Adams's attending physicians. I confidently told the media, "West Adams Community Hospital will be open and treating patients again in six weeks." Then I raced back to the airport. Thanks to the time difference between Los Angeles and New Orleans, I was able to get to the Superdome in the nick of time to see Ali beat Spinks by a unanimous decision.

It took a lot longer than six weeks to reopen the hospital. It took fourteen months, an experience that tested my mettle as a physician, a community organizer, and a business person managing a big-ticket capital transaction. Yet it was an invaluable experience for my later roles in government in Bermuda. It was probably a good thing that when I spoke to the press, I had no idea of the odds against me.

First the receiver, Continental Assurance, had to be persuaded to consider selling the hospital to the physicians rather than to the Catholic diocese of Los Angeles, like many American Catholic dioceses a big hospital operator. The second problem was the price of $5 million (almost $20 million in 2017 dollars). In addition, as a less certain quantity than the Catholic Church, my fellow physicians and I were going to have to put a lot more cash on the table as a down payment—30 percent, or $1.5 million. With these obstacles looming, I solicited my good friend Donald Henderson, a busy gastro-intestinal specialist, to work with me.

Finding physicians to invest $35,000 each for the down payment was not easy. But we got a vote of confidence from Continental Assurance's lawyer, Lew Geyser. He thought enough of our proposal to say he would invest $35,000 of his own money, if we got enough doctors lined up. We finally had a group of thirty investors, with several of us taking more than one $35,000 stake. It didn't hurt that one of the first doctors to join the group, Dr. Richard Williams, had attended Harvard with Geyser.

At the eleventh hour, however, when it was time for everyone to deposit their money in a designated escrow account, half a dozen doctors bailed out with various excuses. In hindsight, I think most if not all of them had the money available and believed the physicians group would succeed in buying the hospital. With that in sight, they figured on being free riders. The hospital would reopen, they could go back to treating patients there and billing profitably for that care, and they wouldn't be on the hook to see that the hospital as a whole ran efficiently enough to pay off the mortgage and remain open.

For a minute, I didn't have the faith in myself that at least some of the renegade physicians apparently had. It looked like the deal was going to collapse, and there wasn't a single stone I could think of turning over to find replacement investors. It occurred to me that Los Angeles had a relatively new group of physicians who were either Korean immigrants or first-generation U.S.-born Korean-Americans serving the city's increasing Korean population. I sought out some of those doctors and their participation made the deal happen in return for Korean signage along with English signage at the hospital entrances and on top of the building. It was the first joint venture of any kind between the Korean, Black, and Latino communities in Los Angeles.

On November 4, 1979, we reopened the hospital under its new name, Western Park Community Hospital. A common family name in Korea, "Park" had very positive associations for the Korean-American doctors and their patients. Five years later the hospital was healthy enough financially that the physician group was able to sell it to a German firm for $15 million (a little over $35 million in 2017 dollars). There was not a huge cash profit for each of us because we had also invested a lot of money beyond the down payment and mortgage payments to update equipment and refurbish the hospital. But the original investors all enjoyed significant tax breaks. A few of the physicians who had promised to invest $35,000, only to back out at the last minute, were upset at not benefiting from the sale. They felt I should have done a better job persuading them to stay in the deal five years earlier. It was only a step from there to acting as if I had unfairly maneuvered them out of the deal.

It had taken meeting after meeting to put together the deal to rescue the hospital. It was the only period during my years in Los Angeles when I was not spending the vast majority of my time seeing and treating patients in my practice. The practice kept going only because the clinic had established a good reputation and I had a good associate physician, Beverly's cousin Dr. Wallace McLeod.

As a side effect of leading the physician group's purchase and operation of the hospital, I also became quite active in Los Angeles medical politics. Getting a hospital in a disadvantaged community reopened and participating in the medical society put me on the radar of Governor Jerry Brown. In 1979 Governor Brown invited me to serve on a special year-long California state commission on maternal and child health. This gave me another opportunity to use my expertise in family practice and public health in a way that prepared me for being an MP and Government Leader in Bermuda. The commission's work resulted in a number of progressive steps, such as ensuring that testing children for lead contamination from peeling paint would be wholly covered under Medi-Cal. Previously that test and similar cost-effective tests and treatments had not been covered at all.

DURING MY FIRST YEARS IN PRACTICE IN CALIFORNIA, my main focus for community or public service was as an enthusiastic alumnus of Howard. My criticisms of the university as a student were part and parcel of my love for the place, and I'll always be grateful for the superb education I got there. For five years in the mid- to late 1970s, I organized and emceed an annual Howard Alumni Dinner in Los Angeles as a reunion and fundraising occasion. Each year's event was bigger than the last. I also served as an admissions interviewer and informal liaison for prospective Howard students throughout Southern California.

Over the same years, Aunt Gloria found her efforts as an MP and Cabinet Minister stymied by her colleagues in the UBP. During a little over twelve years in Parliament she served in the Cabinets of the UBP's first four Government Leaders: Henry Tucker (remember he called her the UBP's "secret weapon"), Edward Richards, John Sharpe, and David Gibbons. At various times she held the portfolios of Health and Social Services; Education and Libraries; and Planning, Housing, and the Environment.

As Cabinet Minister for Education and Libraries from 1972 to 1976, Aunt Gloria was a key figure, together with Bill Cox, Dr. Stanley Ratteray, and Dr. David Saul—the "famous four"—in the drafting, passage, and implementation of the Bermuda College Act 1974. This legislation called for amalgamating the Bermuda Hotel and Catering College, the Bermuda Technical Institute (BTI), and the Academic Sixth Form Centre into a single institution offering both professional certifications and associate's degrees that could be applied to bachelor's degree programs abroad. Dr. Saul has said, "Mr. [sic] Ratteray was the father of Bermuda College and Mrs. McPhee was the mother. I . . . was the midwife."

The creation of Bermuda College was a signal achievement, and the institution has done an enormous amount of good in Bermuda. It might have done even more, if successive UBP Governments had supported it well enough that its constituent parts, including the old BTI as I touched on earlier, could continue and increase their effectiveness in step with Bermuda's needs.

Frustrated by the UBP leadership's foot-dragging on race relations, Aunt Gloria formed the UBP Black Caucus in 1975 with my mother, Arnold A. Francis, Dr. Clarence E. James, Dr. Ratteray, Anita Smith, and C. V. "Jim" Woolridge. With assistance from Kenneth Clark, who as I mentioned played an important role in resolving the sit-in crisis at Howard University in 1968, these seven MPs drafted a report to the UBP on resolving increasing racial tension and addressing the wounds inflicted by Bermuda's history of racism. Among other things they were looking ahead to the outcome of the murder cases against Buck Burrows and Larry Tacklyn and the unrest that the likely guilty verdicts might trigger.

The UBP Black Caucus did not include all the party's Black MPs. Moderate though the Black Caucus was by any objective standard, some Black MPs sitting on the UBP's side of the House of Assembly considered it too radical.

On December 29, 1975, John Sharpe succeeded Edward Richards as UBP Leader and Bermuda's Premier. The next general election took place on May 18, 1976. Although the UBP retained a sizeable majority in the House of Assembly, the balance of power shifted slightly with the PLP increasing its representation from 10 to 14 seats and the UBP winning 26 seats.

My mother lost her seat in the House of Assembly in that election, and she was not a candidate in future elections. Frustration with the pace of change led the remaining four members of the UBP Black Caucus—Aunt Gloria, Dr. Clarence James, Dr. Stanley Ratteray, and Jim Woolridge—to resign from John Sharpe's Cabinet on February 14, 1977.

Despite this, Aunt Gloria clung to her faith in the party of her mentors, Henry Tucker and Edward Richards, and she and my mother still hoped I might change my views and join them as a member of the UBP. My mother and aunt expressed this desire in a teasing manner that involved Julian Hall, a talented young Black Bermudian.

Clarence Terceira, a leading member of the UBP who served more than once as its chairman, had taken Julian Hall under his wing and paid for his higher education at Mount Allison University in New Brunswick, Canada, and the London School of Economics. After returning to Bermuda, Julian founded the UBP's Under 40 Caucus and for a time became the party's deputy chairman. My mother and aunt said, "We have Julian now. We don't need you, Ewart," hoping that would spur me to compete for UBP laurels with Julian.

Julian Hall was brilliant. In 1974 he passed the Bermuda bar exam without taking the exam prep course, was called to the Bermuda bar, and became one of the first Black lawyers at one of Bermuda's powerful White law firms. In short order he established himself as modern Bermuda's finest courtroom advocate.

I didn't know Julian well, although we later became very close friends. From all I heard of him, I thought he was making the same mistake about the UBP, out of gratitude for educational opportunities, that my mother and Aunt Gloria had been making since 1964. I wondered what it would take to open their eyes to the truth about the UBP. The events of 1976 to 1980 provided the answers

On July 20, 1976, Larry Tacklyn was found not guilty of murdering Richard Sharples and Hugh Sayers. Buck Burrows had confessed to murdering the two men as well as George Duckett (Tacklyn was never charged in the Police Commissioner's death), and he was tried separately on those counts. On November 18, 1976, both Burrows and Tacklyn were found guilty of murdering Victor Rego and Mark Doe, and they were sentenced to death. Tacklyn appealed his death sentence, but Burrows, who seemed resigned to his fate, did not. Burrows's attitude did not change on July 6, 1977, when he was also sentenced to death for murdering George Duckett, Richard Sharples, and Hugh Sayers.

At the end of August, the UBP held a leadership vote. Aunt Gloria controlled a bloc of 6 votes, which in the end provided the edge a White UBP MP, David Gibbons, needed to defeat a Black one, Jim Woolridge, and become the new Leader of the UBP and the new Premier of Bermuda. Aunt Gloria did not think Jim Woolridge was ready for the top job.

In October, the next session of Parliament having convened, the UBP appropriated funds at Aunt Gloria's urging for a study by Kenneth Clark and his consulting firm. The Clark Study was to recommend a program for achieving racial equality in Bermuda. Looking on from the PLP's side of the aisle, Opposition Leader Lois Browne-Evans and Deputy Opposition Leader Freddie Wade must have seen this for what it probably was in Premier David Gibbons's own eyes: the least he could do for the MP who had handed him the

Premiership. The PLP's leaders welcomed the Clark Study, but they could harbor little hope that the UBP would implement any substantive recommendations it made.

On November 25, the UBP Government announced in the House of Assembly that the executions of Buck Burrows and Larry Tacklyn would be carried out by hanging at Casemates Prison on December 2. Since early in the year a campaign against capital punishment had been building, collecting thousands of signatures on a petition for Tacklyn's death sentence to be commuted to life imprisonment. Over the next few days, a "Peoples' Parliament" petition collected thousands more signatures.

Meanwhile Lois Browne-Evans was leading the Tacklyn appeal as it wound through Bermuda's court system. Ignoring the displeasure of his UBP colleagues, Julian Hall threw himself into assisting her with the appeal.

However, on December 1, the Court of Appeal meeting in the Sessions House rejected the final appeal on Tacklyn's behalf. When Lois Browne-Evans exited the Sessions House at 10 p.m., she sadly told the waiting crowd of the outcome. In a repeat of its casting blame on the PLP for the April 1968 disturbances because of the party's fiery electioneering, the UBP pilloried Browne-Evans for "inflaming" the crowd and portrayed her as a cause of the unrest that followed.

The night of December 1 saw the use of bottles and firebombs by protesters and tear gas by the authorities. In the early morning hours of December 2, Burrows and Tacklyn were hanged, and at 9 a.m. the Governor declared a state of emergency. Unrest continued through December 2 and 3 but was beginning to settle down when two hundred British troops arrived on December 4. Over the following days the unrest petered out, and the state of emergency ended on December 9.

Just as in 1968, a Government commission was empaneled to account for the disturbances and offer recommendations. The Pitt Commission was chaired by David Pitt, a physician-politician in the mold of E. F. Gordon. Pitt was born in Grenada and after studying medicine at the University of Edinburgh was active in medicine and politics first in Trinidad and Tobago and then in the Labour Party in the United Kingdom. In 1975 he had been appointed to the House of Lords as a life peer, one of the first peers of African descent, and he was formally Lord Pitt of Hampstead, signifying both the Hampstead area of London and Hampstead in Grenada.

The Pitt Commission was asked to report in July 1978. In the meantime, the Clark Study filed its report, which noted the damage racism had done and was doing in Bermuda and made a number of sensible recommendations for improvement. The UBP Government of David Gibbons accepted the report and filed it away. The same thing happened to the Pitt Commission Report and its equally sensible, much more detailed recommendations, when it was submitted in July.

Anyone who cares about Bermuda can learn much from the Pitt Commission Report. In no uncertain terms, it confirmed the findings of the Wooding Commission that the real cause of racial unrest in Bermuda was the country's history of racism against Black people. It went beyond the Wooding Commission, however, in diagnosing how racism had festered in Bermuda for so long, why it was still festering, and what should be done about it.

Among other observations, the Pitt Commission noted that the UBP was wrong to dismiss the December disturbances, in Deputy Premier Jim Woolridge's words, as "the thoughtless actions of a handful." To the contrary, the Commission said, the relatively few people actively involved in the disturbances were expressing the frustration of the vast majority of Black Bermudians. In this regard the Commission highlighted the fact that although shop windows were broken in Hamilton during the disturbances, no looting occurred.

The Pitt Commission also bravely, if diplomatically, pointed out that the UBP was doing little if anything to ameliorate the situation. Henry Tucker's UBP Government had established a Race Relations Council as part of the Race Relations Acts of 1969 and 1970, yet the Pitt Commission Report emphasized "the failure of the [UBP] Government to make use of the institution it has itself created . . . or to give it sufficient resources to carry out its very considerable responsibilities." The Commission also emphasized the unwillingness of successive UBP administrations to create bipartisan standing committees with the PLP on finance, planning, education, and social services. In short, the Commission called out the UBP for giving only lip service to the struggle for racial equality and justice in Bermuda.

In 1979 Julian Hall left the UBP and joined the PLP, where he became an important asset in that struggle for equality and justice. To punish Julian, in 1984 the UBP passed a law, unique in the free world, to ban practice by bankrupt lawyers. Julian had had to declare personal bankruptcy in 1977 because of a failed concert promotion, Summerfest, featuring Peter Tosh, Richie Havens, and Wild Cherry.

As 1979 drew to a close, Aunt Gloria was wrestling with her feelings about the UBP, her long-standing loyalties at odds with facts that were more and more difficult for her to ignore. But she continued to serve in David Gibbons's Cabinet as Minister for Planning, Housing, and Environment.

By early 1980 Aunt Gloria was contemplating leaving the UBP and electoral politics, but not quite ready to make the move. As Minister for Planning, Housing, and Environment, she oversaw the Development Applications Board, all of whose members served at Ministerial pleasure. Like most government agencies in Bermuda under UBP rule, the Development Applications

Board functioned as an extension of White economic power, in this case that of White property developers, who relied on it to approve their applications without a fuss. A White property developer named Buddy Franklin was on the board, but after he missed several important meetings and made racist remarks in her presence, Aunt Gloria sacked him.

In a private meeting Premier Gibbons told Aunt Gloria she was completely within the bounds of her Ministerial authority, right reason, and human decency. Considering the matter settled, she left Bermuda to come to Los Angeles, where her daughter Karen was then living and was about to give birth to her first child, Karmen.

While Aunt Gloria was in California for her granddaughter's birth, however, Buddy Franklin's fellow White property developers were raising a ruckus in Bermuda about his being fired from the Development Applications Board. Showing where his allegiances truly lay, Premier Gibbons told the press that the sacking of Buddy Franklin had been the result of "an emotional outburst" on Aunt Gloria's part and that she had promised not to do it again.

That left Aunt Gloria no choice but to resign, and she asked me to draft her letter of resignation from Gibbons's Cabinet, the UBP, and Parliament. The final draft of the letter drew on the arguments I'd long been making to Aunt Gloria as well as her own recent experiences. I telexed it to Julian Hall, who tweaked it a little, had it typed properly, and then signed it for Aunt Gloria as her attorney. He personally took the letter to Premier Gibbons's office, but the Premier left it unopened on his desk while he went to lunch. He was still at lunch when Julian Hall issued a press release about Aunt Gloria's resignation.

After sending that letter to David Gibbons, Aunt Gloria naturally also stopped urging me to join the UBP. Instead she was now eager for me to return to Bermuda and help the PLP win its first majority in Parliament. The time wasn't yet right for that in my view, however. Among other things, my personal life was then seriously in disarray.

Throughout the 1970s I had continued to keep Kevin's existence a secret from Beverly. I only visited him three or four times during these years, telling myself it was best for his mother and her husband to continue to raise him, while I contributed financial support.

In the spring of 1980 Beverly graduated from dental school. To celebrate, I took her on a round-the-world trip. We got tickets that covered the whole trip on TWA and its partner airlines around the world. The only condition for the tickets was that we had to go around the world in one direction, westerly or easterly, with no backtracking. We headed east, stopping briefly in New York to see friends from Howard before making our first international stops in London, Paris, and Rome.

It was a great trip until near the end. In Tahiti I played soccer on the beach—it was France against travelers from the rest of the world—and I hit my foot on a rock and tore a tendon. I just wrapped it up for the time being while Beverly and I continued on to Hawaii and then home to Los Angeles. But that's not really what turned the trip sour at the end. It was telling Beverly about Kevin when we were in Hawaii.

I had given up thinking that I could wait to tell Beverly until after she got pregnant. Kevin was nine years old now, and I felt I had to make an effort to be part of his life. Beverly did not take the news well, and I cannot blame her for that. It was not just the nature of the news, but my having kept it secret for so long, which justifiably angered her. If Beverly and I had been able to conceive a child, I think things might have gone more positively between us at this juncture. Unfortunately, the gulf between us grew greater and greater over the following months. In 1983, we separated, preparatory to an amicable divorce in 1984.

In 1983 I brought Kevin to Los Angeles for a visit and introduced him to Emelita and my friends. This was a lot for Kevin to digest, but I thought it went reasonably well.

Another major event for me in 1983 was meeting Priscilla Murray through Marvin Johnson, who was dating her roommate. Priscilla was from Detroit and planned on going back there to attend law school. In the meantime she was working at CBS, with an eye toward eventually becoming a lawyer in the entertainment industry.

Priscilla began studying for her law degree at the Detroit School of Law in the fall of 1984, and I visited her there several times. Her mother, who by herself had raised Priscilla and her two brothers and two sisters, quickly became one of my favorite people. Priscilla, her mom, one of her sisters, and I were all driving together in Detroit one day when we were rear-ended by a guy who was speeding to get away from the police. I was knocked unconscious for a minute, and when I came to I saw that Priscilla's mother's scalp was lacerated and bleeding. An ambulance reached us very quickly, and we were soon being well tended to at Henry Ford Hospital downtown. (It turned out that I had sustained damage to one of my cervical disks, which did not cause any trouble at first but eventually required surgery, as I will discuss.)

After one year at the Detroit School of Law, Priscilla transferred to Loyola Law School in Los Angeles. Our relationship was steadily growing more serious, but neither of us wanted to rush into marriage. We both needed to be sure it was the right choice for us. Among other things, Priscilla had to feel reasonably confident that she would want to move with me to Bermuda when the time came.

Bermuda's politics and the PLP kept tugging at me, directly and indirectly, and in the latter part of 1986 I began to feel that it was time to engage actively with them both. Drawing on my student and part-time job experiences on newspapers and radio, I chose to do that through journalism. The Forty Thieves party, the UBP, basically had a stranglehold on the news media in Bermuda. The one daily newspaper, the *Royal Gazette*, was as loyal to British colonialism in sheep's clothing, the national policy of the UBP, as the paper's name suggests. And the UBP Government carefully controlled the Bermuda Broadcasting Corporation, which shared the initials but none of the journalistic independence of the British Broadcasting Corporation.

The weekly *Bermuda Sun* tended to be a bit more even-handed but was not remotely a voice for the Opposition PLP. So in 1987 I founded the *Bermuda Times* newspaper. The first editor was my lifelong friend Murray Brown, and the chief reporter, and later the editor, was my cousin LaVerne Furbert. We printed the papers in Silver Spring, Maryland, and flew them into Bermuda to go on sale at news agents and neighborhood shops.

There were two newspaper printing presses in Bermuda. They were both quite willing to print the *Bermuda Times* for what they considered a fair price. I saw the almost identical prices they quoted me differently, however, because they were triple what it cost to print 4,000 copies of each edition in Baltimore, air freight them to Bermuda, and distribute them throughout the Island.

To start we were a monthly, and the first issue appeared on March 4, 1987. The October issue included a story on Priscilla's and my wedding in Detroit on September 5, with Kevin standing by me as best man. Priscilla was twenty-nine and I was forty-one years old, and we soon had two sons, Trey and Donovan. Trey was born on June 3, 1988, and Donovan was born on November 24, 1989.

The following spring, Freddie Wade, the head of the PLP, called me in Los Angeles. "If you want to be part of what the PLP is going to do over the next decade and more, you need to come back to Bermuda to stay sometime soon," Freddie said.

My gut told me he was right. It was time to get ready to move back home. If I delayed too long, it would become much harder to contribute to Bermuda's growth and maturation as I had always hoped to do.

7. "This Is Our Country!"

"I AM A BERMUDIAN," I SAID, TO STIRRING APPLAUSE. "This is our Country!"
"Yes, brother!" "Right on!" "We hear you!" members of the audience sang out, warming to call and response as in Sunday service.

"We're taking it back."

The audience roared approval.

"After twenty-eight years of living outside of Bermuda, if you think I've come home just to practice medicine, you couldn't be more incorrect."

Laughter rippled through the audience. They knew my words were not meant only for the few hundred people gathered at Pembroke Hamilton Club that Thursday evening, July 23, 1992.

"I have scores to settle, accounts to pull even."

Gasps of mingled shock and delight, along with shouts of "Tell it, tell it," answered me.

"I don't overestimate my ability to change things. But I believe the strongest powers in existence are working with me, first the Almighty God, then the people. Together we are going to make a change."

The applause ratcheted up a notch.

"And, if you're not willing to work, as Malcolm X said, get back in the alley, because this Progressive Labour Party train is on the way!"

The audience stood and cheered as one as I stepped back from the podium, arms raised in salute to them.

When I left the stage, I expected members of the Bermuda news media, particularly the *Royal Gazette* and the Bermuda Broadcasting Corporation, to ask what I meant by "scores to settle, accounts to pull even." Although my speech had been basically improvised, with no written text or notes, I had been planning what to say for some time. The "scores to settle, accounts to pull even" were not personal ones. In the most immediate sense I meant the eight consecutive elections in which White Bermuda's political representatives had defeated the Progressive Labour Party, the first time in 1963 as nominal independents who followed the lead of Henry Tucker and thereafter as formal members of the United Bermuda Party under his explicit command and control. I wanted to change the won-lost record to UPB 8 and PLP 1 at the next general election.

To my surprise, the *Royal Gazette* and BBC reporters had already raced away to file their stories. However, I suppose I should not have been surprised to see myself described as "Dr. Revenge" on the front page of the next day's *Royal Gazette* and in much the same terms on the Bermuda Broadcasting Corporation's news programs. At least they quoted me accurately. It was also good to see their highlighting my quoting Bob Marley's "Redemption Song," which calls on people to "free their minds" and escape "mental slavery." But for the next fourteen months, the combined forces of the UBP and the *Royal Gazette,* and to a lesser extent the Bermuda Broadcasting Corporation, portrayed me as a mad villain intent on the "politics of revenge" and employed a policy of non-reporting and silencing to limit my efforts to elaborate on "scores to settle, accounts to pull even."

"Revenge" was a word I never used and a concept I rejected in politics as well as other areas of life. My goal was then, and still is, equity, redressing and eradicating racism in Bermuda and on that basis at last achieving national unity, which the country has not yet experienced in fact.

The news coverage in the *Royal Gazette* and on the Bermuda Broadcasting Corporation highlighted comments by Quinton Edness, a UBP MP for Warwick West who was also a Bermuda Broadcasting Corporation radio announcer. He voiced the UBP's view of me as one of the PLP's "would-be overseas politicians," although I was the only PLP candidate who had been living outside Bermuda until recently. To continue quoting the *Royal Gazette,* "Mr. Edness said voters should ask [Dr. Brown], who still has a clinic in Los Angeles, 'Where will you represent me, in California or Bermuda?' and 'Where will you be when we need to see you or call you? Do I have to call California?'"

While we were both in politics, Quinton Edness regularly opposed me and apologized afterward. He was good friends with my mother and Aunt Gloria.

My prospective constituents did not have to call California, although to my dismay I still had to return there frequently. When Freddie Wade called in the spring of 1990 to say it was time to come home and campaign for a seat in Parliament, I could not make the move immediately. I was responsible for over a thousand patients at the Vermont-Century Medical Clinic. From the day I opened the clinic in 1974, I strove to build a practice that would outlast me and serve patients effectively far into the future. When I am in Los Angeles I enjoy driving by the corner of Vermont and Century and seeing the well-kept office of a successor practice—in a community that remains underserved by other medical providers.

To make that possible I had to arrange a transition that made sense financially and medically. Not long after Freddie's call, I began spending three days a month in Bermuda. My first objective was to establish a medical practice. I had already completed an essential preparatory step by taking the Bermuda medical licensing exam again in 1988. This time I was said to have passed.

Following a model that served me well at Vermont-Century in Los Angeles, I set up my first medical office in Bermuda, which I incorporated as Bermuda HealthCare Services (BHCS) in 1991, at 17 the Lane in Paget Parish, close by the country's busiest intersection. The present office is right next door to the first location, a stone's throw east of Foot of the Lane Park on Hamilton harbor and a few hundred yards from where Bermuda's most heavily traveled roads feed into a roundabout. Aunt Gloria suggested the current site. She came by my office one day to tell me that the Berkeley Institute had received the building at 19 the Lane as a bequest and wanted to sell it.

Bermuda HealthCare Services quickly attracted an increasing patient roster, and I was eager to sell the Vermont-Century Medical Clinic. What promised to facilitate a sale was Emelita's deciding to purchase the physical therapy side of the clinic. She was going to remain in Los Angeles and divide her work time between running the physical therapy business at Vermont-Century and consulting on medical practice management, for which she was increasingly in demand.

A young Black physician who had been working for me at Vermont-Century wanted to buy the practice. Emelita's purchase of the physical therapy business meant he had to come up with less money as a fair price for the physical premises, medical equipment, patient roster, and associated good will, which was considerable. As I began to spend more time in Bermuda, Emelita said my loyal patients were joking about suing me for patient abandonment. The physician who took over the Vermont-Century Medical Clinic would be walking into an extremely favorable situation in terms of quality of prior medical care, volume of satisfied patients, and positive cash flow.

I had hoped to complete the sale long before the July 1992 rally at Pembroke Hamilton Club. Just before the contract was to be signed, however, the prospective purchaser tried to change the terms of the deal. He knew how eager I was to live and work full-time in Bermuda, and he thought he could pull a fast one on the price. So I had to hold on and continue to commute back and forth between Los Angeles and Bermuda, until I could arrange a sale at a fair price to another young Black physician.

It was a grueling thirty-four months before that happened in 1993. At one point I woke up on an airplane and did not know whether I was coming home to Bermuda or going back to Los Angeles yet again. Too embarrassed to ask a flight attendant to tell me which direction the plane was headed, I asked for my suit jacket instead. My ticket was in the inside pocket, and it said the flight was going to New York, where I would change planes for Bermuda.

One very satisfying break in the Los Angeles–Bermuda circuit, however, was being invited to give the commencement address at Howard University College of Medicine on May 8, 1992. The disturbances in Los Angeles connected with the Rodney King incident were still fresh in people's minds, and I spoke about the unrest in terms of the individual and collective challenges that young Black physicians faced. This was also a time when the health maintenance organization (HMO) model was becoming a big factor in medicine, and I urged Howard's new medical graduates to avoid letting that model, rather than quality of care, determine how they treated their patients. The HMOs were shaping a generation of what I called "slot doctors," who interacted with patients according to corporate HMO guidelines rather than their sense of the best treatment for each individual. I considered that approach to be dangerous for the medical profession and patient outcomes.

Throughout the second half of 1992, the UBP hammered at me as an "overseas politician." In October the PLP held a press conference at Alaska Hall, its headquarters in Hamilton, so that Freddie Wade could introduce three other members of the party and me as candidates for the four House of Assembly seats from Warwick East and Warwick West. My cousin Calvin Smith, then one of the PLP's appointees to the Senate and previously an elected member of the House of Assembly, was going to run in Warwick East with Alex Scott, then the Senate Opposition Leader for the PLP. Union leader George Scott and I were going to run in Warwick West.

It wasn't only that the four Assembly seats for Warwick East and Warwick West were held by UBP MPs. Those same UBP MPs—Gerald Simons and Irving Pearman in Warwick East and Quinton Edness and former Premier John Sharpe in Warwick West—were also all Cabinet Ministers. The prominence of the four incumbents meant tough campaigns for Alex Scott, George Scott, Calvin, and me. However, the demographics of Warwick were becoming more favorable to the PLP as Black people moved there from elsewhere in Bermuda. With about 2,500 voters, Warwick West had become the most populous constituency in Bermuda..

Although the three other PLP candidates each got a share of attention at the press conference, most of the questions were, directly or indirectly, about me. The discussion came to a head when a reporter for the *Royal Gazette* asked how many months of the year I was off the Island.

It was a disingenuous question on two counts. One was the form of the question, asking how many months I was away, as if it were one continuous block of time, rather than how frequently I left the Island. The question was also fundamentally disingenuous because there was nothing unusual about politicians in Bermuda spending a great deal of time off the Island pursuing their careers or business interests. Both the PLP and the UBP had MPs who were constantly coming and going throughout the year.

Freddie Wade noted this point in responding to the *Royal Gazette*, saying, to quote the newspaper, that it was "a non-issue given that many MPs are never questioned about their off-island business travel."

I answered the question myself by saying, "I haven't counted, but I'm here every month. I'm a Bermudian, born and raised here. I have been involved in the life of Bermuda since my younger years . . . [and] I've decided to return home to contribute to the development of my Country." I also stated that the voters of Warwick had never raised the question with me.

The *Royal Gazette*'s asking me how many months I was off the Island, a question it would never pose in the same form to a UBP politician, typified its acting not as an impartial news organ, but as an arm of the Island's White elite. It expressed a key policy of Bermuda's White supremacists with regard to education and the labor market, which had been part of Henry Tucker's effort to make Bermuda the Switzerland of the Atlantic and remained central to the UBP's agenda. The policy was to force ambitious young Black men and women to leave the Island to pursue higher education and training in the professions while importing White workers to fill jobs created by our fast-growing international business sector. Since its inception in 1964, the UBP had been executing this policy in order to shift the balance between White voters and Black voters and drive talented Black change agents out of the country. The same policy animated the ridiculous attempts to misrepresent me as no longer Bermudian.

One of the great ironies of Bermuda's recent political history is that from the early 1990s on the UBP had more Black MPs than White MPs, yet the party adhered steadily to an agenda of resisting and postponing racial equality. Many of those Black MPs ultimately went through the process of disillusionment with the UBP that my mother, my aunt Gloria, and Julian Hall went through. But the UBP always found Black politicians who believed, or could be persuaded to believe, that the best path to change was working within the existing power structure. In 1992 the UBP's roster of Black MPs and Cabinet Ministers included Warwick West incumbent Quinton Edness, the Minister for Health and Social Services, and Premier John Swan.

The UBP had been particularly fortunate in tapping John Swan to be the "secret weapon" with Black voters it so desperately needed after my aunt Gloria resigned from David Gibbons's Cabinet, Parliament, and the UBP in the spring of 1980. The December 1980 election showed the extent of the need, with the PLP, which had gone from 10 seats to 14 seats in the 1976 election, gaining another 4 seats. That gave the PLP its highest total to that date, 18 seats in the House of Assembly, and the UBP its lowest, 22 seats.

The margin of only 4 seats set the stage for a bitter leadership struggle within the UBP to unfold over the next year. Since winning the leadership on January 15, 1982 (other Black UBP MPs vied for the honor, and were surprised by his victory), John Swan had restored most of the UBP's dominance in Parliament and been Premier for more than a decade, longer than anyone before or since. His signature achievement was to negotiate a tax treaty with the United States in 1985. This gave Bermuda's economy—and Henry Tucker's Switzerland-of-the-Atlantic vision—a new lease on life.

Any Black UBP politician who wanted to advance Black Bermudians from their still-less-than-equal status had to walk a tightrope. Whatever the individual said and did had to be couched and limited to avoid antagonizing the White supremacists who controlled the UBP behind the scenes.

John Swan walked that tightrope in two main ways in my view. He made more scholarships for study abroad available to less advantaged Bermudians, which in practice mainly meant Black Bermudians, given their low share of the country's prosperity. And he followed a consistent policy of recruiting talented young Black men and women into Bermuda's civil service. He recognized that Bermuda's civil service had to grow and modernize to keep pace with the country's international business sector. Like Lord Martonmere in the 1960s, he also saw that civil service jobs were a medium for nurturing the Black middle class and supporting the entry of succeeding generations into good private sector jobs, the professions, and small business entrepreneurship.

UBP Premiers who came after John Swan lowered the recruiting bar that he raised. PLP Governments later managed to raise the bar again, but I don't think our efforts have yet matched the collective IQ that John Swan brought into the civil service through his recruitment of talented young Black Bermudians.

That's a view I take very much in hindsight. I certainly wasn't focusing on this aspect of John Swan's leadership in 1992. Like everyone else in Bermuda politics, I was wondering when he was going to call the next general election.

John Swan's snap elections in February 1983 and October 1985 had bedeviled the PLP. The 1983 election took the PLP down to 14 seats, and the 1985 election dropped it to 7 seats, only one more than the PLP won on its first foray at the polls in 1963.

A leadership struggle within the PLP had contributed to its problems in 1985 with my cousin Gilbert Darrell opposing Lois Browne-Evans and being expelled from the Party along with other dissident MPs. Gilbert Darrell and Austin Thomas had then won House seats under the banner of the dissidents' new National Liberal Party (NLP).

It was a low point for the PLP. But Lois Browne-Evans then demonstrated good leadership by stepping down as Party Leader in favor of her protégé, Freddie Wade. Under Freddie and Deputy Leader Walter Roberts, the PLP had rebounded at the most recent general election in February 1989, gaining 8 seats and pushing its total back up to 15 seats. Gilbert Darrell had held onto 1 seat for the NLP, there was 1 Independent MP, and the UBP retained a comfortable majority with 23 seats.

The conventional political wisdom was that the next general election, whenever John Swan chose to call it, would not change the balance of power much, if at all. I was one of a few within the PLP who read the mood of the country differently and thought it was ready to give the PLP a majority in Parliament and an opportunity to form its first Government—if we really put our shoulders to the wheel in the campaign and worked nonstop for victory.

That, I believe, was why John Swan was keeping everyone in a state of expectation. He saw that the Black supporters of the UBP were growing weary of its failures to deliver meaningful change, that they were readier than they had ever been to consider voting for PLP candidates. Black voters were the key for both the PLP and the UBP because Black Bermudians voted for both PLP and UBP candidates. White Bermudians voted almost exclusively for the UBP. Swan was holding off calling an election, not from overconfidence or failure to appreciate the political moment, but because he read the moment well. He hoped delay and uncertainty would confuse and distract the PLP and provide opportunities to derail its progress.

As 1992 came to a close without John Swan calling an election, I worried that he was achieving exactly that. I remained impatient for the election to be scheduled on that ground as well as on two others. The first was frustration over selling my Los Angeles medical practice, which would take several more months to complete. A second, more serious source of frustration was my personal life.

ONLY TWO AND A HALF YEARS AFTER PRISCILLA and I were married, I was becoming concerned for our future. Sadly, our different approaches to parenting gave me my most serious qualms. It was early in 1990 and Trey was just over a year and a half old. Donovan was only six months old. Trey's diaper was wet, and I changed it while Priscilla and I finished a conversation we were having. Then I handed Trey the wrapped-up diaper and told him to put it in the diaper pail.

"What?" Priscilla, who had been on her way out the door, turned around and asked, "Why would you tell him to do that?"

My immediate reaction was, "Why not?" I couldn't grasp Priscilla's objection. I added, "If he can't help dispose of his own diaper, then I don't stand a chance."

My model for child rearing was, naturally enough, the way my parents had raised Emelita and me. That meant unconditional love including tough love, setting limits and imparting responsibilities in an age-appropriate way.

Over the next three years there were many instances in which I wanted to set a limit of some kind on the boys' behavior or remind them of a responsibility. No matter how I tried to do so, however, Priscilla objected in the moment or after the fact. She didn't see it as tough love, she just saw it as harsh, and overly so. From my perspective she erred in the other direction by coddling the boys.

As these experiences accumulated, frustrating both of us and doing the children no good, I realized that the differences between us on child rearing exemplified a profound difference in our mindsets and world views. We had both so wanted to be parents, and we both delighted in our precious, healthy sons. But if we couldn't see eye-to-eye on raising the boys, the marriage had nowhere to go and no room to grow. We were just setting ourselves up for unresolvable conflict. And that was bound to have a bad effect on the boys.

While I was doing the groundwork for moving to Bermuda, gradually spending longer periods of time there, Priscilla and the boys remained in our house in the Ladera Heights area of Los Angeles. Flying back and forth, I wrestled over what to do. Finally I suggested to Priscilla that we divorce in California. That way I could try to start over in Bermuda, and the boys would experience the least disruption in their lives and benefit from a consistent environment without a daily clash of parenting styles. I would see Trey and Donovan on the same sort of schedule on which other divorced dads saw their children. I'd have to fly back to California a lot. But that was not going to be a problem compared to all the flying back and forth I was now doing and my divided energies because of the delay in selling my Los Angeles practice.

Priscilla disagreed. She argued in turn for following through on our long-standing plan for all of us to move to Bermuda together. That way we could start fresh as a family.

She was so insistent that the marriage deserved more of a chance and that the boys deserved to have their parents remain together, that I felt in good conscience I had to go along with her. But it was against my better judgment and gut feelings that I did so.

In the summer of 1993 we made the move to Bermuda permanently. Our plan didn't call for buying a house right away. I first wanted to build up Bermuda HealthCare Services and make sure it was on a firm financial footing. Priscilla and I found a very nice house for rent on Idle Acres Road in Smith's

Parish. It was close to my parents and other relatives and near the schools I attended as a boy.

We settled into the house and established our daily routines easily enough, but I remained extremely frustrated as a father to Trey and Donovan. I felt somewhat better about how things were going with Kevin.

My relationship with Kevin had progressed in fits and starts through the 1980s. As I later would with Trey and Donovan, I sought to apply tough love on my parents' model when I thought it was needed. As Priscilla later would with Trey and Donovan, however, Kevin's mother, Georgia, saw my applications of tough love as overly harsh.

Meanwhile my pride in Kevin's accomplishments and hope for his future made me feel he was a great candidate to attend Howard. Kevin wasn't keen on the idea, however, and Georgia thought he should go wherever he wanted to go. His grades and other credentials gave him plenty of options.

After a knock-down, drag-out discussion of the issue on the phone with Georgia, I offered Kevin a deal. If he went to Howard for one semester and didn't like it, I would pay for him to go anywhere he liked and could get accepted.

In due course Kevin matriculated at Howard as a freshman undergraduate in the fall of 1989. At the end of the semester I asked him if he wanted to transfer. Like me twenty-five years earlier, he no longer had the slightest wish to do so. He loved Howard. Since then he'd done very well there, and he was getting ready to follow further in my footsteps by also attending medical school at Howard. Our relationship was still often rocky, but I was enormously proud of Kevin and very hopeful for his future.

IN LATE SUMMER 1993 THE POLITICAL TENSION IN BERMUDA was building again in anticipation of John Swan calling an election. He had to do it by February 1994 and waiting until then smacked of desperation, which wasn't his style. The summer was just drawing to a close when the word came: Bermuda would be going to the polls again on October 5, 1993.

Over the prior year and a half I had met the majority of Warwick West's voters. Now I redoubled my efforts, trudging up and down hills to knock on every door and speak to every single one of the constituency's 2,500 or so voters. My cousin Calvin Smith, the PLP's deputy campaign chair, had warned me, "If you want to beat Jack Sharpe, you're going to have to work your tail off." Indeed, I found that many constituents were going to vote for both Quinton Edness and Jack Sharpe out of habit and misguided loyalty. Several elderly voters said they had to save a vote for Jack Sharpe because he brought them grapefruit at Christmas.

Behind what these and other voters told me, however, I sensed a readiness for change and a welcome for my and the PLP's focus on the inequities in Bermuda. It strengthened my hunch that an all-out effort could win the PLP's first majority in Parliament and see Freddie Wade become the first Premier from the Party.

Not all of the PLP's candidates shared my belief or demonstrated the same energy. Julian Hall, who had won a seat from Hamilton West for the PLP in 1989, refused to canvass at all, saying the voters knew him well enough already. That was no way to demonstrate respect and concern for constituents, and they accordingly turfed him and fellow PLP MP Eugene Blakeney out of their seats in favor of the UBP's Maxwell Burgess and Wayne Furbert.

My running mate in Warwick West, George Scott, canvassed with me for most of the campaign, but two weeks before the election he went missing in action. I couldn't even get him on the telephone. Although George was in good physical shape, I think he was mentally exhausted by campaigning. He had never run the 440, which requires psychological as well as physical stamina. I needed to draw on my experiences as a competitive athlete to keep up my own campaign pace, and I never worked as hard in any subsequent election.

On the eve of the election the *Royal Gazette* evaluated the candidates' chances in all forty constituencies. Echoing its "Dr. Revenge" rhetoric of the previous fifteen months, the paper blithely opined, "As for Dr. Brown, he is simply unelectable."

A friend of a friend in Washington, D.C., was visiting Bermuda at the time, and that night he helped put up posters for me in Warwick West. He was almost seven feet tall, and he put the posters on the lampposts as high as he could reach while standing in the back of a pick-up truck. When the UBP sent out a crew early the next morning to tear my posters down, they found they couldn't do it without a ladder. That led Quinton Edness to excoriate me for bringing "American ghetto politics" to Bermuda. He was apparently unaware of how racist his absurd rhetoric was.

On election day the Warwick West voters put me 14 votes ahead of John Sharpe and only 2 votes behind Quinton Edness. That meant Edness and I both had seats in the next Parliament. The PLP and the UBP also split the results in Warwick East with Alex Scott winning a seat for the PLP and the UBP's Irving Pearman defeating Calvin Smith by 43 votes. Overall the PLP matched its best previous showing in 1980, and won 18 seats to the UBP's 22. It was only then that some others in the PLP realized how close we had come to a historic victory.

As for the UBP and Bermuda's White establishment, they were not gracious winners; they were practically apoplectic. And they pinned my face up as their target. Over the following days the *Royal Gazette* repeatedly lamented the voters' foolishness in electing me. It also prominently published a letter from Jack Sharpe's daughter berating the voters of Warwick West for ingratitude. The Forty Thieves and their minions were more than surprised, they were shocked and frightened to discover that a few grapefruit at Christmas might not be enough to continue securing their privileges as the overlords of Bermuda. In her only political statement during our marriage, Priscilla wrote a stinging reply to Jack Sharpe's daughter, which the *Royal Gazette* also published.

At the age of forty-seven I had achieved a major part of what had been foreseen for me from the time I was a boy. I had won a seat in Bermuda's Parliament. But I was a member of the Opposition, not the party forming the Government. In a parliamentary system that is not a form of purgatory, but of political hell.

Part Two: Joining the Fight

8. Powerless in Parliament

ECHOING DANTE'S *INFERNO*, PARLIAMENTS SHOULD BE POSTED, "Abandon all hope, you who enter as Members of the Opposition." Absent coalition government, parliaments are winner takes all. The majority party calls the shots, and the Opposition suffers perpetual frustration. My first five years as a Bermudian politician, from 1993 to 1998, were all about learning how to survive and build a following while serving as a member of the minority party—as well as coming to grips with the lengths that the majority was willing to go in an effort to maintain its hold on power.

An anecdote from early in my parliamentary career illustrates some of the challenges minority members face. House of Assembly sessions usually begin midmorning on Fridays and may run late into the night. Speakers often hold the floor for an hour plus.

At 3 a.m. one Saturday, I turned to Freddie Wade and said, "We know we're going to lose the vote. Why don't we say what we have to say and get out of here at a respectable hour?"

Freddie said, "It's not that simple. Our people want to hear us representing them."

"There's got to be a better way."

Bermuda's Parliament is broadcast on the radio, and Freddie was right. PLP supporters were listening. Quite a few shared their reactions to what they heard. But I thought from my first session as an MP in fall 1993 that Bermuda would benefit from quality, rather than quantity, in parliamentary debate. I liked to make my points short and sweet. As Shadow Minister for Youth and Sport, I often debated related UBP policies. I also spoke in support of Freddie, my fellow Shadow Ministers, and other PLP MPs.

Outside politics, I found satisfaction in my medical practice. I enjoyed caring for patients and growing the business financially. But at home Priscilla and I failed to find common ground on raising Trey and Donovan, then respectively five and four. I worried about the discord's effect on the boys, but kept trying to make things work. Kevin was then beginning medical school at Howard, and I was glad to see him advancing on a good path for the future.

On January 3, 1994, the UBP announced an independence referendum that summer. Independence was a foundational goal for the PLP. The UBP had always categorically opposed it. John Swan probably broke with UBP tradition on independence for two reasons, external and internal. The external, much discussed reason was the impending closure of U.S. Navy installations in Bermuda. Our airport was a U.S. Naval Air Station with commercial flights on the side. There was also a listening post on Tudor Hill and a supply area, the U.S. Navy Annex Station, at Morgan's Point.

The Canadian Royal Navy had a small facility at Daniel's Head. Smaller still was HMS *Malabar*, not a (British) Royal Navy ship but a token shore establishment at Dockyard. HMS *Malabar* recalled the time when Bermuda was Britain's western Atlantic stronghold. In 1958 the British sold their installations, except HMS *Malabar*, to Bermuda for £750,000.

After the Soviet Union dissolved in 1991, the United States announced plans to leave Bermuda. The Canadians acted first, leaving their Daniel's Head establishment on December 31, 1993. As for the Royal Navy, the shore establishment HMS *Malabar* would set sail, so to speak, when the U.S. bases closed.

Seeing this coming, John Swan pointed out an obvious fact. Bermuda was now alone in the world. Implicitly, Swan made the case that if the British were going to withdraw their last military forces, remaining a dependent territory no longer had concrete benefit.

Bermuda's economic future depended more on the United States than the United Kingdom. This situation was the outgrowth of Henry Tucker's positioning Bermuda as the Switzerland of the Atlantic. Tucker envisioned Bermuda operating more or less in competition with the City of London and more or less in cooperation with Wall Street in financial services. But few Bermudians appreciated the extent to which our future depended on financial services for businesses and high net worth individuals in America or how British oversight limited us in that regard.

Fewer still appreciated the domestic political considerations behind Swan's independence move—the PLP's growing appeal to voters.

Swan saw the country shifting toward the PLP. Achieving independence, stealing the PLP's thunder on the issue, might extend UBP Government for another generation. In newly independent countries since World War II, the party bringing independence has often put itself at the heart of a new national identity and become hard to supplant.

The PLP wanted the political advantage of achieving independence. We also distrusted UBP-brokered independence. As Freddie Wade said, South Africa had become independent in 1910, yet apartheid was ending only that year in 1994. Independence under the UBP might derail our drive for racial equality for a generation or more. UBP policies and actions displayed no willingness to dismantle Bermuda's covert apartheid. To set the terms of independence, Swan wanted a Commission of Inquiry chaired by Governor Lord Waddington. Freddie compared this in the House to "asking the slave master to investigate slavery." Slavery might disappear in name, but remain in fact.

I worried that blocking John Swan's independence plans would sour the country on the issue. However, I agreed that the PLP should oppose the referendum.

Addressing a PLP rally a few days later, I said, "You don't want a Johnny-come-lately convert taking you to a place he originally said was a bad destination." Following PLP policy, Freddie called for rejecting an independence referendum in favor of deciding the question in a general election. An election was a more appropriate forum because a referendum would have a lower turnout and be less reflective of popular will.

Except for the independence referendum, the UBP Government conducted business as usual, White interests first and foremost. Looking to private development opportunities, the UBP took no apparent steps to hold the United States accountable for abandoning the bases without provision for repurposing them.

It was certainly UBP business as usual in the budget. Recessionary unemployment and declining tourism revenue should have spurred efforts to foster small Black-owned businesses and train Black Bermudians for our international business sector. It should have checked the UBP's reflex of issuing work permits for White workers from abroad for every managerial post or skilled job.

The primary employment message of the UBP, voiced in the *Royal Gazette* by Jack Sharpe, still a power in the party, was that Black Bermudians should appreciate their unskilled job opportunities. The paper quoted him: "There is a future for unskilled workers in Bermuda but attitudes have got to change. People have got to respect those jobs more and realize they require commitment and hard work." The implicit disrespect for workers typified UBP policies.

It was fortunate for the PLP that so many White Bermudians lacked John Swan's understanding of the benefits of independence and the fate of the UBP if it failed to redefine itself. Most Black Bermudians also feared independence. A *Royal Gazette* poll indicated that 59 percent of those planning to vote in a referendum would vote no. We in the PLP saw that as ratifying our agenda for achieving independence: win a general election, educate people on the pros and cons of independence, and then decide the issue in a subsequent election.

Division in the UBP grew so bitter that Freddie Wade said John Swan was leading a virtual minority government and should resign. In early May, following UBP rebels' failed attempt to oust him as leader, Swan withdrew the Independence Referendum Act, which had not passed its final hurdles in the Senate, and canceled the Commission of Inquiry. He vowed to reintroduce a referendum bill after the UBP prepared a Green Paper on independence for discussion in Parliament.

Meanwhile the *Royal Gazette* lost no enthusiasm for attacking the PLP. In my case, it reported a leaked confidential finding of Bermuda's Human Rights Commission that I had discriminated against a pregnant woman by firing her. The finding forced me to agree to pay her $6,800 in a secret settlement, which the newspaper also revealed.

I had not fired the employee for being pregnant. I have hired pregnant women in my medical practices, and I have always made reasonable adjustments for an employee's pregnancy or similar life-changing event. The problem was that the employee, a good ultrasound technician, began to insist on running her own appointment book, something that violates sound medical practice management. She could have kept her job except for that. Ignoring my side of the story, the *Royal Gazette* portrayed me as a hypocrite on human rights.

Human rights were in the air. On May 10, a huge crowd gathered at Hamilton's City Hall to celebrate Nelson Mandela's inauguration as South Africa's first Black president. White self-congratulation in South Africa and elsewhere over Mandela's election rang hollow in my ears. Considering Mandela's leadership qualities, I could not help thinking of what he, South Africa, and the world had lost during his twenty-seven years of imprisonment under apartheid.

Four days later, the House of Assembly voted on the Criminal Code Amendment Act 1994, UBP MP Dr. John Stubbs's bill to decriminalize male homosexual activity between consenting adults. Long overdue though it was (the United Kingdom had passed a similar bill in 1967), the Stubbs bill was as controversial as the independence referendum. Most Black Bermudians were religious and social conservatives, no matter what their party.

Because it was a private bill, offered by Dr. Stubbs in the last months of his terminal cancer, the MPs of both parties were free to vote their consciences. In the early morning of May 14, the bill passed 22 to 16. Fourteen yes votes came from the UBP and 8 from the PLP. I voted yes with fellow PLP MPs Freddie Wade, Lois Browne-Evans, Jennifer Smith, David Allen, Renee Webb, Alex Scott, and Leon "Jimmy" Williams. Six UBP MPs including Premier Swan voted no, as did 10 PLP MPs.

Although the *Royal Gazette* supported the bill, I was still surprised by the post-vote editorial, which said, "It was one of Mr. Wade's finest moments and

Mrs. Browne-Evans demonstrated that she can be the conscience of the House. . . . the Hon. Pamela Gordon's spectacularly delivered early morning speech, Mr. Richard Spurling's thoughtful and very sensible speech and Dr. Ewart Brown's passionate plea for human rights must mark the new MPs as future stars."

As UBP MPs, Pamela Gordon and Richard Spurling would not have to wait long for more praise from the *Royal Gazette*. As leaders of the PLP's drive for racial equality, Freddie Wade and Lois Browne-Evans would have to wait until their deaths to be spoken of so well by the paper. That will doubtless be the case for me, too, if then. But I don't mind having one 1994 human rights issue on which the *Royal Gazette* and I agreed.

The *Royal Gazette*'s attitude toward the PLP quickly reverted to form. In June the PLP announced Rolfe Commissiong as the Party's candidate in Paget East. Rolfe had served five years in prison for robbing a Bank of Butterfield branch at gunpoint in 1984 while caught up in substance abuse. Since his release, he had turned his life around and become a role model for young Black Bermudian men who were disaffected from society. He was working as a paralegal for the lawyer who prosecuted his case and the lawyer who defended him. Introducing him to prospective voters, Freddie Wade said, "By his own boot straps, he has pulled his life back together."

The UBP loved "boot strap" rhetoric. But faced with the principle in action, it turned vicious. Quinton Edness said of Rolfe, "I do not think a bank robber should be an example to young people. The *Royal Gazette* sang the same song in a headline: "Convicted bank robber gets PLP's backing."

Not "ex-convict" but "convicted bank robber," as if Rolfe had robbed a bank the other day rather than a decade before. As if he had not paid his debt to society with five years in prison. And as if he had not become a law-abiding member of society.

I could not understand how anyone could fail to embrace Rolfe's redirection of his life. If you don't help people who are responsibly rebuilding their lives, what trash heap are you consigning them to?

The criticism of Rolfe contradicted everything the UBP and the *Royal Gazette* claimed to support. The UBP had commissioned, and with the newspaper had endorsed, a 1992 report calling for rehabilitating prisoners. As Health and Social Services Minister, Quinton Edness was responsible for rehabilitation services. He also knew the Commissiong family and Rolfe's hard work to rehabilitate himself. Yet he was prepared to kick Rolfe in the teeth as he pulled himself up by his boot straps.

It was an example of how Black people in the UBP trampled on their own. The criticism of Rolfe exemplified a larger agenda of the UBP and the *Royal Gazette*. It fit with Jack Sharpe's condescending remarks about Black Bermudians—especially low-skilled Black men—having a poor work ethic.

I agreed then and still agree that the work ethic of some disadvantaged Black Bermudians needs to be kindled and strengthened. In my medical business, it took considerable time to develop a top support staff.

However, a poor work ethic generally characterizes downtrodden communities, including poor White, methamphetamine- and opioid-troubled communities in today's America. When people have been driven into the ground, they need a helping hand, with judicious tough love, not a kick in the teeth.

We should also not forget "Bermuda's Stride Toward the Twenty-First Century" by American economist Dorothy K. Newman, published by the Finance Ministry in November 1994. It reported, "The median income of Black managers with a college degree is below that of White managers who have not even attended high school." Such racist disparities hardly encouraged a strong work ethic.

The biased portrayal of Rolfe Commissiong in 1994 also fit with policing methods that targeted young Black men. As Shadow Minister for Youth and Sport I spoke out against warrantless stop-and-frisk tactics, which ruined futures on the basis of small amounts of marijuana. Refusing to recognize the counterproductive nature of the tactics, the UBP and the *Royal Gazette* instead misrepresented me and the PLP as endorsing drug abuse and drug crimes.

The UBP and the *Royal Gazette* had the same response when Bermuda's under-23 football team played an important match in Jamaica at the end of 1994. With its much smaller population, Bermuda is an underdog in any sporting competition with Jamaica. Yet Bermuda's under-23's won 1-0, qualifying for the Pan-Am Games.

The *Royal Gazette* made little of the victory and much of the arrest of seven players, while changing planes in Miami, for trying to bring marijuana home for their personal use. The paper's reportorial zeal was out of proportion to the mistake the seven young men had made. The paper and the UBP attacked me when I said the team's victory for Bermuda was being ignored, the arrested players were being condemned while the legal process was in its early stages, and their youthful mistakes should be treated as such with appropriate discipline and compassion. These were Bermuda's children, yet the UBP and the *Royal Gazette* were acting as members of the prosecution.

War-on-drugs hysteria was so rampant, John Swan suggested a presumption of guilt in alleged drug crimes. In more or less the same breath, he said the "glass ceiling" through which many Black Bermudians were looking up at White jobholders existed only in the minds of those who bumped their heads against it. This "bootstrap," "tough on crime" talk made it impossible to have an evidence-based discussion on the abuse of drugs, legal and illegal.

As a physician-politician, I wanted to limit all drug abuse and favored efforts focused on harm reduction rather than punishment. Yet I also called for vigorous, effective policing and law enforcement against illegal drug trafficking, saying I saw the same early warning signs of gang violence in Bermuda in 1994 as in Los Angeles in 1974. The question was how to address the problem effectively, which was where I differed from the UBP and the *Royal Gazette*.

By all objective measures the war on drugs has failed. It has only exacerbated the violence and corruption associated with large-scale drug trafficking and antidrug policing in poor communities. It has succeeded only from the point of view of keeping Black people down. It has dovetailed with "bootstrapping" labor policies and an education system that warehouses young Black people rather than developing them into productive members of society. As in the United States, racist sentencing biases helped make Bermuda's prison population disproportionately Black. Fellow PLP MP Nelson Bascome pointed out, "Our young people . . . see the disparity in our justice system."

UBP policies on crime, employment, and education were tailor-made to undermine the work ethic of many disadvantaged Black people. The most pernicious result of these policies has been to demonize young Black men as feared subhuman "others," who must be treated harshly to keep law and order.

The UBP/OBA and the *Royal Gazette* have for decades refused to acknowledge the connection between these policies and Bermuda's covert apartheid. It was no surprise that following the late 1994 resignations of Bermuda's White British expatriate Police Commissioner and Deputy Police Commissioner, news quickly came that their successors would also be White British expatriates.

In response to protests from the PLP and the Black community, the UBP said Bermuda should be proud of attracting top cops from abroad. But well-paid positions in Bermuda were not a hardship for people who had risen as far as they could in their British jobs and already secured full pensions from them. The UBP and the *Royal Gazette* took it as given that no senior Black Bermudian officers were qualified for leadership.

The same White power agenda lay behind UBP management of the base closures, with little allowance for input from the PLP and the public. Late in 1994 the UBP Government awarded a contract for civilian management of the airport after the U.S. Navy departed in June 1995. The bidding for the contract was such that, Freddie Wade argued, all the business opportunities associated with the base closures would go to "UBP cronies." I spoke in the House on the related issue of having no Black concessionaires at the airport and said, "If we are going to fix this Country, we have to secure the economic empowerment of Black people." Freddie's words and mine fell on deaf ears in the UBP.

As my first year in Parliament drew to a close, PLP Senator Terry Lister spoke of challenging Freddie Wade for the Party's leadership. Although I admired and liked Freddie, I didn't yet know him very well, and I was receptive to Terry Lister's move on two counts. One was Freddie's poor health: in addition to a bad heart scare in 1986, he had polycystic kidney disease, which had killed his mother at the age of 40. I was also concerned about the age of the other leading members of the Party and thought we needed younger, more vigorous leadership. I changed my mind when Freddie bullied Terry into withdrawing his leadership bid by saying, "If you run against me, you'd better win. Because if you don't, you'll never have a position within the PLP again." Terry caved, and I reckoned that he was not destined for leadership.

Freddie only had to worry about a leadership contest because of voting for the Stubbs Bill. Deputy Leader Walter Roberts was one of the PLP MPs who voted against the bill, and he did not want to reaffirm support for Freddie. However, the PLP as a whole rejected Walter Roberts in favor of another leadership term for Freddie and elected Jennifer Smith as Deputy Leader.

That fall the *Bermuda Times* was at risk of being struck off the Bermuda Register of Companies because of back taxes. Lack of advertising, except from small, mostly Black-owned businesses, continued to hobble us. Earlier in the year an investor had sued for the loss of his money and damages, but the other investors and I were in the same boat. There were no profits. In March we'd had to part ways with my cousin Charles Brown as the paper's general manager, and in July editor James Ziral had resigned. However, I wasn't willing to fold the only majority-Black-owned newspaper in Bermuda.

Two fall events brought better news. In late September I was reelected as a vice president of the Union of American Physicians and Dentists (UAPD), which I had joined in California. I would not be able to help lead the UAPD much longer, given my Bermuda responsibilities, but I wanted to stay involved while I could.

In November, Howard University ended a steep surcharge for international students instituted by President George H. W. Bush's administration. As a university trustee, I had worked to roll back the surcharge, which affected students from Bermuda and the Caribbean. The number of international students at Howard had fallen 57 percent, meaning the increased fees did little for the university's bottom line. Recognizing that it was good for America to educate leaders at Howard, the Clinton administration eliminated the surcharge.

That month I had my first opportunity for parliamentary debate on the Throne Speech, which describes the governing party's objectives for the coming year and which the Governor reads in Parliament on behalf of the British monarch. The November 1994 debate reflected the usual UBP versus PLP divisions on major issues.

Among its other plans, the UBP announced a Commission for Unity and Racial Equality (CURE). The PLP welcomed the idea of the commission but wondered whether the UBP would actually empower it in keeping with its ambitious name. As I said then, no country in the world had cured racism and the UBP was promising to do so on its first attempt. CURE became a bone of contention between the parties, even as other PLP MPs and I supported it as best we could.

In May 1995 the UBP's board of inquiry into the seven footballers' drug bust delivered its report. As PLP Shadow Minister for Youth and Sport, I gave credit to the board for bringing "critical issues into the light." However, the board had not really gotten to fundamentals. The most striking omission was that the board had secured no input from the arrested players, and I observed that the average age of the board's members, closer to sixty than fifty, was a factor. The board needed the perspective of someone younger, who would have been able to elicit the views of the athletes. It was also unfortunate that the board's recommendations were all on the side of punishment with nothing substantive on prevention. The UBP appropriated money for random drug-testing of athletes but offered nothing to guide youngsters before they got into trouble.

The *Royal Gazette* responded to my criticisms by describing the PLP in general and me in particular as giving Bermuda's young people "permission to abuse" and being "soft on drugs." PLP MP Renee Webb rebutted this nonsense with heartening vigor and a solid dose of the facts on the PLP's efforts to address the crime and other harms associated with illegal drug use.

I said in the House, "I expect pigs to oink. That which comes from pigs is oink. The *Royal Gazette* reminds me of pigs' language."

Premier John Swan immediately asked, "Do you mean the editor of the *Royal Gazette* is a pig?"

Refusing to be baited, I observed that the vast increase in illegal drug use in Bermuda over the previous thirty years "has happened on the UBP watch. But we [in the PLP] would never say the UBP is soft on drugs. The world . . . is struggling with the drugs problem. To say it is linked to the softness or hardness of a particular party . . . is at best immature, at worst just plain nasty."

Spring 1995 also brought the UBP Government Green Paper on independence, and the PLP asked its supporters to boycott the referendum vote in mid-August. We continued to distrust the UBP to secure independence in a way that didn't undermine progress toward racial equality.

For example, the UBP continued to support importing White workers at the cost of developing talented Black Bermudians. Aside from the jobs in question, the importation of White workers who frequently acquired status as Bermudian citizens provided more votes for the UBP. Although Blacks voted for both the UBP and the PLP, depending on their personal views, 98 percent or more of Whites voted only for the UBP. The percentage of foreign-born voters among UBP supporters was rising steadily.

To express the frustration of Black Bermudians, the PLP had put forward a motion in February to cut the Governor's salary from $126,063 a year to $1. Just before this, Freddie Wade had presented Governor Lord Waddington with a petition signed by some 6,000 voters, a hefty percentage of Bermuda's electorate, calling on him to rescind the hiring of White Englishmen Colin Coxall and Michael Mylod as Bermuda's next Police Commissioner and Deputy Police Commissioner.

Rather than accept the petition gracefully, Lord Waddington displayed anger bordering on contempt. Even the *Royal Gazette* admitted that the Governor "appeared angry." The UBP then presented the ironic spectacle of a governing party whose leader was bent on independence arguing, in Deputy Premier Irving Pearman's words, that a direct representation to the Governor was "beyond reason," and that the PLP was "totally disregarding the fact that we are a British dependent territory."

We in the PLP knew our petition would go nowhere. But we took satisfaction in bringing out the contradictions between John Swan's plan for an independent Bermuda and the UBP's wish to preserve a racist status quo. That is why I said at a July PLP rally, "I would rather sprint through hell in . . . gasoline shorts, than give independence in Bermuda to the United Bermuda Party."

The referendum vote was scheduled for August 15. Hurricane Felix's arrival, mercifully without loss of life or great damage, postponed the vote one day. Only 58.8 percent of the electorate turned out, well below the 70 percent or more who voted in Bermuda's general elections, and well below the two-thirds the PLP felt was necessary for legitimacy. Of the 58.8 percent who went to the polls, almost 74 percent voted no. Fulfilling a promise he made before the vote, John Swan resigned as leader of the UBP with his departure as Premier awaiting the party's choice of his successor.

The fight over the referendum soured the country on the whole question of independence and has since prevented an accurate appraisal of its pluses and minuses. If John Swan and Freddie Wade had had the sort of relationship where they could talk heart to heart or there had been a mediator they both trusted, they might have gone into seclusion for a weekend and hashed everything out. Then independence would have been a slam dunk. To Bermuda's loss, the old suspicions and reservations persisted on both sides.

If the failed independence referendum was 1995 Bermuda's biggest political story, the second biggest was probably my dual citizenship in the United States. Although my U.S. citizenship was never a secret, in June the *Royal Gazette* sounded the headline alarm "Brown in breach of Constitution." The paper quoted section 30(1)(a) of the Constitution: "No person shall be qualified to be appointed as a Senator or elected as a member of the House of Assembly who is, by virtue of his own act, under any acknowledgement of allegiance, obedience or adherence to a foreign power or state."

I knew about this provision before I ran for office in Bermuda, but received legal advice that it concerned oaths of office, not citizenship. Parliament had many dual nationals. Almost all were born in other countries of the British Commonwealth, but there was also one UBP Senator, Lawrence Scott, who had been born in the United States. Based on the legal advice, the PLP and I thought there was no problem. Yet a hullabaloo erupted, with the UBP and the *Royal Gazette* calling on me to resign my seat in the House.

I explained that I had only become a U.S. citizen in order to serve as a trustee of Howard University from 1990 through 1993. The *Royal Gazette* quoted me, "My desire to serve was so strong that I would have become a German." The *Royal Gazette* also quoted me, "If it is required, or if it is determined, that I can only serve in the Bermudian Parliament by resigning from my U.S. citizenship, then that's an easy decision for me." I was first and last a Bermudian.

Springing into action as my lawyer, Julian Hall found Bermuda's election law allowed objections to the service of a new MP or Senator only within twenty-eight days of election or appointment. My continuing to serve as an MP was beyond challenge for the present, but the challenge was bound to resurface.

The UBP soon chose as leader Dr. David Saul, a Ph.D. in physical education who had left teaching for business and politics and was John Swan's last Finance Minister. Dr. Saul and his Cabinet were sworn in as Bermuda's Government in late August.

Freddie Wade shuffled the PLP Shadow Cabinet in order to give the other Shadow Ministers and me exposure to different portfolios before the next general election. I became Shadow Minister for Human Affairs. Over the next thirty-eight months relations between the UBP and PLP in the House of Assembly continued along the usual lines.

In November, a year after its announcement in the 1994 Throne Speech, the UBP finally established their "cure" for racism with the appointment of the twelve members of the Commission for Unity and Racial Equality. Although the commission included a few PLP supporters, the UBP had not appointed anyone the PLP had specifically recommended.

CURE's chairman, Mr. Michael Mello QC, immediately stuck his foot in his mouth by saying racism was not yet a major problem in Bermuda. Shadow Labour and Home Affairs Minister Alex Scott and I immediately challenged this statement in the House.

Mr. Mello's response would have been comical except for reflecting the UBP's decades of pretending racism did not trouble Bermudian society. He said, "We must make every effort to change negative community attitudes and behavior now, so that there will not be 'major problems' of a destructive nature . . . in the future."

This was historical amnesia. What about slavery? What about the legal segregation that held sway until the 1970s? What about the racial unrest of the 1960s and 1970s? What about the major problems of a destructive nature in employment, education, and policing, which the UBP and PLP had been debating for the past thirty years?

Late 1995 also saw the UBP Government purchase land from a wealthy White person for a new post office in Paget Parish. Over PLP objections, the UBP appropriated $325,000 to buy a quarter-acre lot, claiming the existing post office location was much too congested. In House debate PLP Shadow Works Minister Stanley Morton described significant traffic congestion at the new site. He also noted that regular mail volumes were dropping fast because of email. PLP MP Ottie Simmons, Sr., said that at $1.3 million an acre, he had some land he could offer the Government.

Watching the UBP push through the purchase, I recalled an older gentleman in my Warwick West constituency saying, "Hamilton is the capital of Bermuda, but Paget is the capital of White Bermuda." Enough said.

THE YEAR 1995 ALSO INCLUDED UPHEAVAL IN MY PERSONAL LIFE. I received messages at Bermuda HealthCare Services to call a number "about your son," which I did not understand. After the third or fourth message I called the number and found myself talking to Maureen Pitt. My first thought was, "Maureen who?"

It turned out I knew her. In 1981 when I was separated from my first wife, Beverly, I had gone to Bermuda for a brief vacation and met Maureen on the beach. What started out as an afternoon of innocent fun ended up being much more.

Maureen gave birth to a son, Maurice Pitt, on March 31, 1982. When I first learned of and met Maurice in 1995, I felt a fatherly love connection, just as I had on meeting Kevin for the first time. A few days later, a lawyer called on Maureen's behalf to ask if I would take a DNA test. I said yes, and the test confirmed my paternity.

Again I wanted to do my duty as a father outside marriage, and I began contributing to Maurice's care financially. Also again, however, there were obstacles to my being a father on a daily basis. Maurice was thirteen years old, with his character and personality already developed, if still immature. He was obviously bright and strong-willed. Physically he was tall for his age, but slender, as I had been. Until recently he had been doing well academically, but he was now beginning to get into trouble in school. He was deeply distrustful of authority and very doubtful about me, natural attitudes considering the circumstances.

It was difficult for everyone involved, but toughest on Maurice. I tried to see him regularly, and I introduced him to Trey and Donovan. For better or worse, my model was the matter-of-fact way my father revealed that Emelita and I were not his only children.

At the same time, my marriage to Priscilla had run its course. Again there were a few issues, including our having divergent personal interests and activities. But the most serious issue remained our different approaches to child rearing.

An episode with Trey, then seven, typified this difference. I was working with him on his math homework, which included multiplication problems. Trey knew his basic 1-to-9 multiplication tables, but he was having trouble with bigger numbers. I was showing him that with multiples of 10, 100, 1,000, you can first put down however many zeroes there are and then work more easily with the other numbers.

It wasn't sinking in, and Trey was distracted. In exasperation, and to get his attention back, I thundered, "Just add the damn zeroes!"

Hearing this, Priscilla intervened rather than let me work through the moment with Trey.

After other such episodes with the boys, she agreed to a separation in 1995. We divorced in August 1996. The divorce was hard on our sons. However, I believe the change was good overall. I remained closely involved with Trey and Donovan. They knew what to expect at home with their mother and what to expect with me. I think they were calmer and less troubled as a result.

ON APRIL 26, 1996, THE BERMUDA TIMES PUBLISHED its last issue, and later its few assets were liquidated. I regretted our three full-time employees' need for new jobs and our no longer being able to counter the Royal Gazette's relentless anti-PLP coverage. But I remain proud of the Bermuda Times's contribution to news coverage and political debate for over nine years, with zero support from Bermuda's major advertisers.

In July 1996 my neck injury from the 1986 car accident in Detroit required surgery to relieve nerve pressure. Dr. Gary Dennis, a good friend from medical school, performed the successful operation at Howard University Hospital. The surgery kept me from voting on a PLP-supported plan, devised by Sandys' residents, to make the Daniel's Head Canadian Royal Navy installation a nature and recreation area. PLP MP Reverend Trevor Woolridge was also in the United States to attend a church conference. The UBP defeated the plan 19 to 18, with one UBP MP breaking party lines to vote for it. It was only so close, however, because some UBP MPs also missed the vote.

The *Royal Gazette* said, "Dr. Brown has been off the Island reportedly getting medical attention for a neck complaint. He is also believed to have had a speaking engagement in the Caribbean." It was interesting to read those lines, as if my medically necessary surgery were a cosmetic procedure, and as if I had gone abroad to give a speech rather than attend to important House business. An objective observer could only have concluded that the UBP had scheduled the vote for when Trevor Woolridge and I were away.

On August 13, at only fifty-seven, Freddie Wade collapsed and died on his doorstep as he was leaving to attend a Commonwealth Parliamentary Conference in Malaysia. I was in the United States, planning to return in early September, but I quickly arranged to fly home.

The Black community mourned Freddie as a champion of racial equality and social justice. The PLP was at a crossroads. Thanks to Freddie's leadership, the *Royal Gazette* editorialized, "The PLP is closer to power now than it has ever been." The choice of our next leader would determine whether we won the next general election. The editorial said Freddie's likely successor was Deputy Party Leader Jennifer Smith and praised her leadership. But it called "centrist" PLP Senator Terry Lister "the most universally acceptable leader for the PLP," adding that "Alex Scott or Ewart Brown would frighten the middle class whom the PLP need for success."

I didn't frighten the middle-class constituents of Warwick West, and I was flattered to be mentioned as a candidate. But I thought my time for party leadership was in the future.

Following its constitution, the PLP met to elect an interim Party Leader and Deputy Leader. Jennifer Smith became Party Leader, taking 26 votes to Shadow Labour Minister Alex Scott's 18 votes and Shadow Finance Minister Eugene Cox's 5 votes. Alex Scott then became Deputy Party Leader with 25 votes to Terry Lister's 15 votes and Nelson Bascome's 7, with Trevor Woolridge receiving none.

The PLP held a regular leadership vote at its November Delegates Conference. Only Jennifer Smith and Alex Scott stood for the leadership, with Jennifer winning 48 to 29. To gauge how far I might be from a serious challenge for one of the top two spots, I ran for Deputy Leader against Eugene Cox, losing 52 to 22. The *Royal Gazette* described this as "a landslide result." However, I thought taking 22 votes, almost 30 percent of the total, as a first-term MP was not too shabby.

Between the two leadership votes, CURE held its first workshop. Only three MPs—Premier David Saul of the UBP and Renee Webb and I of the PLP—attended. The turnout from Bermuda's international business community was also poor. More MPs from both parties should have attended, but the relative showing of the UBP and the PLP indicated which party really wanted to see racial equality in Bermuda. CURE continued its efforts over the following two years, but there was little substance to them.

That fall I addressed Bermuda's increasing homeless problem. Knowing that many homeless people suffered mental health problems, I wanted to organize resources for diagnosis and treatment as well as public education. I first went to meet the homeless, confirming my suspicions that quite a few had psychological problems that could benefit from treatment. I then contacted Dr. Hameen Markar, chief of Psychiatry at Bermuda's only mental health facility, St. Brendan's Hospital (now Mid-Atlantic Wellness Institute or MWI). I hoped Dr. Markar and his staff could assess the homeless where they were. After discussion with him, I asked the community to help bring homeless individuals to St. Brendan's for evaluation. I took several myself, but the public response was disappointing.

The response probably resulted from "compassion fatigue." People were inured to seeing the homeless and felt they could do little to improve things. Indeed, homelessness is a difficult problem to ameliorate, in part because many homeless people resist help for fear of being institutionalized. All the same, the attention we brought to homelessness triggered some positive change. The Salvation Army opened a homeless day center, which at least provided a refuge from cold winter rains. I resolved to keep doing what I could as a physician and MP.

When I established Bermuda HealthCare Services, Bermuda had no mammography facilities. Yet Bermuda had a higher incidence of breast cancer than the United States. I offered mammography at BHCS through an association with the Lahey Clinic, a hospital associated with Tufts University School of Medicine in Boston. Lahey radiologists read the mammograms done at BHCS, fulfilling my aim to provide state-of-the-art care for my patients.

Within a year or so King Edward VII Memorial Hospital (KEMH) sent an emissary, Eugenie Brown (no relation), to BHCS. She said KEMH had no intention of offering mammography, but simply wanted information on equipment sources and costs. I smiled and gave her the information. KEMH soon began offering mammography, as did the Health and Cancer Center.

In January 1997, the Health Insurance Association of Bermuda (HIAB) cut mammography reimbursement 33 percent. To my protests HIAB responded that it was distinguishing between initial and follow-up mammograms, as if follow-ups cost less to do. HIAB's previous schedule of reimbursements only listed "bilateral mammogram," which is how BHCS submitted its claims. We did follow-ups in line with recommendations by cancer specialists and public medical authorities.

The UBP Government and the *Royal Gazette* were hesitant to criticize HIAB, but in the short term they were reasonably evenhanded in addressing BHCS's mammography services. BHCS had to withhold submitting mammography claims for several months until the HIAB finally acknowledged the facts were on our side. In the meantime I arranged with the Lahey Clinic to provide free mammograms to uninsured Bermudians. BHCS did the scans and Lahey radiologists read them pro bono.

With the mammography issue pending, I questioned why HIAB reimbursed the hospital up to 80 percent more for a variety of services including mammography than it reimbursed my clinic. I also discovered that Dr. Charles Dyer, who offered ultrasound, had never been subjected to a cut in his reimbursements for that service.

I'd grown up hearing about Bermuda's White establishment using economic assassination against opponents, including my uncle George. The mammography reimbursement cut was phase one of attempts to assassinate me economically. UBP Cabinet Ministers began saying private medical providers were responsible for Bermuda's increasing health costs, directly or indirectly pointing at BHCS. Yet care at BHCS or just about any private doctor's office in Bermuda was much cheaper than the same care at KEMH.

A big cost driver was Bermuda's covering treatment for the elderly only in a hospital, not in a doctor's office. Seniors naturally avoided paying for care out of their own pockets by treating the hospital as a doctor's office. Among other counterproductive results, this practice filled the hospital's beds with non-acute care patients. I sometimes faced delays in admitting patients who needed hospital care; on one occasion I was denied a bed for such a patient. When I spoke out on these problems, the *Royal Gazette* editorialized against me.

Early in 1997 I applied to hire an associate physician from the United States, the kind of thing White employers in Bermuda got rubber-stamped without question. But the Bermuda Medical Society, controlled by White physicians from the United Kingdom, turned me down. I said, "What right do you White English doctors, leaving the British National Health Service to make a lot of money in Bermuda, have telling me what to do in my clinic?"

A member of the medical society's board, Dr. Valerie James, a White Australian, wrote me she was "incensed" by this "verbal attack." I replied that protesting unfair decisions was not an "attack" and added, "That you were so incensed by my remarks probably has more to do with the fact that it was unexpected that I should climb out of my 'proper place' and express my intention to resist certain conduct which I find incorrect." Dr. James's husband,

Sanders Frith Brown, filed a complaint against me with the Bermuda Human Rights Commission. The commission took no action because there was no basis for Mr. Brown's contention that I had made "a racial attack . . . sinister to the extreme."

This was 1997, not 1897. Yet White people in Bermuda still felt Blacks should defer to them on account of their skin color. While in no way retreating from my position—I continue to stand by my remarks to the Bermuda Medical Society—I did my best to cool off the exchange with Dr. James and Mr. Brown. He claimed to be 1/32 Black, so I said for all I knew we were cousins and I didn't want to prolong a family squabble.

A UBP squabble broke out at this time affecting John Swan and his business partner, UBP MP Maxwell Burgess, who wanted to open the first McDonald's in Bermuda. There had been a KFC in Bermuda since 1975, but no other international fast-food franchises.

To my surprise, some in the UBP still wanted to punish John Swan for the independence referendum. UBP MP Ann Cartwright DeCouto, who had resigned from John Swan's Cabinet over the issue, drafted the Prohibited Restaurants Bill, which on iffy constitutional grounds retroactively banned any fast-food franchise restaurant not in operation before 1996 (protecting a KFC owned by a UBP supporter). The bill was pending through the first half of 1997.

In March, the UBP replaced David Saul as leader with Pamela Gordon. The party wanted an appealing Black woman at the top of their ticket to counter Jennifer Smith at the top of the PLP's ticket. At the end of March both David Saul and John Swan resigned their seats in the House of Assembly.

When the "hamburger vote" on Ann Cartwright DeCouto's anti-McDonald's bill came in June, it passed into law with PLP support. Freddie Wade also remained angry about the independence referendum and felt we should not help rich guys in the UBP get even richer. Maxwell Burgess, who remained a UBP MP, was allowed to vote despite the rule prohibiting MPs from voting on matters in which they had a direct personal or financial interest. He plainly had a direct interest in the prospective McDonald's.

Around this time Shadow Labour and Human Affairs Minister Alex Scott introduced a motion to change 30(1)(a) of the Constitution to allow native-born Bermudians with dual citizenship to serve as MPs. For his part, Jack Sharpe obtained a legal opinion from a Queen's Counsel (QC) in England saying that my sitting in Parliament was illegal. Alex Scott pointed out that despite the title, a QC could only give a private, not an official, opinion. If one wanted the most impressive possible legal opinion, one hired a QC.

Adding to the absurdity, Premier Pamela Gordon suggested I resolve matters by applying for naturalization as a Bermuda citizen, a status I held by birth. I replied that if the UBP wanted me to swear an oath superseding my

U.S. citizenship oath, I had already done that by swearing an oath to the Queen on entering Parliament.

Alex Scott's motion came up for a vote just after the "hamburger vote." In contrast to letting Maxwell Burgess vote on a matter of direct interest to him, Speaker of the House Ernest DeCouto banned me from voting on the Scott motion and officially reprimanded me when I complained about the disparity.

Later in the year Shadow Health Minister Renee Webb introduced a motion calling on the British government to address the fact that 30(1)(a) violated the European Convention for the Protection of Human Rights and Fundamental Freedoms and the International Covenant on Civil and Political Rights. The United Kingdom had signed both agreements, and British law had no equivalent to 30(1)(a). Given Bermuda's status as a dependent territory of the United Kingdom, something was amiss with 30(1)(a).

Renee Webb's motion was scheduled for debate in early December, and had been on the Order Paper since late November. The UBP had said there would be two more pre-Christmas sessions of the House, on December 5 and December 12. At 3:30 p.m. on December 5, the UBP Whip asked if Renee Webb was going to proceed with her motion. At 5:50 p.m., the PLP Whip said she was. This was standard parliamentary procedure.

But that evening, when Renee tried to advance the motion, the UBP said it had not had time to consider it and the House was going to adjourn for Christmas. Renee led all the PLP MPs out of the House in protest, leaving our side of the aisle empty for the last fifteen minutes of the session. We sent Deputy Speaker and PLP MP Stanley Lowe back inside, however, to wish the Speaker, the Governor, and their families a merry Christmas.

Another important 1997 issue was the United States government's "stop list" of Bermudians barred from traveling there. I was the most vocal of several PLP MPs and Senators calling for the UBP Government to request the list from the United States and inform Bermudians who were on it, so they could petition for travel waivers for medical treatment or other reasons. Lack of transparency meant people regularly began journeys to the United States only to be stopped at the airport.

Questioning the stop list again brought UBP and *Royal Gazette* charges that the PLP was soft on crime, particularly drug crime. Even without access to the list, it was safe to assume most people were on it for drug crimes. That was clear from the testimony of those who learned they were on the list when they tried to travel.

The United States has the right to stop people from entering its territory, including major drug dealers and other serious criminals. But American citizens can do time for murder in the United States and travel to Bermuda as soon as they have served their sentences. A Bermudian arrested on the Island for a single marijuana cigarette might be permanently barred from the United States.

I mentioned speaking in the House in late 1994 about increasing violence in Bermuda. I could see that gangs were becoming a problem, but I tried in vain to get the UBP to give the issue serious attention. In March 1997, I introduced an Ambassadors for Peace program at Warwick Secondary School, which Maurice was then attending. And in September, Bermudian sportsmen Calvin Symonds, Leroy Lewis, Kenneth Bascome, Rudolph Laurence, and I brought youth activist Mark Charley to Bermuda.

During my involvement in community programs for young people in Los Angeles, I learned of the impressive work of the Breakthrough Foundation in the San Francisco Bay Area. That led to my contacting Mark Charley, who worked with the Breakthrough Foundation and then set up Uncommon Results. One meeting with Mark convinced me it would be valuable to bring his ideas and program to Bermuda.

I invited Premier Gordon, her Cabinet, and Governor Thorold Masefield, among others, to a presentation by Mark and associate Denise Ochoa at the Elbow Beach Hotel. The turnout exceeded my expectations as did the response to Mark and Denise. Video of an Uncommon Results camp attended by forty-two youths from inner-city Louisville and Cincinnati blew everyone away. Men and women had tears in their eyes and were passing tissues around.

Afterward, Premier Gordon and other members of the Government said they would do something with Uncommon Results. All too predictably, those promises fell victim to UBP politics as usual and nothing happened.

Early in 1998, Dr. Wendy Woods, a Black Bermudian with an exemplary academic record at Howard University and its medical school, was denied a license to practice her specialty, obstetrics and gynecology, in Bermuda. She had recently completed a multiyear residency at Parkland Hospital in Dallas. She had also passed the U.S. board exam in obstetrics and gynecology. In Canada or the United Kingdom, passing a written exam would have been all she needed for full licensing in her specialty. In the United States she was "board eligible" and could practice in any state, but to be "board certified" there she needed a two-year case log as the basis for an oral examination. Her visa would not let her stay in the United States that long, so she came home to accumulate her case log in Bermuda, on the understanding that KEMH would give her full privileges to admit and treat her patients.

No sooner had Dr. Woods returned home and used a bank loan to set up her practice, than the hospital board yanked the rug out from under her. They said they would only give her "minor privileges" in obstetrics and gynecology at KEMH. She asked me for help, and I brought her dilemma to the attention of the House.

The major obstacle to a fair resolution was White Bermudian Dr. Jack Patton, then Chief of Staff at KEMH, aided and abetted by the UBP Government and the *Royal Gazette*. They all spouted about "standards," long a code word for denying Black people opportunity. When UBP MP John Barritt uttered that word in the House about Dr. Woods, I walked out for a few minutes in protest. When I returned I described KEMH as "a hot pocket of racism, dripping out of the windows and doors."

As I told the House and the media, Dr. Woods's training exceeded that of someone who was fully licensed by British medical authorities by virtue of only passing a written exam. She was already an accomplished obstetrical surgeon. If you are looking at hiring a third-year ob-gyn resident in the United States, you know they've delivered at least X number of babies, performed at least X number of hysterectomies, and so on. In the United Kingdom much depends on the senior specialist a young doctor studies under, and there isn't the same clarity and uniformity of experience.

Nearly all the White physicians in Bermuda had trained in the British system. Their discomfort with Dr. Woods's American credentials displayed ignorance, prejudice, or a combination of the two. Bermuda had a shortage of ob-gyns, and a Black ob-gyn was especially needed given our majority Black population.

At first the hospital refused to reconsider its decision. But CEO Sheila Manderson had worked in the United States and understood the system there. Eventually I persuaded her to reconsider the matter, and Dr. Woods received the major privileges her training warranted. Since then, Dr. Woods has had a flawless career as one of Bermuda's best ob-gyns.

At one point, Dr. Patton sat a few chairs away from me in a conference room at KEMH with Sheila Manderson on the other side of the table. She emphasized compromise, and Dr. Patton said, "Madam Chair, Dr. Brown would not recognize compromise if it was staring him in the face."

I said, "Dr. Patton, if I did not understand compromise, you would not be breathing."

BY MIDYEAR 1998, ELECTION FEVER WAS HEATING UP. The next general election had to be soon. The PLP knew victory was within reach.

Warwick West was then what is known as a marginal constituency, because the 1993 margin of victory for both of its MPs was quite narrow, as well as being split between one UBP MP, Quinton Edness, and one PLP MP, me. Polling indicated I would be reelected by a good number of votes, and my colleagues in the PLP and I accordingly wrestled with the choice of my running mate. The first choice was Cromwell Shakir, a barber in Warwick West who was a very nice gentleman and politically wise. But polling suggested he might not fare well against Quinton Edness, and in June we chose Elvin James, popular former cricket international for Bermuda and President of the Bermuda Cricket Board of Control. Polling on him was extremely positive. Cromwell Shakir was disappointed by our decision, but we wanted to win.

In early July the *Royal Gazette* reported that former employees of mine said I was a bully. Any employer in business for more than a minute is bound to have former employees who are disgruntled for one reason or another. The timing of the story showed it was a pre-election smear.

The claim that I was a nasty boss came and went. The accusation that would not die was that my U.S. citizenship oath meant I was sitting in the House of Assembly as the agent of a foreign power. Quinton Edness attacked me for spending too much time out of Bermuda and arriving late to House sessions, and said El James did not know Warwick West well enough to represent it, which was nonsense. Quinton Edness's running mate, UBP Senator Yvette Swan, was Jamaican-born, but the PLP did not object to that. When I proposed that all the candidates in Warwick West sign an "oath of integrity" to refrain from personal attacks, Quinton Edness increased his attacks on my dual citizenship.

In light of the discrepancies between the Bermuda Constitution and United Kingdom law as well as the many foreign-born members of Bermuda's Parliament, I believed then, and still believe now, that justice was on my side. My colleagues in the PLP continued to give me strong support, and I was very grateful for that. In September, however, I decided enough was enough, and I renounced my American citizenship.

Quinton Edness said he didn't believe I had renounced my citizenship. He also said I could reclaim my citizenship with a phone call within a ten-year grace period. Asked to comment by the *Royal Gazette,* I said, "It is not important what Mr. Edness thinks about my honesty. If he believes that I have not done what I said I would do, then he should do whatever his owners tell him to do." To his credit, the next day he apologized, acknowledging that renouncing U.S. citizenship was a final act with no grace period.

DESPITE ALL THE JOCKEYING BY THE UBP AND PLP FOR THE ELECTION, Premier Pamela Gordon had not yet set a date for it. The big reason was the base closings. The extent of the pollution created by the U.S. Navy had come to light, and the U.S. disclaimed any clean-up responsibility. The cost was going to be astronomical. In mid-October, Premier Gordon and Finance Minister Grant Gibbons secured a meeting with U.S. Secretary of Defense William Cohen. Making that known, Premier Gordon also called the election for November 9, 1998, no doubt hoping to return from Washington with good news for Bermuda's taxpayers and voters.

In the event, the results would be quite different from those that Premier Gordon and her colleagues wished. They'd usher in a new chapter in my political history.

9. A Seat at the Table

AFTER PREMIER PAMELA GORDON CALLED THE GENERAL ELECTION for November 9, 1998, the UBP stepped up its usual scaremongering about the PLP. This time, however, Bermudians no longer paid heed to claims that the PLP was by definition incapable of governing. The Island's voters repudiated the UBP, ousting many of its most prominent MPs, including Deputy Premier Jerome Dill, Labour and Home Affairs Minister Maxwell Burgess, Health Minister Wayne Furbert, former Cabinet Minister Quinton Edness, and former Cabinet Minister and former Deputy Premier Ann Cartwright DeCouto. They put on a good face for the most part, saying they had anticipated a PLP victory and accepted the people's decision. But they were shocked by the landslide of support for the PLP, and Mrs. Cartwright DeCouto told the *Royal Gazette*, "I was a bit surprised by the result, but we will be back." It was clear that they had really expected to hold on to power and were unprepared for the loss of it. The UBP would return, but only after undergoing cosmetic surgery, as we'll see.

More than 80 percent of registered voters went to the polls, and the final tally was 26 seats in the House of Assembly for the PLP and 14 for the UBP. Later in the month, when Governor Thorold Masefield read out the first Throne Speech of the first PLP Government at the commencement of the new parliamentary session, he added a comment of his own, saying, "The very high levels of voter registration and of voter turnout for the election demonstrate the full involvement of the vast majority of Bermudians in the process, as well as the clarity of their choice and wish for change."

The PLP had finally achieved its dream of a peaceful "green revolution" in Bermuda. Only Cuba's Fidel Castro had held power longer than the UBP. The new Opposition hated that comparison, but it was and is a telling one.

In mentioning the Throne Speech I've jumped over the immediate post-election buzz about who would be in the new Cabinet. The election took place on a Monday, and the usual pattern is for the new Premier to be sworn in as

soon as possible, followed by the swearing in of the new Cabinet. On this occasion Jennifer Smith was sworn in as Premier of Bermuda on Tuesday, November 10, and the members of her Cabinet were to be sworn in just before
midday on Wednesday.

Was I going to have a seat at the Cabinet table? According to the talk in
political circles throughout the Island, there was good reason to think that I
should. Over the previous five years in Opposition I had become a leading
voice in the "new PLP" that Freddie Wade had carefully constructed. My constituency of Warwick West was no longer remotely a marginal one. It had
come out solidly for the PLP, and El James and I had each beaten the UBP's
Quinton Edness and Yvette Swan by hundreds of votes. On any objective cri-
teria, political friends told me, my contributions to the PLP in Parliament and
on the campaign trail had earned a Cabinet seat.

I thought so, too. But as that Wednesday morning wore on, and news
came in of this or that PLP colleague being offered this or that Cabinet post,
no call for me came from Premier Smith's office. It looked like I was the odd
man out.

My friends protested, "What is going on? Why are they disrespecting
you?"

I said, "It is the Premier's choice. If I don't get the call, then I'll be on the
back benches. If I do get it, I'll be in Cabinet."

Later that day I was sitting in the back of a car outside Alaska Hall with
Nelson Bascome, part of the motorcade to Government House for the swearing in of the Cabinet by Governor Masefield. One of Premier Smith's aides
came to our car and said she would like to see me inside.

Premier Smith told me, "Well, the only Ministry I have left is Transport.
Would you be willing to do that?"

I said, "Yes. I just want to be in the room."

"Okay. This is not an invitation to travel to every airport in the world.
But if you're willing to accept it, welcome."

"Thank you, Premier."

I meant it, too. Transport was a problem area where no UBP Minister had
ever made much progress, and it didn't have the profile with the public that
ministries like Tourism, Finance, Labour and Home Affairs, or Health and
Family Services had. However, I was happy to be in the room, I thought my
own time as Party Leader and Premier was far off, and I was determined to
make lemonade out of the lemons I'd been given.

November 1998 marked a changing of the guard at the *Royal Gazette* as
well as in Government. David L. White, who had been editor for twenty-two
years, retired, and he was succeeded by William J. "Bill" Zuill, who was then
thirty-four and had worked at the paper since he was twenty-two. Although
the change in Government was the most substantive one imaginable, the

change at Bermuda's only daily newspaper was imperceptible, at least insofar as the rest of the PLP and I were concerned. From time to time the paper pleasantly surprised us by agreeing with something we did, but overall it continued to carry the UBP's water, commencing its service as part of the PLP's Combined Opposition, as I dubbed it.

Back to making lemonade out of lemons. The UBP Government had commissioned and approved a very capable study called Transport 2000, but had done little to act on it. I took Transport 2000 as the basis for my initial agenda to be adapted and modified as circumstances required. There was much to be done in every area.

Bermuda's laws on motor vehicles were behind the times in terms of safety—in 1998 we still lacked a mandatory seat belt law—and our fatality rate was much higher than in the United Kingdom or the United States. That rate was in large part the result of a good deal of drunken driving. It was also the result of the high proportion of motor bikes and a penchant for aggressive, even reckless riding by too many Bermudians, especially young men. Restrictions on car size, established with Bermuda's narrow roads and lanes in mind, meant that many cars had their original bumpers removed before they were sold and then put back on illegally by their owners. The Island needed an emissions testing facility. Among other problems the Transport Control Department (TCD), which issued driver's licenses and license plates and inspected vehicles, regularly caused enormous frustration and inconvenience to Bermudians. Everyone rued going to TCD and losing hours or even whole days waiting one's turn, and then winding up being treated rudely or having a vehicle fail inspection for a nitpicking infraction.

The taxi industry was a notorious hornets' nest, and outgoing UBP Transport Minister Erwin Adderley warned me against getting bogged down trying to address its problems. There was no shortage of taxis or taxi drivers, but their availability when and where they were needed was seriously out of whack. More than once the airlines called me at home to complain that there were no taxis at the airport for passengers on arriving flights. Taxi availability was a question of safety as well as convenience. In the summer of 1996 a seventeen-year-old Canadian visitor, Rebecca Middleton, had been raped and murdered when repeated calls to a local taxi service failed to produce a taxi and she then accepted a ride offered by some men on motorbikes. The trial of the accused took place in November and December 1998, ending in an acquittal that caused dismay in Canada and a lot of bad publicity for Bermuda. There was also an increasing problem with violent holdups of taxi drivers. The taxi industry plainly needed some kind of central dispatch system to improve service, as well as security for drivers and passengers. But there was no consensus among the taxi drivers, most of them individual owner-operators, about what should be done.

Traffic on the roads was often jammed up, and we needed to improve both bus and ferry service as alternatives to private vehicles, especially for daily commutes to work and school. However, the Island's bus fleet was aging. On a visit to the maintenance facility I saw a bus that should have been in a transit museum being virtually remanufactured. And as with TCD, the standard of customer service for bus passengers was unacceptably poor.

The ferries were also coming to the end of their useful life. The UBP had announced its intention to replace them with faster modern vessels, but again had done nothing to make that a reality. In opposition, my fellow PLP MPs and I regularly protested the UBP's penny-wise, pound-foolish budgeting and failure to maintain and improve Bermuda's infrastructure. On forming the first PLP Government, we discovered the situation was even worse than we thought.

The Bermuda International Airport, formerly the U.S. Navy's Kindley Field, was the brightest spot on my Ministerial map. Yet it, too, was hardly what it needed to be after more than three years of civilian management under the UBP. Air links were truly Bermuda's lifelines to the rest of the world, essential for both of the two mainstays of our economy, tourism and the international business sector. There were too few flights and the fares were too high for Bermuda to flourish. Although flight operations were being handled competently and safely, the airport was not a welcoming place. In early December the *Royal Gazette* ran an article about a French traveler who had visited Bermuda in 1994 and decided to come back on the spur of the moment without a hotel reservation, only to get off the plane and find there was no longer a visitor's information and help desk at the airport. The UBP had axed this standard service without any regard for the impact on business and holiday visitors and on Bermuda's reputation among travelers generally.

Improving the airport and Bermuda's air links was going to require a major effort in concert with the new Minister of Tourism, David Allen, whom the *Royal Gazette* described as "valuable as the only White face on the [PLP] Government benches." David and I already had a good working relationship from our time as Shadow Ministers, and we quickly built on that.

I had good working relationships with my fellow Cabinet Ministers in general, and I found myself enjoying the challenges of the Transport portfolio because it cut across so many major issues for Bermuda and Bermudians. Transport affected everyone's daily quality of life and safety, law enforcement, environmental concerns, labor affairs, and so on, as well as tourism and international business. I felt that my lemonade stand was giving me a great opportunity to develop as a member of Government and prospective leader for the PLP and Bermuda.

Along the way I had to fend off a series of unfair attacks on my integrity and my livelihood. The economic assassination attempts on me by the UBP and its allies ratcheted up at the start of my time in Cabinet. Somehow or other it was just then that "a letter came to light," in the *Royal Gazette*'s words, "regarding the need for visiting overseas medical specialists and questioning [local doctor and Government MP Ewart Brown's] clinic's 'integrity.'" Judy Panchaud-White, then president of the Health Insurance Association of Bermuda (HIAB), had written the letter to UBP Health and Social Services Minister Wayne Furbert on July 29, 1998, enclosing a copy of a Bermuda HealthCare Services (BHCS) announcement of upcoming visits from Lahey Clinic specialists. Ms. Panchaud-White wrote, "This type of advertising will encourage residents to book appointments without their own general practitioner concurring that such a consultation is medically necessary." Further she blamed overuse of specialist care for rapidly increasing healthcare costs, and she asked what "financial incentives" BHCS might be receiving as a result of its association with Lahey Clinic.

So many things were turned Alice-in-Wonderland upside down in this letter. To begin with, as I said in the House, insurance companies and physicians are on opposite ends of the healthcare spectrum. Helping people get the care they need is not the prime motivation of insurers. The most profitable business model for insurers is to maximize what they receive in premiums and minimize what they pay in claims. Some insurers would be happier if there were no specialist healthcare and no advances in medical science.

Nobody's money should be wasted, and healthcare costs must be managed in the public interest. But what's often missed in discussions of healthcare cost and healthcare innovation is that better healthcare is not just a product of prosperity. It is also an enhancer and driver of prosperity. It enables people to do more with their lives, and in that sense medical innovation is one of the greatest prosperity engines that modern society has.

As for BHCS, the only financial incentives were the normal ones of charging reasonable fees for high-quality medical services. More than two-thirds of the referrals to Lahey through BHCS were made, not by me and my associate physician at the time, Dr. Sonia Meade, but by other doctors on the Island who wanted to facilitate necessary specialist care for their patients. Again, BHCS's fees were well below what the hospital charged for the same services.

More than that, however, BHCS was pioneering a medical services model called for in Bermuda's recent Oughton Healthcare Review Report, which the *Royal Gazette* described as finding "that Bermuda needed to establish overseas links with 'Centres of Excellence' to support the local healthcare system." This is exactly what I did in linking BHCS to the Lahey Clinic, and it bears repeating that Lahey is a state-of-the-art facility and affiliated with the Tufts University School of Medicine. The association with Lahey Clinic has saved many patients from having to incur steep travel expenses to see a specialist off the

Island, and it is obviously more efficient for one physician to fly to treat 30 patients than for 30 patients each to fly somewhere for treatment. HIAB president Ms. Panchaud-White made an obligatory reference of support for the Oughton Report in her letter about BHCS, but she was writing out of both sides of her mouth.

The sequel to this attack on my business and on my integrity as a physician and a politician came the next year in two main forms. One was that a few physicians, including some in high-level positions at KEMH, were actively bad-mouthing the Lahey Clinic. It was any physician's right to refer or not to refer patients to a specific provider or institution, but to say that the Lahey Clinic should be avoided for some unspecified reason was a clear violation of medical ethics. Not to mention that it was absurd because Lahey Clinic was and is equal or superior to KEMH in every category of medical services they both provide.

In part Lahey's superiority stems from its greater size and resources. It may be impossible for the only hospital in a small community, like KEMH in Bermuda, to equal a medical center of excellence in a major metropolis. But not every small jurisdiction is as riven with racism as Bermuda.

I also got lots of flak for trying to help an old colleague from Los Angeles, a Black surgeon, open a practice in Bermuda. Research then and since has shown that racial disparities in all areas of medical treatment, including surgery, occur with high frequency, and that one of the best ways to ameliorate this situation is to have more Black healthcare providers. Yet my arguing that a highly accomplished Black surgeon would be of great benefit to Bermuda was "playing the race card." It evoked mental echoes of my late 1960s and early 1970s efforts to convince U.S. medical schools to admit qualified Black students.

In 1999 there was also renewed talk about conflicts of interest for physicians who offered diagnostic testing and their role in driving up healthcare costs. Then UBP Shadow Finance Minister Grant Gibbons again directed those attacks not at the physician community in general, but at me in particular, citing as an ethical standard U.S. laws against Medicare and Medicaid claims for referrals to physician-owned diagnostic facilities. However, those U.S. laws, the Stark Amendments, concerned stand-alone diagnostic labs owned by physicians outside their practices, whereas I was providing diagnostic services as part of BHCS. Other physicians in Bermuda were also offering diagnostic services as part of their practices.

As I said in the House, "Offering testing is not a conflict of interest, it's an integrity challenge. The issue of testing was never raised in this House when the testing was done by White doctors."

As for conflicts of interest, Grant Gibbons never touched on the fact that one of the Gibbons Companies, Colonial Insurance, sold health insurance. His personal financial interest obviously lay in limiting reimbursements for medical treatment.

In this regard, I also said in the House that the UBP would be better advised to consider the impact on healthcare costs of the unregulated pricing of prescription medications in Bermuda. Doing that, however, would have meant questioning the business model of UBP Senator and Shadow Health and Family Services Minister Kim Young and her husband, Ward Young, wholesale prescription drug importers and owners of the Phoenix pharmacy chain.

Politically motivated attempts at economic assassination periodically forced me to address the House about issues affecting BHCS. But I disliked doing so, and I strove to keep my political responsibilities separate from my medical and business responsibilities. My model in that regard was Ottie Simmons, Sr., who always kept a wall between his duties as president of the BIU and a PLP MP. Following his retirement from the BIU, Ottie became our Government Whip. His successor as BIU president, Derrick Burgess (he came into the House after winning a by-election to fill the seat vacated when PLP MP Reverend Trevor Woolridge resigned because of legal issues), also admirably separated his BIU and PLP roles. Ottie and Derrick, products of the labor movement, will always have my deep and abiding respect.

At a fundamental level there was a link between my political career and my medical practice, to be sure, and that was my ambition to serve others. I enjoyed being a physician because of the opportunities to improve patients' lives. In politics I was looking for opportunities to improve Bermudians' lives, especially by rooting out racism and ameliorating its pernicious effects on both Black and White Bermudians. As a Cabinet Minister in a parliamentary system, I finally had the chance to do what I first felt called to do as a boy, when my parents, Aunt Gloria, and other family members told me, quoting Luke's Gospel, "From everyone to whom much has been given, much will be required; and from the one to whom much has been entrusted, even more will be demanded."

In my role as Transport Minister I focused on improving service to Bermudians across all transportation sectors. The length of time it took to draft and enact legislation, even with a commanding PLP majority in the House of Assembly, frustrated me at times. By temperament and problem-solving style, I would have preferred to roll things out more quickly and amend them as good government and Bermuda's best interests required. But along the way my Transport Ministry colleagues and I accumulated measurable victories that enabled continuing progress to occur.

The first legislative victory came quickly enough. In December 1998 my fellow PLP MPs and I won a vote to lift feudalistic restrictions on driving a car to the owner, members of the owner's household, or employees of the owner. The UBP protested that we were rushing this legislation through the House with unseemly haste, as if it required long and deep study. It was not the protest of an Opposition seriously committed to the public interest, but of an old regime upset at the loss of any element in the White oligarchy's superstructure of societal control.

The extent to which UBP MPs were living in the past soon showed itself with regard to traffic safety. Responding to calls from me and others in the PLP for a mandatory seat belt law, Shadow Transport Minister Erwin Adderly, my predecessor as Transport Minister, opined that if drivers observed Bermuda's 35 kilometers per hour (kph) speed limit, they didn't need seat belts. This statement ignored the facts of physics and human nature. Even assuming that every driver always obeys the speed limit, serious lasting injury or death can result from hitting one's head against the windshield or another part of a car at sub-35 kph speeds. Objections of equal absurdity kept coming from the UBP over the years as my fellow PLP MPs and I worked to bring Bermuda's vintage traffic laws up to speed with modern automobiles and modern technology in general, especially regulation against the use of cell phones for talking and texting while driving. In addition to appropriate legislation, I also sought to encourage safe driving through public education efforts like Project Ride, a motorbike safety course.

The Opposition howled in protest in February 1999 when the Government reestablished permanent secretaries for both Environment and Transport. UBP MPs complained about the salaries for these civil service positions and claimed that the two ministries had been getting along fine without them. Medicine has the concept of benign neglect of a problem that does not need immediate treatment. But the prior neglect of significant environment and transport issues in Bermuda was anything but benign. Permanent secretaries had an important role to play in ensuring continuity of knowledge and expertise and sustained follow-through on major public issues and projects. Not to have them was, again, penny-wise and pound-foolish.

Another important development in February 1999 was upgrading the computer links at the airport with fiber optics and 40 Common User Terminal Equipment (CUTE) terminals, which had the capacity to check in 1,000 passengers an hour instead of 700 an hour with our existing equipment. The CUTE terminals could be deployed as needed and as such were an essential infrastructure for attracting new airlines to operate flights to and from Bermuda. The flexibility of the new equipment allowed us to phase out permanent check-in and departure desks and avoid the much greater expanse of expanding the whole departures terminal in order to increase check-in capacity.

Together with Tourism Minister David Allen, I also worked on improving the atmosphere of the airport for both arriving and departing passengers. Over the course of 1999 and 2000 we reestablished a visitor's information and help desk, brought in Bermudian musicians to play for arriving visitors (Island entertainer Gene Steede became the airport's director of entertainment), revamped the departure lounges, and experimented with having one of Bermuda's signature companies, Gosling Rum, give out free rum swizzles to arriving adults. We also brought in the Charles Tucker Art Gallery on the departures level, along with the airport's first duty-free shop.

In March 1999 Bermudianization took a step forward when Marshall Minors became the airport's general manager designate. The current manager, Jack Gordon, was soon to return to his native Canada. Marshall had risen by merit in a number of civil service postings. The choice was up to the Public Service Commission, subject to the approval of the Governor, and I was glad when Marshall got the nod for the job. With the change from UBP to PLP Government, the Public Service Commission began to select more Bermudians, Black and White, for top jobs.

I mentioned that poor customer service was a problem throughout Bermuda's transportation system. Working with the Monitor Company as consultants, in the spring of 1999 I expanded the existing Ambassadors Program in customer service. A series of modules on customer service and human relations, the program had been offered to Public Transportation Board employees since 1991 and had cut customer complaints about bus service by over 60 percent. We selected government employees from throughout the transportation sector to go through the course and take the learning back to their colleagues and coworkers.

That spring I also began to expand Transport 2000 into a formal National Transportation Management Plan (NTMP), drawing input from a wide range of stakeholders. The NTMP then guided the transport agenda over the following years, and we checked off objectives for ferries, buses, trucks, cars, motorbikes, and the airport as we achieved them. Larry Jacobs, a White Bermudian, contributed a great deal to the development of the NTMP, and he remains a valued consultant to the Transport Ministry.

From the start of my tenure as Transport Minister, I gave special attention to upgrading the ferry system. Fast ferries had a huge potential to improve Bermudians' daily lives and boost tourism. The Opposition repeatedly said that I was moving too fast, that the proposed ferries and associated infrastructure were too expensive, and that too few people would want to use them. I knew the Opposition was wrong, and I kept trying to accelerate the process.

IN JULY 1999 THE PLP TOOK A BIG STEP to more equitable taxation by increasing the taxes on land. The UBP had established an extremely regressive tax regime with most revenue coming from consumption taxes in one form or another. Such taxes unfairly burden middle-income and lower-income people compared to the affluent. The PLP's efforts to change that situation ran up against not only the UBP's intransigence, but many Bermudians' fears that a progressive income tax, say, would hit them harder than the taxes they were already paying. The new land taxes were one way we in the PLP could shift some of the tax burden to where it rightly belonged, on Bermuda's wealthiest people.

The preeminent political development of 1999 also had nothing to do with transportation, but it was one I wholeheartedly participated in as a Cabinet Minister and MP. This was the naming of the first day of Cup Match as Emancipation Day, thanks to passage of the Public Holiday Amendment Act in November.

The two-day holiday of Cup Match occurs every year on the Thursday and Friday closest to August 1. It centers around the annual cricket match, contested over the two days, between St. George's and Somerset, which take turns hosting the event. As I touched on earlier, the holiday began as an informal celebration by Black Bermudians of Great Britain's Slavery Abolition Act 1833, which took effect in most of the British Empire, including Bermuda, on August 1, 1834.

In 1947, Bermuda's original Public Holiday Act gave the Friday of Cup Match the name of Somers Day, commemorating the first British landing on Bermuda and its beginnings as a British colony. On July 28, 1609, Admiral Sir George Somers—formerly a Royal Navy captain, he was admiral of the Virginia Company's supply fleet, bound from Plymouth, England, to Jamestown, Virginia—deliberately drove his sinking flagship, the *Sea Venture*, onto the Bermuda reefs in a storm to save those on board. The survivors spent ten months building two small ships with Bermuda cedar and spars and rigging from the *Sea Venture* before sailing on them to Jamestown.

Admiral Somers subsequently sailed back to Bermuda where he died of illness on November 9, 1610. For quite some time the islands of Bermuda were also known as the Somers Isles. They were administered by the Somers Isles Company, an offshoot of the Virginia Company. Leading members and agents of the Somers Isles Company brought the first Black slaves to Bermuda from the West Indies in 1616. In describing my family's lineage I noted that in the late 1670s, English colonists in Massachusetts sold a great many American Indians into slavery in Bermuda.

The settlement of Bermuda is something every Bermudian should know about and honor—without honoring the slave economy that followed. The near perfect coincidence of the *Sea Venture*'s arrival on July 28 and the end of British slavery on August 1, separated though they were by two hundred twenty-five years, makes Cup Match an appropriate time for Somers Day.

But with no official association of emancipation with Cup Match, the designation of Somers Day in effect hijacked a holiday begun by former slaves to celebrate their freedom and coopted it to celebrate the event that quickly led to slavery in Bermuda. After the Friday of Cup Match was named Somers Day in 1947, increasing numbers of Bermudians, Black and White, had no idea of the two-day holiday's true origins. They knew it only as a holiday for cricket and honoring Admiral Somers.

Fairness and honesty demanded official recognition of Cup Match's connection with emancipation. Yet when we in the PLP introduced the bill to designate the Thursday of Cup Match as Emancipation Day, while preserving the Friday as Somers Day, the UBP behaved as if we were proposing a day for devil worship.

Sir John Swan said, "We do not want to send a message to the outside world that we are now developing a divided society through the symbolism of two separate holidays—one for Whites and one for Blacks."

Reading that statement still makes my mind reel. It amounts to saying, "It is okay to have a holiday implicitly connected with the establishment of slavery in Bermuda. But it is not okay to have a holiday directly connected with the end of slavery, because that is divisive."

Should White Bermudians not also celebrate the end of slavery? White Bermudians often ostentatiously declare their British identity and allegiance. Should they not be proud that Great Britain ended legal slavery in its dominions almost thirty years before Abraham Lincoln's Emancipation Proclamation in the United States? Was John Swan saying that White Bermudians still wanted to preside over a slave state?

Remember this was 1999, not 1799, 1899, or even 1969, when school segregation remained the law of the land. John Swan was no longer in the House of Assembly, but the UBP MPs echoed him loud and clear. Black UBP MP and Shadow Works and Engineering Minister Jim Woolridge said in the House, "[The PLP] come here and try to destroy one of the few things which is totally Bermudian," and he called the bill "a waste of time." Other Black UBP MPs also spoke of Emancipation Day as somehow undermining and diminishing Cup Match.

The objections of John Swan and other Black members of the UPB to Emancipation Day as a full partner with Somers Day make no sense. Their comments illustrate the extent of the persistent racism in Bermuda; they show the evil that racism does to Black people's sense of themselves and of reality.

PLP MP and former star cricketer El James, who played in many a Cup Match, offered perspective when he stood up in the House and said, "When I first played in Cup Match I wasn't aware of the rich historical reasons behind it. It's our responsibility to maintain this part of our heritage. . . . [S]chool kids . . . [do] not know the history of Cup Match."

For my part, and with no disrespect to the PLP's women MPs, I said that the Government had the "testicular fortitude" to enshrine Emancipation Day on the calendar of Bermuda's public holidays, and I wondered "how anyone can be opposed to anything that counteracts the effects of racism."

Thanks only to the PLP's majority, the bill passed into law. The week before the vote, in one of its rare agreements with the PLP, the *Royal Gazette* editorialized, "Sir John [Swan] and other opponents of the change have failed to acknowledge that the two days . . . do mark significantly different milestones in the Island's history. Arguing that recognition of the two separately may cause discord is similar to claiming that the celebration of Independence Day and Martin Luther King, Jr. Day in the United States is divisive. It is very sensible to give both days the attention they deserve, particularly in light of the ignorance which still exists among Bermudians—particularly the youth— about the origins of Cup Match."

Well said. Since then, the celebration of Emancipation Day and Somers Day on the two days of Cup Match has been nothing but positive for Bermuda. Far from diminishing Cup Match, it has only enhanced the event. Over the years, the vocal objections to Emancipation Day have gradually faded, at least from public discourse.

I heard much the same sort of objections when I mounted a campaign in 2000 to rename KEMH's Memorial Ward for Dr. E. F. Gordon. Memorial Ward was the only ward at KEMH not yet named for an individual, and I thought it was the perfect opportunity to honor Dr. Gordon as a physician-politician whose overriding goal was to build a healthy society. One of the PLP's campaign pledges in the 1998 general election was to honor Bermuda's Black heroes. Government is about both symbolism and substance, and it is important for any society to commemorate its best representatives appropriately. At that time you could search Bermuda from end to end and not find a single significant monument to a Black person or any public institution or department named in honor of one.

There was no question of Dr. Gordon's importance to the evolution of modern Bermuda. In mid-twentieth-century Bermuda, when there was no effective counterweight to the White oligarchy, Dr. Gordon stepped forward to build one. Although he never led the Government of Bermuda, he led the way to the beginnings of Bermuda as a democratic society for all of its people, Black and White alike. Even the *Royal Gazette* once called Sir Henry Tucker and Dr. Gordon the two most important leaders Bermuda has ever had.

The cadre of White physicians who have always run KEMH greeted my initial overtures with barely concealed disdain. They complained that Dr. Gordon had never been part of KEMH's staff or an admitting physician there.

I said, "When Dr. Gordon was practicing medicine in Bermuda, you refused to hire Black physicians or give them admitting privileges. You didn't have any Black nurses, either, until he led the fight for them."

It took months of persistent effort to persuade the hospital to name the ward for Dr. Gordon. Although until his death in 1955 he was the fiercest opponent that Bermuda's White establishment and the UBP ever had, the Opposition had to keep silent about my campaign—at least in public. Remember, two of Dr. Gordon's daughters, former Premier Pamela Gordon and Patricia Gordon-Pamplin, had become UBP politicians and in 2000 they were both in the House of Assembly.

On the evening of Wednesday, September 6, 2000, with Dr. Gordon's children in attendance, I had the privilege and pleasure of announcing the naming of Dr. E. F. Gordon Ward at KEMH. Both Pamela Gordon and Patricia Gordon-Pamplin thanked me briefly in private. No doubt their pride in the naming of the ward was tempered by knowing it would never have happened if their own party was in power.

Two days later the *Royal Gazette* ran a brief story of 133 words, which limited its description of Dr. Gordon's contributions to Bermuda to his being "instrumental in the formation of the predecessor of the Bermuda Industrial Union, which lobbied for workers' rights." The article ended, "Dr. Brown assured those gathered the PLP did not intend to honor only Blacks nor will less progressive people be ignored or discarded."

The last sentence of the article should speak for itself. Given the racist historical amnesia so prevalent in Bermuda, however, I have to add that it is indeed remarkable, if unsurprising, that I had to give such assurances in announcing the first public memorial to one of Bermuda's Black heroes. The anxiety and fear the first PLP Government's initiatives triggered in the White establishment and the White citizenry generally can probably only be understood in terms of their guilty consciences. No matter what state of conscious denial they were in, I suspect that deep in their hearts they knew how brutally they had treated Black Bermudians and feared righteous retribution for their crimes against humanity.

Retribution of that kind has never been on the PLP agenda, however. We wanted then, and continue to strive, to unite all of Bermuda to acknowledge the truth about our shared history and present and work together to build a just society.

From late 1999 through the end of 2000 the PLP made considerable progress, however. In transportation, that included a December 1999 agreement for the BIU to represent taxi owner-operators and drivers in talks with the Government. In order to improve conditions in the industry, Government needed to work with the taxi drivers as a group that had a united voice. Since the drivers were nearly all owner-operators of their own taxis, the UBP responded that it would be much more appropriate for that united voice to come from a taxi industry association rather than a union.

I'd been urging, and then challenging, the taxi drivers to form an organization of some kind since I became Minister of Transport. None of them stepped forward, individually or as a core group, to form and lead an organization on their own behalf. So I finally asked Derrick Burgess if the BIU would step into the breach. Unlike the UBP, with its knee-jerk antiunionism, the PLP saw unions as prospective partners rather than inherently evil enemies. After consultation with his colleagues at the BIU, Derrick agreed that the union would provide the organizational structure the taxi drivers needed. There was much conflict and controversy to come over taxi issues, as I'll explain, but the BIU's involvement was vital to the industry-wide improvements we eventually were able to make.

In July 2000 the government of the United Kingdom agreed to give Bermuda autonomy in negotiating with air charter companies. This enabled us to arrange direct charter flights from Europe and North America, and helped build up the airlift.

That same month, I took a six-person team to the United States to see the operations and vessels of the three companies that had submitted the most attractive bids to supply Bermuda with fast ferries. As happened regularly with my official travel, the UBP complained that I was taking too many people and spending too much money. They whined that I should have taken two people at most.

Again, penny-wise and pound-foolish. No matter what kind of ferries we purchased, and no matter who made them, we were going to be spending millions of dollars of the taxpayers' money. We had to get it right. Everyone on the trip was an important stakeholder in the decision process: Marine and Ports director Ron Ross, Ports Authority chairman Philip Richardson, BIU Marine Division president Randolph Smith, ferry service supervisor Mike Dolding, senior pilot Terry Spencer, and consultant Larry Jacobs. They not only had important perspectives to bring to our tour of inspection, they also each had to communicate our findings to important constituencies in Bermuda, from the business community to the people who would actually operate the vessels. We visited three boat yards—Gladding-Hearn in Boston; Austal in Mobile, Alabama; and Derecktor in New York—and what we saw gave us a good foundation for signing a $5 million contract with Gladding-Hearn later that year for our first two fast ferries.

The ferry vessels were only part of the cost. We also had to upgrade the ferry docks. In the House in July, the UBP claimed we could cut the total expenditure by $10 million if we went with side-loading ferries rather than

front-loading ferries. Side-loading ferries are much less convenient and efficient to operate because they do not allow a seamless transition between boat
and dock. If the new ferries were going to achieve their full potential for Bermuda, they had to be front-loading, and I held firm to that decision.

In November I welcomed the appointment of White Bermudian Kevin
Monkman as head of TCD, another step forward for Bermudianization. Kevin
joined Marshall Minors, the general manager of the airport, and Daryl Bean,
the airport's recently appointed U.S. Navy-trained senior fire safety officer, as
well-qualified Bermudians who had ascended to top transport-related jobs
since the PLP's victory in the 1998 election.

November was also when the PLP Government enacted the first statutory safeguards for workers' rights in Bermuda. The UBP said we were coddling workers and creating nightmares for employers. That was neither the
PLP's intention nor the legislation's result.

In my speech in the House supporting the statutory workers' rights bill,
I emphasized my own dissatisfaction with the poor work ethic of some Bermudians: "All the legislation in the world won't improve the ethic in the work-
place." Acknowledging that Bermuda needed workers from overseas in many
job categories, I added, "We must out of self-respect . . . be as self-contained
and self-sufficient as we can possibly be. Our education system, if we want to
make ourselves self-contained, must promote the talent, energy, and vision
we need. It is embarrassing to me as a Bermudian to acknowledge the number
of positions that Bermudians should be occupying and they are nowhere to be
found. . . . We must begin to set high standards [for ourselves] and not be
afraid to reach them, and not be associated with suboptimal performances.
There is no substitute for hard work. Hard work is acceptable, it is necessary,
and it is critical if we are to become self-contained. [Bermudians] must stop
confusing service with servitude."

At the same time, workers' rights laws are necessary to a productive
economy and a just society. They help ensure that those who work hard and
strive to succeed are not cast aside on a whim or to make room for someone
who appeals to an employer's biases.

As I said above in relation to John Swan's dismissive remarks about the
"glass ceiling" for Black people in Bermuda, a poor work ethic is a consequence of both generational poverty and institutional racism. These forces
create sullen workers who have been burned out by a combination of history's
impact on their families and their personal experiences. For the disadvantaged
and disaffected members of a society to exert themselves to becoming productive, they must see people like themselves earning high-level jobs through
ability and hard work. That was, and is, why Bermudianization has been an
important complement to workers' rights protection.

It has never been easy to find staff of any background who can keep up with the high standards and fast pace in my clinics. We are also known for giving candidates with less than perfect credentials a chance in our entry-level jobs. That means we have sometimes run into problems with our hires and had a lot of turnover, but it also means we have found true diamonds in the rough.

In December 2000 the PLP achieved one of the party's foundational goals by enacting legislation, pending the United Kingdom's approval, to amend Bermuda's Constitution so that voting districts could be redrawn fairly and single-seat constituencies created. Our legislation also called for striking 30(1)(a), the provision that was the basis for challenging my 1993 election to the House of Assembly in order to bring the Constitution into conformity with U.K. law.

The PLP's bill followed the protocol used throughout Bermuda's history as a dependent territory of the United Kingdom from its origins to the arrival of party politics in the 1960s and the first UBP Government under Henry Tucker. Although the Bermuda Constitution was drafted in the late 1960s via a Constitutional Conference in the United Kingdom, that conference decreed that there would not be a sequel except as part of Bermuda's becoming independent. Until then, amendments to the Constitution were to proceed via legislation in Bermuda's House of Assembly and then be submitted for the U.K. government's approval or rejection.

Redrawing voting districts to contain approximately the same number of voters and making them single-seat constituencies would level the playing field in Bermuda politics. Frightened by this prospect, the UBP forgot all about the protocols enshrined in the laws of the United Kingdom and Bermuda and frantically argued that any amendment to our Constitution should only come in a Constitutional Conference, where they might strangle any substantive change.

It would be some time before the United Kingdom gave its verdicts, yea or nay, to each of the proposed changes. Even so, passing the bill to submit the changes to the United Kingdom was an enormous achievement for Jennifer Smith as PLP Leader and Premier of Bermuda. And her contributions as head of Government were by no means over. But there were already rumblings against her, inside and outside the PLP, as I'll discuss in the next chapter.

10. Personal Changes and Political Upheaval

T HE EARLY YEARS OF THE 2000S SAW A CONTINUING STRUGGLE for leadership of the PLP. But before I recount that struggle and the role I played in it, I have to tell you about events in my personal life at this time, some of which spilled over into political controversy.

Priscilla and I continued to view bringing up Trey and Donovan in very different terms. But now that Priscilla and I were divorced, we no longer had so many wrangles about the boys.

During the late 1990s I dated women without seeking or finding anyone who might be another life partner. After two divorces I figured I was through with marriage. With four sons of varied ages, I wasn't looking to have any more children—on purpose or by accident. Believe me, I became very careful about birth control, as I admittedly always should have been rather than assuming that the lady in question was taking care of it.

The late 1990s were also when I began really getting to know Philip Butterfield, the brother my father had told me about, and his younger brother, Vincent, who I had discovered was also my father's son with Mrs. Marie Butterfield. Vincent's legal name is Butterfield, but after his mother married Mr. Edmund Hollinsid she enrolled him in school with that last name. As Vincent's passport says, he is "also commonly known as Vincent Hollinsid" and for all practical purposes that is his name in Bermuda. After high school Vincent went to work for the Bermuda Telephone Company while also volunteering as a fire fighter. A year later he joined the Bermuda Fire Service as a paid fire fighter and began working his way up the ranks. Under the last UBP Government, he had become Deputy Fire Chief and was in line for the Chief's job. Thanks to an initiative Vincent proposed in 1989, Bermuda Fire Service personnel had started training as both fire fighters and emergency medical technicians, and he had other improvements in mind.

Vincent and his wife, Karen, had two sons, Robin and Ramon, who were six years apart in age. In May 1996, their younger son, Ramon, who was only twenty-two years old, had a seizure and died inside his paternal grand-mother's house. Shortly after Ramon's tragic early death I began to spend more time with Vincent, who was strikingly like our father in both looks and manner. One of the joys of that experience was getting to know Robin, who was then well along in a productive career in the Bermuda Police Service, and seeing the wonderful relationship he had with both his parents. I quickly came to count Robin as a friend.

For his part, Philip had made a fine career in banking in the United States. After earning his bachelor's degree at New York University and his MBA at New York University Stern School of Business (he was one of only two Black students in his business school class), Philip had gone to work at Citibank. Of the new executive trainee hires at Citibank in the summer of 1972, Philip was one of a small handful of people of color. He stayed at Citi for twenty-eight years, ultimately rising to become a senior vice president in the wealth man-agement division.

Philip and his wife, Roz, and two daughters, Charlene and Vernée, lived in Connecticut. In 1999, however, he began coming back to Bermuda fairly frequently because his and Vincent's mother was in failing health.

We had that in common, because Emelita's and my mother was also in very poor health, suffering from accumulating problems related to her heart condition and diabetes. The burden of seeing to Mom's medical care fell heav-ily on Emelita, who accompanied her when she went for treatment to Lahey Clinic for gallbladder surgery and complications ensued. In the first half of 1999 Mom bounced back and forth between Lahey and a rehabilitation center, never quite getting well enough to return home to Bermuda. On June 25, 1999, Helene Darrell Brown passed away in Boston at age seventy-one. Emelita and I were both at her side.

Our father, D. A., had only minor health issues until shortly before he died. He suffered a mild heart attack in 1959. When Uncle Bert tried to admit him to a semi-private room at KEMH, the hospital said no, there was already a White patient in the room. Luckily there was no recurrence, and his slightly high blood pressure was easily managed. He seemed in vibrant health when he flew to Los Angeles in spring 2000 to see Emelita and her family, and get her help in buying an outfit to wear to the graduation from Tufts University of Philip's younger daughter, Vernée. Dad became ill in his hotel in Boston, went into the hospital there, and then returned home to Bermuda. Eventually he too was admitted to Lahey Clinic for treatment, and he passed away there on August 27, 2000, at age eighty-two. Emelita, and I were at his side, and Philip was in transit to Boston. It was good that Emelita, Philip, Vincent, and I had each other's support.

I was also happy that in the previous couple of years, Phil, Vincent, Robin, and I had enjoyed some excellent times with D. A. I organized the first of what became a series of annual trips for the guys to places like Turks and Caicos. We went on fishing excursions with Dad, and my brothers and nephew and I played golf. These experiences really solidified the bond between us, and they gave Dad a lot of joy.

Unfortunately our outings did not include Dad's fourth son, Maxwell Trott, who was about the age of Philip and Emelita. Dad didn't tell me about Maxwell's existence until some time after I learned about Philip and Vincent. Maxwell had a rather troubled life, and Philip, Vincent, and I never forged a close relationship with him.

Emelita knew Maxwell better because they were friends as teens. At sixteen Maxwell was dating one of Emelita's best friends. However, because of our mother's insistence, Emelita had no idea she was related to Maxwell. It was not until 1986 that Emelita learned that Philip, whom she'd also known as a teenager, Vincent, and Maxwell were her brothers.

Dad tried to do all he could for Maxwell, including setting him up in a car cleaning and detailing business. But Maxwell wound up dying of a stroke at fifty, following a long struggle with substance abuse.

After that, Philip, Vincent, and I made a special effort to get to know Maxwell's son, Errin, better. We consciously emulated our father, D. A., in doing so, and we are all glad to have formed a close bond with Errin. He has built a thriving business as a plumber, and he and his wife, Martha, have added to the extended family with their son, E. J.

Although Philip and Roz kept their house in Connecticut, in 2000 they both began spending a good deal of time in Bermuda because of a new development in Philip's career. On a visit in 1999 he had bumped into Henry Smith, CEO of the Bank of Bermuda. They had long known each other as senior banking executives. Learning that Philip was soon going to be leaving Citibank because of the change in regime following Citi's merger with Travelers Group to form Citigroup, Henry Smith asked him to come see him at the Bank of Bermuda. In the discussions that followed, Philip learned that the Bank of Bermuda wanted to move its stock listing from Bermuda to the Nasdaq in New York and eventually pursue a sale to a larger bank.

There were a number of financial reasons for the move, not the least of which was that the Trimingham family wanted to divest their remaining shares. The family had long controlled the Bank of Bermuda as well as Trimingham's Department Store. The department store had been declining for some time, but now that decline was accelerating. Discomfort with political change also played a part. When the PLP gained power, more than one old White Bermudian family chose to abandon the country rather than live under the first non-White–controlled Government. A branch of the Trimingham family had settled in the United States in colonial times, and more of the family was moving there. In any case, relisting the Bank of Bermuda on the Nasdaq exchange required a waiver of Bermuda's law that businesses be at least 60 percent owned by Bermudians.

Given Philip's distinguished career at Citibank, Henry Smith saw him as a perfect candidate to arrange the Nasdaq listing and lead the bank after his own retirement. On June 1, 2000, Philip joined the Bank of Bermuda's senior leadership team, and a year later he became chief operating officer and heir apparent to Henry Smith.

DURING THE YEARS 1998 TO 2000, MAURICE WAS coming of age. It had long since become clear to me why his mother, Maureen Pitt, had finally gotten in touch with me thirteen years after the brief encounter that produced Maurice. She saw her teenage son heading down a bad path, and she reached out for help in correcting his course.

So far, I had not been able to do much. As I've mentioned, Maurice was deeply distrustful of authority and of me when we met in 1995. He was very bright and very headstrong, qualities I had when I began to sink into hopelessness at the Bermuda Technical Institute (BTI) at much the same age. Since then he had been in a succession of public and private high schools, and dropped out at sixteen as soon as he legally could. I gave him a part-time job at Bermuda HealthCare Services, and I tried to connect with him the way my father connected with me when I was suspended from BTI.

My father's telling me, "They don't make doctors in prison," started a change in me based on my history of trust in him and my mother, and on the state of my own development both intellectually and emotionally. Even so I needed to go to high school in Jamaica to really get back on track.

Maurice and I didn't have a comparable history as father and son. He was also less emotionally mature and under the surface even more angry and fearful and despairing about what life had in store for him than I was when my parents sent me to Jamaica. In any case, I'm afraid my words didn't get through to him the way my father's got through to me.

In 2000, however, Maurice was making positive strides. He completed his GED, and with my financial support he went to Southern California to attend Santa Monica College, a two-year institution that could be his path to a skilled technical job and/or a four-year bachelor's degree. I hoped it would be as positive a change for him at eighteen as going to Jamaica was for me at thirteen.

A promising aspect of the situation was that he had extended family on both my side and his mother's in the Los Angeles area. In addition to his paternal aunt Emelita and her children, his first cousins Kimberly and Kyle, Maurice also had a maternal aunt and first cousins in Los Angeles. To begin with he shared an apartment with a male first cousin on his mother's side, but the two young men were soon at odds with each other. Maurice next found a room in an apartment right across the street from Santa Monica College. That was convenient, but he was moving into a complicated sharing arrangement with two single guys and a couple, all a few years older than he was. Maurice had what passed for street savvy among his peers in Bermuda, but he was naïve when it came to the urban culture he tried to navigate in Los Angeles.

For one semester he was a diligent student, working toward an associate's degree in computer science, and he compiled a 4.0 grade point average. But he also started, in his words to me much later, "smoking weed like a train." He was soon more in sync with his disordered surroundings and living situation than he was with his studies.

At one point he moved in with Emelita's son, Kyle, but here, too, the relationship took a negative turn. Despite everyone's best intentions, a promising change was turning sour. Things reached the stage where I told Maurice I wouldn't send him another dime until he got himself back on track academically. Kevin, who was then doing his residency in family practice in Los Angeles, was trying to be a good older brother to Maurice, but that relationship also fell prey to misunderstanding and wounded pride.

By mid-2001, Maurice was living on his own and selling drugs to support himself. He was arrested for bank robbery in May 2002 and received a ten-year prison sentence.

Although I felt I had tried my best to help Maurice, I also felt a deep sense of failure as a father. I could only hope that years of imprisonment would not damage Maurice beyond recovery, and strive to be there for him when he was released.

Meanwhile there was a tragic loss for my extended family early on the morning of Saturday, January 27, 2001, when Vincent's older son, Robin, died in a traffic collision with a drunken driver. Robin was thirty-one years old and a highly commended narcotics detective with the Bermuda Police Service. There was an outpouring of grief from his colleagues and superiors in tribute to Robin as a police officer and a person. My brother Vincent and sister-in-law Karen had to endure his loss only five years after losing his younger brother, Ramon. Robin left a six-year-old son, Rakeem, to whom he had been absolutely devoted.

I did my best to console Vincent, Karen, and Rakeem, as our extended family did. I also mourned for Robin as a nephew, a talented and dedicated public servant who was contributing significantly to Bermuda and could have gone on to make even greater contributions, and most of all as a goodhearted and joyful friend.

DURING THIS TIME BERMUDA HEALTHCARE SERVICES (BHCS) continued to grow. Unfortunately the business side of the clinic was not keeping pace. Bills and insurance claims were not going out in a timely way, and cash flow, which would otherwise have been robust, was becoming problematic. As a result BHCS was falling behind in paying payroll taxes To my dismay, the clinic began to appear on Bermuda's "list of shame" of tax-delinquent companies.

By late 2000 I decided that I needed to bring in a very experienced practice manager from the United States, and I asked for Emelita's help in identifying candidates. She immediately thought of Kelley McKinney, who had shown her the ropes of the U.S. healthcare system when she moved to California to work with me at Vermont-Century Medical Clinic. Kelley turned out to be ready for a new adventure in her life, and in March 2001 she came to Bermuda on a one-year contract. She was such a great addition to BHCS that we kept extending the contract and adding to her responsibilities. She soon put the business side of the clinic on a firm foundation to match our extensive patient roster, and then helped manage the clinic's growth throughout the rest of the decade and beyond.

The other invaluable addition to BHCS was Dr. Mahesh Reddy, a general practitioner originally from India who came to Bermuda by way of Jamaica. Dr. Reddy is one of the most skilled practitioners around. More important, he's also one of the most caring. As a result, he has become one of Bermuda's most popular doctors, widely respected by his colleagues and patients. The combination of Dr. Reddy and Kelley McKinney took a heavy weight off my shoulders. They enabled me to concentrate on being a physician and treating patients when I was at BHCS and to focus otherwise on politics and on getting my personal life in order.

My political enemies later seized on and distorted the temporary cash flow problem at BHCS, the result not of inadequate business but inadequate office management, as they sought to smear me with false allegations of corruption. In doing this they also misrepresented how I built my house in Bermuda.

Since moving back to Bermuda I had been renting a house, but I always wanted to buy or build one. In early 2000, I decided the time was right financially. Despite the brief cash flow crunch at BHCS, my personal finances were in good shape. Since my freshman year at Howard, I have always followed my father's sage advice to "take care of your breakfast first." That is, protect your quality of life against any business risks you might take by planning ahead and being prudent.

My friend and fellow PLP MP Arthur Pitcher alerted me to a property for sale on A. P. Owen Road in Smith's Parish on Bermuda's South Shore. It was a great location and I loved having an ocean view. There was a house on the property, but it wasn't in very good shape.

The original plan was to do an extensive remodel incorporating the existing structure with additions. After work commenced in 1999, however, it became clear that the house was too far gone to be saved in any form and had to be demolished. My architects drew up plans for a new house, and construction recommenced. My understanding was that the original planning approvals covered this, but in the fall the local inspector issued a stop order.

The inspector's first concern was the use of prefabricated walls, which was a well-tested construction method elsewhere and had been used with no problems on a house less than a half-mile away. In addition the inspector challenged the change from renovating and remodeling an existing structure to building a new one.

Controversy ensued when PLP MP and Environment Minister Arthur Hodgson visited the construction site and then lifted the stop order. Eventually it was determined that the demolition of the existing house was covered by the original planning approvals, but the drawings for new construction had not all been submitted for approval. The use of prefabricated walls had also not been specifically approved. There was really no reason to bar either the new building or the construction method, and in early December retroactive approval was granted for them.

Along the way the *Royal Gazette*, which put the story on its front pages, also used up a lot of ink about normal construction problems like a dispute with a neighbor over a right of way to the ocean and damage to a couple of trees and steps leading down to the water on the neighbor's property. As soon as those issues were brought to my attention, I resolved them amicably with the neighbor. From the start my intention was to do something that would enhance the neighborhood and boost everyone's property values, and that in fact was what happened when all was said and done.

Unfortunately, this was not the end of trouble with the house construction.

THE YEAR 2001 BROUGHT TWO SIGNIFICANT CHANGES in my personal life. In the summer of that year Priscilla moved to West Bloomfield, Michigan, with Trey and Donovan, so that the boys could go to high school there. The West Bloomfield school system was first-rate, and I was in favor of the move. Priscilla continued to practice Bermuda corporate law from Michigan, and I saw Trey and Donovan on holidays and extended visits in the summers. I also burned up the phone lines talking to them and once joked to Trey that I had set a new record with AT&T. He made that remark the basis of a speech he gave in a public speaking class. The move turned out to be positive for all of us.

The second big change of 2001 in my personal life began early in the year, but for quite a while I wasn't sure where it was leading. On Wednesday, January 10, I got a message that Wanda Henton had called me at the suggestion of Flash Wiley, a mutual friend and Wanda's former boss when she practiced law in Boston. Wanda and I had met in August 1992 at a party on Martha's Vineyard and again in passing at Martha's Vineyard Airport in August 1995. I knew she was in investment banking and, moreover, a pioneer in that field as a Black woman, but nothing more than that and the fact that we had had a lively rapport at our first meeting. When I called her back late on Thursday evening, she said that she was in the running for some business in Bermuda, would appreciate the opportunity to get some pointers on the local business scene, and wondered if she could arrange to meet me there. I was leaving Bermuda early the next morning to fly to California, with a two-hour layover to change planes at New York's John F. Kennedy Airport, so I suggested we meet at the American Airlines Admirals Club lounge at the airport at 8 a.m.

Wanda was punctual to the minute, dressed in a sober business pantsuit, but somehow imbued with a sense of style that made her seem anything but an ordinary business person to me. As we sat down, she asked after my family, and I explained that Priscilla and I had separated and divorced shortly after she saw us with our sons at Martha's Vineyard Airport in 1995.

Wanda had married in her twenties. But she was already divorced from her husband when we met on Martha's Vineyard, and I guessed from the bare ring finger on her left hand that she had not remarried. Somehow that and my saying I had been divorced for almost six years immediately changed the atmosphere. I felt a remarkable energy between us, and it looked as if Wanda felt it, too. Not forgetting the reason for our meeting, we talked about the business scene in Bermuda. By the time Wanda walked me to my gate two hours later, however, that was not top of mind for either of us. We exchanged all our contact information and promised to talk again soon.

Back in Bermuda on Sunday evening, I called Wanda and left a message that I had lost my Palm Pilot with all my phone numbers in it and was wondering if that might be an omen. Wanda called back and left a message saying there was no question it was an omen; the question was whether or not I would heed it.

Unbeknownst to me at that point, after leaving our meeting Wanda had called two of her closest friends, including Flash Wiley's wife, Bennie, who was a Howard classmate of mine. Wanda told Bennie she had worn the wrong clothes to meet me and was ready to move to Bermuda the next day. She had made an equally big impression on me, but as a little time passed I failed to call her again. The reason was simply that I was scared of commitment after two divorces, and I sensed that any relationship I had with Wanda would have to be a serious one.

It was late February before I called Wanda and we spoke again. By coincidence she was on the phone with Bennie Wiley. Fed up with my not calling over the previous six weeks, Wanda had just told her, "I have not heard from Ewart Brown. I have quit him. We do not need to discuss him." That was vintage Wanda, decisive and clear.

When her call waiting beeped and she found out I was on the other line, she put Bennie on hold and spoke with me briefly. I was going to a medical conference in New Orleans in March. Knowing that Wanda was from Alexandria, Louisiana, and still had lots of family there, I asked if she would meet me for dinner in New Orleans. She politely declined, the call ended, and I told myself I had messed up big-time.

Thank heavens for friends, as Wanda says about this moment. When she got back on the line with Bennie and related what had just transpired, Bennie said, "Wait a minute. You still need to learn more about doing business in Bermuda, and I've known you to fly to Holland for a business meeting and turn around and fly straight back to New York. Why don't you give it a shot?"

A little later Wanda called me back and said she would be glad to meet me for dinner in New Orleans in a few weeks. She arrived late on the evening of the first day of the medical conference, and we had a drink before retiring to our respective hotel rooms. All through the next day I was like a kid with a first crush trying to keep my mind on the medical conference.

That evening we had a wonderful dinner at the Pelican Grill. Finding that we both liked to gamble, we then went to the casino next door to play blackjack. We both won at blackjack, and the chemistry between us was so obvious that everyone around seemed to assume we were husband and wife. Neither of us bothered to correct anyone who voiced that assumption. When we left the casino we still said good night to each other, however, and went to our own rooms. This was very different for me.

The next day Wanda told me that she only wanted to be in an exclusive relationship. I "dummied up," as she likes to say, and asked what she meant by that. She said that no one could guarantee the future, but that she could not be involved with me while either of us was seeing or intending to see someone else. She said that at the point when we began staying together, she would need to know that we both intended the relationship to be exclusive. The energy between us was not only intact when we parted, it was increased. Yet the question of a next step in the relationship remained unanswered.

We got into a pattern of talking all the time on the phone as well as meeting now and then in New York or elsewhere. Ironically, Wanda was the first woman I was deeply attracted to who cared or knew much about politics. Like me, Wanda had grown up in a household where politics was trumps. Her father was active in community politics, and both her parents had regularly assisted other Black people in preparing for the onerous voting registration test with which Louisiana suppressed the Black vote. As a teenager Wanda had been involved in NAACP voter registration drives. As a law student at Southern University in Baton Rouge, she became the first Black assistant clerk on the floor of the Louisiana House of Representatives. After practicing civil rights and criminal law in Alexandria, she had married and moved with her husband to Boston, where she practiced corporate law and worked in civil rights.

Following her divorce, she moved to New York City, where she became actively involved in David Dinkins's successful 1985 mayoral campaign and Carl McCall's successful campaigns for the office of state comptroller. With Carl McCall's guidance she made a career switch, going to work for two of New York State's main bond-issuing agencies. Within a few years she was being recruited by white-shoe Wall Street firms, and she took a job at Dillon Read, where she became a vice president. She was recruited from that post by the even-more prestigious firm of Lazard Frères, where she became a senior vice president, and a few years after that she went into business for herself connecting private equity and real estate funds with institutional investors such as pension funds. Her combination of political and business expertise was formidable, and her point of view never less than incisive.

I had never felt so much on the same wavelength with any other woman. However, Wanda's involvement with politics had led her to tell friends she would never date a politician. She'd seen too much of the political realm's unfairness and the damage it could do to personal relationships. I was delighted that she was considering making an exception as far as I was concerned, and I applied myself to persuading her to do so. We talked on the phone practically every day. By the summer I was extremely frustrated about her still insisting that a romantic relationship would have to be exclusive, and I asked her if she was playing games with me.

Wanda said, "No, Ewart, I am not playing games."

We arranged to spend some time together, very happily, at the end of which she said, "Good-bye, Ewart. I wasn't playing games with you. But I'm not going to be with you if the relationship is not exclusive. When you're ready for that, call me."

I was stunned, angry, and confused. For a couple of months I didn't call. But I couldn't shake the feeling that life was offering me an extraordinary opportunity, one I shouldn't squander. In late August I called Wanda and suggested we get together to talk seriously.

On Sunday, September 9, 2001, we met in Orlando where I had a timeshare. I asked Wanda again what she meant by an exclusive relationship. She repeated what she had said before, emphasizing that no one could guarantee the future and that she was simply asking for clear intentions, honesty, and that neither of us have any present intention to see anyone else. By this point I was ready to acknowledge the reasonableness of her position.

We were supposed to fly home to Bermuda and New York respectively on Wednesday, September 12, but the events of 9/11 grounded all flights until that Friday. By then we had agreed that we would spend every weekend together, taking turns traveling to Bermuda or New York to see each other. That became a wonderful extended courtship for us.

During this time I began to get to know Wanda's family. Unfortunately, her older brother, Mack Henton, Jr., had died of lung cancer in 1989 at the age of forty-seven, but the fondness with which everyone recalled him gave me a sense of him and of the strength of the Henton family. They were also devout Christians—Wanda spent much of her young life in church.

Wanda's mother, Evangeline, known as Van, was in the late stages of cancer, and I never knew her when she was fully herself, so to speak. All the same, I saw many similarities between her forceful personality and Wanda's. When Van had to go into the hospital, her three daughters stayed at her bedside in eight-hour shifts: Deloris, the oldest; Shirley, known as Tiny, the middle daughter; and Wanda, the youngest. Wanda's oldest nephew, Reginald, also took a regular shift. Relieving them as needed were Wanda's nieces Angel, Kim, and Dion, nephew Shaun, and other family members. Van was never alone. In all my years of practicing medicine, I had never witnessed such family glue. It greatly impressed not only me, but the hospital staff. Caregivers work harder when they see the kind of support Van's family exhibited.

After Van's passing in 2002 at the age of eighty, I began to develop a close relationship with Wanda's father, Mack Henton, Sr. The cliché "tower of strength" was made for people like Mack and Van Henton. All through the Civil Rights Movement, they were a focal point of grassroots activism in Alexandria, Louisiana. Wanda had told me how her parents helped their kin and neighbors learn what they needed to know to pass the racist voting tests that Louisiana used. I loved going to the family homestead in Alexandria and sitting with Mack while he hosted his extended family. I soaked up his great stories and wisdom.

Gradually it dawned on me that Wanda and I got along so well and had such similar approaches to life because her mother was just like my mother and her father was just like my father. However, it took me until March 2003 to propose marriage by saying to Wanda, "When are we going to close our deal?"

She laughed and said, "How romantic, Ewart."

"Well, we're not getting any younger."

She laughed again, and said yes. Our wedding took place at St. Monica's Church on Turks and Caicos on May 31, 2003, and we had a reception in Bermuda in June just before the next general election was called. The election of

July 24, 2003, would prove to be a pivotal one for my ambition to lead Bermuda. But before I tell you about that, I have to fill you in on political events beginning in early 2001.

FROM LATE 2000 TO MID-2003—FOR ME and many others in the PLP—Jennifer Smith's leadership as the head of the Party and Premier traversed an arc from solid to unsure. Discontent with her leadership spread as her leadership habits gradually became more extreme.

At first her leadership persona was an effective one of judicious reserve. As time went on, however, reserve became secrecy and she kept her views on key questions unknown outside a small inner circle, announcing decisions without first consulting or informing the PLP backbench MPs. Even Cabinet Ministers found themselves out of the loop.

Premier Smith was equally unwilling to engage with the media and the public except in carefully controlled photo opportunities. The Premier's unavailability gave the impression of shrinking from the possibility she might say something she'd be held to later. This became a bigger and bigger negative in the public's attitude toward her.

In her office the Premier cocooned herself behind a limited access policy, even for members of Cabinet. And she engaged with the public only in carefully controlled photo opportunities. Gradually this behavior eroded voters' confidence in her. Thanks largely to her aloofness, which I always felt was rooted in shyness and which became more marked the longer she was in office, by pre-general election polling in 2003 she had lost so much support that it put the whole PLP on dangerous ground. I could not envision continuing to serve in her Cabinet and thought I would join the backbenchers after the election, assuming the PLP squeaked through to a victory.

Through the summer, rumors circulated about discontent in the PLP with Jennifer Smith's leadership. News stories focused on Environment Minister Arthur Hodgson, who was reportedly interested in challenging her.

Named Bermuda's first Black Rhodes Scholar in 1964, Arthur had, then as now, a well-deserved reputation for being able to drill down to the intellectual base of an issue. Yet he also had a well-deserved reputation for carrying such analyses past the point of being practically useful, and administration was never his strong suit. Nonetheless, Arthur has often given me solid advice, and I have always valued his contributions to Bermuda as a teacher, lawyer, magistrate, Senator, MP, Cabinet Minister, and committed member of the PLP.

In mid- to late 2000, I was convinced that it was not yet time for a new leader of the Party or the Government and that the Premier's overwhelming support among PLP delegates meant that any challenge to her leadership at that point in time was dead in the water.

Arthur is several years older than I am, and perhaps he saw the clock ticking on his chance for leadership. In any case, he declared himself a candidate for Party Leader when the PLP Delegates Conference opened at the end of October. Two aspects of this announcement were problematical for Arthur's political future. First his declaration came so late he had no time to make his case to the various delegates one by one or in small groups, which signaled to me that he was acting out of frustration. Second he declared his candidacy to replace the Premier without the usual step of first resigning his Cabinet post.

I continued to make no secret of my own leadership ambitions, and over the previous two years my profile in the Party had risen because of my handling of the Transport portfolio and my role in parliamentary debate across all issues. So as a learning experience and to see where I stood with the PLP branch delegates, on the day of the vote I put myself forward for the role of Deputy Leader against Finance Minister Eugene Cox. Because I was a candidate for Deputy Leader, not Party Leader, there was no tradition calling for me to resign from Premier Smith's Cabinet first.

Both Arthur and I went down to defeat by large margins. Premier Smith defeated Arthur's challenge to her leadership by 81 votes to 35, and Eugene Cox defeated my challenge to his deputy leadership by 87 to 31.

The result in my case told me it would be some time yet before I could hope to attain one of the PLP's two top leadership roles. The result also encouraged me, however. Getting 25 percent of the votes from scratch, with no campaign period, showed I already had a base of support among PLP branch delegates. So I carried on with my work in Transport as a loyal member of the Premier's Cabinet.

For Arthur, however, the sequel to his leadership challenge was ouster from Cabinet and relegation to the PLP backbench. He continued to contribute significantly to the PLP and Bermuda in that role. Life is full of "what if" situations, however, and there is no telling what he might have been able to contribute in a larger role.

AFTER ARTHUR HODGSON WAS AXED FROM CABINET, talk of replacing Jennifer Smith as PLP Leader and Premier, insofar as I heard it, subsided to the level of occasional grumbling from fellow Cabinet Ministers and PLP backbenchers. The next scheduled PLP leadership vote was November 2002, and it was unlikely the Premier's leadership would be questioned until that date approached. The intervening period promised to be one of politics as had become usual between the PLP Government and the UBP. But that inevitably set the context for the next leadership fight, whenever it was to come.

I mentioned in chapter 9 that Kevin Monkman became head of the Transport Control Department (TCD) in November 2000. The mandate I gave him was to take TCD, the Government department that citizens and residents most hated to deal with, and transform it into one they applauded for its efficiency and customer friendliness.

One afternoon in February 2001 I went down to TCD to see how things were going. What immediately caught my eye was a sign that read, "If you are not at the counter by 4:30 p.m., please reschedule your appointment."

I was incensed. The sign meant that an appointment scheduled with TCD to renew a license, register a vehicle, or conduct any other business was basically worthless. TCD appointments were only placeholders in an interminable wait for service. I turned to Kevin and said, "This sign must come down."

After about a week I called Kevin and asked if the sign had been taken down. He said no. We briefly discussed why the sign needed to go, and I left the matter in his hands. After about another week I called and asked again about the sign. Kevin said he had not taken it down because "the union will have a problem with that."

"They probably will," I said. "But that's okay. We will resolve that with the union the way we resolve any other grievance. It's a ridiculous sign. If you don't remove it within the next couple of weeks, I'm coming down there with the media so they can watch me take it down."

I bolstered the message early in March during an address to the House of Assembly announcing the preparation of a comprehensive National Transportation Management Plan. I made special note of the fact that the TCD sign about rescheduling appointments was coming down. The next day the *Royal Gazette* included that promise in an article on my speech.

This attention brought the sign down at last. It was a tough but important lesson for Kevin Monkman as head of a Government department and for the department's employees. The union pushed back, but I held to the principle that people must be able to rely on TCD's appointments and be served in a timely manner. It proved to be a turning point in infusing TCD with a positive commitment to serving the public. The employees found they felt a lot better about themselves and their jobs when efficient procedures were in place and people walked away from the counter satisfied and happy, rather than frustrated and resentful.

March 2001 was also when I moved to upgrade airport security with x-ray screening of bags. Even before the tragic events of 9/11/2001 in the United States, I knew we had to improve security at Bermuda International Airport. Our x-ray scanning equipment put us well ahead of many busy metropolitan airports in North America in terms of security, and the improvement went hand in hand with other measures to make the airport more efficient and passenger-friendly.

EVERY SUMMER THE SMITHSONIAN FOLKLIFE FESTIVAL TAKES PLACE over two weeks on the Mall in Washington, D.C., and in June and July of 2001 the focus and name of the festival was Bermuda Connections. Minister of Development and Opportunity Terry Lister (in late 2000 he also became Minister of Environment, replacing Arthur Hodgson) led negotiations with the Smithsonian to arrange the festival, which also drew on a major effort by the Department of Community and Cultural Affairs within the Ministry of Community Affairs and Sport and significant cooperation by Tourism, Transport, and Education. The festival was supported by generous funding from the Bank of Bermuda.

Bermuda Connections was an unprecedented opportunity to show Bermuda's folkways to the American public and international travelers visiting Washington. The exhibition ranged from craft, construction, farming, and fishing methods to cuisine, cricket, art, music, and dance. The demonstrations on the Mall by master artisans and agriculturalists included constructing a house with hand-cut limestone, building the hull of a classic Bermuda dinghy, furniture-making, and beekeeping, among other traditional practices. The musicians, dancers, and comedians who performed on the Mall ranged from the spit-and-polish, redcoat-uniformed Bermuda Regiment Band to Gombey dancers and musicians in handmade multihued attire and the satirical group Not the Um-Um Players. Fulfilling Terry Lister's January 2001 promise in announcing the festival, it amounted to a "mini-Bermuda" at one of the world's most prominent public venues.

The PLP Government approached this opportunity in a bipartisan spirit that embraced all of Bermuda's traditions, whatever their origin, and that celebrated exemplary individuals whether they were PLP or UBP supporters. The exhibition succeeded on every level from the reaction of more than a million attendees to the positive public relations for Bermuda tourism. It also resulted in a superb cultural resource guide for use in Bermuda's schools.

Yet there was no support from the UBP side of the aisle in Parliament. Instead of helping to celebrate Bermuda in partnership with the Smithsonian, one of the world's greatest cultural institutions, the Opposition sat on their hands until the festival was over and then nitpicked the costs involved. What we spent was a fraction of what we received in marketing and promotion of Bermuda as a tourist destination, but you would not have known that from the UBP's response.

The UBP's allegations of mismanagement and overspending had no basis in fact and expressed nothing so much as White establishment Bermuda's ambivalence about the African, Native American, and Caribbean elements in our culture and history. For example, UBP Governments always depended on Gombey troupes to provide entertainment and local color, if you will, for both visiting dignitaries and tourists. But the UBP never wanted to acknowledge that the Afro-Caribbean strands in Bermuda's history began with the importation of Black slaves from the West Indies, that the commercial activity of White-establishment Bermuda in the Caribbean was a continuing fact, not a distant memory, and that Bermuda's majority Black population continued to have and develop ties of kinship throughout the Caribbean.

The attention the Smithsonian Institution gave Bermuda's folkways must have made the UBP and the entrenched White power that ran the party deeply uncomfortable. Their wish to ignore the legacies of slavery and colonialism had been on full display in the debate over naming the first day of Cup Match as Emancipation Day. The same attitude reared its head from late summer 2001 in the UBP's aversive reaction, echoed in many *Royal Gazette* articles and editorials, to the PLP Government's plan for Bermuda to become an associate member of the Caribbean Community and Common Market (Caricom).

From the perspective of the PLP, joining Caricom as an associate member was a moral responsibility. It honored countless common threads in our island cultures, our histories under colonial rule, and our prospects for advancing our societies for the benefit of all our peoples, not just a ruling elite. To take the earliest and most important example, colonial Bermuda's White establishment ran a busy slave trade to Turks and Caicos. The Turks and Caicos National Museum documents this history, but I grew up in Bermuda without ever learning about it.

Sad to say, the UBP's attempt to deny these common threads exemplified its agenda as the servant of Bermuda's traditional ruling class. Also sad to say, the Combined Opposition of the UBP, the White Bermuda business establishment, and the *Royal Gazette* (in its editorials if not always in its news coverage) spoke as usual out of both sides of their mouths. On the one hand, they protested that joining Caricom as an associate member would subject Bermuda to collective decisions that were not in our national interest. On the other hand, they said joining Caricom was worthless and we would get no return on the $98,000 yearly cost, precisely because the PLP refused to subject Bermuda to those collective decisions.

In setting forth Bermuda's prospective associate membership in Caricom, the PLP Government precluded participating in a common market and single currency or allowing a free flow of labor into the country from the Caribbean. We ceded first place to no one in enhancing Bermuda's status as the Switzerland of the Atlantic, a role that many jurisdictions in the Caribbean were competing to fill. Strengthening our international business sector and maintaining control of our labor market were complementary parts of our duty to improve opportunities for all Bermudians. Joining Caricom did not conflict with this duty in any way.

There was considerable irony, however, in UBP claims that the Caribbean was a dangerous place to do business and that joining Caricom was "gambling" with Bermuda's national interest. The UBP's Grant Gibbons knew this well, as the Gibbons Companies had extensive interests in the Caribbean. It was misguided of the UBP to dismiss any possibility that membership in Caricom might be useful for supporting Bermudian businesses like the Gibbons Companies in the Caribbean.

Responding to Grant Gibbons in the House, I said, "I wish those who oppose the idea would be a little more direct and a little more honest about why they have misgivings about this Government and this country joining Caricom. And I find it somewhat offensive for the Opposition to speak in such derogatory terms about the Caribbean region, despite that Honorable Member's intimate knowledge of businesses which thrive in the Caribbean." I concluded that, in contrast to viewing Caribbean countries simply as arenas of exploitation, we in the PLP believed that it was important "to find cultural and educational common ground" with them.

It was surely no coincidence that in the midst of the Caricom controversy, the UBP attacked a recent link between Bermuda College and Grenada's St. George's University School of Medicine, which was founded in 1976 by an American lawyer whose son had been unable to gain admission to medical school in the United States. Following a familiar pattern, the UBP said its questions about this link were only about quality standards. Under the headline "Concerns raised over Caribbean medical school," the *Royal Gazette* reported on March 7, 2002, that Shadow Health Minister Michael Dunkley said in the House, "I would like to stress when we make these medical alliances, we should make them with quality educational institutes because Bermuda is a first-class business destination and a first-class visitor destination and Bermudians have a high regard for our Island." The article also quoted a Bermudian physician, Dr. William Cooke: "Bermudian students have long been successful in well-established, academically superior institutions and I would have expected Bermuda College to aim higher."

In attacking the quality of St. George's University School of Medicine, the UBP should have looked beyond the circumstances of its founding and location. As I replied to Michael Dunkley in the House, standards for graduation and medical licensing were and are much more important than standards for admission. St. George's University School of Medicine had established itself as an academically superior institution with regard to the quality of its instruction and the accomplishments of its graduates. A primary factor in establishing the link with St. George's was that in 2001 its graduates had passed the U.S. Medical Licensing Exam at a rate of 93 percent, higher than any medical school in the United States. St. George's has sustained this excellence: between 2011 and 2012, for example, it placed more doctors into first-year U.S. residency positions than any other medical school in the world.

Bermuda College was not alone in linking with St. George's University School of Medicine in the 2000s. New York City has a program with St. George's called CityDoctors, begun in 2012, the second-to-last year of Michael Bloomberg's mayoralty, to train primary care physicians for the city's public hospitals.

If you assume anything Caribbean must be substandard, these are uncomfortable facts. Like the convoluted, contradictory argument against joining Caricom, the ill-informed criticism of Bermuda College's link with St. George's University raised the flag of racism for anyone willing to look honestly at the matter.

Dealing with so many controversies contrived for purely political reasons was a regrettable waste of energy that could have been put to better use. However, the positive momentum I was able to develop as Transport Minister was establishing a track record of positive results. They would stand me in good stead when the time came for the next upward step in my political career. But as I'll explain in the next chapter, that time had not yet arrived.

11. Dissident MPs, Triumphant Premier

I N JANUARY 2002 I DELIVERED MY PROMISED National Transportation Management Report. Among the facts stressed in the report, which had been very ably prepared by experts within the Transport Ministry, were the dramatic increases in people and cars in Bermuda between 1980 and 1999. Thanks to the growth of the international business sector, the population had increased 14 percent and the number of cars had increased 71 percent. The result was daily gridlock, which we could only unlock by improving bus, ferry, and taxi service. Densely populated Bermuda had no space available for widening roads or adding new ones, which was one of the main reasons Transport was traditionally a thankless lemon of a Cabinet Ministry.

A *Royal Gazette* editorial headlined "Ferries or gridlock" said, "Transport Minister Ewart Brown and the team who put together the [report] deserve credit for a study which delves deeply into the problems confronting transport and for coming up with some innovative solutions." I appreciated that and the rare occasions afterward on which the newspaper offered support for legislation or other action embodying those solutions. In most such cases however, the newspaper seemed to prefer to look past the solution and remain part of the Combined Opposition.

FOLLOWING THE TERRORIST ATTACKS ON THE UNITED STATES ON 9/11/2001, I worked with my team in the Transport Ministry to devise a post–9/11 aviation strategy to counter the panic mode that dominated the airlines for several months. The result was, I believe, that Bermuda experienced much less disruption in its air service than would otherwise have been the case.

In the fall of 2001 Marshall Minors announced that he was retiring from the civil service to go into private business. He had done a creditable job as the airport's first Black Bermudian general manager, and it was important for

Bermudianization that the job not revert to being held by a succession of managers from abroad. However, there was not a Bermudian candidate available to run the airport, although there were a few potential candidates who might grow into the position.

Again, it was up to the Public Service Commission to decide who would run the airport, and all I could do as Cabinet Minister was to support a good search. I encouraged the Permanent Secretary in the Transport Ministry, Herman Tucker, to identify candidates to serve as interim general manager and eventually mentor a young Bermudian manager. In the meantime, Bermudian Lester Nelson served as acting airport manager.

At the top of Herman's short list after a first round of interviews in Washington, D.C. was James "Jim" Howes, the vastly experienced general manager of the St. Petersburg–Clearwater Airport in Florida. There he had overseen an extensive upgrade of facilities, including construction of a new terminal, and attracted a number of new airlines to serve the airport. Those were major objectives for Bermuda's airport.

Without telling anyone in the Transport Ministry, Jim made a late 2001 weekend visit to Bermuda. By happenstance Herman Tucker found out he was here, and I invited him to lunch. Jim said he had come unannounced and at his own expense because he wasn't sure he wanted to pull up stakes and move to a foreign country. The beauty of the Island and the friendliness and upbeat character of Bermudians—not least of all the friendly spirit and good work ethic he saw at the airport—had won him over, he added, although he still had questions about the job.

The more we talked, the more Jim and I found we were on the same wavelength. There was further discussion after Jim returned to Florida, pending the Public Service Commission's deliberations. But in relatively short order he accepted the commission's offer of a three-year contract as the airport's general manager, beginning May 2002.

During the same time, in late 2000 to early 2002, Herman Tucker and I also looked for a new director for the Department of Marine and Ports, where Ron Ross was retiring after many years. As for TCD and the airport, I was keen to find a talented, accomplished young Bermudian who could lead Marine and Ports in the new century. Francis Richardson was an excellent long-term prospect to do this job, as he had risen through a succession of civil service posts in other departments. We looked to fill the post in the interim.

The assistant director at Marine and Ports, Mike Dolding, was an expatriate manager who had acquired Bermudian status. He struck me as typical of the UBP hires from abroad and unlikely to provide the fresh leadership Marine and Ports needed. UBP Governments had traditionally hired expatriate senior managers who did little or nothing to develop Bermudian managers.

Dolding wanted the director's job and pursued legal action when he didn't get it. But he was not really ill treated and in the end he retired with a full pension.

Herman Tucker again identified a short list of excellent candidates from abroad for the Public Service Commission to consider. The commission brought in Barry Coupland from New Zealand as interim director on a three-year contract beginning March 2002, and Francis Richardson became director designate. Barry Coupland made a major contribution to Marine and Ports during those three years, and Francis Richardson succeeded him on schedule in 2005.

Both Barry Coupland and Francis Richardson were on hand when the first fast ferry arrived in March 2002. This was *Serenity*, whose name came from a student contest won by young Keaton Tannock. In addition to helping welcome and, with Premier Jennifer Smith, christen *Serenity*, Keaton won two round-trip tickets to Florida.

As I said at the time, I was like a kid with a new bike. I was extremely proud that the Transport team and I had brought the fast ferry concept to reality—and done so more quickly and cost efficiently than the critics had thought possible.

Serenity went into service on a Hamilton–Dockyard–St. George's route. In June, the second fast ferry, *Resolute*, arrived and went into service on a Hamilton–St. George's route. The faster, more comfortable, and more convenient services were a success from the start, although the UBP kept up a chorus of nay-saying that ignored the public's growing enthusiasm for the new vessels.

IN ADDITION TO *SERENITY*'S ARRIVAL, THERE WAS ANOTHER EVENT in March 2002 to celebrate. My brother Vincent Hollinsid became Chief of the Bermuda Fire Service (BFS), where he had been Deputy Chief for several years. At his swearing-in Vincent called for the amalgamation of Bermuda's three fire services, the BFS, the St. George's Volunteer Fire Brigade and the airport fire service. This made undeniable sense in terms of public cost and safety, and Vincent, who had done much to upgrade the BFS, was the logical person to lead a unified, Island-wide fire service.

As Transport Minister I cooperated with Vincent in this effort, which had very positive results, as we'll see. It bears noting that Vincent had now reached the height of his profession in Bermuda, I was a Cabinet Minister, and our brother, Philip Butterfield, was COO of the Bank of Bermuda and designated successor to CEO Henry Smith.

Some in Bermuda assumed the three of us must be cooperating secretly outside the bounds of our responsibilities and ethical conduct. That never occurred. Following our father's example, we made it very clear that each of us would do his job as he saw fit and that we would consult and work together only as our positions properly required. With that mutual understanding, we also shared a commitment to Bermuda's progress and did our best to support each other in our individual and joint efforts toward that goal.

Some who assumed we connived unethically behind the scenes were downright disappointed to find that we didn't. They couldn't understand why we didn't behave like the traditional old boys' network in Bermuda.

A revealing incident, which I heard about only after the fact, concerned the expansion of Trimingham's Department Store on Front Street into an adjoining building. BFS fire inspectors visited the combined spaces where holes had been cut in the walls to create passageways, and they found the work had been done without regard to fire safety codes. Alarms in the two original spaces had not been linked into a single system, and there was no plan for evacuating the combined space in an emergency.

Trimingham's executives were shocked when BFS denied the space a fire safety certificate, said the company would have to make a number of changes to obtain one; and warned that if it did not comply, the store would be shut down. This was very different for them.

One executive called Vincent and complained about all the money they'd spent on combining the spaces. Vincent responded that they should have consulted the BFS before they began the work. The executive then said, "Listen, we've never had a problem in the past getting what we need from the Fire Service."

Vincent said, "You're not a very observant person."

Incredulous, the executive asked, "What do you mean?"

Vincent said, "Be careful now. Things can change."

The head of the Trimingham family, which not only owned the store but had also founded and remained major shareholders of the Bank of Bermuda, then called Philip and said, "You need to tell your brother to back off."

Philip asked, "Which brother?"

"The Fire Chief."

"Why?"

After listening to the explanation, Philip said, "You need to make your case to the Fire Chief, and he will decide what action is appropriate."

"But—"

"No but. Regardless of how you are used to doing things, this is how it works where either of my brothers is concerned. We each deserve respect in our separate roles."

To comply with the requirements issued by the BFS, Bermuda Fire and Marine, which insured Trimingham's Department Store, brought in an expert consultant from the United States. The insurer and the store may have hoped the consultant would give them ammunition for challenging the BFS, but he told Vincent, "You've already gone easy on the store. In the United States they wouldn't have been able to open the doors. We would have shut them down."

This was by no means the last time my brothers and I were found insufficiently willing to go along to get along. From Henry Tucker on, UBP Governments had functioned as an extension of Bermuda's White business establishment. The PLP's efforts to govern on behalf of the whole country frustrated that establishment, which lashed out furiously at any opportunity.

IN 2002 BERMUDA HAD SOME 600 LICENSED TAXIS, plenty for the country's size and population. But as I mentioned earlier, they were seldom where they were needed when they were needed. The newly formed Bermuda Taxi Operators Association (BTOA) advised people in need of a taxi to call an hour and a half to two hours ahead—and the night before for service first thing in the morning. Bermuda needed taxi availability to be such that taxis arrived anywhere on the Island within fifteen minutes of a call, day or night.

The only viable solution was computerized central dispatch, but my proposals for this continued to meet opposition from a vocal segment of taxi operators, amplified by the UBP and the *Royal Gazette*. My attempts to reason with my opponents fell on deaf ears. They did not see that a central dispatch system with GPS was fast becoming the "new normal" around the world and would improve driver safety in the event of an accident or mugging (the proposed system included a "panic button").

The taxi operators opposed to centralized dispatch with GPS complained about two things: the cost of installing equipment for the system and its functioning as a "spy in the cab."

The equipment a taxi needed for centralized dispatch was reckoned to cost $1,500 to $2,000, but using it would enable the operator to cut expenses (such as gasoline consumption) and maximize profits. It would pay for itself over time. I was sympathetic to taxi operators' concerns about cost, however, and I explored ways to increase their revenue, such as allowing bigger taxis and shared rides with multiple fares from the airport, which would let operators collect a fare for each passenger drop-off. I also proposed a grace period of twelve months, later increased to eighteen months, for drivers to install the necessary equipment in their vehicles. There were already tax concessions for taxi operators, and the possibility existed for additional concessions. My door was always open to the taxi operators for any reasonable negotiation on implementing centralized dispatch. When a group of taxi drivers ages sixty-five and older had their health insurance canceled, I was the first to speak up on their behalf and urge my fellow Cabinet officers, the Finance Minister and Health Minister, to intercede for them.

The "spy in the cab" protests were fundamentally misguided, however. They seemed to emanate from a group of drivers who feared that GPS would expose that they were using their cabs to visit their girlfriends when their wives thought they were working, and/or that it would show TCD that their cabs were not in operation for the required sixteen hours a day.

From time to time I recalled that my UBP predecessor as Transport Minister, Erwin Adderley, had warned me against getting involved in Bermuda's taxi mess. But taxi licenses were a public franchise, and the taxi fleet was too big a part of our transport system to let go unmanaged and unimproved, as UBP Governments had for so long.

The unhappy taxi operators called for my head on a plate and petitioned the Premier to sack me from Cabinet. I was grateful for her support in response to those pleas and threats of strikes by the BTOA, which claimed to represent the majority of taxi operators. How many operators the BTOA represented was a question, however, because the threatened strikes never amounted to much and caused little disruption.

In a close vote at the beginning of June 2002, the House of Assembly passed the Motor Car Amendment Act, including computerized central taxi dispatch with GPS. Some fellow PLP MPs cast votes against the bill or abstained, rather than oppose friends and acquaintances among the taxi operators. I understood the MPs' decisions and held no grudges. The important thing was that the bill passed.

However, at the end of June the Senate rejected the bill, as too many PLP and Independent Senators voted in sympathy with taxi-operating friends. This meant I could not reintroduce the bill in that form for at least a year.

For the present, those taxi operators unwilling to modernize and their supporters had their way. They insisted that existing law, if enforced, was sufficient. So it was time for enforcement.

Lo and behold, the first steps toward enforcement—spot checks for two-way radios in taxis and requests for radio call records from taxi companies—triggered howls of protest. BTOA spokesman Lee Tucker claimed that requiring taxi operators to use their radios on picking up or dropping off passengers was a huge burden because they might miss a fare trying to reach dispatchers. He was apparently blind to the fact that this claim underlined the need for computerized central dispatch and the automated data collection it would enable. So it went, with the BTOA and the group of taxi operators it represented angry that I had taken them at their own word. They thought the Senate vote meant they had won the war, not the battle. However, I was still determined to clean up the taxi mess.

THE AIRPORT'S NEW GENERAL MANAGER, JIM HOWES, had only been on the job a few weeks when the International Air Transportation Association (IATA) announced that passengers rated the Bermuda airport number one among airports of similar size in North America, and number nine in the world, for staff courtesy and helpfulness over the prior year. Bermuda's category was airports with passenger volumes under 15 million a year, putting it up against 159 North American facilities and 701 worldwide.

This was an unprecedented honor for the Bermuda airport, and Jim was as delighted by it as I was. We agreed it called for recognition of the airport staff's excellent work and provided a unique opportunity for raising the bar even higher. We accordingly decided to hold an Airport Appreciation Day on July 24 on Clearwater Beach with team-building games and other activities. We invited everyone who worked at the airport and their families from flight agents and baggage handlers to weather station, fire, and police personnel. Around 1,000 people attended, and we provided soft drinks and food, musical entertainment by DJ Craig "Bubbles" Darrell, and beach towels, pins, and tee shirts emblazoned with the airport's logo and "Bermuda—Number One in Service."

The total cost was around $35,000, a reasonable sum by any normal human resources standard for the size of the airport and the number of attendees. Flushed with excitement and pride during the party, when a *Royal Gazette* reporter asked about the cost, I spoke off the cuff and said, "We scraped around in our budget and pulled together funds." My focus at that moment was emphasizing that we had done something out of the ordinary for airport employees, at least as far as Bermuda work culture was concerned, because they had achieved something extraordinary.

In the next day's *Royal Gazette* an article headlined "Minister spends $35,000 on staff thank you party" seized on my statement to suggest we might have misappropriated public funds. The following day another article raised the same question and, while acknowledging that the airport staff deserved recognition, argued that public employees should do their jobs well for their pay checks alone. This article also quoted UBP Opposition Leader Grant Gibbons and Shadow Transport Minister Erwin Adderley as saying the expense was excessive and should be looked at by Bermuda's Auditor General. Four days later an editorial headlined "Airport party" repeated these points, clinging to the hope that I had somehow done something illegal by spending money allocated for the airport on a team-building event for airport personnel.

The negative news coverage for what he thought was a normal organizational event, including an entertainer to rev up the group, flabbergasted Jim Howes. But the editorial really shocked him. Bermuda was being applauded on the world stage by an impartial third party in a way it had never achieved before. Yet instead of joining in to celebrate the achievement and the hardworking people responsible for it, the UBP and the *Royal Gazette* clutched at straws and imagined malfeasance where there was none.

Jim wrote a letter to the *Royal Gazette*, noting that "astute management in any large organization realizes that there is far more to motivating employees in the pursuit of excellence than a pay cheque alone" and that the Airport Appreciation Day was a cost-effective way of enhancing a great work ethic at the airport. He also explained that the $35,000 for the July 24 event had come out of the airport's promotions budget as had the cost of the airport's *Royal Gazette* advertisements trumpeting the IATA rankings. "Funny the editorial didn't mention the money spent on [the ads]," Jim wrote.

To its credit, the *Royal Gazette* devoted an August 8 article to Jim's letter and quoted extensively from it, including his comment on the ads in the paper. All it took was a simple explanation—by a White general manager!

The silver lining to the attacks on Airport Appreciation Day was that airport employees were delighted to see Jim Howes go to bat for them in public. Jim had already built the foundation of a good relationship with the staff. His letter to the *Royal Gazette* solidified the relationship because it too was unprecedented, as far as I am aware, for an expatriate manager in Bermuda.

Jim was proving his value to the airport and Bermuda's air service in myriad ways. In addition to his leadership skills and managerial acumen, he was ingenious at finding ways to upgrade the airport's amenities without big expenditures. For example, at the time of Airport Appreciation Day he had just brought the airport's Wi-Fi lounge into being, far ahead of most other airports in North America large and small. Over the course of his long career, he had earned a lot of trust and good will with key players in commercial aviation and he was putting all of it to work for Bermuda's benefit. We became an effective team in strategizing how to secure more and better air service for Bermuda, and in making presentations to airline decision makers.

Disappointed they could not pillory me for Airport Appreciation Day, in mid-August my critics took aim at Transport Ministry ads thanking Bermudians for flocking to the new fast ferries and urging those who had not yet tried them to do so. Although it was plainly in the public interest to push ferry use as an alternative to driving on Bermuda's congested roads, the critics said the ads were campaign ads in disguise. In reply I said, "Everything a sensible Government does should help them to be reelected."

A month later the target on my back was for the parties the Transport Ministry hosted for the public in connection with the launches of *Serenity* and

Resolute. I sensed a palpable air of frustration on the part of the UBP and the *Royal Gazette* when I explained that the money for the parties came appropriately from a $50,000-per-vessel promotional budget allocated by manufacturer Gladding-Hearn.

Refusing to be satisfied with this explanation, the Combined Opposition kept blowing smoke and looking for fire. They argued that I should have negotiated the price of each ferry down $50,000, and that Gladding-Hearn's promotional budget amounted to a discount that should have been paid back into the Government's general funds. They did not want to hear that as normal in such purchases, Gladding-Hearn would not discuss a promotional budget until we'd agreed on the price of the ferries or that the money was paying not only for parties to introduce the ferries to the public but also for print and television advertising with the same objective in Bermuda's interest.

As with Airport Appreciation Day, the facts spoiled the fantasies that I was the "Minister of Frivolous Parties" and that I was wasting the public's money. The facts never stopped the Opposition from spinning fantasies about me, however.

IN THE COURSE OF THESE DEVELOPMENTS, A DISSIDENT GROUP of PLP backbench MPs asked for a meeting of the party's MPs to discuss our progress under Jennifer Smith's leadership. On the evening of May 16, 2002, all but seven of the PLP's twenty-six MPs gathered at Sessions House. The absent MPs were off the Island or otherwise unable to attend.

We had been the governing party for three and a half years. Although Premier Smith was not tipping her hand on the date, she would have to call the next general election within a year and a half. Also on the horizon was the PLP's Party Conference in November, when both MPs and party delegates would vote on the Party's leadership.

With an eye on the general election and the party leadership vote, PLP backbencher Wayne Perinchief introduced a motion calling on Jennifer Smith, in the *Royal Gazette*'s words, "to jump ship before she was pushed." The dissident backbench MPs were upset with the Premier for being unavailable to them and not consulting or informing them about Government moves. They also said her leadership was becoming an electoral drawback for the PLP and an asset for the UBP.

The meeting reached an impasse after Education and Development Minister Paula Cox had left. The Premier refused to resign, and the 18 MPs still present voted on her leadership in a secret ballot that resulted in a 9–9 tie.

The issue subsided for most of the summer. But it rose up again in August, when the *Royal Gazette* reported, "Government backbenchers have issued a blunt warning to Premier Jennifer Smith—stand down or you will cost us the election. Wayne Perinchief said a leadership challenge was likely at the Progressive Labour Party Delegates Conference in November and urged the Premier to resign or spark a damaging coup. He warned potential challengers to start their campaigns now or suffer the fate of Arthur Hodgson, whose challenge by stealth failed two years ago."

The newspaper quoted PLP MP Elvin James as saying about the Premier, "I think at this point in time it's best she goes." And it wrote, "[Wayne Perinchief] said a new leader was needed to take Bermuda to another level on fundamental issues . . . He said Cabinet Ministers Dr. Ewart Brown, Alex Scott and Paula Cox had all shown promise." This made it necessary for me to announce that I would not be a candidate for Party Leader at the PLP's November conference.

In late August the Public Service Commission announced that Marc Telemaque, a young Black Bermudian lawyer and Bermuda Regiment captain who had just completed a tour as aide-de-camp to the Governor, would replace the retiring Herman Tucker as Permanent Secretary of the Transport Ministry. I had nothing to do with the appointment. Only the Premier has say over civil service appointments at this level, which are made by the Governor based on, but not subject to, recommendations by Bermuda's Public Service Commission.

Rumors beget rumors. The unfounded talk about me as a potential challenger to Premier Smith's leadership in November stimulated talk that she had persuaded Marc Telemaque to apply for the job of Transport Permanent Secretary, so he could keep an eye on me for her. I ignored the rumors, and Marc and I found we worked well together.

By the time the PLP held its annual Pre-Conference Policy Symposium in September, the political buzz said no one would challenge the Premier in November. This talk was largely the result of another August announcement: after nine months of work, Bermuda's latest and most controversial Boundaries Commission on electoral districts was ready to deliver its report. That in turn was going to trigger one of the most important debates and votes in the history of Bermuda's Parliament.

THE STORY OF THAT 2002 DEBATE AND VOTE goes back to the beginning of party politics in Bermuda. A founding goal of the PLP in 1963 was to achieve electoral reform on the principle of one person, one vote, each vote of equal value. I've discussed the battles to end "plus votes" for wealthy landowners and a number of other reforms achieved by Roosevelt Brown's Committee for Universal Adult Suffrage and the PLP, beginning with the Parliamentary Election

Act 1963, which brought universal suffrage, and the Parliamentary Election Act 1966, which abolished the plus vote.

What kept eluding the PLP and the majority of Bermuda's voters, however, thanks to the UBP's intransigence, was a fair electoral map with single-seat constituencies of as near as possible equal size. When the Bermuda Constitution was drafted at a 1966 conference in the United Kingdom, the hopelessly outnumbered PLP delegation tried and failed to achieve single-seat constituencies of equal size. Instead, with the approval of the Labour government then in power in the United Kingdom, the UBP got double-seat constituencies of very unequal size, with both the double seats and the unequal sizes giving White voters vastly disproportional sway over electoral results. This unjust system kept the UBP in power for more than thirty years.

The Labour government of Prime Minister Harold Wilson must have understood how it was helping the UBP, choosing to sustain White power rather than form common cause with its fellow labor party, the PLP. I mentioned that a Labour MP of that day questioned how democracy could advance in Bermuda under Henry Tucker, with his multiple conflicts of interest. No surprise, that MP was a backbencher, not a member of Wilson's cabinet.

After the 1978 Pitt Commission Report (see chapters 5 and 6) laid bare the continuing racism in Bermuda, the British convened our Second Constitutional Conference at Warwick Camp, Bermuda in 1979. To quote the PLP's official history, "No agreement could be reached on the adoption of a new, more equitable electoral system. . . . [But] it was decided that whichever party actually campaigned in the next general election or any general election on its preferred electoral system and won a majority of both the parliamentary seats and the popular vote in that election—then that party would be granted permission by the U.K. government to amend the Bermuda Constitution of 1968 accordingly; and thus introduce its preferred system."

In addition the British government decreed at Warwick Camp, and both the UBP and PLP accepted, that another constitutional conference would not be convened except in connection with Bermuda's becoming independent.

From 1979 to 1998 the UBP remained in power and used its control of government to preserve double-seat, unequally sized constituencies. The PLP always ran with a fair electoral system as a central plank of its campaign platforms, and finally in 1998 we won the government and the popular vote—and the opportunity to act on the Warwick Camp Agreement.

Although I thought we could have acted immediately on that basis alone, in the summer of 1999 a U.K. government White Paper, "Partnership for Progress and Posterity: Britain and the Overseas Territories," gave democratic progress a spur. The document had three remarkable features. First, it said Britain would grant independence "willingly" to any Overseas Territory that wanted it. Second, it emphasized the need for new human rights legislation, calling on Caribbean Overseas Territories to legalize homosexual acts between consenting adults in private, on the British Virgin Islands and Bermuda to ban corporal punishment from their justice systems, and on Bermuda to end capital punishment. Third, it asked Overseas Territories to propose amendments to their respective constitutions.

Implicit in the last regard was that the British government did not want the expense of overseeing and attending constitutional conferences; it wanted specific amendments to be put forward through the legislatures of the various Overseas Territories and then submitted to the Privy Council in London. Constitutional conferences were an exception, not the rule, when it came to amending the constitutions of the Overseas Territories.

To its credit, the last UBP Government—with the crucial help of a number of PLP MPs' votes, as I described earlier—had decriminalized homosexual acts between consenting adults in 1994.

In December 1999, PLP Development and Opportunity Minister Terry Lister tabled the Abolition of Capital and Corporal Punishment Act in the House of Assembly. The British government had warned in its White Paper that it would abolish these punishments by an act of parliament in Westminster if the Overseas Territories did not get them off their statute books themselves. Despite this, the UBP responded to the bill by saying that because the majority of Bermudians supported the death penalty, the matter should be put to a referendum. As Telecommunications Minister Renee Webb said in the House, if it had required a referendum to emancipate Black Bermudians, "we would still be slaves."

Later that month, the bill passed the House and Senate by narrow margins. A few PLP MPs and Senators abstained from the votes because of their constituents' support for the death penalty or because the bill as tabled lacked the option of a life sentence without parole.

As for referendums, they are unwieldy tools at best and vulnerable to being gamed by an unscrupulous government or the side with the most advertising dollars. They confer less, not more, political legitimacy on outcomes, because they attract fewer voters than general elections. Political scientists and constitutional scholars generally endorse referendums on constitutional issues only if the country's original constitution was subject to a referendum. The Bermuda Constitution had been drafted in secret and imposed without any public input, much less a referendum.

Under the first PLP government, however, the UBP called so often for referendums that it was virtually a reflex action. They also called for a constitutional conference, in hopes of diluting electoral reform. After agreeing to rules set when they had the upper hand and never questioned by them while they won a series of elections, the UBP, having lost in 1998, became obsessed with changing the rules.

In August and October of 2000, respectively, Premier Jennifer Smith tabled a paper outlining a process for achieving single-seat constituencies of as near as possible equal size and a motion asking the U.K. government to amend the Bermuda Constitution to enable this. In doing so she was not dictatorially or arrogantly imposing a process on Bermuda, as the UBP repeatedly claimed; she was following the British government's process as defined at Warwick Camp and agreed to there by both the UBP and the PLP.

Around 9:30 p.m. on December 1, 2000, Premier Jennifer Smith opened debate on the motion in the House of Assembly. Citing the election platform on which the PLP campaigned successfully in 1998, she explained that if the motion passed, a Boundaries Commission made up of two members from the Government, two members from the UBP, and two independent members chosen by the Governor would recommend 20 to 39 new single-seat constituencies after deliberations including public input through written and oral submissions as well as public forums; that the Boundaries Commission's report would undergo debate in the House; and that finally the commission's report, together with a report of the House debate, would go to the British government, which would determine any subsequent steps.

Equal numbers of PLP and UBP members made the proposed Boundaries Commission unprecedentedly bipartisan. As governing party the UBP consistently stacked commissions to reflect its majority in the House of Assembly and ensure that it was easy to outvote the PLP.

Equal representation on the Boundaries Commission and public input during its deliberations did not satisfy the UBP, however. It wanted a constitutional conference and a referendum. In calling for these measures, the UBP's MPs, beginning with Shadow Legislative Affairs Minister John Barritt, spoke as if they had never heard of the Warwick Camp Agreement. Even more amazing, they spoke as if they did not understand Bermuda's parliamentary system or its status as a British Overseas Territory.

Following Premier Smith's initial remarks, John Barritt said, "The PLP say they have got a mandate. What about the 46 percent who didn't vote PLP? Don't we have a mandate?"

The Parliamentary Procedures 101 answer was, and is, no; there is no mandate for the minority party in opposition. And with regard to Warwick Camp and electoral reform, there was especially no mandate for the Opposition.

Barritt also complained about the heavy hand of the British Foreign and Commonwealth Office (FCO), and he accused the PLP of instilling fear in UBP supporters.

I responded in the House to these remarks by noting that based on the lack of substance in them, John Barritt was apparently trying to buy time. Indeed that proved to be the case for all of the UBP's MPs, as they dragged out debate for hour after hour repeating the same irrelevant points and making the same baseless motions—irrelevant and baseless in light of Warwick Camp—for a constitutional conference and referendum. They knew they could not win a vote on these things, but they desperately hoped to prolong debate to the point of the House's adjournment.

As for the fear voiced by the UBP on behalf of itself and its supporters, I said I wondered if it was humanly possible to allay this fear because it was plainly racist at its root and expressed the Opposition's unwillingness to accept the results of the 1998 election. Urging the UBP to "embrace the inevitable" and "work together [with the PLP] for a brighter future," I said, "Discussion, yes. Openness, yes. Transparency, yes. Arguments, yes. But kowtowing to you, no. When people don't want the outcome, they argue against the process. The UBP benefited for years from gerrymandered seats."

Thanking John Barritt for pointing out the decisive role of the FCO, I said, "That's how it goes when you're a colony."

Around 10 a.m. on Saturday morning, after almost twenty-five hours, we were finally able to move to a vote on the motion for the Boundaries Commission, which we won on party lines. Frustrated its delaying tactics had not worked, the UBP blamed us for the length of the debate. Although the *Royal Gazette*'s article on this included rebuttals from the PLP, it mostly quoted the UBP, and the headline of "Opposition slams Government over late night debate" declared the newspaper's favoritism.

The Opposition vowed to fight on for a constitutional conference and referendum. As a purely partisan political position, that made sense. A constitutional conference was the best way to prevent or dilute electoral reform, and a referendum with the usual low voter turnout could bless the result and delay democratic progress by a generation.

A group including my aunt Gloria, who despite her disenchantment with her old party was susceptible to appeals to tradition, sprang up to help the UBP. The group called itself the Association for Due Process (ADP), but its intellectually threadbare attempt to wish the Warwick Camp Agreement out of existence made it an association for delaying progress.

In January 2001 Opposition Leader Pamela Gordon delivered an 8,500-signature petition for a constitutional conference and referendum to the British government, which by all accounts gave her a perfunctory welcome. In April an FCO team spent four days in Bermuda gathering views on the motion for a Boundaries Commission.

The weirdest vibe I have ever experienced in Bermuda was attending the FCO team's meeting at Government House with members of the ADP. It was like a scene out of a horror movie with a number of old, pale, gaunt White women sitting there looking angry and scared, and one establishment-loving Black woman, Aunt Gloria, standing up to speak for them.

The result of the team's visit was that the FCO recommended that the British government grant the motion via an Order in Council. The vehemence of the Opposition's complaints was such, however, that the FCO added that after the Boundaries Commission report was debated in the House of Assembly and a record of the debate sent to London, there should be a "cooling off" period before the British government decided on the next steps, if any, before changing the electoral system.

Black people around the world are all too familiar with "cooling off" periods before any step toward racial equality. What was more serious was that Tony Blair's Labour government said via the FCO that although the possibility was very unlikely, it would not rule out a constitutional conference or referendum. The official view in London was perhaps that White Bermudians would trust the proceedings more if they knew the British government was willing to consider a conference as a last resort. Instead the possibility of a constitutional conference, however slim, added fuel to the fire the UBP was stoking.

Black Bermudians are all too familiar with the fact that British governments, Conservative or Labour, give a high priority to not making White people in the Overseas Territories psychologically uncomfortable. In this case, whatever its intentions, the FCO's statements meant Bermuda had to endure almost two more years of false claims from the UBP about the conduct and constitutional basis of the Boundaries Commission. The British government's failure to loudly reaffirm the Warwick Camp Agreement undermined not only the PLP but the principles of representative democracy. However, as I said in the twenty-five-hour House debate, that's how it goes when you're a colony.

In July 2001 a High Court in London threw out the ADP's challenge to the Boundaries Commission motion and ordered the association to pay the British government's court costs. In August the U.K.'s Privy Council issued an Order in Council duly amending the Bermuda Constitution to enable the Boundaries Commission to proceed. And in November the Boundaries Commission formed with Attorney General Dame Lois Browne-Evans (she accepted a damehood in 1999) and Deputy Premier and Finance Minister Eugene Cox from the PLP, and MPs John Barritt and Pamela Gordon (Grant Gibbons had succeeded her as Opposition Leader) from the UBP. The Governor named Sir Frank Blackman of Barbados as chair of the commission (he had also been chair of the last previous Boundaries Commission in 1994) and retired British High Court judge Sir Brian Smedley as the commission's judicial member.

Over the nine months from December 2001 to August 2002 the Boundaries Commission fulfilled its charge, including ample provision for public input through written submissions and oral testimony in public meetings. The commission submitted its report to the Governor on August 30, and Premier Smith tabled it in a special session of the House of Assembly on September 6, calling for debate in another special session on October 11.

The report recommended 36 single-seat constituencies, with no more than 5 percent variation in size, and included a map of the new districts. According to a news article in the *Royal Gazette* of September 7, "Members of both sides predicted bipartisan support for the report." That made sense given that the Boundaries Commission was unanimous in its recommendations. Unanimous though it was on the number of House seats and their boundaries, however, the report contained what a *Royal Gazette* editorial the same day called an "admirable dissenting view from Opposition MP John Barritt."

John Barritt had no problem with the report's recommendations, which he endorsed. After the tabling of the report in the House he even said that everyone in the Boundaries Commission had gotten "a fair shake." The problem, he claimed, was that there could have been more public input and that the commission had refused to take up matters that were not part of its official charge, such as whether the House of Assembly should have an appointed speaker, whether voters should have to reregister in their new districts, or how future Boundaries Commissions should operate. And he expressed the UBP's desire for a constitutional conference and referendum.

The UBP, the ADP, and the *Royal Gazette*'s editorials immediately formed a chorus repeating these criticisms. The editorial calling the dissent admirable said, "It is to the eternal shame of the majority of the Commission that they shut the public out" and "The secrecy under which the system was born may taint it forever."

Strong words for weak arguments. Far from shutting the public out, the 2001–2002 Boundaries Commission was more open to public input than any similar process in Bermuda had ever been. All who made a modest effort to express their views were able to do so in writing or in person. Although the commission kept the confidence of those who addressed it in writing or orally and did not disclose the back-and-forth deliberations of its members, its report was completely transparent about its recommendations and the drawing of the proposed boundaries of the constituencies. It kept no explosive secret from public view.

Of course, a process may be better than what preceded it and still not be good enough. But the Boundaries Commission did an exemplary job of gathering public input, reaching agreement on the number of single-seat constituencies, and drawing their boundaries. The UBP, ADP, and the *Royal Gazette* wanted public input on the actual boundary lines, which was a recipe for never reaching agreement. In calling for such input, John Barritt himself warned against fiddling with the boundaries and said they couldn't be drawn any better or more fairly.

The call for reregistering voters was one of many signs that the Combined Opposition wanted to torpedo the new electoral system by any means, fair or foul. Voting registration hurdles limit voting by the less educated and less affluent. The powerful use them to keep those without power from exercising their political rights as citizens.

The demand for an appointed Speaker of the House was a manufactured controversy. The claim was that if as customary in democratic parliaments the world over, the Speaker was a majority party legislator who abstained from debate and only voted to settle ties, then his or her constituents would lose representation and not enjoy the benefits of one person, one vote, each vote of equal value. This argument ignored the reality of party politics. The Speaker's colleagues maintained their majority and could express the views and fight for the goals for which the voters in question had placed their ballots. The constituents who had successfully elected the person who became Speaker in no way lost the value of their votes.

It very quickly emerged that the public, even the UBP-supporting public at large in contrast to party functionaries, was quite happy with the proposals. On September 10 the *Royal Gazette* reported, under the headline "UBP pushed to drop calls for conference," that "an audience of over 100, most of them White and elderly" had "openly questioned the wisdom of the UBP's insistence on a constitutional conference before moving to a single-seat electoral system." According to the article, these core UBP voters recognized that the time had come to abandon double-seat constituencies and thought that the 36 single-seat constituencies and their boundaries were reasonable enough. Instead of fighting for a constitutional conference and referendum, they wanted the UBP to "focus on winning the next election."

On September 24 the *Royal Gazette* printed John Barritt's dissenting opinion in full with the apparent hope that it would spark outrage against the Boundaries Commission's recommendations. However, the newspaper ignored the most remarkable thing about the dissenting opinion, which was that the other UBP member of the commission, MP Pamela Gordon, had declined to sign it. This was unheard-of behavior for a UBP MP.

The next day, the *Royal Gazette* editorial "Changing the Constitution" said, "This is a case where the end does not justify the means, and the precedent set by the current Government for constitutional change is a dangerous one, because it would permit changes to all areas of the Constitution on, effectively, a simple majority decision of the House of Assembly." The statement ignored the facts that the Bermuda Constitution could only be changed by the British and that we were following a process approved by the British government and regularly used by it in amending the constitutions of the Overseas Territories. By the editorial's logic, racial equality and political justice did not justify following a constitutionally valid process.

On September 26, Tourism Minister David Allen died of abdominal cancer diagnosed only six weeks earlier. His passing at the age of fifty-nine was a significant loss for the PLP and Bermuda as well as those close to him personally. I consider it an honor to have known and worked with him, and I will always remember his enthusiastic dedication to social progress in Bermuda.

Politics won't allow for long mourning periods, however, and there was soon talk about who would succeed David as Minister of Tourism. On October 7 a *Royal Gazette* headline declared, "Webb, Brown front runners to take over Tourism." The Ministry of Tourism was traditionally one of the more sought-after Cabinet portfolios, and there was speculation both that it made a natural fit with Transport and that Premier Smith would not want me to have such an important dual role. On October 8 the Premier announced that Renee Webb was adding the Tourism portfolio to her duties as Minister of Telecommunications and E-Commerce; that Housing, formerly part of the Health and Human Services Ministry, was becoming a separate Ministry under Senator David Burch; and that Neletha Butterfield, a PLP backbench MP but not one of the dissident group, was becoming Minister without Portfolio.

It was no surprise when the October 11 debate in the House of Assembly featured UBP MPs repeating the "Changing the Constitution" editorial's absurd argument.

Premier Jennifer Smith opened the debate with an incisive speech. She rightly said, "With this move, the long-cherished dream of many Bermudians and certainly of the PLP, that of establishing a modernized and reformed electoral system predicated on the democratic ideal of 'one person, one vote, each vote of equal value' will become a reality. Every meeting day in this House is important, but today is historic. Our actions today can help to bring Bermuda's electoral system into the 21st century, and a quest begun 40 years ago can finally be concluded."

Opposition Leader Grant Gibbons asked, "How could anyone do otherwise" than support single-seat constituencies and votes of equal value? But this was just a prelude to arguing for a constitutional conference and a referendum. He also insisted, "From the beginning, the approach of the PLP has created anxiety and suspicion and polarization in the community, which would not have been necessary if it had been handled properly."

Speaking after Grant Gibbons, I said that as the manufacturers of the current unjust system, the UBP had no moral authority to question the introduction of democratic changes. I asked, "If your boot is on my neck, are you qualified to judge how your boot is removed?"

The debate went on for ten hours. The second to last member of the Government to speak was Attorney General Dame Lois Browne-Evans. She spoke for about an hour, and every minute was a gift to Bermuda. She gave the House and the many Bermudians listening on the radio a history lesson that had the authority of her lifetime's pursuit of justice and equality. She was disarmingly comical, deeply moving, and unmistakably direct in setting forth the facts. As the *Royal Gazette*'s Ayo Johnson put it, "she was in her element as the *griot* of the House of Assembly, holding court on her most passionate lifelong ambition for the country and frequently dissolving the entire House into paroxysms of laughter."

Describing entering the House as its youngest member in 1963, a distinction she still held, and being "even then known as a mouthy young person," Dame Lois recalled that colleagues warned this could get her thrown out of Parliament. "I have been here 37 years–40? Well, I haven't been thrown out yet and I hope I don't get thrown out."

She explained why the architects of the UBP "had a lot to live down," along with the British Labour government of the day, for quashing single-seat constituencies of equal size at the 1966 Constitutional Conference in London. At that time the UBP's Edward Richards argued that double-seat constituencies would foster racial harmony. Dame Lois said, "I certainly do not believe that that political chicanery has brought racial harmony to this country. The racial harmony that we do have has been brought by some other fights," especially "the integration of the schools." Unfortunately the UBP had only let integration start in the middle school years after racism had already poisoned young minds, rather than have "their little ones coming up [with] our littles ones, which is the best way to have started the process."

Noting that the PLP and Black Bermudians spent decades "in the wilderness" before nearing "the Promised Land" of electoral equality, she said, "It is now another century, 2002, and I hope the United Kingdom doesn't fail us again, before we can bring about equality of the vote."

In a rousing conclusion she fired a warning shot across the UBP's bow: "Some people are praying that we never win again. But, Mr. Speaker, it don't make any sense to pray for something that's not good. Lord punishes you"— she pointed at the Opposition benches—"for praying for something that's bad. But I can assure that whatever happens, Mr. Speaker, the PLP at the next election will be smiled on by God and they will win the next election. . . . Even in England they will hear the message."

After Dame Lois finished speaking to thunderous applause from the Government benches and chastened schoolboy clapping from the Opposition, former Premier and Opposition Leader Pamela Gordon rose to speak. The *Royal Gazette* described her "hard hitting, passionate speech" as "likely to be her swan song." Certainly it was difficult to imagine her standing for another election as a UBP MP when she said, "I could not comfortably in all my own morality support a call for a constitutional conference or a referendum." We on the Government benches applauded loudly while those on the Opposition benches sat in stunned dismay or looked daggers at their former leader.

Having read up on the constitutional conferences of 1966 and 1979, Ms. Gordon was forced by her own conscience to recognize that everything the PLP maintained about the Warwick Camp Agreement was true. Her speech exploded the UBP's flimflam and, in the *Royal Gazette*'s words, "transformed what would otherwise have been regarded as a foregone, predictable conclusion to a moral victory for the ruling party."

Premier Jennifer Smith then rounded off the debate with a straightforward dismantling of the UBP's arguments and a salute to Pamela Gordon for her integrity and courage in publicly breaking with UBP dogma. At last we were ready to vote.

The Government's motion to approve the Boundaries Commission report not only passed, it received unanimous support from both the PLP and the UBP.

The special session of the House concluded with a voice vote defeat of the UBP's motion for a constitutional conference and referendum. The defeat was assured by the PLP Government's majority, but Pamela Gordon's refusal to vote with her UBP colleagues made it extra sweet.

In that meeting of the House of Assembly, three gifted political leaders and wise women transcended party politics to mark a great advance for Bermuda. It was a triumph for Lois Browne-Evans and Jennifer Smith, and it was Pamela Gordon's finest hour. Dr. E. F. Gordon must have been smiling in heaven then.

The matter now moved into the British government's hands. By the end of November, the Foreign Office announced that there would be no constitutional conference or referendum and recommended an Order in Council to make the necessary changes to the Bermuda Constitution.

The UBP still hoped to dilute electoral reform by making it necessary for voters to reregister in their new districts. But on February 27, 2003, the British Foreign Office quashed this last vain hope and the Order in Council took effect.

The next election, which had to occur sometime that year, would be fought in single-seat constituencies. The sooner the better for the PLP, I thought, especially because Opposition Leader Grant Gibbons had stuck his foot in his mouth on February 24, saying in the House of Assembly that Bermudians had "voted with their hearts" in electing the PLP to Government in 1998. The next day he tried to walk the comment back by saying he understood that Bermudians had voted with their hearts and minds, while I stated in the House that when heart and mind were one, there was no shame in voting with the heart, and that it was a fundamental error to try to banish the heart from politics.

The sooner Premier Jennifer Smith called the election, the sooner she could tie Opposition Leader Gibbons's condescending remark to the UBP's efforts to undermine and dilute electoral reform. And the more the public and the PLP would see her as the champion who led the culminating battle for single-seat constituencies.

The glow of this political triumph had certainly surrounded her at the November 2002 PLP conference. That was why she and Deputy Premier Eugene Cox had run unopposed for reelection as Party Leader and Deputy Leader. Moreover, the PLP had set a new leadership term of four years rather than two.

At this juncture, Premier Smith might have used her enhanced prestige to begin mending ties with the dissident PLP MPs who called for her resignation in the summer of 2002. Instead she seemed to think she had beaten them for good and no longer had to worry about them. As far as both the PLP and the public were concerned, she withdrew back into her cocoon, squandering her political capital. This was a political mistake for which she would soon pay a price.

12. Election and Rebellion

D URING THE FIRST MONTHS OF 2003, Premier Smith may have hesitated to call an election because of controversy over the PLP Government's handling of the construction of a new senior secondary school building for the Berkeley Institute and allegations of misconduct at the Bermuda Housing Corporation (BHC). To fill in that context, I have to go back to events in 2001 and 2002.

After decades of neglect under UBP Governments, the Berkeley Institute desperately needed a new building to provide up-to-date facilities in the twenty-first century. The construction sparked controversy before it started. Given the size of the project, the largest construction firms on the Island, all White-owned, assumed that one of their number would win the contract. There was consternation throughout White establishment Bermuda, when in 2001 Cabinet awarded the job to Black-owned ProActive Management Systems rather than to White-owned Bermuda Tech.

Critics immediately clamored that Bermuda Tech had projected a cost of $65 million, compared to Pro-Active's $70 million. The claim was that the Government was putting taxpayers on the hook for $5 million more than necessary.

Cost projections for major projects must always be taken with a grain of salt. Cost overruns often occur, and the lowest bidder in a particular instance may or may not be able to complete the contract at the promised price. A government, corporation, or other entity deciding between competing bids must factor in its own best sense of what the project will cost and whether a contractor is deliberately bidding low and counting on approval for cost overruns to make up the difference. UBP Governments were no strangers to cost overruns on their projects.

Talk about the lower bid was also disingenuous for another reason: Bermuda Tech was said to be in very poor financial condition. Indeed the firm would go bust in 2002.

Both the Bermuda Tech and ProActive bids fell within the ballpark of what Works and Engineering projected as a best case. Whichever firm won the business, the Government had to be prepared for cost overruns while doing all it could to avoid and minimize them.

In March 2002, UBP Shadow Health and Family Services Minister Michael Dunkley alleged overbilling by contractors and possible kickbacks at the Bermuda Housing Corporation (BHC). The BHC was a quango (quasi-autonomous nongovernmental organization) established by the UBP Government in 1980 in response to persistent PLP calls for a public housing program. It was part of my Cabinet colleague Nelson Bascome's portfolio as Minister of Health and Family Services.

Responding to the UBP in the House of Assembly, Nelson noted that rumors of overbilling and self-dealing at the BHC dated back to its operation under UBP Governments. Although he omitted mentioning it in his speech, it was not rumor, but fact, that Leonard Gibbons, the last UBP Minister of Works and Engineering, had had his own outside firm broker the renting of space for Bermuda Government offices—a blatant, sustained conflict of interest.

Nelson informed the House that Bermuda's Auditor General, Larry Dennis, was already carrying out an audit of the BHC. Finally, Nelson mentioned two instances of impropriety that his team had recently identified and corrected, and pledged his and the PLP Government's commitment to cleaning up any further problems.

The BHC controversy typified how Bermuda's White establishment-controlled media dealt with alleged PLP scandals. On Fridays the weekly *Mid-Ocean News* trumpeted the latest allegations, and on succeeding days its sister publication, the *Royal Gazette*, echoed and amplified the charges. Although the *Royal Gazette*'s articles usually gave fairly equal space to both PLP and UBP politicians and supporters, most articles ended by quoting or paraphrasing someone on the UBP's side. This undermined the apparent balance of the articles and subtly endorsed the UBP version of events as correct.

Bermuda soon heard about payments of more than $800,000 over seven months to a painting contractor married to a friend of Premier Smith, allegedly almost $70,000 over three months to a gardener, and more than $480,000 over seven months to a carpentry and general construction firm. Echoing the *Mid-Ocean News*, the UBP began to describe the BHC as "Bermuda's Enron."

In the second week of March, Health Minister Bascome asked the Auditor General to expand his audit of the BHC and pledged that any wrongdoing would be dealt with "to the fullest extent of the law." Among the issues requiring investigation were a mortgage deal for BHC general manager Raymonde Dill's secretary; property officer Terrence Smith's running private companies from his BHC desk and asking contractors to work on his own house in exchange for being hired on BHC projects; and a planning inspector's doing unauthorized work on Mr. Smith's house. Both Mr. Dill and Mr. Smith were suspended with pay, as was Finance Manager Robert Clifford.

In April Auditor General Larry Dennis submitted his report to the Director of Public Prosecutions (DPP), who immediately forwarded it to the BPS for investigation. Late in May the Auditor General published the parts of his BHC audit that were not being investigated by the BPS. He expressed concern about more than $1 million in unsecured loans and "control failures" associated with the BHC's recent expansion of a program to prepare vacant and derelict buildings for occupancy. The expansion was much needed, and it fulfilled the PLP's 1998 campaign promise to put more energy and funding into the BHC in order to get disadvantaged Bermudians into decent housing.

Raymonde Dill and Terrence Smith lost their jobs in the summer. In September two financial fraud experts from Scotland Yard came to Bermuda to assist with the investigation by the BPS. The same month, Mr. Dill dragged my name into the BHC mess by contending that delays at the BHC's Southside project stemmed in large part from my withholding payment of $400,000 to contractor Bermuda Composite Construction (BCC), which was also building my house on A. P. Owen Road on the Island's South Shore. I immediately made known that I was withholding payment because of major quality issues on my house and overbilling of more than $200,000. I said that "it boggled the mind" to think I was therefore responsible for problems at Southside.

Mr. Dill also claimed that Housing Minister Bascome had ordered him to violate procedure by awarding an untendered $300,000 landscaping contract to Island Construction, one of BCC's unpaid subcontractors on my house. Nelson Bascome was flabbergasted, having no notion that the landscaping contract might violate procedure and having no wish to do so on anyone's account, least of all mine.

My opponents immediately began to twist Mr. Dill's strained assertion about BCC's work on my house into the claim that Bermuda's taxpayers funded a cost overrun on my house through the BHC. This was and is nonsense, but the allegation lives on to the present day.

Another controversy in September 2002 was my outsourcing vehicle emissions testing to Bermuda Emissions Control Ltd (BECL). I caught flak from the Bermuda Public Services Union because the function was being outsourced, and from the UBP because the contract was not tendered for bids from other providers.

A central feature of the UBP's caricature of the PLP was that we were hostage to Bermuda's unions. However, my approach was always to look for the best steward for a public initiative, whether it was a Government department, a quango, a union, or a private commercial enterprise.

As for not tendering the contract for multiple bids, there were no other providers in Bermuda at the time. The previous UBP Government had opened negotiations with BECL, and I saw no reason to end those negotiations simply because of party politics. It was one of many occasions on which my refusal to toe an ideological line and my focus on pragmatic outcomes baffled both the left and right in Bermuda.

The Berkeley construction was not an issue for me personally but for the PLP Government as a whole. Auditor General Larry Dennis submitted a seventeen-page report on the project, and in late November 2002 the *Royal Gazette* spun a long series of repetitive articles out of those pages. The report praised the accounting and payment processes on the project and found no corruption. But Auditor General Dennis questioned the legitimacy and security of ProActive's $6.8 million performance bond. He also questioned Works and Engineering's advances to ProActive, although he acknowledged that they were properly approved and made at 9 percent interest.

After being rejected by all of Bermuda's banks and insurance underwriters, ProActive had obtained the performance bond from Union Asset Holdings Limited (UAH), a wholly owned subsidiary of the BIU established expressly for this purpose. The Auditor General saw corner-cutting in the sequence of the bond's being signed after the PLP Government said it was awarding the contract to ProActive and eleven days before the BIU actually incorporated UAH. Works and Engineering Minister Alex Scott responded that the sequence by which the bond was obtained was not unheard of under UBP Governments, and that the Attorney General had okayed the arrangements.

The Auditor General's larger concern about the performance bond was whether the BIU would pay UAH's $6.8 million obligation if the bond was called. In his report he stated that he considered this "unlikely." And he wrote that he had unsuccessfully asked for, and still wanted to see, a receipt for the $700,000 bond premium ProActive had to pay UAH, for which Works and Engineering had reimbursed ProActive as a project expense, releasing that sum out of the total monies due to the builder over the course of construction.

As president of the BIU, Derrick Burgess was incensed and issued a press release attacking Mr. Dennis's questions about the bond and description of the BIU and UAH as racist. Derrick is a fighter, which together with his sharp intellect and other abilities meant that any PLP administration was stronger with him than without him. But he would be the first to admit that he sometimes spoke a little rashly.

Derrick also mistakenly asserted that Mr. Dennis had not pointed out similar problems on projects by UBP Governments. In response, Mr. Dennis pointed to his audits of the construction of Westgate Correctional Facility and CedarBridge Academy under UBP Governments. In the case of Westgate, he had brought to light a $2 million bailout of contractor Sealand Construction and the failure to secure a performance bond until the project was half done.

At CedarBridge Academy he had exposed a cost overrun of $11 million. And he said that he had written that the BIU was "unlikely" to meet the UAH's bond obligation simply because the union's subsidiary was incorporated on a limited liability basis. Yet in his capacity as BIU president Derrick had already written to inform the Auditor General that if the bond was called appropriately, the UAH would meet its obligation, and that ProActive had paid the bond premium.

The UBP, the *Royal Gazette*, and even PLP activist Rolfe Commissiong deplored the description of the Auditor General as racist and cited his audits on UBP Government projects. Nonetheless, I do not think Derrick was wrong to feel insulted by Mr. Dennis's saying it was "unlikely" that the BIU would meet the obligations of its limited liability subsidiary, UAH, without ever asking the BIU if it would do so. This was tantamount to saying that the performance bond was a scam, and, as far as Derrick was concerned, to saying that he was not as good as his word.

No one who knew and worked with Derrick could doubt that his word was truly his bond. And Derrick was surely right to feel that no White executive at the helm of a Bermuda enterprise as big as the BIU would ever have been subjected to such insinuations.

Before Parliament adjourned for the Christmas 2002 holiday, a bill passed for Bermuda to become an associate member of Caricom. And I summed up the increasing success of the first two fast ferries, *Serenity* and *Resolute*, and announced plans to buy two or three more of them.

In February 2003 I took up the cudgels on taxi service again, proposing that the Government might buy or subsidize the purchase of over a hundred taxi licenses held by operators seventy years old and older. In addition to being resistant to computer technology, the older operators tended to have their taxis on the road less than was desirable—or legally required. Transferring the licenses to younger people, with a suitable payment to the older operators, would alleviate both those problems. It was more than once suggested to me that the Government should get around taxi operators opposed to GPS by issuing a lot of new taxi licenses. I rejected that idea because I did not want to devalue the licenses and undermine the livelihoods of taxi operators. I wanted to enhance both as part of improving taxi service for Bermuda.

That month I made a rare speech for a PLP MP at the Hamilton Rotary, which regularly hosted speakers from the UBP. I used the occasion to repeat my concern about the increase in gang youth violence. I also addressed other negative societal trends in Bermuda, including what I felt was the BIU's tendency to call labor strikes before giving negotiation a full chance and Bermuda's growing number of "unemployables," especially among Black men. Bermuda was small enough, I said, that we could identify young people heading down the wrong path before it was too late, and our economy was healthy enough that we could still reverse the trends in Black male employment. But if we didn't soon "get down to brass tacks," we were putting all of Bermuda society at risk.

One measure the PLP Government wanted to take in this regard was to provide Bermuda's first unemployment insurance. The UBP and the *Royal Gazette* dismissed this proposal with classic "boot-strap" rhetoric.

Rolfe Commissiong was then organizing a Black Agenda 2003 discussion, and I returned to my Hamilton Rotary themes before a packed crowd of several hundred Black Bermudians at St. Paul's Centennial Hall. The Hamilton Rotarians had given me polite attention and mild approval for my analysis of societal dysfunction—at least the parts they heard as criticizing Black misbehavior. But the audience at St. Paul's reacted with enthusiasm born of bitter experience to my pointing out the racial inequities that were persisting and even worsening in Bermuda's Switzerland-of-the-Atlantic economy. They were struggling every day with the cultural damage wrought by the very different employment opportunities in that economy for Black women and Black men.

With regard to the hiring of Black women in lower-level administrative and clerical jobs and White Bermudians and expatriates in higher-level jobs, I quoted Malcom X: "You could put so much cream in your coffee that you forgot you had coffee." And with regard to the PLP Government, I urged the gathering, "Light a fire under me and my colleagues, because I believe that is one of the things that has been missing in the first five years of our 25-year term." They knew exactly what I meant by twenty-five years. It was going to take a lot longer than one five-year term for the PLP to redress the damage to Bermuda of forty years of UBP rule.

In April, I directed $200,000 in Transport Ministry funds to a purpose not specifically designated by the House of Assembly. Unlike Airport Appreciation Day the previous summer, however, this drew no protests of possible illegality from the Combined Opposition because the money went to emergency sewer system repair in St. George's Old Town, a World Heritage Site. The White Bermudian-controlled tourist businesses in St. George's were desperate for the repairs to be made after years of neglect under the UBP and the town corporation, because otherwise cruise ships would have no way of pumping out their waste and be unable to dock there. Without the money from Transport, Bermuda would have lost the entire cruise season.

The same month, the PLP Government called in Parliament for cultural links with Cuba. Remember, my paternal grandfather had come to Bermuda from Cuba, and many Black Bermudians had kinship ties there. My Cabinet colleagues and I saw cultural links with Cuba as going hand-in-hand with our associate membership in Caricom, and there was an opportunity for Bermuda to become something of a tourist gateway to Cuba. To help establish the relationship, I suggested we donate some of the old buses we were replacing to Cuba, which could make good use of them. That seemed much better than dumping them in the ocean off Bermuda's shores.

Unfortunately, our proposal became a political football throughout the rest of the year. It is absurd in hindsight, but the Combined Opposition acted as if we were proposing to establish a communist dictatorship in Bermuda.

As spring progressed, the question of when Premier Smith was going to call the election loomed larger in every political discussion. However, she continued to keep everyone guessing.

In addition to the election date, people wanted to know what the PLP platform was going to be. At the Black Agenda 2003 meeting, a young man asked me if independence remained a PLP goal and if it was necessary to educate Bermudians about independence first, as the party had said since the days of Freddie Wade. I answered that independence remained a fundamental PLP goal and that I no longer thought it was necessary to educate Bermudians about independence. After all, I said, there was no example in history "of a people who had a comprehensive educational programme to seek independence. Political independence is as natural as night follows day. And I don't believe for one minute that my people need any special preparation. I will never discuss the 'ifs' of independence, because I have studied lower animals and they want independence." There was no reaction to this, publicly or privately, from Premier Smith or her office.

Responding to media questions in May, I sent up another trial balloon by saying that four other Cabinet Ministers and I would probably push for independence as a plank in the PLP platform. Again the Premier and her office made no statements about independence or any other aspect of the prospective platform.

On May 9, 2003, the *Mid-Ocean News* spun out a total fantasy about changes in the PLP's leadership. According to this article and follow-up articles by the *Royal Gazette*, all citing unnamed "political insiders," Jennifer Smith was going to be eased out of her roles as Premier and Party Leader in favor of backbench MP Reginald Burrows, one of the most senior and widely admired members of the PLP. The basis for this assertion was that Premier Smith might be named in Queen Elizabeth II's birthday honors list on June 13, and that Reginald Burrows was going to receive the first Salute to Service Award of the Bermuda Health Foundation on June 14. Both papers cited polls showing that Premier Smith's personal approval rating had plummeted to a point even lower than that of Opposition Leader Grant Gibbons.

Along with my friend Murray Brown, my brothers Philip Butterfield and Vincent Hollinsid and I had established the Bermuda Health Foundation in 2001. The main purpose of the foundation was to raise scholarship funds for

Bermudians entering the health professions, and the Salute to Service Award provided an occasion for that. Our goal for the first event was to raise money for scholarships in nursing, because fewer than half of Bermuda's nurses were Bermudian.

The media speculation about Reginald Burrows was nonsense on many counts. The Queen had honored Premier John Swan in 1990 without his stepping down. And it was an insult to Reginald Burrows, not to mention the Bermuda Health Foundation, to suggest we were honoring him for partisan political reasons. In choosing the first recipient of the Salute to Service Award, we sought nominations from across Bermuda, including members of both the PLP and UBP. Reginald Burrows was a bipartisan choice. To top it off, he was not going to stand in the next general election.

(On the plus side, we raised a good deal of money for nursing scholarships at the black-tie dinner in his honor. To date the Bermuda Health Foundation has raised almost $450,000 for scholarships, and we have enjoyed seeing recipients return to Bermuda as doctors, dentists, nurses, and other healthcare professionals.)

With no word on the date of the election, I kept plugging away on Transport initiatives, including preparing to retable legislation for computerized dispatch with GPS in taxis. Not at all to my surprise, the *Royal Gazette* had amnesia on its editorial of twelve months earlier saying that if taxi service did not improve in a year, the Government should make GPS dispatch mandatory. For its part the UBP said that if it won the election, it would ban mandatory GPS.

At the end of the first week in June, the IATA honored the Bermuda airport for the second year in a row as number one in customer service and satisfaction. During that week U.S. Airways began regular service between Fort Lauderdale, Florida, and Bermuda.

Finally, on June 10, 2003, Premier Smith called a general election for July 24. The six weeks in between made for the longest campaign period in Bermuda. Day by day my Cabinet colleagues and I looked for some word from the Premier on the PLP election platform. In the normal course of events, drafts of the platform would already have been circulating for comment by party leaders inside and outside of Parliament.

At the Premier's direction, the PLP assigned me as a candidate to the new single-seat constituency of Warwick South Central. Like many in the PLP and others outside the UBP, I thought 36 constituencies were more than Bermuda needed and provided too many safe seats for both the PLP and the UBP. Nonetheless, the 36 single-seat constituencies were far better for the country than the 40 double-seat constituencies they replaced. For me personally, campaigning became easier because I had fewer doors to knock on in Warwick South Central and the district was pro-PLP.

I did not take the campaign lightly, however. In addition to personal canvassing, I ran a television ad, "Doc Delivers," paid for with campaign funds I had raised over the previous year and more. Although the PLP disbursed some campaign money, candidates shouldered most of the fund-raising burden for their campaigns.

One evening in mid-June, PLP Government Whip Ottie Simmons, Sr., one of the dissident MPs in 2002, asked me to come to his house. When I arrived I found four other 2002 dissidents were already there: Deputy Speaker Walter Lister, Derrick Burgess, Dale Butler, and Wayne Perinchief. So were Health Minister Nelson Bascome, MP Larry Lowe, and PLP candidate George Scott. They said they'd been meeting for weeks and their group also included Labour and Home Affairs Minister Terry Lister, Environment Minister Dennis Lister, and Youth and Sports Minister Randolph Horton.

The members of the group were determined that Jennifer Smith should not continue as Premier, and they asked me to join them. Assuming the PLP won the election, they were going to press for an immediate Government leadership vote by PLP MPs. The PLP's Constitution said the Party Leader should be Premier if we held a majority in the House of Assembly. But the Bermuda Constitution said only that the Governor should designate as Premier an MP who commanded majority support.

As I said earlier, by this point I was so frustrated by the Premier's leadership style that I could not see continuing to serve in her Cabinet. But after helping the PLP win the election, I was expecting to join the backbench, not an internal rebellion. Seeing the commitment to a change in Premier on the part of Ottie and the others, I decided to join them.

It may be difficult for some people to believe that I did not see myself as the next Premier. I didn't think this was my time.

All the polls indicated the popular vote was going to be close. Announcing our intentions before July 24 would have put the PLP at much greater risk of losing the election, betrayed the entire party going back to its founding members, and undermined the party's ability to continue working for racial and social progress. My dissident colleagues and I had no choice but to fight as hard as we could for a PLP victory, and then address the party's internal divisions. At that point we would announce our position.

In late June ongoing progress in Transport enabled me to announce the signing of a contract for two more fast ferries. Somewhat shorter and narrower than *Serenity* and *Resolute*, which each carried 210 seated passengers at speeds up to 23 knots, the new vessels would carry 170 seated passengers at speeds up to 34 knots. For cost-effective maintenance, however, the new fast ferries would have the same engines as the existing ones. The UBP responded that if elected to Government, they would cancel the contract. I was happy to inform them the deal was done and could not be revoked.

I was also able to announce the start of work on a TCD website by a young Black Bermudian, David Burt. Whenever I traveled, I always tried to meet Bermudian students, and I first met David on one of my trips to Washington, D.C. He was then a master's degree student at George Washington University (GWU), where he also did his bachelor's degree and was centrally involved in building the GWU website. He had recently come home to Bermuda, and I had encouraged him to bid on the TCD website. I also encouraged him to mentor other young Bermudians, and he was going to build the website with the assistance of a Black Bermudian teenager, Deon Seymour.

Voters knew this was not just an election move on my part. They saw that it was the latest of my continuing efforts to advance Bermudianization and improve TCD operations and service. But I make no apologies for the advantageous timing of the website announcement.

With regard to the timing of the election, the UBP charged that it was meant to postpone the tabling in Parliament of the Auditor General's Annual Report to the Governor, which this year included his special audits of BHC and the Berkeley construction. According to the UBP, Governor Sir John Vereker had shown Premier Smith the reports and she had then immediately called the election. Deputy Governor Tim Gurney immediately said this was not true, but that didn't stop the UBP's strained allegations of a cover-up.

On July 20, four days before the election, the Auditor General's report was leaked to the press. This blatant attempt to influence the election was almost certainly the action of a civil servant devoted to the UBP cause. Then and later, the PLP urged the Governor to investigate the leak, but nothing much was ever done about it.

In an editorial headlined "Out of Control," the *Royal Gazette* justifiably railed against the overbilling the Auditor General had identified at the BHC (not all the original allegations of overbilling turned out to be true). But the main detail it chose to highlight from the report had nothing to do with overbilling. Instead the newspaper fired away at me for the sale to BHC of a property my parents had given me, a two-family house on North Shore Road for which the BHC paid $602,000, including $152,000 in renovations to prepare it for occupancy by BHC clients. According to the Auditor General, I had failed to disclose my financial interest in the property and the BHC could not produce an outside appraisal for it.

The appraisal, or lack thereof, was outside my control. But I responded that it was common knowledge I was the seller—the property was in my name, not a shell company's—and that the price was a fair one. The sale had even been mentioned in a Cabinet meeting. What I had not done was enter the pending transaction in the House of Assembly's voluntary Register of Interests, which UBP and PLP MPs almost uniformly ignored.

Follow-up stories claimed that then-BHC general manager Raymonde Dill was coerced into buying the house by Health Minister Nelson Bascome and me. To his credit, Mr. Dill said this was not so. He told the media that he had twice turned down the house because it fronted right on North Shore Road and thus was not suitable for families with young children, but he eventually decided to buy it because BHC had plenty of people without children on its waiting list and the price was right. He also said he had indeed obtained an appraisal for the property.

Originally the BHC was just going to manage the property and pass along to me the rental income in excess of its costs. After it spent so much money on renovations, I decided it was better to sell the property outright. I could likely have obtained more from a private buyer, but reimbursing the BHC for its costs would have made that a wash.

About fifty-seven hours before the polls opened on Thursday, July 24, Premier Jennifer Smith released the PLP election platform. The *Royal Gazette* noted the platform's forty-four pages contained very little that was new. The Premier said that the PLP's 1998 election platform was really a two-term platform, and so the platform, which mainly summarized the work of the PLP Government over the previous five years, was all it needed to be. Among other things, this left independence on a back burner turned down very low.

The substance of the platform was one concern. Even more troubling for me and the dissident MPs I had so recently joined, however, was the lack of consultation and discussion before it was released to the media and the public. Notwithstanding that, the good of the PLP, and the good it hoped to do in Bermuda, demanded that we grit our teeth, smile, and keep fighting to win the election.

On July 23 the PLP held its final campaign rally at Bernard Park, with a crowd the *Royal Gazette* numbered in the thousands and an atmosphere it called "electric." The description in the same article of the final UBP press conference, on the steps of the House of Assembly, gave no sense of a crowd or indeed anyone at all in attendance except for the thirty-six UBP candidates.

The PLP rally celebrated the fact that this was the first election in Bermuda's history in which each person's vote was really worth the same as every other person's. To quote the *Royal Gazette*, when I asked if those present wanted to wake up after the election to a UBP Government, "The answer from gathered thousands was: 'No!'"

There were roars of approval, however, when I said, "We must not take a step back. We must not go back, we must go forward. Have you ever heard of any people on the planet who voted their way back onto the plantation? No? Then you do not want to be the first!"

In the end the PLP won a comfortable majority of seats, 22 to the UBP's 14. The popular vote was close, however, with 51.6 percent for the PLP and

48.4 percent for the UBP. Helping the UBP enormously on the popular vote was that 53 percent of White voters in the election were foreign-born, the payoff for its policy of filling as many jobs as possible from abroad when it held power. It continued to be the case that Black Bermudians voted for candidates from either party, depending on their personal preferences, but Whites voted almost exclusively for those from the UBP. The final vote tallies showed that if 80 votes in four constituencies had gone the UBP's way, the UBP would have returned to power.

Premier Smith was contesting a tough constituency where victories for either side tended to be very close. Her 8-vote victory over the UBP candidate fit that historical pattern. In contrast my constituency had become a PLP stronghold since I first beat Jack Sharpe.

After the polls closed that night, instead of going to PLP headquarters at Alaska Hall, I joined the other dissident MPs—Health Minister Nelson Bascome, Youth and Sports Minister Randy Horton, Environment Minister Dennis Lister, Labour and Home Affairs Minister Terry Lister, Deputy Speaker Walter Lister, Government Whip Ottie Simmons, and backbenchers Derrick Burgess, Dale Butler, Wayne Perinchief, and first-time MP George Scott—in a room at the Hamilton Princess Hotel. It was the first time the eleven of us were together as a dissident group.

We were in touch by telephone with Alaska Hall and we asked the Premier to meet us. She refused, but we knew from the reaction at the other end of the line that she and her supporters were shocked by what was happening.

I got on the phone a bit later and asked again for a meeting with the Premier. She apparently conferred with Lois Browne-Evans, and the message came back: "If you intend to be PLP MPs, you'd better come over to Alaska Hall now."

It was reminiscent of when Lois Browne-Evans expelled my cousin Gilbert Darrell from the PLP for challenging her leadership. That wasn't going to work now. The eleven of us at the Hamilton Princess were half of the PLP's new House of Assembly caucus and nearly half of the incumbent Cabinet Ministers.

We didn't go to Alaska Hall, and early Friday morning Premier Smith—she was Premier until the Governor said otherwise—named what the media called a "crisis Cabinet." She also called a PLP Special Delegates Conference for that evening at Devonshire Recreation Hall.

A bit later that morning, the Progressive Parliamentary Group of the PLP, as we called ourselves, met at the BIU. We were encouraged by that day's edition of the *Bermuda Sun*, which published a midweek poll showing that 60 percent of Bermudians thought Premier Smith should step down following the election. We agreed that we would all boycott the PLP delegates meeting, and we voted on who should be our group's nominee to replace the Premier.

The nod went to me by one or two votes, and I don't think Terry Lister ever forgave me for that.

I had not thought it was my time to vie for leadership and I was the last one to join the dissident group, yet I was now at its head. As happens in politics, the unexpected occurs, subsequent events gather momentum, and you have to sink or swim in a strengthening tide.

The other dissidents and I then went to Alaska Hall for a meeting of the twenty-two PLP MPs. A vote on whether Premier Smith should step down ended in a tie, and the stalemate continued.

That afternoon, Ottie Simmons read a statement to the press on behalf of the Progressive Parliamentary Group. The statement expressed our regret that our actions had become necessary, and it emphasized that choosing a Government Leader and choosing a Party Leader were two different things. The Bermuda Constitution required that the Premier have the support of the majority of the House of Assembly. It was up to the MPs in the majority party to select someone for the Governor's approval in that capacity.

On Friday evening the Special Delegates Conference ended only with the decision to meet again on Sunday evening. That the meeting failed to produce a collective statement of support for the Premier was telling. We in the Progressive Parliamentary Group would probably have attended Sunday's meeting in any case, but this gave us a strong sign that the delegates were no longer committed to Premier Smith as they once had been. Our hope now was that she would resign as both Premier and PLP Leader. The *Royal Gazette* quoted prominent local corporate lawyer Tim Marshall that we were playing "high stakes political poker," and so indeed we were.

Sunday evening, July 27, 2003, at the Devonshire Recreation Club was the most raucous and bitter political meeting I've ever attended. People were calling each other names and giving each other the finger from across the room. The Premier very reluctantly agreed to resign as Party Leader, but the atmosphere in the room grew even rougher. The group loyal to the Premier nominated Alex Scott as Party Leader, the Progressive Parliamentary Group nominated me, and the tension in the room kept increasing.

Both Alex and I addressed the meeting. For the past two days Premier Smith's loyalists and the UBP had been saying the rebel MPs were guilty of "misleading" the electorate because of our show of unity with the rest of the PLP during the campaign. In my remarks I used that term, because it was so much in the air, and I tried to explain to the PLP delegates why "we had to mislead you."

In hindsight "mislead" was inaccurate at best. We all fought the election as loyal members of the PLP, for the PLP, and by the PLP. In a parliamentary democracy, the vote is not for a person, as in U.S. presidential elections, but for a party. Lois Browne-Evans had lectured the House of Assembly about this nine months earlier in the ten-and-a-half-hour debate on single-seat constituencies. Rejecting the UBP's call for an appointed Speaker of the House, she said, "People kid themselves when they come out of the ballot box and announce that they voted for an individual" rather than a political party.

I made the same point in my speech, and I believe I got it across to many of those present. Quoting Dame Lois might have given everyone pause, but hindsight is 20-20 and some people will never agree that it was time for Jennifer Smith to step down for the good of the PLP and Bermuda.

The speeches by Alex and me only sharpened the tension in the room. The meeting was about three hours old with no resolution in sight. According to the *Royal Gazette*, what happened next was that Finance Minister and Deputy Premier Eugene Cox, "without prompting or any deal-making, asked for the microphone and told the conference that he was resigning his position as the party's deputy leader in the interest of party unity. A hush descended on the conference floor, then a standing ovation. Moments later, Ewart Brown, who had made a passionate speech in his bid for leader, said he was withdrawing his name from the contest, leaving Mr. Scott as the only contestant in the running."

That is almost how it happened, but not quite. Before Eugene asked for the microphone, he and I were sitting together off to the side of the room. His health had not been good for some time, and he said, "You know what, Doc? Now might be a time for me to step down and for you to be become the deputy."

I said, "Well, I'll tell you what. If you get Alex to agree to that, I'll do it. But if he reneges, we'll be right back where we are now."

Eugene went to the back of the room to confer with Alex. A few moments later he told me Alex had agreed. And then Eugene went to the microphone to withdraw his candidacy as Deputy Leader, and I followed by withdrawing my candidacy as Party Leader "in the interest of party unity." The room exploded with jubilation. People cried and laughed, they hugged each other.

Ten minutes later Alex Scott and I were outside addressing the media. They were stunned by the outcome. Instead of the blood on the floor the reporters were looking for, the PLP was singing in harmony and celebrating in unity.

On Monday, July 28, Jennifer Smith submitted her resignation as Premier to the Governor. When her resignation took effect on Tuesday, Alex Scott was sworn in as Premier. And on Wednesday the Governor swore in the new Cabinet. I retained the Transport portfolio and also became Deputy Premier. The rest of Premier Scott's Cabinet were Community Affairs and Sports Minister Dale Butler; Environment Minister Neletha Butterfield; Finance Minister Eugene Cox; Education Minister, Justice Minister, and Attorney General Paula Cox; Minister without Portfolio Ashfield DeVent; Labour and Home Affairs

Minister Randolph Horton; Works and Engineering Minister and Housing Minister Terry Lister; Health and Family Services Minister Patrice Parris; Legislative Affairs Minister Senator Michael Scott; and Tourism Minister and Telecommunications Minister Renee Webb.

After Jennifer Smith's resignations as Party Leader and Premier, some of her supporters portrayed the rebel MPs as male chauvinists who opposed her leadership on sexist grounds. As I have tried to show, I was happy to serve in her Cabinet until her leadership style became so problematic. And I think Premier Smith will always deserve a place of honor in the history of Bermuda and the PLP for two great victories: leading the party to its first general election win and achieving single-seat constituencies.

It is unfortunate that the PLP and the country could not have had a smoother transition of Premiers. But politics, like the rest of life, is often inconveniently messy. With the transition accomplished, I looked ahead, eager to contribute to Bermuda's further progress and happy to serve in Premier Scott's Cabinet.

13. Now or Never

I N EARLY SEPTEMBER 2003, BEFORE WANDA AND I LEFT for a brief vacation on Turks and Caicos, I announced that a joint Transport and Tourism delegation would begin meeting with airlines. We aimed to add two or three flights a year to Bermuda's air service.

No sooner had Wanda and I reached Turks and Caicos than Hurricane Fabian hit Bermuda. Forecast to miss the Island by 200 miles, the storm struck from the south on September 5 with 120-mile-per-hour winds. Sadly, a water surge killed four Bermudians crossing the causeway connecting St. George's and St. David's with the main island. Property and environmental damage included downed power lines and trees and torn-off roofs. Fabian was Bermuda's biggest hurricane since 1963 and the first to cause loss of life since 1926.

The Island came together in the wake of the storm. Radio broadcasts of names of the elderly and others most in need brought groups of volunteers to their assistance. Hotels sheltered those whose homes were wrecked. As Chief of the Bermuda Fire Service, my brother Vincent Hollinsid played a leading role in storm response. And my brother Philip Butterfield, COO of the Bank of Bermuda, and other banking leaders arranged emergency loans and deferred credit card payments for three months without interest.

Closed for three days, the causeway was not fully repaired until November. During that time, the fast ferries helped get Bermuda functioning again, which ended most of the UBP's claims that we did not need such advanced seaworthy vessels. The airport was ready to open as soon as the causeway could be used, thanks to the great work of general manager Jim Howes and the entire staff. Until Wanda and I could return, I kept in touch with the situation by phone and email.

Wanda and I repeatedly checked online for information. At one point Wanda said, "This must be horrible." She was reading a woman's report that her house was okay, but a lower-lying house across the street had waves crashing over it.

I looked at the story and said, "Honey, the lady is talking about your house."

"What?!"

Still new to Bermuda, Wanda didn't yet know all our neighbors' names. We arrived home to find that sea water had swept through Gombey House, covering the ground floor with mud and dead fish. We had to replace many things, including doors and windows, and couldn't live in the house for two weeks.

We were lucky the house kept its structural integrity. Our losses were small compared to the families of the four Bermudians who lost their lives and others whose homes and property were destroyed.

Throughout the rest of 2003 and beyond, Jim Howes and I worked with the Transport and Tourism departments to gain more flights for Bermuda. We lost flights along the way, but kept making net gains. New origin-and-destination data showed that Bermuda's air passengers were no longer overwhelmingly tourists, but one-third each tourists, foreign business travelers, and Bermudians.

October 2003 saw the launch of the TCD website. It was an immediate time-saver for Bermudians, and David Burt progressively added functionality.

At the end of October the Bank of Bermuda announced an agreement to be acquired by HSBC for $1.3 billion, or $45 a share, after which CEO Henry Smith would retire and my brother Philip would become CEO of HSBC's new subsidiary. I assumed the sale was a done deal as far as the major shareholders were concerned. Again, the Trimingham family, which had founded the bank and held an unknown number of shares through trust arrangements, wanted to cash out, especially in light of the precipitous decline of Trimingham's Department Stores.

The sale had internal business impetus, too. As part of HSBC, the Bank of Bermuda would be able to grow its business in and out of Bermuda more aggressively than it had recently been able to do. Some people saw the sale as a loss of independence. But the Island's business community enthusiastically endorsed it.

Over the next two and a half months Henry Smith and Philip held shareholder meetings about the proposed sale. Shareholders questioned the price per share, payouts to senior management for their stock options, and job losses. The Bank of Bermuda was one of the country's most important financial institutions, and these were appropriate questions.

In advance of the meetings the bank provided shareholders with information on every aspect of the sale, including Philip's qualifications for becoming CEO. Those very distinguished qualifications left no doubt that Bermuda was lucky to have him lead the Bank of Bermuda in its new incarnation.

At the last shareholder meeting, however, a White Bermudian woman said, "Mr. Smith, there is a question on the minds of many people in Bermuda, but some have been afraid to ask it. Many of us believe that the Government of Bermuda, the PLP, gave permission for this transaction so that Dr. Brown's brother could become CEO of the new bank. What can you tell us about that?"

Obviously shocked by the question, Henry Smith said, "It's been part of our succession plan for some time that Philip Butterfield would become CEO after me, and that is in no way dependent on the Government of the day." He asked Philip if he wanted to add anything.

Philip then stood up, looked directly at the questioner, and in a sober tone said, "This is truly a sad moment. You've chosen to negate my professional experience by suggesting that the only reason I'm going to be the new leader of this enterprise is because of familial connections. That is disgusting and unacceptable, and you should be ashamed. And I'm not going anywhere, so you should get used to that."

The next day a *Royal Gazette* reporter came to Philip's office and said, "I'm here to follow up on a question at the shareholder meeting last night."

Philip asked, "What question?"

"A woman asked about Government approval hinging on your becoming CEO. Your response has been described as aggressive and intimidating."

Philip said, "We recorded the meeting. I'm happy to have you sit in the conference room and listen to the recording. And then we can talk."

After listening to the recording, the reporter told Philip, "I don't see that anything you said was aggressive or intimidating. I'll tell the editor that."

An hour later the reporter returned and said, "The editor says he believes his source and not your recording."

Philip brought the reporter into his office, locked the door, asked for *Royal Gazette* editor William Zuill's direct phone number, and dialed it. When William Zuill answered, Philip said, "Bill, your reporter is in my office and is staying here until we have a conversation about this so-called story."

Bill Zuill said, "I have full confidence in my source."

"Your reporter has heard the recording, and there's no raised voice, no intimidation, no threat. So what is the story?"

"We're going to report what my source has told me."

Philip said, "The moment your paper hits the street with that story, I'm calling a press conference. I'm going to play the recording of the meeting. And I'm going to call you a motherfucking racist, and I'm going to call your source a motherfucking racist." He slammed the phone down.

Thirty seconds later the phone rang. It was Bill Zuill: "Phil, please, that's not necessary."

Philip said, "Bill, if you're going to publish an untruth, after your own reporter has verified it to be untrue, I have to respond appropriately."

The story never ran, which speaks for itself. On February 16, 2004, the sale received shareholder and regulatory approval. On February 18, the sale closed and Philip became HSBC Bermuda's CEO.

Before that happened, Bermuda lost a dedicated public servant when Finance Minister Eugene Cox, age seventy-five, died of cancer at the Lahey Clinic outside Boston on January 9, 2004. Premier Alex Scott soon named Eugene's daughter, Education Minister and Attorney General Paula Cox, as Bermuda's first woman Finance Minister. Terry Lister became Education Minister, Senator Larry Mussenden became Attorney General, and Ashfield DeVent replaced Terry as Works and Engineering Minister.

The next month Premier Scott called for a national discussion of independence. In March he appointed a PLP independence committee, and in December he formed a fourteen-member Bermuda Independence Commission chaired by Bishop Vernon Lambe, with the mandate of reporting on the costs and benefits of independence.

AT TRANSPORT IN 2004, WE CONTINUED TO WORK on improving Bermuda's transportation system. For buses, that included expanded service, new vehicles, plexiglass bus shelters to replace most of the old stone shelters, and in July groundbreaking on a new Hamilton bus terminal.

In late July my brother Philip was in his office when a colleague said, "Your nephews are here." Expecting to see Trey and Donovan, Philip went down the hall, where his colleague pointed out the window at the third and fourth fast ferries, the *Tempest* and the *Venturilla*, being delivered. To test their seaworthiness, they had shakedown cruises in Bermuda waters by Cup Match, and we christened them on August 6. They joined *Serenity* and *Resolute* on commuter runs between the west end of the Island and Hamilton, where car traffic was heaviest. To begin serving the east end of the Island with regular ferry service, I urged that the 2005 budget provide for a fifth fast ferry.

Taxi issues continued to be controversial, as Transport did the preparatory work for retabling GPS dispatch legislation in the House of Assembly. Taxi operators were pushing for a fare hike, and I proposed that a 20 percent increase be linked to service improvements.

My opponents never seemed to realize that I was seeking to enhance taxi service as part of updating Bermuda's entire transportation system. Again, taxi service was too important to remain hobbled by obsolete technology.

In a May 5, 2004, "Taxi Wars" editorial, the *Royal Gazette* still had amnesia about its May 2002 editorial saying Bermuda should make centralized GPS dispatch mandatory if service did not improve within a year. The new editorial said that if GPS dispatch was such a good idea, Government should let taxi companies adopt it or not in a free market. UBP MPs soon made the same argument in Parliament.

As the *Royal Gazette* and the UBP surely knew, the value of GPS dispatch depended on network effects. Unless almost all taxis used GPS, there would be little incentive for a taxi company, much less an individual owner-operator, to install the equipment. A voluntary system was doomed to failure.

After I retabled GPS legislation in mid-June, about a hundred owner-operators belonging to the BTOA pushed their way into the Cabinet Office. They battered on the doors of the room where Premier Alex Scott, Labour and Home Affairs Minister Randolph Horton, and I were holding a press conference about emergency transport measures in the event of a threatened strike. We finished the press conference, and then went outside to meet the protesters. A week later, a similarly sized protest occurred at the House of Assembly. The BTOA also protested along the road to the airport.

Despite the BTOA's protests, Bermuda kept moving. A shameful act occurred on the night of June 28, when someone torched the taxi belonging to my seventy-four-year-old first cousin, Vincent Simons, one of many drivers who served the public during the BTOA's strike.

The House of Assembly passed the GPS dispatch legislation on July 2, but the Senate killed it on July 14. If I waited a year and the bill passed the House a third time, the Senate could only delay its becoming law by a month. Nonetheless we went ahead with a 20 percent fare hike for taxis, as well as shared multiple-fare rides from the airport, with both becoming effective September 1. Likewise, despite poor taxi service at the Bermuda Music Festival in early October, Transport developed the 300/300 plan for the Island's 600 licensed taxis, offering a 50 percent equipment subsidy on the first 300 taxis to install GPS and a 25 percent subsidy on the remaining 300.

In the meantime Tourism Minister and Telecommunications Minister Renee Webb resigned from Cabinet on July 20, 2004. Rumor had it that her slamming of the door as she left the room could be felt throughout the building. In her public comments, she cited "irreconcilable differences" with Premier Scott and leveled charges of sexism at the Premier and the male members of the Cabinet and PLP backbench.

Wanda and I were on a vacation cruise in the Mediterranean, and Transport Permanent Secretary Marc Telemaque communicated that Premier Scott wanted to speak to me. The cruise ship was off Tunisia when the Premier called to offer me the Tourism portfolio. I was eager to see what synergies I could achieve for Bermuda as Minister of both Tourism and Transport, even though Premier Scott told the media my handling Tourism was "an interim move." The media echoed the general buzz that, like Jennifer Smith, the Premier did not want me to achieve too much success and advance my well-known ambition to lead the PLP and the nation.

In August 2004 the Bermuda Police announced that a two-year investigation had found no basis for criminal prosecution of alleged wrongdoing at the BHC. The investigation included a visit to Bermuda by two Scotland Yard fraud experts, a visit to London by two BPS detectives to consult those experts, and Police interviews of members of the PLP Government.

The investigators never asked to speak to me. That plainly indicated there was nothing wrong with my selling a house on North Shore Road to the BHC. However, the Combined Opposition kept charging that I'd ripped off taxpayers.

In a press conference I repeated the facts proving the sale of the property was aboveboard. I offered to buy the house back for the $602,000 the BHC paid to purchase and renovate it. In October, Colonel David Burch, then serving as deputy chairman of the BHC, declined my offer because the house's increasing value was well over that amount.

August also saw the PLP Government terminate ProActive Management's work on the new Berkeley secondary school. Delays and cost overruns continued to be a problem with ProActive's replacement, Somers Construction. But Somers was better capitalized and could roll with the punches common to such a big project.

I don't believe this decision invalidated the original choice of ProActive. Governments are made up of fallible human beings, and their decisions don't always work out. But that doesn't mean things couldn't have worked out better if, for example, a number of construction firms in Bermuda hadn't refused to work as subcontractors for ProActive, hampering its progress. Other adverse circumstances were also not inevitable. For example, I wish ProActive had maintained its relationship with a larger U.S. construction firm.

Serious problems of some kind were bound to occur because of the size of the project. But ProActive completed most of the construction, none of which had to be redone or modified. And it was not paid beyond the work it accomplished. But because ProActive was not able to increase the pace of work, Cabinet decided to bring in Somers. Again the true cost overrun and delays were not out of the ordinary for Bermuda or other jurisdictions.

AS SUMMER 2004 CLOSED, NEW TOURISM DIRECTOR CHERIE WHITTER and I announced a formula for improving tourism: more hotel beds, cheaper fares, more flights, more visitors, and a Bermuda which made them want to return. Making the formula deliver required hard work by everyone in the tourism industry and a change in attitude by the country as a whole. We had to stop taking Bermuda's tourist appeal for granted, and Bermudians had to stop equating service with servitude, one of the most pernicious legacies of slavery and racism.

In August I drew on Transport and Tourism expertise to propose a redevelopment of Hamilton's waterfront. The plan included moving the cargo docks from their Front Street location and creating an esplanade with offices, apartments, and shopping. John Swan praised the plan and suggested a casino as the centerpiece. I welcomed his suggestion. We needed to get the boredom out of Bermuda and be a destination for more than the "newly wed and nearly dead."

In September, BHCS unveiled an open magnetic resonance imaging (MRI) facility. Practice manager Kelley McKinney did a superb job on this project. Following the model of our mammography arrangements, our MRI scans would be read by Lahey Clinic's accredited radiologists.

We had chosen to install an open MRI to serve those who were too claustrophobic or obese for KEMH's closed MRI. I never imagined that enhancing Bermuda's medical infrastructure in this way would eventually become the pretext for a politically motivated attack on BHCS and me.

During her last year as Tourism Minister, Renee Webb had commissioned a study by American travel consultant Elliot Ettenberg. The Ettenberg Report recommended that tourism marketing continue to focus on the eastern United States, eastern Canada, and the United Kingdom.

I was convinced we had to cast our net wider. We might get more short-term bang for the buck in our traditional markets, but long-term growth needed high-spending tourists from the Midwest and West Coast, continental Europe, and emerging markets like China. Our success in gaining new flights for Bermuda made it feasible to market more widely.

Previous attempts to penetrate the European tourism market had faltered because of the lack of flights. European tourists would not put up with the inconvenience and cost of traveling via London, where British Airways milked its U.K.-Bermuda monopoly with exorbitant fares.

From the PLP backbench, Renee Webb criticized my abandoning the narrow focus of the Ettenberg Report. So did UBP Shadow Tourism Minister Kim Swan, who complained I was also ignoring a study of Bermuda's golf resources by the sports marketing giant IMG. The IMG report and golf tourism had my attention, however, as the first advertising on my watch showed.

Advertising was one area where Tourism could definitely improve. Arnold Worldwide had Bermuda's then $10 million-a-year account. Arnold's contract had another year to run. Its campaigns struck me as formulaic, but I wasn't ruling out continuing to work with them, if we could move the needle on visitor arrivals and spending per visitor.

For some time our tourism industry had wanted to attract more visitors from November to March by making it known as golf-and-spa season. To that end, in November 2004 we introduced a new television ad produced by Arnold with the tagline "Just a putt away." Running in the eastern United States and Canada, the ad showed golfers striking putts in winter-bound offices and homes with the balls rolling to Bermuda's sunny golf courses.

At the end of 2004 we also announced a new focus on African-American tourists. As I said on a number of occasions, money the world over had become younger, more diverse, and browner. To help attract newly affluent demographics as well as traditional luxury travelers, we hired African-American advertising entrepreneur Don Coleman as a consultant in January 2005.

There were going to be charges that Don Coleman was a friend of mine from Howard University and got PLP Government contracts because of that. In fact, he was a University of Michigan graduate who never attended Howard. About a year earlier he had visited Bermuda and been introduced to me though a Michigan classmate.

After attending the University of Michigan, where he played defensive end on the football team and excelled academically, Don Coleman had become a linebacker for the New Orleans Saints and New York Jets, earned an MBA, and gone into advertising. He quickly rose to senior vice president at Detroit's Campbell-Ewald agency and lead executive on the Chevrolet account. He then founded Don Coleman Advertising, which became GlobalHue. Through organic growth and acquisition, GlobalHue gained prominence in multicultural marketing, with a host of A-list corporate clients.

With the new year I announced ambitious Tourism goals:

- Increase annual air arrivals to 400,000 within three years
- Increase visitor satisfaction by 10 percent
- Increase per-capita visitor spending by 7 percent

The announcement noted that a new American Airlines flight to Miami would open up Bermuda for travelers from Los Angeles and the rest of the West Coast, as well as South America. A coming Northwest flight from Detroit would do the same for the Upper Midwest and Central Canada.

Tourism Ministers going back to the last UBP Governments had vainly tried to get a Miami flight. Bermudians bound for the Caribbean or Florida were sick and tired of having to go north to New York to get south.

My effort was failing, too, until I insisted on visiting American Airlines senior vice president Peter Dolara in his Coral Gables office. Peter said, "I'd like to give you the flight. But your passenger load is over 90 percent tourists, which means the planes will return to Miami empty."

"No, Peter, you have it wrong," I said. "Bermuda's air passenger profile has changed dramatically. When you look at total numbers, Bermuda's air passengers are about one-third tourists, one-third international business people, and one-third Bermudians."

I gave Peter the new origin-and-destination surveys. After follow-up discussions, we agreed that American would start a Miami-Bermuda flight with twice a week service in March 2005, increasing to five times a week in June. Bermuda had to furnish a $1.5 million revenue guarantee for 2005 by putting that sum in escrow and paying it to American depending on passenger loads.

Escrowed revenue guarantees were a painful necessity for gaining most new flights. Of a potential $820,000 in 2004 airline guarantees, we had to pay out $529,000 for shortfalls on a U.S. Airways flight from Fort Lauderdale and a United flight from Chicago. The Fort Lauderdale flight had since been canceled.

In 2005 Bermuda had to guarantee $200,000 for United's Chicago flight, up to $300,000 for prospective European flights, and $1.5 million for American's Miami flight. Early in the year we asked Bermuda's hotel industry and international business community for contributions to a $3 million airline revenue guarantee fund. The additional $1 million was to be a reserve for any additional flights we were able to secure. The hotel industry recognized the benefit of this and contributed to the fund, as it had in 2004, thanks in no small part to the leadership of Bermuda Alliance for Tourism chair Mike Winfield.

No matter where the escrowed revenue guarantees came from, we wanted to avoid paying them. We preferred to spend money promoting Bermuda in our target markets. If the promotions succeeded, the Island would enjoy a substantial return in tourist spending.

To support American's new flight, I asked GlobalHue to do a promotion campaign in the Miami area. This was a test case of the firm's capabilities for Bermuda. The results, including a sponsorship deal with the Miami Heat, exceeded expectations. The Miami flight became one of American Airlines' most successful start-up flights, with passenger loads typically over 75 percent. Thanks to GlobalHue, Bermuda never had to pay revenue guarantees on the Miami flight. But we had to pay them on United's Chicago flight and a few others.

The *Royal Gazette* editorialized that "the Ministry of Tourism risks losing its focus by widening its marketing efforts." But the newspaper also said our new goals "made sense." It was a welcome departure from the newspaper's usual attitude to my initiatives.

In the first week of February I went to Jamaica for a China-Caribbean Trade and Economic Forum. There I learned what Bermuda had to do to become an "approved tourist destination" for China's rapidly expanding new affluent class.

At Premier Scott's request I also worked to revive Bermuda's African Diaspora Heritage Trail, a signature project of David Allen's as Minister of Tourism. I agreed the African Diaspora Heritage Trail had an important role to play in bringing visitors to Bermuda and should link with UNESCO's multinational Slave Route Project.

At an African tourism summit in Lusaka, Zambia, I met the tourism ministers of Zambia, Angola, Tanzania, and Uganda, and invited them to attend a planning conference in September for Bermuda's second African Diaspora Heritage Trail Conference in 2006. The first conference in 2002 had set a much-needed precedent as Bermuda's first major effort to appeal to Black tourists, especially African-Americans. There'd been no follow-up since David Allen's death.

I was putting a lot more Tourism irons in the fire without much increase in budget. Instead we shifted resources where they could do the most good. A key budget issue was Tourism's five North American sales offices in North America, set up under UBP Governments, which cost a lot of money to maintain. When I visited these offices, I was appalled at the lack of energy in them. Even more shocking was hearing employees say, "Minister, our job is not selling, it is educating people about Bermuda."

That had to change. I announced that we would close our sales offices in Toronto, Boston, Chicago, and Atlanta as the office leases expired. The employees would work from home offices and would have the sales quotas they should always have had. We would keep an office in New York City, but seek a cheaper location for it.

Tourism and Transport cost-cutting generated enough savings for a fifth fast ferry, our largest. A small team in Transport led by consultant Larry Jacobs worked up specifications for a catamaran that would withstand winter storms and carry 300 seated passengers. In late February, following the annual budget debate, the team began looking for the right company to build the boat.

Closing ineffective sales offices was financially prudent and part of a larger message. We had to work smarter and harder to revitalize our tourism industry. Despite the decline in tourism, the attitude persisted that high-spending tourists would always come to Bermuda. Yet by any objective measure Bermuda's appeal had waned a great deal, especially in comparison to what was on offer elsewhere. This included the physical amenities and service levels of our hotels and resorts. As Minister of Tourism and Transport, I continued to beat the drum on distinguishing between service and servitude.

To encourage Bermudians, whether living abroad or on the Island, to help boost tourism, in March 2005 we announced the Points of Light program. It offered cash awards to anyone who helped bring groups of 25 or more people to the Island. The program had some initial success, but it could not flourish without hardworking salespeople rather than "educators."

That month I also tried to broaden Hamilton's tourist venues. Court Street in Back o' Town had a block of historic buildings that bore comparison to the French Quarter in New Orleans. The Spinning Wheel Entertainment Complex already attracted locals. Why shouldn't it draw tourists bored with Front Street's offerings?

We provided free paint to the area's business owners so they could spruce up its looks. The change was a dramatic improvement. To counter fears of crime, the Bermuda Police Service briefly assigned officers on bicycles. However, the larger community did not cooperate. Front Street merchants and taxi drivers still warned tourists against venturing to Back o' Town. The French Quarter in New Orleans is a high street-crime area, but many adventurous visitors go there.

A surprising vote of confidence in Bermuda's ability to appeal to more than "the newly wed and nearly dead" came from the retailer Old Navy. Its spring 2005 promotion centered around fashion-forward updates of Bermuda shorts. The advertising showed Bermuda could be repositioned in consumers' minds, if we evolved our tourist offerings.

Randy Brangman replaced the retiring Kevin Monkman as director of TCD in March. An up-by-his-bootstraps success, Randy had first gone to work for the Transport Department as a mechanic and risen from job to job. I was proud to see Bermudianization continue with well-qualified appointees like Randy.

ON APRIL 1, 2005, THE *MID-OCEAN NEWS* and the *Royal Gazette* initiated a new tag-team attack on me. Although the facts should have made this at most a malicious April Fools hoax, the Combined Opposition wasn't fooling. Following the sister newspapers' pattern, the *Mid-Ocean News* sucker punched me with an error-filled article claiming a 2002 campaign fundraising lunch in Washington, D.C., was an example of "pay-to-play" corruption. The *Royal Gazette* piled on with a pretense of impartiality, acting as a megaphone for misplaced outrage from the UBP.

According to a 2010 PricewaterhouseCoopers white paper, "'Pay to play' is . . . making campaign contributions and related payments to elected officials . . . to influence the awarding of lucrative contracts for the management of public pension plan assets and similar government investment accounts." For pay to play to occur, the elected official has to be someone who can, directly or indirectly, decide who will receive contracts for managing government investments. In 2002 I had no such power, direct or indirect. Nor was I likely to acquire it in the next general election. The 2003 election left this authority in the Ministry of Finance where it had always been.

Ministerial prerogatives were jealously guarded in the Cabinets of Premier Smith and Premier Scott. No Cabinet Minister could meddle in the portfolio of another Minister. As everyone conversant with Bermuda's politics knew, then Finance Minister Eugene Cox, a man of very strong will, was in a different camp of the PLP from me.

In March 2002 Tina Byles Poitevien (she is now Tina Byles Williams) hosted a $2,500 a plate fundraising lunch for me in Washington, D.C. The CEO of Fiduciary Investment Solutions (FIS), a Philadelphia firm, Tina had in late 1999 won an investment advisory contract for the Bermuda government pension fund from the Finance Ministry.

The *Mid-Ocean News* insinuated that Tina got the 1999 contract because of her friendship with Thaddeus Fletcher, a friend of mine. My future wife, Wanda, knew Tina from Wall Street. But in 1999, Wanda and I had not begun our relationship, I did not know Tina, and Thaddeus Fletcher was not doing business in Bermuda.

Among the *Mid-Ocean News* errors was the claim that FIS received twice as much for its work on Bermuda's then $1 billion Government pension fund as it did on Philadelphia's $4 billion fund. Bermuda was paying much less than the newspaper claimed and much less than Philadelphia. The fee structure was well within industry parameters. Moreover, FIS produced Bermuda's best-ever pension fund returns.

The luncheon guests were other African-American financial services professionals who wanted to support progressive Black change agents. The guests knew I had no influence over management decisions for Bermuda's pension fund or any other Government investment account.

I used the contributions from this lunch for my "Doc Delivers" television ad and other campaign expenses in the 2003 election. It is interesting that the pay-to-play allegations came up almost two years later. In April 2005 I had been Tourism as well as Transport Minister for nine months and I was committing the unforgivable act of succeeding in both roles.

A secondary target of the spring 2005 articles in the *Mid-Ocean News* and the *Royal Gazette* was Calvin White, chairman of Bermuda's Public Funds Investment Committee (PFIC). He had invited several other investment managers to a PLP golf fundraiser.

In the House, Opposition Leader Grant Gibbons called for FIS to lose the remaining term of its consulting contract, which again dated from late 1999, more than two years before the lunch. He also called for Calvin White to lose his post as chair of the PFIC. And he wanted me sacked from the Government.

When Premier Alex Scott did not fulfill these demands, Grant Gibbons called him "a political eunuch" in the House. The insult reeked of slavery and racism.

Showing testicular fortitude, the Premier said the Gibbons Company had sold cars and other products and services, including insurance, to UBP Government entities. He asked if Bermuda was to believe the company never contributed to the UBP. The Premier also expressed confidence that the Finance Ministry had been well stewarded by Eugene Cox and was in good hands with Paula Cox.

I stood up in the House and said Dr. Gibbons had dragged Bermuda's politics to a new low. I urged UBP MPs, who claimed high standards for their party, to call on Dr. Gibbons to resign as UBP Leader.

Finance Minister Paula Cox commissioned an outside review of the pension fund. The review confirmed the fund's good governance as well as FIS's stellar returns. The newspapers' error-filled sources turned out to be disgruntled FIS employees in Philadelphia. Emails showed that erroneous information reached the newspapers via David Bolden, co-owner with his Bermudian wife, Antoinette, of businesses offering financial services. Tina Byles Williams had declined to include them among the firms handling parts of the Government pension fund. "Follow the money," the saying goes. Sometimes you have to follow the trail of those disappointed at not getting any money.

As THE COMBINED OPPOSITION TRUMPED UP PAY-TO-PLAY CHARGES, I worked on Tourism and Transport goals. In May 2005 we renewed Jim Howes's contract as airport general manager for another two years, during which he would mentor Black Bermudian Aaron Adderley as general manager designate.

At the beginning of June, the *Royal Gazette* editorialized, "Set tourism free." The newspaper urged me to support a tourism authority quango, echoing UBP calls in both the House and Senate. Although the editorial acknowledged the progress I was making as Tourism Minister, it argued for "freeing tourism from the political shackles that it has been locked in for decades."

Those decades were mainly ones of UBP Government. After the 1998 election, the UBP had murmured about a tourism authority. But in mid-2005 they cranked up the volume. The clear implication was that the Combined Opposition really wanted to set tourism free from me. I was not opposed to a tourism authority on principle, but I also did not think it was a silver bullet. In any case, the time for such a change was not while the Tourism Ministry was gaining significant traction.

A bit later in June the Queen's Birthday Honours List for 2005 included the damehood for Jennifer Smith some had predicted for 2003. Although British honors for Bermudians have never been my ideal seal of approval, given our colonial history, I do not begrudge anyone their enjoyment of them. That year I was happy to see the pleasure two of my boyhood idols, my uncle Bert and Dennis Wainwright, took in being named OBE, Officer of the Order of the British Empire, for their contributions to Bermuda.

Also in June the Tourism Department introduced "Pop-By" flags as part of a "Pop and Sizzle" campaign. The idea was that Bermudians could take the brightly colored Pop-By flags with them on their regular routines, signaling willingness to talk to tourists. We distributed the flags to schools in keeping with the bipartisan consensus that Bermuda's schoolchildren should help make the Island tourist-friendly. UBP Shadow Tourism Minister David Dodwell frequently emphasized this idea.

However, the leading private schools on the Island—all with predominantly White student bodies—called the flags a danger to their students who might run afoul of predatory adults. In my immediate response, I charged a "deliberate campaign of destruction."

I appreciated, and shared, concern for the well-being of schoolchildren. But I never imagined students should use the Pop-By flags without guidance from parents and teachers. Like many other good ideas, the Pop-By flags were torpedoed by the Combined Opposition. However, at the end of June we went ahead with the first annual National Tourism Student Debate.

As July began I spoke in the House about the UBP's responsibility to acknowledge that it and its members were beneficiaries of the plantation system rather than treat festering wounds of slavery and racism with "Band-Aids and perfume." The Combined Opposition said I was playing the race card and should shut up.

That same month the retabled taxi GPS legislation passed the House of Assembly by 3 votes. The Senate could only delay the bill's going to the Governor to be signed into law by one month. The BTOA grudgingly accepted the outcome and gave itself a shot in the arm by hiring Julian Hall as an advisor.

Before July ended I was in Washington, D.C., summoning my old cricket bowling skills to throw the first pitch at a Nationals game to promote Bermuda tourism. April-June visitors were up 5.5 percent over the second quarter of 2004. American's Miami flight had just gone to five times a week with passenger loads averaging 78 percent. A new head of sales, Glen Bean, was energizing our remaining North American sales office in New York. In addition we terminated an expensive marketing contract in London and hired a British public relations firm, which was more cost effective.

Grant Gibbons vented the UBP's frustration with my tourism progress by slamming Andre Curtis's appointment as chair of the Tourism Board, because a bankrupt construction firm in which he'd been a partner owed around $500,000 in payroll and pension taxes. The Tourism Board was largely a talking group, but it was a statutory entity set up under UBP Government. We had to maintain it or vote it out of existence.

In September the Government published the Bermuda Independence Commission (BIC) report, which detailed the costs, benefits, and misconceptions associated with independence. It found that Bermuda could well afford independence at a cost of "$5.3 to 14.7 million, depending on an independent Bermuda's ... policy" on international representation.

A few days later former Premier John Swan demonstrated that he had not "gone PLP" in a speech at Hamilton Rotary. He said construction problems at Berkeley's new senior secondary school and the low-income housing project at Southside did not "inspire confidence that this Government can take us to independence in a judicious ... way." He also said, "The PLP has failed and the UBP has not changed. Therefore the country remains divided."

I didn't agree on the failure. However, I understood former Premier Swan was mainly speaking to his own party. He apparently hoped dollops of criticism of the PLP would help the medicine go down with the UBP.

As 2005 drew to a close I signed the contract for our fifth fast ferry, the largest yet. I pointed out that much of Bermuda's hotel product looked shabby compared to our competition in the Caribbean and elsewhere. An angry backlash grew muted, when the chief visiting judge at Bermuda's dog show coincidentally complained about the shabby state of his hotel room and the show moved him to a new hotel.

In November the Tourism Department put Bermuda's now $13 million advertising account out for bids. Arnold Worldwide declined to participate, citing a $90 million account from candy giant Hershey as the reason it no longer wanted our account. Several leading agencies bid for the business, including GlobalHue.

Toward the end of November UBP Shadow Minister of Labour, Home Affairs and Public Safety Maxwell Burgess said that the delays and cost overruns on the Berkeley construction were "nothing short of criminal" and that the PLP Government should call a general election. His UBP colleagues claimed that the project was 70 percent over budget and that this was a dismal new record for Bermuda. The *Royal Gazette* echoed them by typically describing the project as "heavily delayed [and] massively over-budget."

ProActive, which began construction in 2001, had completed 80 percent of the original contract in August 2004, when the PLP Government replaced it with Somers Construction. Somers had completed the remaining 20 percent of the original contract, and the building was basically finished. However, considerable work remained to ready the building and its surrounding campus for teachers and students.

Senator David Burch was back in the Government as Minister of Works, Engineering, and Housing. In November 2005, he noted that the total cost of the project had risen from the final pre-construction budget of $71.5 million to almost $122 million. But $27 million was for work commissioned later, including a sewage-pumping station, a dedicated electrical feed, additional land purchases, and landscaping. As far as the initial contract was concerned, the cost overrun was $23 million or—final cost minus budgeted amount, divided by budgeted amount, times one hundred—32 percent, not 70 percent.

A cost overrun of 32 percent is significant, but UBP projects had incurred similar and even greater overruns. The Ministry of Works, Engineering, and Housing was hoping to hand the new senior secondary school to the Ministry of Education in January 2006. That date would have to slide back to September 2006, as we'll see, for a total delay of three years. Again, that is significant, but not out of the ordinary for major public works projects.

AT THE START OF 2006 *EBONY* DESCRIBED BERMUDA as the ideal winter getaway. I said we would mount faith-based tourism marketing and increase efforts to bring major events to Bermuda. At the end of January JetBlue announced twice-daily service from New York in May.

I had been courting JetBlue since 2002, redoubling my efforts with the addition of the Tourism portfolio in 2004. It is astonishing in hindsight, but in early 2006 there were still those in Bermuda's tourism industry, and even the Tourism Department, who questioned whether a budget airline like JetBlue would bring high-spending tourists. They seemed unable to grasp that people don't become and remain affluent by wasting money and that one airline seat is as good as another on relatively short flights like those from the eastern United States to Bermuda. They also missed the high-value profile JetBlue had achieved in the minds of U.S. consumers.

After JetBlue's announcement, Continental and American said they would lower their fares to Bermuda in May. Knowing JetBlue's service would raise awareness of Bermuda as a tourist destination, United said it would add a Washington, D.C.–Bermuda flight.

There were also important developments on the hotel front. Saudi Arabia's Prince Alwaleed bin Talal Alsaud was buying the global Fairmont Hotels group for $3.9 billion. The purchase included Bermuda's Fairmont Hamilton Princess hotel and Fairmont Southampton resort.

Unfortunately the Government was forced to terminate an exclusive two-year window for the Renaissance Consortium to redevelop the abandoned Club Med overlooking St. George's. The site's history as a hotel location began in 1973 with a Holiday Inn, which successively became a Loew's Inn and Club Med. Each venture failed because its midmarket brand appeal didn't fit Bermuda's upscale image and costs.

Renaissance Consortium head Wanda DeRosz claimed she had Four Seasons lined up as a partner. It is easy to throw around the names of luxury hotel brands like Four Seasons, Ritz-Carlton, and St. Regis. The brands don't mind because it's a form of advertising. But they are hotel operators, not builders. They make modest investments, if they contribute any capital, only if a deal is coming to fruition. The Renaissance Consortium could never line up the money to break ground. So we gave developer Jack Avedikian's Connecticut-based firm, KJA, a two-year exclusive on pretty much the same terms.

January 2006 was also when we awarded Bermuda's tourism advertising account to GlobalHue on a three-year contract. In promoting American's Miami flight, GlobalHue had introduced the tag line "Bermuda—Feel the Love," and it made a compelling case for building on this theme. GlobalHue offered more insight into Bermuda's tourism challenges than other agencies, and its Miami results showed it could supply both substance and sizzle.

January and February saw developments connected with the taxi GPS law. Because the value of taxi GPS depended on network distribution effects, a centralized dispatch system was the wisest course for the taxi industry. Yet the industry could not unite on a shared system as I had urged. Instead three competing GPS dispatch firms prepared to begin operations. This seemed likely to hamper the success of GPS dispatch, but how much remained to be seen.

Almost no taxi operators had purchased and installed the necessary equipment. Rather than be heavy-handed about this failure, we provided a six-month grace period to install the equipment, with no import duty.

At the beginning of February the Transport Ministry and the Works, Engineering, and Housing Ministry together opened the new Hamilton Bus Terminal. As part of my emphasis on remembering Bermuda's heroes, my Transport colleagues and I had arranged to name the terminal for driver Hubert "Sparky" Lightbourne (1924–2000), whose famously entertaining tours of Bermuda had won him an MBE (Member of the Order of the British Empire) in his lifetime. It was gratifying to bestow a Bermudian honor posthumously, with his widow, Betty Lightbourne, and other family and friends in attendance.

On February 17, the *Mid-Ocean News* claimed that Berkeley's new senior secondary school was "a death trap," according to a Canadian construction auditor formerly employed by Somers Construction. The *Royal Gazette* echoed this view until it accepted that as both Somers and the Ministry of Works, Engineering, and Housing argued, the alleged whistleblower was retaliating for being fired. Sure, there were all sorts of little problems in the new school as in any new building of that size. But the construction was fundamentally sound.

The new senior secondary school would not be ready for teachers and students until September. But it began to be used for other purposes in March, when it housed a conference on addiction treatment with several hundred attendees.

Before February ended, the Tourism Department found a Wall Street location for our remaining North American sales office. The rent was dramatically lower than what we were paying in midtown Manhattan.

The same month, UNESCO's Slave Route Project formally linked with Bermuda's African Diaspora Heritage Trail. On the day of the UNESCO announcement a *Royal Gazette* reporter asked me if GlobalHue had won Tourism's account because Don Coleman was Black. Like the shareholder who asked if the Government approved HSBC's acquiring the Bank of Bermuda so my brother Philip could become CEO, ignoring his track record as a senior vice president at Citibank, the reporter ignored Don Coleman's achievements. It was as if Don Coleman could become the account executive for a brand like Chevrolet and build a leading agency from scratch simply by virtue of being Black. The supposed justification for the question and a subsequent *Royal Gazette* editorial was that GlobalHue had no history of travel-related advertising. The agency's Miami work had just shown such a history was unnecessary.

I told the reporter, "The answer is no. But that is a plantation question, and in the future I will refuse to answer plantation questions." I explained that a plantation question, one a White politician would never be asked, evoked the relationship of master and slave as one between man and boy. If I had a choice to make for myself, it was man, not boy.

The UBP had just replaced Grant Gibbons as Party Leader with Wayne Furbert, heeding John Swan's call for Black leaders in the UBP. Unfortunately the UBP responded with the same old "race card" rhetoric, and new Opposition Leader Furbert said I was divisive. A *Royal Gazette* article described my remarks on plantation questions as a "rant," just as Philip's response to the shareholder was supposed to be "aggressive and intimidating." An editorial voiced the same disapproval. It escaped me why honesty about the continuing racism was supposed to be divisive or inappropriate.

The UBP did not want to face the facts about GlobalHue's widely recognized capabilities. In 2006 GobalHue had $470 million in annual billings, a remarkable achievement for an agency founded in 1988. By 2009 its billings were $833.7 million. That kind of growth, and clients like the U.S. Navy, Verizon, Merck, Wal-Mart, and Chrysler, only came from delivering value.

On the evening of March 21, I joined Mayor Lawson Mapp and other key public and private stakeholders at a meeting on redeveloping Hamilton's waterfront. Over the previous five months the Corporation of Hamilton, along with Tourism and Transport, had been working on a master plan with leading urban planners and development consultants. Estimated to cost $639 million,

80 percent funded by the private sector, and take ten to twenty years, the plan included shifting the cargo docks to another part of the Island, a new park and esplanade, moorings for cruise ships that would not block the harbor view, and office, retail, and residential development The plan left many questions unanswered, but it presented a compelling vision of what the waterfront could become.

My willingness to partner with the private sector and my ability to engage with business leaders on a substantive basis did not fit my opponents' caricature of me as an angry radical. One-on-one, I could usually break down the misconceptions about me fostered by the Combined Opposition. But those misconceptions ensured that prejudicial group-think about me persisted.

The week before I opened the meeting on the Hamilton waterfront plans, Derrick Burgess retired as BIU president after ten years at the union's helm and Chris Furbert succeeded him. My speech at the retirement ceremony shocked many in both the PLP and the UBP.

I congratulated Derrick on the BIU's progress under his leadership, affirmed the shared goals of the BIU and PLP, and acknowledged the BIU's crucial support of the PLP. With Derrick's prior agreement, however, I also stressed that service is not servitude and discussed how the BIU and its members could help renew the tourism industry. I asked the BIU to be less quick to call strikes and more creative in negotiations, to refrain from blocking management when employees deserved disciplinary action, and to encourage union members to provide great service. I said I was making this plea in mid-March, because the summer held great promise for tourism and a single day of interrupted service would sour thousands of first-time visitors' impressions of Bermuda. At the same time, I gave equal stress to the need for Bermuda's largest hotel operators to do their part to advance Bermudianization.

It was unusual, to say the least, for a Bermudian MP or Cabinet Minister to strike such a balance. I spoke from long-held belief and the urgency of the moment. The signs of a big tourism spike were accumulating. GlobalHue's "Feel the Love" advertising was transforming our identity in travelers' minds from stodgy to stylish. And JetBlue's service was going to open a spigot that would not only make its own flights profitable but boost passenger volume on all carriers.

Another encouraging sign was a reinvestment plan for the Ariel Sands Cottage Colony, owned and operated by the Dill family. Academy Award–winner Michael Douglas, whose mother was a Dill, and his relatives were partnering with Hilton Grand Vacation Club to take the old cottage colony upscale. Reinvestment at the Fairmont Southampton also sent the message that Bermuda was renewing its identity as a luxury destination.

In April we announced May to October nightlife promotions to take the boring out of Bermuda. That month I attended the African Presidential

Roundtable 2006 in Johannesburg, South Africa, at the invitation of Dr. Charles R. Stith, Founding Director of Boston University's African Presidential Center and U.S. Ambassador to Tanzania from 1998 to 2001. It was a privilege to participate, and I especially appreciated meeting Kenneth Kaunda, Zambia's inaugural president from 1964 to 1991. Another plus was that Phylicia Rashad, a friend from our undergraduate days at Howard, sat on the same panel with me.

When I returned to Bermuda, Premier Scott was playing down UBP-generated talk of a general election that year. Before April ended, I announced plans to make the Public Transportation Board, the quango operating Bermuda's bus service, into a Government department. Although quangos are sometimes appropriate, and PLP administrations including my own used them, they can take on agendas of their own and become difficult to manage. That was the case with the Public Transportation Board.

In May we held the first National Youth Tourism Day. About 400 students participated, and I encouraged them to consider working in hotels and other aspects of the tourism industry as a first step toward running them.

That month Tourism took over management of the Island's public golf courses from the Ministry of Works, Engineering, and Housing. The shift flowed from the IMG report on golf in Bermuda. Roddy Carr, a leading figure in golf course development worldwide, had written the report, which recommended upgrading our best public golf course, Port Royal, to PGA level. That became an important goal of my administration, and Roddy contributed a lot to our achieving it.

The biggest news of the month was the start of JetBlue's New York–Bermuda service. It immediately transformed Bermuda's travel and tourism picture, increasing air arrivals by 6 percent.

Florida-Bermuda travel increased in June thanks to the GlobalHue-arranged promotion with the Miami Heat. A season after acquiring Shaquille O'Neal from the Los Angeles Lakers, the Heat were on the way to winning the NBA championship, and Bermuda was recording increased advertising impressions with consumers throughout the southeast United States.

Bookings were booming at our hotels and resorts as Tourism opened the second phase of the World Heritage Centre at St. George's, named a World Heritage Site by UNESCO in November 2000. Because of the environmental impact, we decided against widening the Town Cut, the St. George's harbor entrance, for the benefit of mega-cruise ships carrying up to 3,000 passengers. We had to find another way to make Bermuda a viable port of call for this new generation of ships.

The numbers for January to May showed visitor arrivals up 18 percent. The UBP chose this moment to attack my travel expenses, citing my staying in a seven-star hotel in Dubai for the Arabian Hotel Investment Conference, not knowing that I personally paid for half the daily rate. As I said on a later occasion, I didn't like to stay at Motel 6. But my travel expenses were appropriate to representing Bermuda's interests as head of Tourism and Transport. They gave me opportunities (in addition to personal travel at my own expense) to gauge our luxury tourism competition. Each dollar I spent returned multiple dollars to Bermuda through increased air service and rising visitor volume and spending.

In July Tourism incorporated the African Diaspora Heritage Trail Foundation as a quango. This would enable the foundation to raise money from contributions and other nongovernment sources.

That month brought the first discounted fare from British Airways on its London-Bermuda route. A direct weekly flight from Germany began. And the numbers for the April-June quarter were the best of the young twenty-first century, with tourism revenues up $40 million over the second quarter of 2005.

The annual PLP Delegates Conference in the fall marked the end of the four-year leadership term begun by Jennifer Smith in 2002. The Special Delegates Conference after the 2003 general election had put Alex Scott at the head of the party for the rest of the four-year term, not given him a four-year term of his own. Asked by the media if I would challenge Premier Scott to lead the party, and thus succeed him as Premier, I said no. The time did not seem right.

In an August media interview, Premier Scott said he would welcome a leadership challenge as a sign that the PLP was a healthy party. Wanda and I were at her house on Martha's Vineyard when Murray Brown called to urge me to run for party leadership. Triggered by Premier Scott's statement, others in the PLP also urged me to run. They persuaded me the time might be right after all.

That month the grace period for taxi operators to install GPS equipment ended, and TCD began to crack down on those who still had not done so. The immediate benefits of taxi GPS were not as great as they might have been because many drivers refused to use the equipment. Those who did reported positive experiences, however, especially during busy periods like Cup Match.

Berkeley's new senior secondary school opened in September. There was a problem with a leak in the roof. Despite the claims of the firm that had lost the roofing contract and the UBP, this turned out to be a minor issue of flashing in one section of the roof. It was quickly put right.

Teachers and students enthusiastically praised the new building and campus. The *Royal Gazette*'s headline toned this down to "Students give new Berkeley passing grade." The quotations within the article made clear that students and teachers gave the facility top marks.

September also saw the second African Diaspora Heritage Trail Conference in Bermuda. Nobel Prize for Literature laureate Wole Soyinka, African-American civil rights leader Andrew Young, and actor Danny Glover participated, and the conference was a great success. I drew harsh criticism from the Combined Opposition, however, because I said in opening the conference, "Let us end the idea that empowering Black people is evil."

Two other significant events in September were the christening of the fifth fast ferry and a benefit concert by internationally acclaimed opera star Kathleen Battle. We christened the new ferry, which would serve the eastern end of the island by linking St. David's and St. George's with Hamilton, the *Warbaby Fox*. The name honored Charles Hilgrove Gawthorpe "Warbaby" Fox, the Black Bermudian founder of St. David's County Cricket Club. As at the opening of Hamilton's new bus terminal, named for Sparky Lightbourne, I highlighted the importance for Bermuda of recognizing its national heroes.

Kathleen Battle, a friend of Wanda's for many years, was singing to raise money for the T.H.E. Foundation (Tourism Helps Everyone). Wanda had started the foundation to defray costs associated with bringing top performers to the Bermuda Music Festival in October. Kathleen Battle's recital raised a considerable amount of money for this good cause.

At the beginning of October polling measured very high approval ratings for Finance Minister Paula Cox and me. Just over a week later I was proud to announce that a deal was all but signed to bring the PGA Grand Slam of Golf, a competition between the year's four major tournament winners, to Bermuda's Mid Ocean Club in 2007 and 2008. The general manager of Mid Ocean Club told the media to expect a formal announcement soon.

The next day, October 12, 2006, I resigned from Premier Scott's Cabinet to vie for leadership of the PLP at the November Delegates Conference. With Wanda at my side, I humbly presented myself for people's evaluation, emphasizing that I intended to serve only one four-year term as Party Leader and would withdraw from politics if I lost to Premier Scott.

Arthur Hodgson soon backed me, as did Julian Hall and the other most progressive members of the PLP. Paula Cox affirmed her support for Premier Scott.

For two weeks, Wanda and I crisscrossed Bermuda as I spoke to PLP delegates about my goals for the party and the nation. On the eve of the vote at the Delegates Conference, a poll showed the public supported me two to one over Alex Scott.

The choice was up to the PLP's 150 branch delegates and 27 parliamentarians (22 MPs and five Senators). The brief leadership campaign ended with the candidates' speeches at the Delegates Conference. Premier Scott went first, and the *Royal Gazette* said that "the incumbent must have known from the smattering of applause as he made his way to the podium that it was all over."

When I went to the podium, the mic, which had been working perfectly, was dead. Without a moment's hesitation I strode across the stage, told one of the officials on the dais "I need your mic," and began to address the assembly. Warning everyone "If you don't want change, don't vote for me," I presented my vision for the PLP and Bermuda, interrupted by twelve standing ovations.

The vote immediately afterward was 107 for me and 76 for Alex Scott. The next day he resigned as Premier and I was sworn in as his successor, Bermuda's ninth Government Leader since Henry Tucker.

At last I had achieved my lifelong dream of leading the PLP and the nation. Shortly thereafter Wanda and I attended my mother's church, First Church of God, pastored by my dear friend and spiritual guide, Bishop Vernon G. Lambe, Sr., with his amazing First Lady, Elder Ruth Ann Lambe. During the televised service, Bishop Lambe called us to the altar and prayed over us, for my leadership of Bermuda and for our strength and protection under God—prayers we welcomed and needed. The next four years would be tumultuous.

Hilgrove Darrell, my maternal grandfather, was one of Bermuda's most respected ferry pilots. *Courtesy the author.*

Dorothy Darrell, my maternal grandmother. *Courtesy the author.*

The Darrell sisters: my mother Helene, Winifred, and Gloria. *Courtesy the author.*

My final report card for 1951-52, age 6. The line "Finds it impossible to sit still for any length of time" still holds true. *Courtesy the author.*

My sister Emelita and me in November 1961. *Courtesy the author.*

The 1963 cricket team of St. Jago High School in Spanish Town. Center front is our distinguished headmaster, Mr. O. R. Bell. I am seated far left. *Courtesy St. Jago High School.*

Howard University's track team, spring 1968. The whole team was inducted into the Howard Sports Hall of Fame in November 2018. Standing far right is Coach Wilmer Johnson. I am standing far left. *Courtesy Howard University Athletic Department.*

I address the media on March 22, 1968, the last full day of the sit-in at Howard University's administration building. To my left is Alfred Babington-Johnson, who played a significant role in strategy sessions among the student leaders. *Washington, D.C. Public Library Special Collections/Washington Star.*

Outside my new Los Angeles office, the Vermont-Century Medical Clinic, in the mid-1970s. *Courtesy Emelita Johnson.*

Premier Jennifer Smith, the first Progressive Labour Party Leader to be Premier of Bermuda, and her Cabinet, shortly after our historic general election victory in November 1998. Seated: Lois Browne-Evans, Paula Cox, Premier Smith, Eugene Cox, Renee Webb. Standing: Alex Scott, Terry Lister, Dennis Lister, me, Arthur Hodgson, David Allen, Nelson Bascome. *Bermuda Government Department of Communications.*

With Bermuda's first fast ferry, *Serenity,* March 2002.
Courtesy Arthur Bean/Royal Gazette.

Renowned Bermudian caricaturist Peter Woolcock featured me
in several cartoons. This one appeared in the *Royal Gazette* on
March 24, 2004. *Courtesy estate of Peter Woolcock.*

With my Cabinet Ministers and others after being sworn in as Premier of Bermuda by Governor Sir John Vereker, October 30, 2006. *Bermuda Government Department of Communications.*

With my Cabinet and the PLP Caucus, October 2006. *Bermuda Government Department of Communications.*

Dame Lois Browne-Evans speaking at the naming ceremony for L. F. Wade International Airport. *Courtesy Bermuda Ministry of Tourism and Transport.*

Kicking off the general election campaign in November 2007. To my left is childhood sports hero Dennis Wainwright. *Courtesy Akil J. Simmons/Royal Gazette.*

With my fellow Premiers from the Progressive Labour Party: Hon. Paula A. Cox, Hon. W. Alex Scott, Hon. E. David Burt, and Dame Jennifer Smith. *Courtesy Deanna Williams/DW Perception.*

With Trey, Wanda, and Donovan after I received an honorary Doctor of Laws degree from my beloved alma mater Howard University. *Courtesy Howard University.*

With Mirrors graduates in November 2009. *Bermuda Government Department of Communications.*

With Congressman James Clyburn of South
Carolina, Majority Whip of the U.S. House of
Representatives and Dean of the
Congressional Black Caucus. *Courtesy the
author.*

With U.S. Attorney General Eric Holder
during his official visit to Bermuda. *Bermuda
Government Department of Communications.*

With President George W. Bush in the Oval Office at the White House. *Official White House photograph.*

With Wanda and Prime Minister P. J. Patterson of Jamaica. Using a cricket analogy, P.M. Patterson advised me that after I left office I should "retire to the pavilion and watch the game from there." My critics wouldn't let me go so quietly. *Courtesy Tamell Simmons/Progressive Labour Party.*

The June 16, 2009 protest on the Cabinet grounds against my granting asylum to four innocent Uighurs released from Guantánamo Bay. *Courtesy Royal Gazette.*

U.S. Secretary of State Clinton's letter of thanks for our offer of asylum to the innocent Uighurs. *Courtesy the author.*

Wanda and me with Secretary of State Hillary Rodham Clinton and former President Bill Clinton in August 2009. *Courtesy the author.*

The official invitation to our State Dinner in honor of Queen Elizabeth II and the Duke of Edinburgh. *Courtesy the author.*

Awaiting the arrival of Her Majesty. *Bermuda Government Department of Communications.*

Before the State Dinner for Queen Elizabeth II with Her Majesty, the Duke of Edinburgh, and Wanda. Gifts were exchanged during this private meeting. *Bermuda Government Department of Communications.*

Wanda and me with President Barack
Obama at the Summit of the Americas, Port
of Spain, Trinidad, 2009. *Courtesy the author.*

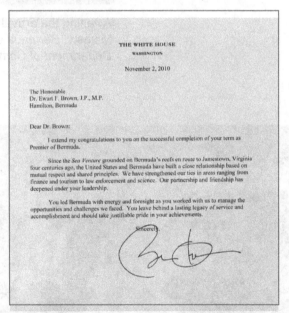

President Obama's gracious letter to me on
the completion of my service as premier.
Courtesy the author.

Wanda and I are married by my first
cousins, Archdeacon James Palacious
and Reverend Angela Palacious, at St.
Monica's Church, Providenciales, Turks
and Caicos, May 31, 2003. *Courtesy
Vernée Butterfield.*

Brushing sand from
Wanda's feet just before our
evening wedding reception
on the beach in Turks.
Courtesy the author.

With Wanda before our Bermuda wedding reception in
June, 2003. *Courtesy Arthur Bean/Royal Gazette.*

Emelita and me. *Courtesy the author.*

With my brothers, Vincent and Philip. *Courtesy the author.*

With Trey and Donovan . . . having fun! *Courtesy the author.*

Donovan and Trey. *Courtesy Donovan Brown.*

My son Maurice.
Courtesy the author.

With my son Kevin at his wedding.
Courtesy the author.

My new life is centered on the rising generations:
Maurice, Donovan, Trey, Kesi (Maurice's daughter), Kira
(Kevin's daughter) and Caleb (Kevin's son). *Courtesy
the author.*

Part Three:
Prescribing for a Nation

14. Looking for a Hammer

O N OCTOBER 30, 2006, GOVERNOR SIR JOHN VEREKER swore me in as Premier, the third Leader of the Progressive Labour Party to head Bermuda's Government. He also swore in my Cabinet.

Heads of parliamentary governments can redefine cabinet portfolios. My immediate predecessor, Alex Scott, had created a National Drug Control Ministry headed by Wayne Perinchief, former Assistant Police Commissioner.

Because substance abuse is entangled with other ills, I created a Ministry of Social Rehabilitation to fight abuse, deliver family services, and reintegrate prisoners into society. Dale Butler, Premier Scott's Community and Cultural Affairs and Sport Minister, accepted my invitation to head the new ministry. Also to address issues holistically, I tapped former high school principal Randolph Horton as Education, Sport, and Recreation Minister. Meanwhile Wayne Perinchief accepted my offer to become Community and Cultural Affairs Minister.

I asked Deputy Premier Paula Cox to continue as Finance Minister. I also asked Derrick Burgess to continue as Labour and Immigration Minister. I reappointed Colonel David Burch, Premier Scott's Works and Engineering and Housing Minister, to the Senate and named him Public Safety and Housing Minister. His military background and good work on housing suited this blended portfolio.

I also decided to keep handling Tourism and Transport, which my critics said was too much for a Premier. However, the ministries were functioning smoothly and I was committed to leading further progress in both areas.

I selected Nelson Bascome as Health Minister, his role from 1998 to 2003 under Premier Smith. Dennis Lister became Works and Engineering Minister. And Neletha Butterfield became Environment, Telecommunications, and E-Commerce Minister.

My Senate appointments also included Phil Perinchief, who became Attorney General, and three young people—Wayne Caines, Davida Morris, and Kim Wilson—as Junior Ministers and a bench of developing talent.

I no longer had time to see patients and regretted giving up practicing medicine, but my official responsibilities demanded it. I left Gombey House by 6:30 a.m. for a gym session before each day's work, usually getting home twelve or fourteen hours later, assuming I had no official evening engagements.

Before the PLP leadership vote I had purchased a beautiful eighteenth-century house, Winterhaven, in Smith's Parish. As young boys, my mates and I passed it on our way to the beach. We skirted it carefully, because it had supposedly been haunted since an early occupant killed her husband. I boasted, "One day I'm gonna buy that haunted house."

As young men, the same friends and I had beach parties nearby. Someone always teased, "Are you still gonna buy that haunted house?" I said, "Sure am."

When I closed on the house, Wanda joked, "You're fulfilling boyhood ambitions, Ewart. Alex Scott better watch out."

Wanda and I planned to refurbish the house as a medical facility, the Brown-Darrell Clinic, named for my parents. In concert with supercharged BHCS practice manager Kelley McKinney, Wanda took the lead in overseeing the arrangements.

On November 1, the *Royal Gazette* reported on an October 17 letter to Premier Scott from Bermuda Public Services Union (BPSU) General Secretary Ed Ball. The letter claimed "a number of senior civil servants" had "serious concerns" about Wanda's creating the Tourism Helps Everyone (T.H.E.) Foundation and arranging for Kathleen Battle's recital to defray the Bermuda Music Festival's excess costs.

Mr. Ball wrote, "The focus of the disquiet is whether . . . it is correct for the wife of a Cabinet Minister to . . . rais[e] funds for a government funded programme." He added that T.H.E. Foundation's not being a registered charity "must put the funds raised in question."

Wanda had tried to register T.H.E. Foundation with Bermuda's Charities Commission. Normally this is easy for any group with a charitable purpose. However, it became clear that the official designation would not be received in time. Wanda carried on, always referring to the T.H.E. Foundation as a "charitable organisation" and advancing her own personal funds to stage the event, which turned out to be a remarkable success.

Mr. Ball had not discussed the matter with anyone else in the BPSU. Union President Armell Thomas was surprised to learn of the letter and said, "I can't really support the comments . . . in [it]."

Whether Ed Ball discussed the letter with "a number of senior civil servants" was also in question. The most senior civil servant, John Drinkwater, about to retire as Cabinet Secretary, said he had no knowledge of it, and other senior civil servants said the same. Ball then told the *Royal Gazette* the letter reflected concerns of "more than three civil servants," dropping any attributions of seniority.

Ed Ball was a long-time associate of Alex Scott, and the letter struck me as a ploy to fight my leadership run. The *Royal Gazette* reported it had received the letter the day before the October 27 leadership vote but delayed publishing a story because the letter's authenticity was uncertain.

At the time I was occupied with rewriting the Throne Speech to reflect the priorities my Cabinet and I would pursue. On November 3, 2006, Governor Vereker read the Throne Speech to open Parliament.

The speech began with a quotation from King Whitney, Jr., on how fearful people shrink from change because "things may get worse," hopeful people welcome it because "things may get better," and confident people embrace "the challenge . . . to make things better." It called on Bermudians to reject passivity in connection with the national motto "Quo Fata Ferunt" ("Where the Fates Lead") and to recognize "the time has come to chart our own fate."

Relatively brief compared to most Throne Speeches, the speech promised:

- a focus on educational basics, apprenticeships, internships, and training, with employers in certain categories being required to hire Bermudian trainees or apprentices as part of securing permits for expatriate workers
- ambitious affordable housing targets
- increased investment in sport, especially football
- abolition of KEMH's "Indigent Care" clinic and other hospital improvements
- a National Health Promotion Strategy
- a national conversation on race relations
- an official poverty line to guide efforts for the disadvantaged
- improved prisoner rehabilitation
- a National Drug Information Network, substance abuse treatment programs, and enhanced anti-drug crime enforcement
- a Council of Economic Advisors
- legislation to strengthen the international business sector
- development of upscale resorts
- further enhancement of public transit and limits on car ownership
- a new recycling plant

The speech as my team and I drafted it ended by quoting Frederick Douglass: "If there is no struggle there is no progress. . . . Power concedes nothing without a demand. It never did and it never will."

Governors usually make bland closing comments of their own. Governor Vereker added, "As your Governor I want to emphasise . . . that each of us on this Island must value the contribution made by each other, regardless of race, or gender, or age, or country of origin. . . . . All parts of this community must now move forward together. I look forward to working with the Government to that purpose."

Black Bermudians could not fail to hear a reproof to anyone who thought our international business sector should hire more Bermudians and import fewer workers. The reproof echoes in ranking country of origin equally with race in a context where White expatriates have historically been favored over Black citizens.

The Governor had never made such pointed comments after previous Throne Speeches. It was one of many signs that I was going to meet more antagonism from the Combined Opposition than my two PLP predecessors combined.

Questioning my leadership agenda, the *Royal Gazette* ran articles on Alex Scott's view that "you can't hurry change" and Bermuda should "make haste slowly."

I make no excuses for trying to speed overdue progress. I had said it loud and clear on the night of the PLP leadership vote: "If you don't want change, don't vote for me."

Among my substantive actions in November was announcing with my brother Vincent Hollinsid, head of the Bermuda Fire Service, that as of April 2007 the St. George's Volunteer Fire Brigade and airport fire service would merge into an expanded BFS. Cost, efficiency, and most of all public safety required this merger. An expert British team had recommended it in 2003. Premier Scott's Cabinet proposed going ahead with it in November 2005, but soon abandoned it because of opposition motivated by a fear of change. My Cabinet was not going to "make haste slowly" where lives were concerned.

Another step was hiring Rolfe Commissiong as a consultant on, and liaison to, young Black men in Bermuda. Rolfe would be my point person in the "Big Conversation" the country needed on race. The Opposition dragged up Rolfe's old criminal record again. That showed they had no interest in honest dialogue about racism. They preferred to pretend racism was in the past, our society was color blind, and those who failed to thrive had only themselves to blame.

When the Combined Opposition acknowledged racism, it was in the language of the Governor's Throne Speech comments, situating it as one among several great social problems. That view evaded the circumstances that make racism loom above Bermuda's other ills.

The Governor said he looked forward to working with the Government. It was time to see if his attitude was really one of partnership. The Premier goes to the Governor's office every week to discuss Bermudian affairs. In our first such meeting, I suggested meeting in my office on alternate weeks.

The Governor said he would consider it. But in less than 24 hours his office said there would be no alternating venues. This response told me the Governor was committed to the vestiges of imperial control in his mostly ceremonial position. I say "mostly" because the Governor controlled the Bermuda Police Service and Bermuda Regiment.

Late November took me to London for the annual Overseas Territories Consultative Council (OTCC) meetings at the FCO. The UPB thought it scandalous that I threatened to boycott future meetings unless territorial heads of government had a session without territorial governors. Grant Gibbons sneered that the British government would quickly learn whatever we discussed. He missed the fact that people engage with each other more forthrightly when they have set the parameters, even if they know their discussions will be monitored. We knew the British would learn whatever we said, but if they weren't in the room they would have to work harder to get the information from their snitches.

The FCO soon found time for the OT heads of government to meet in private session. I subsequently asked Governor Vereker to act more substantively in his largest practical responsibility, law enforcement. The Combined Opposition considered this outrageous.

While I was still in London at the OT meetings, Grant Gibbons questioned Wanda's T.H.E. Foundation in the House on Friday, November 24. Echoing Ed Ball's letter, Gibbons insinuated something fishy must have occurred because consulting firm Kurron, which had a KEMH-related contract with the Bermuda Hospitals Board (BHB), contributed $10,000 as a sponsor of Kathleen Battle's recital. Gibbons also attacked sponsorships by GlobalHue's Don Coleman and his wife and FIS's Tina Byles, claiming again that Tina's fundraising luncheon for me was "pay to play."

My PLP colleagues declared Gibbons out of order in making such allegations when I was not there to respond. Despite his protests, he was not allowed to continue speaking about the matter that evening.

It was no secret that ticket revenues did not cover the Music Festival's costs. The value of the event included tourism revenue from visiting attendees and its appeal to future visitors. On the eve of the 2006 festival, the media had reported that T.H.E. Foundation, although not a registered charity, was producing Kathleen Battle's concert to help defray the shortfall between ticket revenue and festival costs. Everything was in the open and aboveboard.

There was nothing unusual in corporate sponsorship of philanthropic events in Bermuda. The recital sponsors included Bermudian and overseas companies and individuals. I'll say more about Kurron's Bermuda contracts, which it won on merit, but contributions to T.H.E. Foundation by PLP Government vendors and supporters were legal. They paralleled contributions to UBP causes by UBP Government vendors and supporters.

That was the context when I stood up in the House on December 1 as Premier, PLP Leader, and a husband whose wife had been insulted by the UBP's Grant Gibbons. With Wanda in the visitors gallery, I reminded the House that Gibbons had a penchant for disrespecting Black people across the aisle and quoted his calling then Premier Scott "a political eunuch." Addressing Gibbons's claim that "political" silenced echoes of castrating Black male slaves, I said the adjective couldn't save the noun: "If I called that Member [of the House] a racist dog, you see it is the dog that matters."

Gibbons objected, "Mr. Speaker, is he calling me a racist dog?"

I said, "Mr. Speaker, I would never call that Member a racist dog, because I can . . . see that he is not a dog."

The House of Assembly chamber is ample for its purposes but not vast. MPs and House officers occupy a space twenty-eight feet wide by forty-seven feet long. The Visitors Gallery seats 37 people, including 3 seats reserved for the media, and its front row is only a few feet from the nearest MPs. Wanda thus had an excellent vantage point to see Grant Gibbons squirm as I spoke about a hypothetical racist dog. When protest from the UBP and applause from the PLP subsided, I said I wanted "the Honorable Member to know something that has apparently escaped him. There are Black people on the planet who have money. . . . And many of those people . . . support Black politicians all over the world because they see . . . . commonality in their efforts. It doesn't mean that there is anything tricky going on."

I added that Wanda deserved praise for public service to Bermuda and that in my neighborhood men attacked the men they were angry at, not their wives. Saying Gibbons "crossed the line" in criticizing Wanda and I would cross the aisle if he ever mentioned her name in the House again, I concluded, "Mr. Speaker, . . . I say to that Honourable Member that I would like to stay on this side of the House and not have to come to the other side because it wouldn't be in order to vote for the UBP."

Accounting on the Bermuda Music Festival was soon complete, with costs almost double ticket revenue, $1.5 million to $800,000, leaving Tourism a $700,000 shortfall. Fulfilling its charitable purpose, T.H.E. Foundation initially and publicly contributed concert proceeds of $110,000 (with more funds contributed later), lowering the shortfall from $700,000 to less than $590,000. Wanda deserved a bipartisan commendation for saving taxpayers at least 16 percent of the excess cost. Kathleen Battle should forever be thanked for showering Bermuda with her resplendent gift.

IN LATE NOVEMBER, BRITISH PRIME MINISTER TONY BLAIR authored a statement on the approaching bicentenary of Britain's March 1807 abolition of slave trading in its possessions. Prime Minister Blair did not apologize for Britain's participation in slavery, but he expressed "deep sorrow" over the "profoundly shameful" slave trade. I publicly applauded this statement, while the UBP said nothing about it. White members of the UBP whose families profited hugely from slavery and the UBP itself should have echoed Prime Minister Blair. This was beyond them, however.

I've said political leadership must combine substance and symbolism. To support the new Ministry of Social Rehabilitation, I convened a Cabinet meeting at Westgate Correctional Facility in December. The meeting covered all Cabinet business, but it highlighted Bermuda's need to break a cycle of recidivism reflecting entrenched racism.

On December 15, I hosted a dinner for my Cabinet at the Elbow Beach Hotel. When the servers asked which plate was mine, the Australian chef said, "The one with the arsenic in it." The staff reported this remark, and within forty-eight hours the chef, allowed by the hotel to resign rather than be fired, appropriately had his work permit revoked and left the country.

The Combined Opposition was distressed on the chef's behalf. The *Royal Gazette* editorialized, in effect, "Can't the PLP take a joke?"

Imagine the UBP's response if a work-permit-holding African chef had "joked" about arsenic in a White UBP Premier's food. Like all Black Bermudians, Black UBP MPs knew an African chef in such a scenario would have been lucky to depart the country without a prison sentence.

Because of this event and a disturbed man's twice demanding to see me at the Cabinet Building, Public Safety and Housing Minister David Burch ordered a formal threat assessment, a measure also taken for my predecessors. Minister Burch said the threat was such that I needed Police security. I accepted this expert recommendation, although on many public occasions I continued to be accompanied only by Chief of Staff Wayne Caines.

The UBP and *Royal Gazette* declared security unnecessary even as they demonized me beyond any other Bermudian politician. A choice of words was important. Police services refer to protection details as "security officers," not "bodyguards." The Combined Opposition insisted on referring to my "hiring a bodyguard" to portray me as an "imperial Premier."

I had made two hires the Combined Opposition considered "imperial": Chief of Staff Wayne Caines and Press Secretary Scott Simmons. Bermuda might be small, but it had a developed economy and complex domestic and international agendas. A chief of staff and press secretary are part of what any twenty-first-century head of government needs to function.

Imperial trappings, however, were on display in Bermuda—in the office of the Governor. In addition to the Governor's salary, Bermuda paid for the lavish upkeep of Government House, where little governing occurred, and its numerous staff. I could only protest this symbolically, such as insisting that the elected leader of Bermuda should be able to get off a plane, skip Immigration, and go straight to his car, like the Governor.

January 2007 also saw the first Premier's Weekend Gala. A PLP fundraiser, the event triggered chatter about when I would call the next election. I had until fall 2008. Although some in the PLP wanted a snap election, I felt my Cabinet and I should demonstrate our worth before asking voters to give the party another five years in power.

In February we launched the Mirrors Program for young people at risk. Mark Charley and his Uncommon Results organization would run the program for a year, while training Bermudians to replace them. Dianna Taylor, director of the Department of Financial Assistance, proposed the name Mirrors, which evokes how the program aimed to help young Bermudians at risk see themselves in new ways.

In February we also brought David Hopkins, inaugural HSBC professor of International Leadership at the University of London's Institute of Education and a British government advisor, to Bermuda. Professor Hopkins and his team undertook a comprehensive review of our educational system.

The schools were not meeting Bermuda's needs and would clearly be difficult to change. That was why we secured the best possible outside reviewer to examine every aspect of the system.

Similarly, we sought the best possible experts to guide the Big Conversation about race. The program kicked off in February at the Fairmont Hamilton Princess with Professor Robert Jensen of the University of Texas, Austin, and Harvard-trained lawyer Bernestine Singley as facilitators.

Also in February, Nelson Bascome took a leave of absence from Cabinet because the Bermuda Police Service was investigating his maintenance business while he was Health Minister from 1998 to 2003. Apparently some officers in the BPS could not accept the failure of previous attempts to entangle Nelson and me in alleged wrongdoing at the BHC.

It was frustrating to see Bermuda's best Health Minister targeted in this way. During Nelson's leave of absence, Attorney General Phil Perinchief became acting Health Minister.

Bermuda and my extended family suffered a major loss on February 18, 2007, when my aunt Gloria died at age eighty from heart disease. Among many UBP and PLP tributes, John Swan called her "one of the most outstanding Ministers in our history."

At her memorial service I said in part, "Gloria McPhee was no spectator to Bermuda's development; she was a force in it. Part of what she developed is the man you see before you . . . . Others may have seen us as the UBP aunt and the PLP nephew, but she was flesh of my flesh and blood of my blood, and in our common goal to make Bermuda a better place we are forever one."

Aunt Gloria's death brought acknowledgment of her many achievements, from being Bermuda's first woman Cabinet Minister to the integration of the school system and creation of Bermuda College. Since then her name has not been properly remembered on occasions such as Bermuda College's fortieth anniversary in 2014. No doubt this had to do with her efforts to reform the UBP, her 1980 resignation from Cabinet and the UBP, and our relationship.

No doubt it also had to do with Bermuda College's founding. Aunt Gloria's UBP colleagues were prepared to support the college, but not to place it in Paget Parish. Remember my constituent who said, "Paget is White Bermuda's capital." Powerful UBP figures thought Bermuda College should be in a Black-majority parish, where there was no appropriate space. Aunt Gloria persuaded Henry Tucker to support her location, the least he could do for his "secret weapon" with Black voters. I suspect some White Bermudians still wish Bermuda College was not in Paget.

BERMUDA HAD A THIRD-LESS HOTEL CAPACITY in 2006 than in 1989. Tourism and Transport progress was bringing more visitors to the Island for business, vacations, and visits to Bermudian relatives, with vacation travel up 25 percent. Further growth depended on upgrading existing hotels and building upscale new ones.

On December 1, 2006, I promised a minimum of three new hotels in Bermuda in 2007, saying 2010 would open Bermuda's "Platinum Period of Tourism." To reach high, you must aim high.

One reason for stating this goal was the Dubai-based Jumeirah hotel chain's plan for a resort at the 37-acre Southlands estate in Warwick. Bermudians Craig Christensen, Brian Duperreault, and Nelson Hunt had bought the estate and formed Southlands Limited to develop it. A mix of green space, farmland, and woodland, Southlands was subject to a "Section 34" agreement protecting environmental features. The developers wanted this restriction rescinded. Despite the scarcity of green space, I felt a Jumeirah resort, built with sensitivity to the environment, would be good for the country.

The opposition of environmental activists coalesced in early 2007 as the Bermuda Environmental and Sustainability Taskforce (BEST). BEST proclaimed me the enemy of sustainability. I thought all development should be sustainable and preserving Bermuda's environment was essential. In late March 2007 I named ecological engineer, U.N. development consultant, and political activist Dr. Pauulu Karamakafego (Roosevelt Brown) and others to a Sustainable Development Roundtable chaired by Arthur Hodgson.

Two weeks later, on April 3, Pauulu Karamakafego died after a brief illness. It was another significant loss for Bermuda. Dr. Karamakafego's leadership had significantly advanced the cause of one person, one vote, each vote of equal value. He tried conventional politics in Bermuda. But after being ejected from the House for calling a UBP MP "asshole creeper," he opted to work in developing countries.

At the beginning of April Bermuda's fire and emergency services united on schedule. Consolidating the services has been an unqualified plus for the country. As head of the enlarged BFS, my brother Vincent Hollinsid improved operations across the board, including lowering ambulance response times to either end of the Island from twenty-five minutes to six minutes or less.

In March we had completed a master plan for development of the airport, and on April 16 we renamed it L. F. Wade International Airport in Freddie Wade's honor. I was delighted to bring this renaming about in my first six months as Premier. Dame Lois Browne-Evans, Freddie's mentor, shared my pride and pleasure that day. Told she had three minutes to speak about Freddie, she spoke for almost half an hour. They both deserved the time.

At the ceremony, a disturbed man with a box cutter and a past conviction for bodily harm tried to accost me. After that I accepted the recommendation that a plainclothes BPS officer always accompany me in public. In a headline, the *Royal Gazette* asked, "Why are Police babysitting Dr. Brown?" The facts were less important than demeaning me.

Controversy also arose in April over closing KEMH's Indigent Medical Clinic. White physician Dr. Catherine Wakely, who was going to lose her job running the clinic, wrote to the *Royal Gazette* in protest. Dr. Wakely was still a probationary employee, and her letter violated a confidentiality agreement. The BHB appropriately asked for her resignation. (She left Bermuda for a time, but returned to practice medicine and raise her family here.)

A few well-to-do White Bermudians rushed to her defense. They formed common cause with patients who feared the unknown and marched in modest numbers on the Cabinet Building. That disadvantaged people sometimes cling to what they know does not support continuing institutionalized racism, however.

The protestors renewed their efforts at various points. But the Indigent Medical Clinic's reason for being was keeping poor Black people out of White doctors' offices. It was expensive to operate and provided suboptimal care. It demeaned patients, including some who could afford private doctors and had themselves dropped off around the corner before they went in. To give the poorest Bermudians adequate healthcare, it had to close. It shut in July 2007 with none of the negative consequences protestors predicted.

The OBA Government elected in late 2012 restored the Indigent Clinic the following year. To spare White people seeing poor Black people in their doctors' offices, the OBA reverted to more expensive, less efficient care.

ON MAY 3, 2007, WE RELEASED DAVID HOPKINS'S REVIEW of Bermuda's educational system. The review presented a devastating indictment. Based on interviews and observations of teachers, students, and Education Ministry staff, it described:

- inadequate teaching and inconsistent curriculum
- no middle school with better than satisfactory performance
- two primary schools, one middle school, and one senior school performing at an inadequate level
- the other senior school and eight primary schools performing at a good level
- only two schools on the Island, both primary schools, performing at an outstanding level (although in the United Kingdom they would only be rated good)
- a "poorly-led," "mismanaged," "secretive," "dictatorial" Education Ministry

The report recommended:

- sacking senior Education Ministry staff
- a temporary external board to oversee "major restructuring" of the Ministry
- external performance reviews for teachers
- monitoring individual student progress
- consultants to coach school principals
- best practice sharing
- new curriculum
- provision for students with learning disabilities

In presenting the report, I said it confirmed what we knew as a community and we had to face facts to improve the situation. A significant aspect of the report was the "culture of low expectations and lacklustre teaching" in Bermuda compared to higher performing school systems.

I asked Education Minister Randy Horton to make the Hopkins Report his change map. I also turned to my brother Philip Butterfield, HSBC Bermuda

CEO. Philip had previously chaired the Bermuda Board of Education, resigning in frustration at the system's resistance to change. Thanks to him, HSBC Bermuda had contributed half of the Hopkins Report's $241,411 cost. Philip agreed to chair the external review board, hoping the report could generate support for progress.

Around this time I emailed Philip and Vincent that I wanted to have a photo taken of us together during my first months as Premier. We set a date, and agreed to wear dark suits to harmonize in the photo. On the appointed day I wore a dark suit. In due course Philip arrived in a dark suit. Vincent breezed in wearing a light brown suit. I turned to Philip and said, "You and I are going to look like the damn Temptations!"

Philip shot back, "With Vincent as David Ruffin!"

"Exactly."

The three of us had a good laugh, and I love the photo anyway.

In 2007 the high school graduation rate almost doubled to 82 percent. The principals said rates of 48 percent and below from 2004 to 2006 should be recalculated on the same basis as the 2007 rate. The question was whether to accept that at face value or see it as the system closing ranks against reform.

Despite Bermuda's school problems, scores of Black Bermudians went abroad for higher education every year, most of them to Canada and the United States. In May 2007, Britain said Overseas Territories students would pay lower home fees for study in the United Kingdom rather than overseas student fees. This greatly increased the number of young Bermudians getting tertiary education in Britain.

From my first Cabinet post, I sought out Bermudian students on my official travels. As Premier I increased those efforts, building a database of young people who could fill jobs in Bermuda.

No job category in Bermuda should be the permanent preserve of expatriates. The UBP wanted to continue importing White workers. Remember, 53 percent of White voters in 2003 were born outside Bermuda. The percentage has edged up since then.

In May, I moved Scott Simmons from press secretary to a three-month contract helping develop the Government television channel. He could put his strong public relations skills to good use there. Much of my press secretary's job was writing press releases. To replace Scott, I hired Glenn Jones from the *Royal Gazette*. I appreciate the newspaper's bringing Glenn to my attention through his well-written, scrupulously fair articles.

On May 29, 2007, two days before her eightieth birthday, Dame Lois Browne-Evans died of an apparent stroke. She was eagerly anticipating the huge celebration we planned. Sadly, it became her memorial service. I hailed her as a champion for justice, Bermuda's matriarch. Like Freddie Wade, she deserved to be in the pantheon Bermudians learned about in school.

IN TOURISM, I CONTINUED TO SEEK WAYS of attracting more visitors. One promising demographic, given Bermuda's strong Christian community, was Christian tourists. The model for this idea came from the Bahamas, where preacher Dr. Myles Munroe, now deceased, had grown faith-based tourism.

I chose Andre Curtis to make a similar effort in Bermuda. Andre had worked tirelessly on my campaign in the 2003 general election, the first with single-seat constituencies. I didn't know my new constituency as I would have liked, and at a pre-election meeting Andre offered to take me to every single house in the contituency. Several people at the meeting, including prominent pastors, endorsed Andre, so I accepted his offer. Andre did not miss a day of campaigning.

In 2006 Andre proposed a faith-based tourism effort, citing Dr. Munroe, who visited Bermuda to share expertise and discuss cooperative marketing. We never did co-promotions, but Andre began working on faith-based tourism in 2006 as chairman of the Bermuda Tourism Board. He continued that effort as a private vendor on a $400,000 contract (expenses and personal compensation) from spring 2007 to spring 2008.

The contract period got off to a rough start. Rosie O'Donnell's R Family Vacations planned a cruise to Bermuda for LGBT families. A group of eighty Protestant churches in Bermuda, United By Faith, led by Andre, publicly opposed the cruise. Although I assured Rosie O'Donnell the Bermuda Government had no problem with the cruise, she canceled it.

Andre had not balanced his responsibilities to the Government and his religious convictions well. But there was good reason to think his faith-based tourism efforts could succeed.

The UBP criticized Andre's contract as payback for his campaign work. Throughout the democratic world, people who help win electoral campaigns often get government jobs or run government-funded programs. Campaign work is a major way to earn trust with, and demonstrate competence to, politicians. This applies to all political parties in all democracies.

I approved the contract first because of faith-based tourism's potential. Conversations with pastors indicated their congregations would support the effort through church organizations outside Bermuda, following the Bahamas model. The contract objective was 2,000 visitors to faith-based tourism events. If Andre worked as hard as he did on my campaign, I thought he could achieve that and more.

As Premier I was not able to monitor Andre's performance closely. During 2007, civil servants in the Tourism Department began to report he was very disorganized. That summer the UBP made increasing noise about his faith-based tourism effort. The media also asked many questions, and in hindsight were right to do so. Andre's responses were unsatisfactory. However, my trust in him was such that I gave him the full contract term to deliver results.

IN MAY 2007 I TOOK PUBLIC NOTICE OF SIGNIFICANT PROGRESS in affordable housing construction at the Loughlands and Southside sites. Public Safety and Housing Minister David Burch was continuing his excellent management of housing, including the BHC.

Remember, a two-year investigation into alleged misconduct at the BHC did not implicate me for my publicly selling a North Road house to become rental stock.

Nevertheless, some in Bermuda, apparently including elements of the Police, remained determined to find me guilty of something—in defiance of the facts. On May 23, 2007, ZBM Radio indicated it had portions of the confidential BHC dossier. On June 1, the *Mid-Ocean News* published extracts purporting to show Nelson Bascome and I were in fraudulent cahoots with construction company owner Zane DeSilva. Sister newspaper the *Royal Gazette* amplified the allegations from its "impartial" perspective. One false claim was that Zane DeSilva buried part of the cost of Gombey House in a BHC project.

I was furious about the leak and rehashing of BHC issues, which had received a full investigation. In a June 1 television address to Bermuda, I said in part:

> Prior to today's defamatory publication in the *Mid-Ocean News*, I had raised directly with the Governor of Bermuda the issue of the security of the files of the BHC investigation. . . . I take this opportunity to again call upon the Governor to discharge the responsibility of his office by taking swift and meaningful action against the perpetrators of [the leak].
> . . . Should he fail to do this, the constitutionally elected Government of Bermuda will lose confidence in the current Governor. . . . [W]e will have no choice but to suspend further business with him.

Talk of a constitutional crisis followed. In the Senate on Wednesday, June 6, Public Safety and Housing Minister David Burch said he had written the Governor asking him to delegate his authority over the Police. The FCO brokered a meeting between the Governor and me that evening, and then announced:

The Governor assured the Premier . . . that an investigation would be pursued diligently. The Governor has advised the Commissioner of Police to seek outside assistance from Scotland Yard.

The Premier assured the Governor that he and his Government . . . [would] collaborate with Government House, in the best interests of Bermuda, in accordance with their oaths of Ministerial office.

All smoothed over in the best British fashion—except it wasn't. The next day the Police arrested Nelson Bascome and charged him with stealing $60,000. The sum was a loan, in good standing with the lender, which Nelson had taken out legitimately. In effect, the BPS charged Nelson with stealing from himself.

The BHC dossier leak revealed the theft charge against Nelson for what it was. Investigators must have hoped his maintenance firm had overbilled the BHC or committed some other crime. Finding no evidence of that, they seized on the $60,000 loan.

Police Commissioner George Jackson took the dossier's theft seriously. He willingly joined Attorney General Perinchief in seeking an injunction to stop publication about the leaked dossier's contents.

The Combined Opposition portrayed the requested injunction as an attempt to suppress the facts. The relevant facts were on the public record. The injunction sought to stop a UBP-client media from trumpeting innuendo and speculation as if they were facts.

Nelson felt he should resign from Cabinet to give full attention to clearing his name. I appointed Sandys North PLP MP Michael Scott as Health Minister.

A lawyer for Commissioner Jackson and Attorney General Perinchief applied to Chief Justice Richard Ground for a media gag order. While Chief Justice Ground deliberated, the media temporarily stopped quoting the dossier. During these few days, "Son of the Soil" posted a letter on Facebook and inserted it in the Wikipedia entry on me, repeating BHC-related innuendo and claiming responsibility for sharing the dossier with the media. A pro-UBP website, politics.bm, also posted dossier material. It took some time before Facebook, Wikipedia, and politics.bm took the defamatory material offline.

Chief Justice Ground denied the gag order. Commissioner Jackson then forthrightly apologized to Bermuda, announcing that two British police officers were helping investigate the dossier's theft. The investigation never went anywhere, but it included visits to ZBM and the *Mid-Ocean News*, 24-hour detention of Auditor General Larry Dennis for possessing a copy of the stolen dossier, and a search of his office.

The UBP asked the British government for a Royal Commission of Inquiry on the BHC, which was a nonstarter. Any objective observer could see the two-year investigation of the BHC had established that my colleagues and I had done nothing wrong.

My administration pursued an injunction for a gag order through the Court of Appeal in Bermuda and the Privy Council in London. I also pursued personal legal action. However, there was no redress in the courts for the unwarranted character assassination in the media. Any redress would have to come in the ballot box.

THE COMBINED OPPOSITION CONTINUED TO ASSAIL the consulting firm Kurron's work for the BHB. I had met Kurron's Black founder and CEO, Corbett A. Price, through Wanda, who knew him from Wall Street. Corbett Price had started Kurron after a senior role at Hospital Corporation of America. He was unpopular with some U.S. unions because of layoffs at hospitals Kurron advised, but the firm had an excellent reputation for putting mismanaged hospitals into good working order. I introduced Corbett Price to Nelson Bascome when he was Premier Smith's Health Minister. With no further involvement from me, Nelson and the BHB hired Kurron in February 2003 to conduct operational reviews of KEMH and Mid-Atlantic Wellness Institute (MWI), our small mental healthcare facility.

When Alex Scott became Premier in July 2003, he appointed Patrice Minors as Health Minister. Minister Minors kept Kurron's consulting contract in force because of the firm's good work.

In 2005 Premier Scott's Cabinet approved a master plan for a new hospital to replace KEMH, which mainly dated from the 1940s. Aside from the cost of a new hospital, the biggest problem was where to put it. The following year the Cabinet opted to build a new hospital on the grounds of the Bermuda Botanical Gardens. This aroused considerable opposition when Minister Minors announced it in August 2006.

After I became Premier, my Cabinet decided against diminishing limited green space in this way. We chose to refurbish and enlarge KEMH on its existing footprint, adding to the need for expert hospital management consulting.

While Attorney General Phil Perinchief was acting Health Minister, my Cabinet awarded Kurron a five-year, $13.5 million hospital management contract. Disgruntled KEMH staff said a BHB committee wanted to give the contract to Johns Hopkins Medicine International (JHMI), a consulting arm of Johns Hopkins Hospital, and the Combined Opposition accused me of cronyism.

That made for good headlines, not good reporting. I understood many in Bermuda's medical community were more comfortable with JHMI than Kurron. An English doctor at KEMH said hiring Kurron was like rejecting Oxford or Cambridge for a university in Wales.

That remark mainly revealed the doctor's snobbery. JHMI's strength was treatment, not management. My Cabinet had a responsibility to select the vendor with the talent, expertise, and grit to do the job Bermuda needed done. For KEMH's chronic mismanagement, Kurron had more experience and expertise than JHMI.

That is why BHB CEO David Hill and the Health Ministry supported Kurron's contract. Kurron installed a team at KEMH including White executives, and they began achieving significant cost savings and getting more of the right people—competent ones—in the right jobs.

We didn't abandon links with Johns Hopkins. We continued to consult JHMI on treatment issues, and later in the year I announced partnerships with JHMI, Lahey Clinic, and Partners Healthcare in Massachusetts to bring specialist doctors and other resources to KEMH.

Over the years cronyism had taken root between the UBP-established BHB, the White doctors who mainly controlled KEMH and MWI medical departments, and senior civil servants. This cronyism kept KEMH and MWI from performing as they should.

For this reason I asked two of my friends, and two very able Bermudians, Herman Tucker and Wendell Hollis, to become respectively BHB chair and deputy chair. Fortunately they agreed, thanks in part to their own friendship, which they knew would enable them to work well together.

Herman Tucker, my first Permanent Secretary in the Transport Ministry, was retired from the civil service. I met Wendell Hollis and his wife, Margie, in 2001 at a dinner to celebrate the launch of a new ship for Norwegian Cruise Lines, which Wendell has worked with since helping incorporate it.

Wendell, Margie, and I were at the same table, and Wendell and I enjoyed an easy, congenial conversation. That was unusual for a White Bermudian and me at the time, especially because Wendell was a UBP Senator.

Subsequently my father's lawyer, Max Quinn, who worked with Wendell, brought us together for golf. I learned Wendell was raised in fairly modest circumstances on the small farm his father and uncle ran in Harrington Hundreds, not far from Flatts. We had a childhood influence in common in Mr. Billy Wainwright, whom I mentioned earlier. Wendell learned carpentry from Mr. Wainwright, and he was impressed by the mutual respect between his father and uncle and Black Bermudians like Mr. Wainwright and Mr. Ewan Darrell, who both helped out on the farm. The relationship was not just one of employers and employees, but genuine affection among men who worked side by side. Wendell often worked with all four men on weekends and school holidays, gaining a perspective unimaginable to most White Bermudians.

Wendell had left the Island to complete his education, begin his career, and meet and marry Margie. Since returning with Margie to raise their family in Bermuda, Wendell had become one of Bermuda's most successful lawyers.

Herman and Wendell began addressing their BHB challenges, but soon reported interference from Health Minister Michael Scott, who feared being left out of the loop. I said I would talk to the Minister and get them the leeway they needed, which I did. I also suggested they should meet informally with me and others with useful perspectives on Bermuda's healthcare system. The Saturday Group, as we called it, included Minister Scott, Health Ministry Permanent Secretary Warren Jones, invaluable for his deep knowledge of Bermuda healthcare, and my brothers Philip Butterfield, chair of the Bermuda Hospitals Charitable Trust, and Vincent Hollinsid, who brought expertise as a first responder.

At 2007's halfway point, I was not sure when I would call the next election, especially in light of the dossier leak. I did not want to wait until fall 2008, the latest possible time. Calling an election when time is running out usually signals weakness in a parliamentary system.

That summer we introduced several new candidates: businesspeople Zane DeSilva and Jane Correia, the PLP's first prominent White members and candidates in some time; community activist Marc Bean and Big Conversation consultant Rolfe Commissiong; twenty-five-year-old Davida Morris, serving effectively in the Senate as Junior Minister for Social Rehabilitation and chairing the party's youth wing, Progressive Minds; and businesswoman Linda Merritt.

In mid-July we held a rally including a speech by MP Jamahl Simmons, who had resigned from the UBP early in the year and was serving out his term as an independent. Jamahl's father, Lionel Simmons, had been a PLP MP, and Jamahl had started his political career in the PLP before leaving for the NLP and UBP.

Jamahl said the UBP was returning to its White supremacist core. He was not the only Black politician to resign from the UBP around this time. UBP Chairman Gwyneth Rawlins resigned over the UBP's treatment of her as a Black woman. David Dunkley, a respected UBP advocate within the Black community although not an MP, also resigned because of the party's racism. UBP MP Maxwell Burgess ostensibly resigned because of discontent with fellow Black Bermudian Wayne Furbert's leadership; as we'll see, both men eventually decided the PLP was the right place for them.

The Combined Opposition criticized Jamahl's remarks at the July rally about Shawn Crockwell, the young Black lawyer replacing Gwyneth Rawlins as UBP chairman and a UBP candidate in the next election. There was ill feeling between Jamahl and Shawn from their time as colleagues. Jamahl spoke negatively about Shawn's past criminal record. Shawn had served a prison sentence for stealing $600,000 worth of illegal drugs in evidence in a Supreme Court proceeding.

I respected Shawn for putting his life back together. In fact, Shawn asked me to write a letter for him when he sought reinstatement as a lawyer, and I was happy to do so. But politics is a bare-knuckle contest, and I did not hesitate to point out that the UBP placed Shawn in a special category, as a reformed person, that excluded Rolfe Commissiong and others who had also reformed.

At that rally, however, I didn't mention Shawn. Instead, following a speech by Donald Evans, son of Dame Lois Browne-Evans, I promised a national holiday to honor her.

I HAD TWO REFRAINS IN CABINET MEETINGS. One was, "Who or what is the nail, and who or what is the hammer?" That is, where and how could we make the most impact?

The other refrain was, "What's in it for Jeremiah?" It was my way of asking if we had ordinary Bermudians squarely in mind.

For that reason, I instituted Open Thursdays in July. If I was on the Island on Thursday, and official business did not require otherwise, any Bermudian could arrange to see me for fifteen minutes. The day included a Brown Bag Lunch with an invited group of Bermudians with common concerns. Open Thursdays centered me on what the PLP had to do for the people of Bermuda, and I kept that schedule the rest of my time as Premier.

Visitor arrivals in Bermuda ebbed and flowed, but the general trend was up. In the summer of 2007 Bermuda's growth in vacation travelers exceeded that of rival destinations in the Caribbean. Growth continued to depend on more and better hotel offerings. In July Cabinet approved, and Environment Minister Butterfield signed, a Special Development Order (SDO) for a Jumeirah-run resort at Southlands. I also pushed for development with luxury brands such as St. Regis, Ritz-Carlton, and Hilton Grand Vacation Club.

Although it took only a small fraction of my time in office, I planned for life after politics. Late in 2006 an intermediary connected me with two successful medical technology entrepreneurs, brothers Roger J. Howe, Ph.D., and Maynard A. Howe, Ph.D. Their most notable achievement was leading Reliant Technologies to world leadership in medical laser technology.

The Howe brothers had become interested in stem cell technology because of a family member who was left a quadriplegic after an accident. Stem cell treatment had benefited their relative, and the Howes wanted to be at the forefront of extending it. They had formed a San Diego company, Stemedica, for that purpose. Stemedica was preparing for FDA-approved studies linking American physician-scientists and hospitals with researchers and clinics elsewhere, an emerging gold standard for medical innovation.

I had been tracking the development of stem cell medicine, and I saw the potential for medical tourism and unused space at the Brown-Darrell Clinic. The Howe brothers visited Bermuda in July 2007 to discuss their plans. Wanda and I were blown away by their relative's story and impressed by the Howe brothers as individuals and businesspeople, including Stemedica's relationships with prominent American medical centers.

On July 22, the four of us held a press conference to announce the Brown-Darrell Clinic's affiliation with Stemedica for clinical application of research innovations. The patients would be those designated "no option" for existing treatments.

The initial reaction in the Bermuda media was intrigued, but ill informed. We hoped that would change as the media gained knowledge of the stem cell field.

In mid August, Wanda and I attended the PGA Championship in Tulsa, Oklahoma, and saw Tiger Woods win his thirteenth major. It seemed the stars were aligning for the PGA Grand Slam of Golf at Mid Ocean Club in October, with Zach Johnson (the Masters), Angel Cabrera (the U.S. Open), Padraig Harrington (the British Open), and Tiger Woods (the PGA) competing for $1.5 million put up by Bermuda.

That sum was our direct financial guarantee. There were also indirect costs, nowhere near as great, such as waiving import duties for the PGA and television partner TNT. TNT reached 90 million households in North America. Bermuda's return on investment would be a function of how many households watched the PGA Grand Slam.

There were bound to be more viewers with Tiger in the tournament. When I was negotiating for the PGA Grand Slam, the PGA referred to him as the "40 percent man." That was how much his participation increased ticket sales, television ratings, and all golf-related revenue.

Only a month later, Woods withdrew from the PGA Grand Slam, citing the need to spend time with his wife and their newborn daughter, their first child. The PGA chose 2003 U.S. Open Champion Jim Furyk to replace him.

Woods's withdrawal disappointed the PGA, TNT, the world of golf, and Bermuda. But experience showed a Tiger-less PGA Grand Slam of Golf could still draw lots of attention and viewers in our target demographics. I told the country that our collective energies could score a major championship victory for Bermuda tourism.

Not everyone got the message. On September 18, "QLQ" was discovered singed into Mid Ocean Club's 13th green (someone was apparently trying to write "PLP"). The green could be fixed, but we worried the repair would be visible on camera. (Fortunately the television people made it look okay.)

We announced the same day that Bermuda Day (usually May 24 unless that fell on a weekend, in which case it shifted to the following Monday) would become National Heroes Day in 2008, with Dame Lois Browne-Evans the first, and temporarily only, honoree. The UBP reacted with pursed-lip approval, distressed that the first National Heroes Day would not include Henry Tucker.

Another September 18 event was the launch of a "Study of Employment, Earnings, and Educational Gaps between Young Black Bermudian Males and Their Same-Age Peers," conducted by Professor Ronald B. Mincy of Columbia University School of Social Work's Center for Research on Fathers, Children and Family Well-Being. A study of young Black Bermudian men had been commissioned by Premier Scott's Government, but never finished. It lacked the specificity and depth of Professor Mincy's study.

Environmental activists continued to oppose a Southlands resort. Former Premier Scott productively suggested my Government should offer Southlands' owners a swap, letting them build on the 260-acre brownfield site at Morgan's Point. This made a lot of sense, and Deputy Premier Paula Cox, Labour and Immigration Minister Derrick Burgess, and I began negotiating with Southlands owners Craig Christensen, Brian Duperreault, and Nelson Hunt.

Early October's Bermuda Music Festival brought good-sized audiences for well-known entertainers. There were fewer visitors than we wanted and still quite a shortfall between ticket sales and costs. Yet we had grown the event and felt we could keep growing it.

A few days later Sir John Vereker ended his term as Governor. Before leaving Bermuda with Lady Vereker, he did an interview with the *Royal Gazette* that surprised many. He expressed perplexity that Bermuda was not yet independent, and said, "To me, independence is the default option." He added that when the Bermuda Constitution was drafted in 1966, "it was assumed there would be independence in a few years." In other words, the British expectation for Bermuda, that it become an independent member of the British Commonwealth like Canada or Jamaica, was exactly what the PLP has always envisioned.

At the beginning of October the Island's sixth fast ferry, the *J. L. Cecil Smith*, named for a longtime ferry captain on the Paget-Warwick run, went into service. This completed the fast ferry system.

On Monday, October 15, the PGA Grand Slam of Golf kicked off with a Pro-Am segment in which Michael Douglas and Catherine Zeta-Jones participated. It should have been a time for unqualified celebration of Bermuda on the world stage. However, the *Royal Gazette* once again went into tag-team mode with the *Mid-Ocean News*, which on October 12 had published inaccurate statements about Stemedica and its partnership with the Brown-Darrell Clinic.

Two *Royal Gazette* headlines summed up its supposedly impartial coverage. "A miracle cure? Don't believe the hype" reported the view of a stem cell expert at Harvard Medical School that it was too soon for stem cell treatments. There was no attempt to provide views of stem cell treatment proponents at prestigious institutions. Likewise, there was no mention of the Howe brothers' successful medical technology entrepreneurship or Stemedica's partnerships with American medical centers and submission of research protocols for FDA approval. An article headlined "The mystery of Winterhaven" presented our plans for the Brown-Darrell Clinic as something out of a horror story like H. G. Wells's *The Island of Dr. Moreau.*

The sister newspapers had waited since our July announcement with the heads of Stemedica, so they could caricature me before the world as a mad scientist. Although the newspapers regularly trumpeted their devotion to Bermuda, they apparently had no concern about their articles' impact on Bermuda's image in the world. They had clearly given no consideration to the prospect of ethical medical tourism on the model of leading American medical centers.

The *Mid-Ocean News* even alleged Stemedica was a "sham" enterprise for "money laundering." Stemedica's lawyers quickly extracted a retraction and apology. The *Royal Gazette* acknowledged no need to apologize, even though royalgazette.com had published the *Mid-Ocean News* articles.

At the UBP's request, the FCO obligingly expressed "concern" about Bermuda's lacking stem cell regulations. When we said we welcomed regulations in line with international protocols, the UBP accused me of conflict of interest. Either they did or did not want Bermuda to join the world's best. As usual concerning my medical business, they spoke out of both sides of their mouths.

Despite Tiger Woods's absence, the 2007 PGA Grand Slam of Golf, won by Angel Cabrera, scored big for Bermuda. In November the PGA confirmed Bermuda as the site of the 2008 event. Television ratings showed we had reaped the equivalent of $7 million in advertising for our $1.5 million guarantee and modest indirect costs.

At the end of the month I led a small delegation to the Second World Tourism Marketing Summit in Beijing, which Bermuda helped sponsor. The Combined Opposition made much of the $75,000 sponsorship and our travel costs without weighing the benefit of securing Bermuda "approved destination status" for Chinese vacation tours. Eventually we achieved the first step toward this status, but subsequent Governments failed to follow up and Bermuda is not yet on the list.

At this time I also went to London on official business. Bermuda's political tongues were wagging about when I might call an election, but my travel persuaded everyone it would not be before early 2008.

The second Throne Speech of my Premiership began by quoting James Baldwin on each generation's responsibility to advance progress and referring to psychologist Abraham Maslow's famous hierarchy of needs, from food and shelter to realizing one's best potential. The speech outlined initiatives covering the full hierarchy from a national perspective: more affordable housing; improved policing; modernized fire safety codes; fighting elder abuse and providing mediation services in family court; seniors pensions and health insurance; a recognition committee for National Heroes Day; mandatory drug treatment for incarcerated addicts; a national disability advisory council and mental health treatment program; aligning domestic human rights legislation with our international obligations; enhanced environmental protections and a streamlined development process; legislation to support our international business sector and combat money laundering and terrorism financing; education reform, including increased financial aid for students attending Bermuda College; and programs to limit obesity and type 2 diabetes. Acting Governor Mark Capes read the speech on Friday, November 2, with no additional commentary of his own.

SHORTLY AFTER ACTING GOVERNOR CAPES RETURNED TO GOVERNMENT HOUSE, I asked him to dissolve Parliament pending an election on Tuesday, December 18. Political Bermuda was shocked. My official travel had misdirected attention, and it was unheard of to call an election immediately after a Throne Speech.

The Combined Opposition apparently believed the leaked BHC dossier had backed me into a corner and would make me delay calling the election until the calendar forced it. But I knew their baseless mud-slinging could not succeed indefinitely. If we let the UBP and its allies blare their sound and fury, Bermudians would eventually decide they had heard enough. Voters would then be able to recognize my Government's effectiveness, from fast ferries and affordable housing to the PGA Grand Slam.

November demonstrated that effectiveness. Tourism signed a ten-year deal to keep Norwegian Cruise Line ships visiting Bermuda. The first 37 graduates of the Mirrors Program testified to its positive impact. The Big Conversation, also known as the Bermuda Race Relations Initiative, held its final event, and if most White Bermudians chose not to participate, Black Bermudians gave the year-long discussions a positive reception. The PGA was delighted to keep the PGA Grand Slam in Bermuda. Economic vital signs were improving, contributing to increased national optimism.

Fearing BHC-related slander was not enough to defeat the PLP and me, the Combined Opposition manufactured another scandal. True to form, it involved another leak.

On November 13, a *Royal Gazette* headline claimed, "Officials called for rewrite of 'embarrassing' hospital report." Referring to the Saturday Group, the claim relied on handwritten notes Health Minister Michael Scott made at a meeting Saturday morning, August 18, in a Fairmont Hamilton Princess conference room. Someone stole the notes from Minister Scott's office and gave them to the *Royal Gazette*.

The newspaper said the stolen notes showed that BHB CEO David Hill spoke at the meeting, in its words, about KEMH's "poor clinical safety, worsening finances, lack of managerial process and accountability and people being employed in the wrong places," and that Kurron CEO Corbett Price said the reports out of KEMH were "devastating." The supposed smoking gun was a note of Minister Scott's to the apparent effect that a JHMI report "must be written so that it . . . does not become a document that embarrasses GOB [government of Bermuda]."

The UBP immediately attacked the Saturday Group as an antidemocratic cabal and alleged that my Government was dishonestly withholding information from the public. Both assertions were false.

It was absurd to say Minister Scott's notes were "minutes." Also attending the meeting were BHB Chairman Herman Tucker, BHB Deputy Chairman Wendell Hollis, Bermuda Hospitals Charitable Trust Chairman Philip Butterfield, and Health Ministry Permanent Secretary Warren Jones. If anyone in that group kept meeting minutes, it would be the Permanent Secretary, not the Health Minister. We met in an egalitarian spirit, but we didn't ask a Cabinet Minister to change roles with a civil servant, even a distinguished one like Warren Jones.

The JHMI report in question was appropriately confidential. The Combined Opposition strove to create the impression that JHMI's recommendations were at odds with Kurron's. Not at all. JHMI and Kurron agreed on KEMH's critical issues. The only difference was their respective expertise in medical treatment and hospital management.

There can be many valid reasons for keeping reports confidential. It may have to do with timing. Or a report may name individuals who have failed in their responsibilities not through malice or wrongdoing but innocent human causes. It would be irresponsible to publish such things.

The *Royal Gazette*'s quotation of Minister Scott's stolen notes should have shown that the Saturday Group had, in my brother Philip's words, "a very positive story" to share about progress in addressing racism and incompetent cronyism at KEMH. My Government had nothing to be embarrassed about with regard to Bermuda's hospitals.

Calling the Saturday Group antidemocratic was laughable. The group included all the duly elected and appointed officials responsible for KEMH and MWI. If I'd wanted to keep the Saturday Group a secret, we would have met at each other's homes in the dead of night, not on Saturday mornings at the Fairmont Hamilton Princess.

The *Royal Gazette* soon reported that 2003–2005 BHB chairman Jonathan Brewin said that during this period "an inappropriate amount of time had to be diverted towards dealing with one internal disciplinary matter because it had caught the attention of [Premier Smith's] Cabinet. This left the board unable to focus on wider issues . . . said Mr. Brewin."

If true, it was an astonishing admission by Mr. Brewin of the BHB's incompetence under his chairmanship or, worse, its disinterest in tackling KEMH's endemic racism. I often wrote Mr. Brewin about racism at the hospitals, especially the treatment of Black physicians I had identified as candidates to join their staff. These physicians had greater expertise and more advanced skill sets than many of the incumbent White physicians at KEMH and MWI. In one disciplinary matter I asked Mr. Brewin about, KEMH called out a Black physician on Cup Match morning to answer questions about the death of a patient, without also calling out the White surgeon involved in the case. In relation to another disciplinary proceeding, I questioned using a hair root for a drug test, an obsolete technique that produces many false positives. Mr. Brewin's minimal answers evidenced no great expenditure of time and effort by him or the BHB as a whole.

I remain proud of the Black physicians who joined KEMH and MWI thanks in part to my identifying them as candidates: Dr. Council Miller, Dr. James Brockenbrough, and Dr. Chantelle Simmons. They all improved patient outcomes in measurable ways, such as the decrease in amputations because of Dr. Brockenbrough's excellence as a vascular surgeon. Dr. Simmons, a native Bermudian who was at Emory University Medical Center when I asked her to consider returning to work in her homeland, was the first board-certified Black psychiatrist to practice in Bermuda. She joined MWI in 2009, became its director in 2011, and has done a superb job.

Ironically, on November 2 Bermuda Ombudsman Arlene Brock had released a comprehensive report, "A Tale of Two Hospitals." The report confirmed everything I had been saying about KEMH and MWI. The Combined Opposition would surely have preferred that "A Tale of Two Hospitals" had faded from memory before it misrepresented Health Minister Scott's stolen notes. But they succumbed to anxiety about the approaching election.

The six-week campaign was Bermuda's hardest fought. It was also notable for the PLP's effective use of digital technology and social media. I kicked things off by announcing the election to the country with a video clip on the PLP website and YouTube on Friday, November 2.

That weekend, businessman Harold Darrell outed himself as "Son of the Soil." A self-described "lifelong PLP supporter," he had been involved in disparate ventures. Early in my tenure at Transport, he proposed putting televisions in the airport's waiting areas. We negotiated an agreement, but he was unable to fulfill the deal.

About a week after revealing his role in leaking the BHC dossier, he inserted himself into the election as independent candidate in St. George's South. He was running against the PLP's Phil Perinchief and the UBP's Donte Hunt.

The Combined Opposition took every opportunity to portray the PLP as divided and me as a problematical Party Leader. On November 8, the *Royal Gazette* ran an article with the headline "Brown is a liability, say insiders." I e-mailed the PLP, in effect, "Hold the leadership challenges until after we win the election. Then I'll be glad to put the matter to the will of the party."

I never tried to block a leadership challenge from a PLP rival. Only a year before, in presenting myself as prospective Party Leader, I argued that stifling party members' political ambitions was counterproductive.

Again, White people voted almost exclusively for UBP candidates, whereas Black people voted for both PLP and UBP candidates. One reason for this disparity was White distrust of the PLP on the economy and our international business and tourism sectors.

At the prize giving for the PGA Grand Slam, I had asked Wendell Hollis to join the presentation group and walk off the 18th green with me afterward. This was powerfully symbolic, but I had more in mind. Walking to the club house, I said, "Wendell, when I call an election, would you make a television ad on the PLP's stewardship of the economy and our two main business sectors?"

Wendell belonged to neither party. After talking it over with his wife, Margie, because of the social stigma in elite White circles, Wendell agreed. We ran the spot on television and posted it on the PLP website and YouTube channel. In an effective low-key manner, Wendell described how the economy and business community had thrived under three PLP administrations and how conditions continued to improve. Among other things, he noted the PLP had achieved better balance of payments surpluses than recent UBP administrations.

Wendell reports his White friends often ask why he "turned," a question that speaks volumes about Bermuda's slow progress to racial equality. The most frequent comment he hears about me in elite White circles is that I hate

White people. He enjoys saying, "Last I saw in the mirror, I'm White, and I'm by no means Ewart Brown's only White friend."

On November 26, I reaffirmed plans for urgent care centers at the two ends of the Island. This would take pressure off KEMH and be more convenient for much of the population.

At the end of the month I blasted the UBP's negative campaign. I also appeared on stage at Bermudian rapper Collie Buddz's shows, wearing a T shirt emblazoned "Blind to you haters," from his hit song at the time.

As November gave way to December, Alex Scott suggested a close election might force a PLP leadership change. UBP Leader Michael Dunkley responded we were misleading the country as we allegedly had in 2003.

I acknowledged some PLP politicians wanted to replace me as Party Leader and Premier. But as I fulfilled my leadership responsibilities campaigning for all PLP candidates, I saw on a daily basis that rank and file members were united in their support for the Party and, by and large, my leadership.

In the run-up to the election, Social Rehabilitation Minister Dale Butler announced the PLP's new strategy for fighting illegal drug use and associated ills, including crime. The strategy entailed coordinated work by all relevant agencies from Police and Customs to addiction treatment programs, addressing both supply and demand.

The UBP's plan for drug-related crime was "three strikes," draconian punishment, and even preventive detention for illegal drug use. The UBP would never have proposed such measures if they affected young White men equally with young Black men.

The UBP also thought it had a winning plan to enfranchise thousands of foreign residents. With 53 percent of White voters in 2003 born outside Bermuda, enfranchising thousands more new White voters would help the UBP. The question was whether it would help Bermuda.

On December 9 we released the PLP election platform. It called for means-tested free day care, free public transport, and better health insurance for seniors, among other steps to improve Bermudians' lives.

The following day postal workers at the main sorting station at the airport intercepted a bullet in my mail. Shortly after the BPS informed me, I appealed for a peaceful election and post-election unity, no matter who won.

The new Governor of Bermuda, Sir Richard Gozney, and his wife arrived on the evening of December 11. I welcomed them to Bermuda at the airport.

Neither the Throne Speech nor the PLP platform mentioned independence. I tried to make it clear independence would always be on the PLP stove, but was not then on the front burner. However, a Reality on Independence Group ran full-page scare ads on any near-term move for independence. Among the scary things the ads predicted was loss of visa-free travel to the United States.

In the closing days of the campaign I emphasized the harm the UBP's "three strikes" policy would do, imprisoning scores of young Black Bermudian men for minor offenses without reducing the illegal drug problem. And I passionately opposed UBP immigration proposals. At the PLP's election eve rally on December 17, I told an overflow crowd, "The UBP has pledged to give [voting] status to up to 8,000 foreigners and allow them to buy our land, dilute our votes, silence our voices, and deprive our children and grandchildren of what is rightfully theirs."

Ashford & Simpson performed at the rally, singing their biggest hit, "Solid," with its "solid as a rock" refrain. We had made that a PLP theme song in recent years. As PLP supporters sang along, I felt we were headed for victory.

15. Leading in Times of Turmoil

T HE PLP'S THIRD GENERAL ELECTION VICTORY over the UBP on December 18, 2007, included monumental victories by Patrice Minors and Zane DeSilva over longtime UBP MPs Michael Dunkley, the Opposition Leader, and David Dodwell. In Smith's North, Patrice beat Opposition Leader Dunkley—he had run in a new constituency in a show of misplaced confidence—by 92 votes. And in Southampton East Central, Zane beat incumbent David Dodwell by 48 votes. The UBP was forced to name Michael Dunkley to the Senate, fueling talk, which continued throughout 2008, that the UBP's days were numbered.

It was gratifying to lead the PLP to a resounding electoral victory. I hoped it set the stage for another year of progress benefiting all of Bermuda. I didn't yet fully recognize the enormous difficulties we'd face in implementing our policies of reform and growth—difficulties driven by both the intensity of the political opposition we faced and global economic upheaval. My immediate focus was organizing a new Cabinet to work with me in leading the nation forward.

In recognition of her hard work in beating Michael Dunkley and her demonstrated abilities as an MP and Cabinet Minister, I wanted Patrice Minors in my post-election Cabinet, but she respectfully declined so she could devote more time to her family. Zane DeSilva was a first-time MP, and we agreed it was too soon for him to have a Cabinet post, but my eye was definitely on him for the future because of his strong leadership ability and tremendous work ethic.

The new Cabinet included an adjustment of portfolios, combining Community and Cultural Affairs (where Wayne Perinchief had been Minister) with Social Rehabilitation in the Ministry of Culture and Social Rehabilitation with Dale Butler as Minister. Wayne Perinchief told the media that his progressive stances on gay rights and race relations had cost him his Cabinet seat. That was nonsense. I was simply looking for the hardest working and most effective Cabinet Ministers I could find among PLP MPs and PLP members who could be named to the Senate.

Phil Perinchief had lost the seat in St. George's South previously held for the PLP by Renee Webb, who had chosen not to stand for reelection. As with his brother, it was a question of demonstrated work ethic and effectiveness, as both a campaigner and a Minister, that left Phil Perinchief out of the Senate and the new Cabinet. Instead I chose PLP Senator Kim Wilson as Attorney General.

I named Derrick Burgess as Minister of Works and Engineering; Elvin James as Minister of Environment and Sport; Randolph Horton to continue as Minister of Education; Senator David Burch to continue as Minister of Labour, Home Affairs, and Housing; and Terry Lister as Minister of Energy, Telecommunications, and E-commerce. PLP Deputy Leader and Deputy Premier Paula Cox remained in Cabinet as Minister of Finance.

It was a personal pleasure, as well as a positive move for Bermuda, to bring Nelson Bascome back into Cabinet as Minister of Health. This raised eyebrows in the Combined Opposition, including in the *Royal Gazette*'s editorial on the new Cabinet, because of the court case against him. However, I was confident the charges against Nelson would not stand up, and there was no question in my mind that he was the best Health Minister that Bermuda ever had. I needed his sound judgment in Cabinet as we continued to work on rectifying the major problems at King Edward VII Memorial Hospital (KEMH), ensuring healthcare for seniors, and making other much needed improvements in the Island's healthcare system. I also believed that we could not, and should not, acquiesce to the UBP's apparently cozy relationship with senior officers in the Bermuda Police Service and the groundless investigative focus on PLP MPs, Party members, and supporters.

The UBP naturally shuffled its leadership lineup following its election defeat and named new MP Kim Swan as Party Leader. Observing this, I wondered if Kim Swan's course would follow that of others among the UBP's best and brightest Black members and eventually estrange him from the party's retrograde agenda.

Two other events of January 2008 bear noting. In the middle of the month I announced a $13.6 million overhaul of the Port Royal public golf course, with a scheduled reopening in a year's time. Port Royal was a championship level course, but had fallen into disrepair. As I already mentioned in connection with the IMG report on Bermuda as a golfing destination, rebuilding it was an important part of our tourism strategy.

Late in January the U.K. Parliament's Foreign Affairs Committee announced that a delegation headed by Labour MP Andrew MacKinlay would visit Bermuda in March. This was part of a "good governance" audit of all fourteen of the U.K.'s Overseas Territories. What motivated the audit at that time was an interesting question. In addition to endlessly repeated, but groundless, assertions about misconduct at the Bermuda Housing Corporation, a good deal of scandalmongering had been going forward regarding Turks and Caicos, including allegations of corruption against Premier Michael Misick. My personal friendship with Michael Misick was always a black mark against me in the Combined Opposition's eye.

Another factor, which I suspect was even more important, was the global economy. The effects of the subprime mortgage crisis in the United States were continuing to ripple through the world's financial markets. The news had been bad since early 2007, and no one knew how much worse things might get. In September the United Kingdom had been forced to prop up Northern Rock, its fifth-largest mortgage lender. Several of the Overseas Territories had become important financial centers, and the City of London's financial institutions were heavily enmeshed with all of them. The U.K. Labour government under Gordon Brown undoubtedly feared its potential liabilities for bailouts and other financial support in the United Kingdom because of the overseas business of British financial firms. The idea that the British cared about the financial health of Bermuda and its businesses was, of course, laughable.

Bermuda's financial regime was solid, and during the course of the year we were going to be singled out for praise in that regard by various authorities, including high-ranking officials in both the U.K. and U.S. governments. Investigating Bermuda, however, provided cover for audits of other Overseas Territories, including those closer to home in the Isle of Man and Guernsey. It also provided opportunities for the Combined Opposition in Bermuda, as we'll see.

The convening of the new Parliament in Bermuda called for a Throne Speech only four months after the previous one on November 2, 2007, just before I called the general election. Throne Speeches during my tenure as Premier were iterative documents that built on each other, and any reading of them will show their continuities. Among other things the Throne Speech on February 1, 2008, committed the PLP Government to:

- Free day care for children four years and younger
- Continuing efforts in primary and secondary education reform in line with the David Hopkins study of May 2007
- Free tuition to Bermuda College
- Interest-free down payments to extend home ownership to more Bermudians, along with rent subsidies and other affordable housing efforts
- Expansion of the Mirrors Program and other measures to fight youth and drug crime

- Continuation of the Bermuda Race Relations Initiative's Big Conversation
- Beginning construction on the first of two urgent care centers to be located in Southside at the east end of the Island, with a center at the west end to follow as soon as possible thereafter
- Public health campaigns on obesity and Type 2 diabetes
- Better provision for seniors' pensions and health insurance
- A beverage container deposit system
- Further strengthening of our robust anti–money laundering and anti-terrorism financing measures
- Reform of the Corporations of Hamilton and St. George's
- A self-regulating press council

In February we released the final tally by the Transport and Tourism Ministry of business and tourist arrivals in 2007. The total for the year, 663,767 visitors, set a new record for Bermuda. The worsening economic climate indicated that 2008 would not be so positive, but all we could do was press on as optimistically, energetically, and effectively as possible to sustain arrival numbers.

In the middle of the month, Jamahl Simmons became my executive aide, replacing Wayne Caines, who was beginning a career in the private sector. Jamahl had to hit the ground running, and he quickly demonstrated that he was the right person for a demanding and important job.

As usual, we tabled the budget in the House of Assembly in February. For the present, we postponed a move to institute free fares on Bermuda's buses and ferries, but we continued with important infrastructure projects. These included the overdue resurfacing of runways at L. F. Wade International Airport, the equivalent of building a new 25-mile road, and the construction of a mega-cruise ship pier in Dockyard.

In a recession every government has two choices: spend wisely to sustain the economy, provide jobs, and build for the future; or opt for austerity. The forces of wealth always prefer austerity in such instances because it enriches them as creditors. The events of the past decade have clearly demonstrated that governments should be very wary of austerity campaigns and recognize that sound infrastructure spending and other sensible pump-priming measures are much more prudent. As 2008 went on and the economic situation worsened even more, my Cabinet colleagues and I had to stay focused on what was good for Bermuda as a whole and not be swayed by fearmongering critics.

As you no doubt realize from my earlier remarks, after my family and Bermuda, there is nothing dearer to me than Howard University. Early in

March I was proud and delighted to receive the university's Distinguished Alumni Award.

That month Health Minister Nelson Bascome decided the time was right to release the sequestered report by Johns Hopkins Medicine International (JHMI), which had become a matter of controversy. I discussed this in the last chapter, in relation to meetings of the Saturday Group on healthcare reform. There was nothing embarrassing to the PLP Government in the report as our critics had claimed. We had not released it earlier because we wanted to refine our policy goals in light of its recommendations as well as get a second phase of JHMI's work underway.

JHMI's report pointed, not at the PLP Government, but at problems within KEMH. In particular, the report recommended a shift from per diem to per case reimbursements for hospital care. This change was needed to reduce average hospital stays, especially for non-acute care, that were almost three times longer than they should be. The average KEMH stay was then 17.3 days, compared to 5.9 days for a hospital stay in the United States and 6.3 days in the United Kingdom.

In planning a first National Heroes Day, with Dame Lois Browne-Evans as the first honoree, we initially decided to have it replace Bermuda Day on the third Saturday in May. Public response persuaded us that this was not the best choice, and in March we announced that we would inaugurate National Heroes Day in October.

As the 2008 presidential primary campaign in the United States heated up, then Senator Barack Obama made quashing offshore tax havens one of his signature policies. He cosponsored a bill in the U.S Senate that listed Bermuda as a tax haven. This action bore watching as the campaign continued, but I felt it was important to observe publicly that Obama was targeting companies that were domiciled in Bermuda, like the conglomerate Tyco, rather than the insurance and reinsurance industry, which was by far the biggest and most important part of our international business sector.

Presidential candidate Obama kept beating his drum on tax havens as the economy continued to worsen. In the meantime Bermuda was losing some of its airlift because of reduced travel and increased fuel costs during the recession. United canceled its Chicago flight and Delta canceled a flight from New York. My Transport and Tourism colleagues and I responded with landing fee waivers to prevent the loss of other flights and worked to gain new ones.

Good news came Bermuda's way when Gerald Cox, the chair of the Global Institute of Internal Auditors, praised our having internal auditors report their findings to the head of the civil service rather than to elected officials or political appointees. Bermuda's system was a model for the world, Mr. Cox said.

I announced one of my most controversial decisions at the end of March, axing Government advertising in and subscriptions to the *Royal Gazette*. We were spending $800,000 a year to fatten the newspaper's profits while getting much less than a fair shake in its news coverage and editorials. In my view it made more sense for the Government to advertise and announce initiatives, requests for contract proposals, job openings, and the like in less expensive online media, which reached much more of the population than the *Royal Gazette*.

I anticipated that the *Royal Gazette* would cry foul, and that industry associations in the United Kingdom, the United States, and elsewhere would protest that we were trying to throttle the media. But I was prepared to accept any criticism that came our way.

Early in April we reached an agreement in principle to swap Southlands for acreage at Morgan's Point. In return for giving up the 37 acres of Southlands, its owners would receive 80 acres to build a resort at Morgan's Point. Much remained to be settled before the swap went through, including who would pay to clean up the toxic pollution left behind by the U.S. Navy. Unless the U.S. government could be persuaded to assume some or all of the cost, Bermuda taxpayers were going to have to foot an expensive bill for environmental remediation.

Two other positive moves for Bermuda tourism occurred at this time, one with future implications and one with immediate impact. With regard to the future, Park Hyatt agreed to manage the new hotel that developer Carl Bazarian planned for the Club Med site. The immediate, or nearly immediate, impact came with a promotional deal for the 2008 Major League Baseball season with the New York Mets, brokered by GlobalHue. This followed the successful formula GlobalHue had established for Bermuda in earlier deals with the NBA's Miami Heat and baseball's Washington Nationals. Now we would be working that strategy hard in the biggest tourism market in the United States.

I was in Augusta, Georgia, for the Masters golf tournament on the second weekend in April. Although I enjoyed seeing some of the golf (South Africa's Trevor Immelman won), I was really there to discuss keeping the PGA Grand Slam of Golf in Bermuda past 2008. The discussions didn't conclude that weekend, but they definitely moved in a positive direction.

To foster good public broadcasting in Bermuda, the PLP Government had established CITV in 2007. We advanced that initiative by forming a partnership for technical and other training with Pittsburgh's award winning public television station, WQED. George L. Miles, Jr., the president of WQED, went out of his way to ensure that the partnership delivered value for Bermuda. WQED's vice president of content, Daryl Ford Williams, also contributed immensely to CITV's successful launch.

I was happy to join other graduates of Central School in May to celebrate its being renamed for Victor Scott. I was impatient to see progress throughout Bermuda's schools in line with the Hopkins Report, and the topic was always high on the agenda for Cabinet meetings. In the meantime I was happy that we were able to launch a website to link Bermudian students with prospective employers.

That month U.S. Consul General Gregory Slayton, a Republican Party stalwart appointed by President George W. Bush, said that relations between the United States and Bermuda were at "an all-time high." Equally gratifying was that he praised our anti-money laundering efforts, pointedly disagreeing with British Tory MP Edward Leigh, who claimed on no evidence that they were "appalling"

In the middle of May, my wife, Wanda, and I flew to Los Angeles at our own expense for a charity poker night and silent auction at the Playboy Mansion to benefit the Urban Health Institute, a charity started by my oldest son, Kevin, and operated by him out of the same building as his medical office on Crenshaw Boulevard. I had no involvement with the Urban Health Institute, but I was glad to support Kevin's charitable efforts.

Three trips to stay at the Elbow Beach Hotel in Bermuda were items in the silent auction, as arranged by Bermuda's New York Tourism office. The Combined Opposition criticized the auctioning of the trips, saying Bermuda's taxpayers shouldn't be footing the bill for my oldest son's charity.

They weren't footing any such bill. No Bermuda Government funds were involved at all. The Elbow Beach Hotel donated the trips, and Bermuda got good value out of them through the event at the Playboy Mansion, which attracted a very affluent group who were the exact demographic we wanted to sell on visiting our country.

In the following weeks there was also criticism of my visiting the Playboy Mansion, because this supposedly gave Bermuda's youth a bad example. I announced that I would return to the Playboy Mansion for any event I thought equally worthwhile on my own and Bermuda's behalf.

The Combined Opposition tried to link the Playboy Mansion event for Kevin's charity with the tripling of Government travel costs over the prior ten years as part of caricaturing me as a luxury-loving spendthrift of Bermuda's money. I've told you about my significant official travel, and there is no doubt that my colleagues and I went on more official trips than our recent predecessors had done. The greater number of trips was simply because we tried more things and generated more initiatives on Bermuda's behalf than our predecessors—in either the PLP or the UBP. Given the efforts and achievements of my Government in education, sports, transport, tourism, and stewardship of Bermuda's international business sector, I see nothing to regret or change with regard to official travel during my tenure as Premier.

Bermuda is a speck in the middle of the Atlantic. If we want people to vacation or do business in our country, it often takes more than an invitation. Sometimes you have to visit them where they are to persuade them to consider Bermuda.

Wanda and I agreed at the start of my term as Premier that she would accompany me on any trip of three days or longer. Whenever she joined me on official trips, she paid for her own airfare and other travel costs. In addition, at every hotel she scrupulously paid 50 percent of all incidental room charges. In cases where we thought the cost of the room was too high for the Government alone to incur, Wanda paid part of that, too. As I said in a comment to the press that some people in Bermuda consider notorious, I didn't stay at Motel 6. Of course, neither did any other Premiers or Cabinet Ministers, whether they were members of the PLP, UBP, or OBA.

Throughout the first months of 2008, the UBP increasingly tried to drag every topic in the House of Assembly into a discussion of alleged PLP corruption. We heard through the grapevine that the UBP's American political consultants had advised that the only route for the party to get back into power was to sow doubt about the PLP in voters' minds—never mind the facts. I began to look for an opportunity to send a shot across their bows.

On Friday evening, May 23, the chief item on the agenda was a renewed lease with additional operating concessions for the Coco Reef Resort, formerly known as the Stonington Beach Hotel. In her tenure as Minister of Tourism, Renee Webb had negotiated the original lease under which hotel operator and developer John Jefferis took over the hotel from Bermuda College's hospitality training program. The existing and additional operating concessions primarily involved tax relief and a suspension of rent until the hotel was operating profitably. This was typical of Bermuda Government concessions to hotels and resorts, and Coco Reef would begin paying rent later in the year.

When UBP MPs veered away from debating the substantive provisions of the lease and operating concessions to insinuate that there was something fishy going on because John Jefferis was a PLP supporter, I halted debate. By that criterion, every Government hotel concession in the history of Bermuda was unethical.

To an uproar of protest from the UBP side of the aisle, I vowed to end debate whenever the UBP groundlessly accused the PLP of corruption. I said:

> I came to the House today to engage in an energetic and robust debate on this Order [regarding Coco Reef Resort]. I came prepared, and was anticipating the Opposition would fashion a number of arguments

against the Order. I appreciate and approve of that approach, but something happened very early in this debate that causes me to explain something to the House and the Opposition.

This is how we are going to do business. We will engage in debate, we will not suppress it, and we will listen to all members of the House and answer questions and then vote. But every time there is the implication or insinuation of something dishonest or corrupt mentioned by members of the other side, we will shut down the debate and move with the numbers.

To quote the *Royal Gazette* on what happened next, "Dr. Brown then said, 'I move that the Order be sent to his Excellency the Governor.' The Speaker of the House gave the Order to the vote, and despite opposition it was approved by the majority."

The Combined Opposition's repeated raising of groundless corruption allegations made me concerned about how this might be affecting Bermuda's image with tourists. I announced that we were considering hiring a public relations firm to address the issue. After exploring the question with several experts, we decided later in the year that tourists were not paying attention to the news media inside Bermuda, either while they were on the Island or at other times, and we did not need to shoulder additional public relations costs in this regard.

Early in June, Wayne Caines resigned from the Senate to devote himself entirely to his rapidly advancing business career. I was sorry to lose Wayne in the Senate, but happy to see how quickly he was progressing in his new endeavors. He was well on the way to becoming one of Bermuda's most successful business executives. To replace him in the Senate, I chose Marc Bean, a rising young member of the PLP.

With every passing week, the economic picture worsened. The deepening recession in the United States was shrinking travel from our biggest business partner and tourism market. As a defensive measure in relation to rival tourist destinations in the Caribbean, my Government tabled a bill to allow cruise ships with casinos to operate them in Bermuda ports. Unfortunately the bill did not pass, but I was determined to try again later.

In the fourth week of June U.S. Consul General Gregory Slayton and I went to Washington, D.C., for two and one-half days of meetings with congressional legislators and members of the executive branch. A planned highlight was a twenty-minute meeting with President George W. Bush.

Instead of behaving in accord with their self-styled image as Members of a loyal Opposition, UBP MPs dredged up a crack I made in relation to one of President Bush's presidential campaigns—I was pulling for his opponent—about his not being much of a reader and having only two books in his library.

The comment also reflected President Bush's adoption of a down-home Texas rancher persona, even though he was the Yale-educated son of an immensely privileged WASP family. There was no reason to think that my words really got under his skin or that he held a grudge about them. As I told Bermuda's media, I was sure that if the President thought about the remark at all, he shrugged it off as normal campaign chatter.

However, the UBP was determined to try to plant a grudge in President Bush's mind, and the *Royal Gazette* did its best to turn up the volume in the President's ear with a headline about my "joke at Bush's expense." Ignoring Consul General Slayton's public comments about our having achieved an all-time high in Bermuda-U.S. relations, UBP Leader Kim Swan said in the House, "The Progressive Labour Party has generally done a poor job maintaining the best possible relations with the government of the United States, Bermuda's largest and most vital trading partner." Forgive me for finding the U.S. Consul General's assessment more telling than that of the UBP Leader. A week or so later, Consul General Slayton rebutted the UBP by describing Bermuda and the United States as "the best of friends." President Bush could not have given me a more cordial reception, and we had a very enjoyable chat.

On the substantive front, I had a busy round of meetings with legislators on Capitol Hill, particularly with members of the Congressional Black Caucus. I had steadily developed relationships with many of them over the years, and as Premier I leveraged these relationships on Bermuda's behalf in a way that was unprecedented and unparalleled for any Government Leader before or since.

The number-one item on my agenda with U.S. leaders was always to protect and strengthen Bermuda's financial regime and our international business sector. In that regard it was enormously useful to have friendly meetings with legislators such as Congressman Charles Rangel of New York, then head of the House Ways and Means Committee, which has chief responsibility on tax matters; Congresswomen Barbara Lee, Laura Richardson, Maxine Waters, and Diane Watson of California; and Congressman G. K. Butterfield of North Carolina, whose father was Bermudian.

Among my additional priorities for this visit was building a case for U.S. help remediating the brownfield acreage at Morgan's Point. It was a long shot, but my good contacts on Capitol Hill at least got me in front of people with real influence over the outcome.

U.S. Consul General Slayton and I returned from this round of talks with quite a plum: pre-clearance of customs for travelers on private jets from Bermuda to the United States. This perk affected a relatively small number of travelers, to be sure, but it greatly benefited our luxury tourism image, as the Combined Opposition rather grudgingly admitted.

I would be remiss if I did not note that my press secretary, Glenn Jones; a security officer detailed to me by the Bermuda Police Service at its sole discretion; and my wife, Wanda, flew with me from Bermuda to Washington, D.C., on GlobalHue's private jet, which also carried one of the advertising agency's employees. Traveling by private jet enabled me to attend the Bermuda-Trinidad football match at the National Sports Center on Sunday night and still make it to the meeting with President Bush on Monday morning. No commercial flight would do that. The Bermuda Government reimbursed GlobalHue for the equivalent of three first-class air tickets, and Wanda paid the same for herself.

July brought criticism of cost increases on the mega-cruise ship pier Correia Construction was building in Dockyard. The cost had increased from the $35 million projected in 2007 to $50 million. There was no skulduggery involved. The head of the construction firm, Dennis Correia, had duly reported that the initial specifications were not sufficient for the pier to withstand 25-mile per hour winds with 80 percent reliability, the target set by the Transport Department's experts. Following review, we revised the specifications accordingly.

Implying that something fishy lay behind Correia Construction's contract to build the pier, the *Royal Gazette* claimed that Dennis Correia was best man at my wedding to Wanda in 2003. In fact, the best man was my oldest son, Kevin, something that would not have been difficult to establish.

Dennis Correia had already saved Bermuda's taxpayers millions of dollars with the East Ferry floating docks and his solution to the Cockburn Bridge's having only a single lane. (Instead of replacing the existing structure, he built a parallel one to allow travel in both directions.) However, the Combined Opposition refused to concede that Correia Construction received PLP Government contracts because of demonstrated competence and efficiency.

A political poll at this time showed quite disappointing numbers for me, extremely good numbers for Deputy Premier and Finance Minister Paula Cox, and disastrous 4 percent approval for the UBP. Tongues wagged inside and outside the UBP about its uncertain future, and former Premier John Swan appealed to his UBP colleagues not to dissolve the party.

The PLP Government took two important steps for Bermuda in mid-July. The first was to conclude negotiations for Bermuda to ally with the University of the West Indies. This vastly increased higher education opportunities for young Bermudians, while ensuring that they would pay the lowest possible costs in earning advanced degrees and professional certifications.

The second important development came when Health Minister Nelson Bascome announced that the Bermuda subsidiary of Kurron Shares, Kurron Bermuda Limited, had received the contract to develop FutureCare, the new system we had promised to ensure that seniors had health insurance in retirement. Bermuda urgently needed FutureCare because we knew that by 2025 we would have the highest proportion of people fifty and older of any similar-sized jurisdiction.

Mid-July was also when the U.K. Parliament's Foreign Affairs Committee (FAC) released its report on good governance in the Overseas Territories. With regard to Bermuda, the report recommended a Commission of Inquiry into the Bermuda Housing Corporation (BHC) and "related matters," in the *Royal Gazette*'s words, despite the fact that all the alleged wrongdoing at the BHC had been thoroughly investigated. Minister of Labour, Home Affairs, and Housing David Burch observed that the report showed the FAC's delegation to the Island in March had devoted too much time to "the lunatic fringe." In my view, as I said at the time, the report indicated that the delegation had given more of an ear to the UBP than the PLP.

The head of the delegation, U.K. Labour MP Andrew MacKinlay, insisted this was not so and described Bermuda and Gibraltar as "flagship overseas territories. Whatever the criticisms about faults are, they are very good." It was hard to see that view reflected in the actual content of the report, however, which was nitpicking with regard to Bermuda.

In terms of assessments of Bermuda, I was much more concerned about the PLP Government's own finding that 11 percent of Bermudians were below the poverty line. The finding validated our promise to determine the number of Bermudians in serious financial need and set a poverty line for the first time in Bermuda—an essential step for accurately diagnosing the health of the country. The finding was an alarm bell for all of Bermuda and gave renewed urgency to the PLP Government's efforts to advance political, economic, and social justice.

Mid-July brought troubling personal news, when Kevin was arrested in Los Angeles on charges of molesting female patients, including an undercover police officer. He assured me the charges were false, and as any father would, I publicly expressed the hope that he would be exonerated. Kevin was freed on a $400,000 bail bond. But later in the month he was rearrested on additional charges of molesting patients and bail was set at $4 million. Kevin could not pay the bond for such a high bail and remained in custody for some time until other family members and I could arrange the bond for him. We did not pay $4 million in cash as my critics alleged. Kevin's mother, Georgia, worked tirelessly to gather mortgage pledges from her family. Together with mortgage pledges from my family and other security, we were able to secure a bond for the $4 million.

I was shocked and dismayed by these events. However, I strove to do all I could for Kevin, who was eventually convicted and sentenced to prison. I was determined to follow my father's example of doing right by all of his children.

At the close of July, Bermuda hosted the fourth annual African Diaspora Heritage Trail Conference. It was gratifying to sustain the momentum for the African Diaspora Heritage Trail, which I had kept as a signature PLP Government project since it was initiated by then Premier Alex Scott and then Tourism Minister David Allen. It was also good to see the *Royal Gazette* recognize and support the effort in an editorial.

The tourism picture as a whole was not improving, however, because of what was now being dubbed the Great Recession, the worst economic downturn since the Great Depression. That added impetus to my continuing efforts to energize the Tourism Department's North American sales office in New York City. With thirty employees, the office was grossly overstaffed and highly inefficient. Over the years, under both UBP and PLP Governments, the New York office had become a favored destination for some young Bermudians who wanted to live in New York. I've already mentioned my disappointment in observing the lack of energy in the office and hearing such things as "Our job is not to sell. Our job is to educate people about Bermuda."

Wrong. The office's only real purpose was to sell Bermuda as a tourist destination, and it had to start functioning aggressively as a sales office. Accordingly we reviewed the staff to see how many should be retained, with those to be let go receiving appropriate severance and assistance in finding new jobs back home in the Tourism Department or elsewhere. On the basis of a Tourism Ministry search, we also contracted with an American sales organization, Sales Focus, to come into the New York office to rev up tourism sales. The contract was short term because I had doubts—well-founded, it turned out—about Sales Focus's ability to sell in the specialized niche of the hospitality industry. But it was a reasonable move at the time given the problems in our New York office and the recommendations of senior civil servants in Tourism.

Rather than address the issue on its merits, the Combined Opposition vilified me for wrecking the lives of the small number of staff who were going to lose their jobs. It was ironic, to say the least, for anti-trade unionists like the UBP's Michael Dunkley to opine that my "disrespect" of the New York Tourism office staff, who were all represented by the Bermuda Public Services Union (BPSU), would hurt Bermuda's ability to "recruit top quality civil servants."

Renee Webb, my immediate predecessor as Minister of Tourism, spoke up at this time to support the need for an overhaul of the New York office. Although she expressed reservations about how I was handling the overhaul, I appreciated her candor in describing her own dismay at the poor functioning of the office and how then Premier Scott derailed her efforts to fix it rather than upset the BPSU.

Seizing a fresh angle for portraying me as an "imperial" Premier, in August the *Royal Gazette* ran the first of several articles about the Government's hiring a housekeeper-cook for my private residence, where we hosted frequent official functions. These articles paralleled a series of stories on security arrangements for the house.

Government work on a Premier's residence was nothing new. Both my predecessors and successors have had work done on their houses at taxpayer expense. Through no request or desire of ours, but on Minister David Burch's sole initiative, security officers conducted a review of our home and determined that our front wall needed an additional balustrade to make it more secure and that the entrance should be guarded.

But somehow my case was different, even if there was no evidence that the outlays on my house were unreasonable. Thus every article about hiring a housekeeper-cook highlighted the $60,000 salary for the job.

It so happened that in October a search commenced for a new chef at Government House, where Governor Sir Richard Gozney resided with his numerous staff in truly imperial splendor. Yet the *Royal Gazette* never mentioned the salary for the job, which was surely at least $60,000 a year. Nor has the newspaper ever questioned the seven-figure annual cost for the Governor's salary, his staff, and the operation of Government House.

To return to August, that month the first students registered for classes at Bermuda College under our free tuition plan. The plan substantially increased enrollment, as we hoped it would.

Other events of the month included positive and negative developments in tourism. On the positive side, the old hotel on the Club Med site was imploded without incident and without any adverse environmental effects in neighboring communities. The demolition opened the way for new construction at the site. On the negative side, discount Zoom Airlines, based in Canada, went into bankruptcy. Zoom had been bringing travelers from the United Kingdom via Canada, but one of its major troubles was the refusal of British Airways to give up exclusivity on the Bermuda-U.K. air route. British Airways' stranglehold on direct service doomed all our efforts to increase tourist arrivals from the United Kingdom.

Late in August, the Bermuda Hospitals Board forged a link with the Dana-Farber Cancer Institute in Boston. Allying with one of the world's foremost cancer research and treatment centers greatly improved the prospects for Bermudians diagnosed with cancer.

For many years I had been trying to raise awareness and generate effective action against the social cancer of illegal drug gang violence. I actively pursued the hiring of consultants who had dealt with these problems. I thought it was essential that we try to nip Bermuda's gang culture in the bud, and I took a well-documented presentation to the Governor, who rejected the use of American experts. I was deeply disappointed by his decision. It was not the Governor's children who were being caught up in antisocial behaviors. He could not feel the pain I felt for my younger Black brothers.

In the years after the Governor rejected my report, drug gangs would become entrenched in Bermuda and escalate the murder rate. Who knows how many lives we might have been able to save if he had allowed us to bring in anti-gang experts.

One anti-gang measure that was working well was the Mirrors Program. Early in September thirty young Bermudian men graduated from Mirrors, and we celebrated that as Mirrors prepared to enroll a new group of young Bermudians at risk.

An increasing number of young Bermudians attended universities in Nova Scotia, and the province was becoming an increasingly important outsourcing provider for our international business sector. In September I went to Halifax to meet Bermudian students, encouraging them to aim high and to bring their newly developed talents and expertise back home. I also met with the province's premier, Rodney Macdonald, to discuss forging even stronger links. In due course Premier Macdonald and his colleagues came to Bermuda to sign a new memorandum of understanding for cooperation in education, workforce development, trade, transport, tourism, and financial services.

In September we also carried through the reorganization of the Tourism office in New York. Nine Bermudians lost their jobs. I took no pleasure in that, but it was a necessary move for Bermuda. We helped the nine individuals in question as much as we could, and most of them found new jobs in the Tourism Department in Bermuda.

Despite the troubling world economic news, Wendell Hollis gave a presentation to Cabinet on Tuesday, September 9, confirming that $400 million in Lehman Brothers Holdings financing was lined up for redevelopment of the Sonesta Wyndham site in Southampton. Money from Lehman Brothers, the global leader in hotel and resort financing, was also set for redeveloping the Coral Beach Club in Paget. Less than a week later, on Monday, September 15, Lehman Brothers was forced to file for Chapter 11 bankruptcy protection. If President George W. Bush's administration had decided that Lehman was too big to let fail and put it on life support along with Citibank and other major American financial institutions, Bermuda would likely have two or three new hotels today.

These events put the focus of the 2008 U.S. presidential campaign squarely on the financial services industry and its sins. That month, Senator Barack Obama's campaign put out a new television ad attacking Senator John McCain for taking contributions from the "tax haven" of Bermuda. Although the polling at this point remained fairly close, the smart money was betting on a win by Obama. That meant we needed a good strategy to show him the value Bermuda's insurance and reinsurance industry provided to America's economy and consumers.

At the end of September, the judge presiding over Health Minister Nelson Bascome's theft trial threw out the charges, which never made any sense. As Nelson's lawyer said after the judge's decision, the whole affair was a "witch hunt" by "unseen forces."

Every October brought around the annual PLP Delegates Conference. Looking forward to that, the *Royal Gazette* began in late September to run articles about my supposedly shaky standing with PLP delegates and a looming leadership challenge. Throughout my tenure as Premier, the media dubbed various PLP MPs as possible rivals, featured negative comments from former members of my Cabinet, such as Wayne and Phil Perinchief, and played up the views of nameless "PLP insiders" that my leadership was under threat. Yet never once did anyone in the PLP straightforwardly announce their candidacy to lead the Party and the Government, as I did in challenging then Premier Scott in the fall of 2006.

Before I discuss the conference in late October 2008, there are a few things I need to mention from earlier in the month. First, the tally of visitor arrivals was down 12 percent through August. The day after we released this figure, the *Royal Gazette* headlined an October 3 editorial, "It's time for a new Tourism Minister." Certainly I had plenty on my plate, as the editorial said, but I also still had plenty of energy for the job as well as more expertise and useful relationships in the tourism industry than any prospective replacement. I wasn't going to make a change to satisfy my critics, when it was not in Bermuda's interest to do so.

A few days later I had the sad duty of going to Jamaica for the funeral of my aunt Alma. Although my relationship with Aunt Alma and Uncle Basil had its rough patches, as I described in chapter 3, they opened their home to me when I most needed it, and I will always be grateful to them.

On October 14, we held the first National Heroes Day and celebrated Dame Lois Browne-Evans in fine style as she deserved. Although we would reconsider the holiday's timing and eventually move it to a weekend in June, we successfully inaugurated a new Bermuda tradition. The increasing popularity of National Heroes Day—it is now the centerpiece of a popular holiday weekend of great value to Bermuda's merchants—has gradually quieted all the naysaying whisperers against it.

That week Bermuda hosted its second PGA Grand Slam of Golf at Mid Ocean Club. Once again it occurred without Tiger Woods, who qualified by winning the U.S. Open in June but then had season-ending knee surgery. Padraig Harrington won both the British Open and the PGA Championship that year, so the four-contestant field included past major winners Jim Furyk and Retief Goosen. It was Fuyrk who won in a sudden-death playoff over Harrington.

On the eve of the event I was able to announce that Bermuda would also host the PGA Grand Slam of Golf in 2009 and 2010, and that in 2009 it would move to the refurbished course at Port Royal. The reaction from the Combined Opposition was interesting. When I first sought to bring the PGA Grand Slam to Bermuda, my critics said it was pointless to promote golf on the Island unless we had two championship-level courses. Because Port Royal was then in such disrepair, the critics said I was ignoring the recommendations in the IMG report I mentioned in chapter 14. The UBP's Kim Swan, a former professional golfer, was extremely vocal on this score.

The multimillion-dollar renovation of Port Royal was well underway, but the Combined Opposition was no longer sure it was a necessary part of the picture. Why not keep the PGA Grand Slam of Golf at the private Mid Ocean Club, they said. The *Royal Gazette* headlined one of its articles on the matter, "Decision to switch Grand Slam a risky move." With astonishing tone deafness, the paper's sports editor, Adrian Robson, wrote, "As Bermuda celebrated its first National Heroes Day this week, those at Mid Ocean Club might have been taking their hats off to their own heroes—course superintendent Norman Furtado and his staff."

As Premier and as a member of Mid Ocean Club—put forward by my uncle Bert, Dr. Bert McPhee, the club's first Black member, and graciously seconded by the Combined Opposition's Michael Dunkley as well as by Leon Nearon, another one of the club's earliest Black members—I wholeheartedly admired the work Norman Furtado and his staff did for the PGA Grand Slam of Golf in both 2007 and 2008. I made a point of thanking and congratulating Norman and his staff personally and in my official remarks each year. But Adrian Robson's trivializing crack, rejecting Dame Lois Browne-Evans, the mother of Bermudian democracy, in favor of Mid Ocean Club's able course superintendent, showed how fealty to the White establishment colored so much of what the *Royal Gazette* published. Snarkily mixing high and low is commonplace in sports writing. Yet I cannot imagine British expatriate Adrian Robson saying a course superintendent for a British Open or the head groundskeeper at Wimbledon was worthier of praise than Winston Churchill.

On Monday evening, October 20, I addressed the people of Bermuda on radio and television about the state of the economy, the PLP Government's response, and the short- and long-term prospects for the country. In any such address it is important to be accurate but neither unnecessarily alarmist nor unjustifiably optimistic. That was the balance I tried to strike, and I believe I was reasonably successful. The Combined Opposition begged to differ, but I didn't expect them to rise above party feeling in their assessment.

The PLP Delegates Conference began October 22. I opened the conference by reminding the PLP delegates that "I never promised you a rose garden," that I had said in 2006 that those who did not want change should not vote for me. And I closed it by exhorting them, "We must keep going." Their enthusiastic responses showed I still had their support and renewed my own confidence in the path we were traveling.

The following week I was in London for meetings of the Overseas Territories Consultative Council. There the Financial Secretary of HM Treasury, Stephen Timms, singled out Bermuda for meeting the latest standards of the Organization for Economic Cooperation and Development (OECD) on transparency of tax information and anti-money laundering. The Great Recession had triggered calls for anti-tax haven action throughout the developed world, not only in the United States, and Mr. Timms concluded his remarks by saying, "If on tax information exchange everyone had made as much progress as Bermuda, the world would be better off."

I welcomed these remarks on behalf of the PLP Government's continuing work to bolster Bermuda's financial regime, and I praised Deputy Premier and Finance Minister Paula Cox's leadership in this area.

Barack Obama's victory in the 2008 U.S. presidential election gladdened the hearts of all Black Bermudians as it did those of Black people throughout the world. I wrote President-elect Obama to congratulate him on his historic election, but also to note "the critical role" of Bermuda's insurance/reinsurance industry in making tornado insurance more affordable to American consumers and contributing other benefits to the American economy.

The Combined Opposition tried to use the Obama victory against me by contrasting his "inclusiveness" with my supposed "divisiveness." The noise about this rose to screeching levels after I said that if White Bermudians had voted in the 2008 U.S. presidential election as they voted in all of Bermuda's general elections, 99 percent of them would have voted for Obama's opponent, no matter who that was. The statement reflected a demographic fact confirmed by every voting tally and poll in the history of Bermuda.

The unfavorable contrast between President-elect Obama and me in the UBP's statements and the *Royal Gazette*'s editorials missed two facts. One was the greater advance toward racial justice in the United States than in Bermuda. The other was that racism in the United States and against Barack Obama as president remained virulent, even though large numbers of White Americans voted for him. The record of racist attacks, explicit and implicit, on President Obama and First Lady Michelle Obama would fill several volumes as long as this book. According to a *New York Times* article of December 5, 2009, "Threats Against Obama Spiked Early," the number of threats of violence against Barack Obama, many of them racially motivated, increased dramatically before his inauguration and early in his presidency.

A new session of Parliament convened in November, necessitating another Throne Speech. The speech sounded the same themes as my Government's previous Throne Speeches and detailed continuing and new initiatives in areas such as education, healthcare, environmental sustainability, reducing violent crime and gang activity, and stewardship of Bermuda's financial regime and economy during tough times in the global economy. The speech also described plans for an inclusive celebration in 2009 of the 400th anniversary of continuous settlement on Bermuda.

Governor Sir Richard Gozney read the speech and in conclusion he added some remarks of his own. The Governor said, "I intend to be vigilant in my role of overseeing law and order and some of the accountability [Bermuda requires] ... in tandem with the elected Government." Time would tell how rigorous and even-handed the Governor's vigilance was going to be. His remarks suggested, however, that he was listening more closely to the PLP Government's partisan political opponents than to the international authorities praising our good governance, transparency, and internal auditing.

A few days before the Throne Speech I dropped Randolph Horton from my Cabinet, naming El James to replace him as Minister of Education and Glenn Blakeney to take over Minister James's former portfolio of Environment and Sports. Randy Horton told the press he had been "bitten by a lion." In the controversy that followed, I revealed that I had made the change because Minister Horton was moving too slowly on education reform, that I had offered him the opportunity to resign, and that he had refused to do so. This was a personally difficult decision for me, and I struggled with it for some time. I have known Randy Horton almost all of my life, and I hold deep affection for him. However, I had given him ample time to show results and the needs of Bermuda's children had to come first.

Mike Charles, the General Secretary of the Bermuda Union of Teachers (BUT), said I should instead have let go the American education leader we had hired to oversee education reform in line with the Hopkins Report. He was referring to Henry Johnson, former successful school superintendent in Mississippi and North Carolina, as well as former Assistant Secretary of Education in the administration of President George W. Bush. Dr. Johnson was doing a solid job for Bermuda.

UBP Shadow Minister for Education Grant Gibbons jumped into the fray by pointing an accusing finger at my brother Philip Butterfield, the chairman of the special committee empaneled to work for education reform. As a *Royal Gazette* headline put it, "Blame Premier's brother, not Horton, says Shadow Minister." Dr. Gibbons argued that reform efforts should draw on "the existing knowledge base in the Ministry [of Education]" and the teachers union.

The Shadow Education Minister's comment suggested that he never read, or had forgotten, the Hopkins Report. In his analysis of what plagued the Bermuda school system, Professor David Hopkins had said we needed to overhaul the Ministry of Education and replace its leadership as well as address dysfunction in the BUT and inadequate training and performance on the part of teachers.

These factors were what made education reform in our small country so difficult. At every Cabinet meeting I asked Minister Horton, "Is there any blood on the floor?" By that I meant, had he followed through on the Hopkins Report's most important recommendations and made the personnel changes reform required? His answer was always, "Not yet."

Bermuda's children desperately needed someone to take hard decisions and action for reform, despite the impact on friends and/or relatives working in education. I sincerely hoped that Minister El James would show more creativity, resolve, and fortitude in dealing with both the Ministry of Education and the BUT.

Later in November, frustrated by the lack of progress in reform, including Mike Charles's resisting requests to meet and work together on behalf of Bermuda, Philip made some very intemperate remarks. He questioned why Mr. Charles, "a gym teacher" who'd had "his fifteen minutes of fame," should be considered an authority on education by the media. He also said "citizens of this country should be ashamed" that Mr. Charles was "the face of public education" in Bermuda.

Philip immediately regretted the "gym teacher" remark, and it was an aberration for him to categorize anyone on the basis of their job or station in life. But he was not going to resign as chair of the education reform committee on that account as the BUT, the UBP, and the *Royal Gazette* all called on him to do. Instead he apologized publicly to Mr. Charles and Bermuda, humbly asked for the cooperation of the BUT, and redoubled his efforts to improve the school system.

I referred to Bermuda's ultimate need for independence in two November speeches in the House on the United Kingdom's scrutiny of its Overseas Territories. On November 9, I expressed concern that the FAC's report on governance in the Overseas Territories "jeopardized reputations" without proof of wrongdoing. I said, "We may not be far away from the U.K. Government using those legislative measures at its disposal to impose on territories standards and laws which may not be desired by their people."

On November 28, I spoke about the "colonial ties" restricting Bermuda and criticized an announced U.K. review of the financial services industries in Bermuda, Cayman, Isle of Man, Guernsey, Anguilla, Turks and Caicos, and the British Virgin Islands. In October the U.K. government had had to provide a £500 billion ($850 million) bailout package for U.K. banks. U.K. authorities were obviously worried that the FAC's good governance audit had not probed deeply enough into the City of London's ties with financial centers in the Overseas Territories.

Given that Bermuda had received a clean bill of health that year from the International Monetary Fund (IMF) as well as the other international authorities I've mentioned, I told the House that we had "just reason to be offended and insulted" and that the prospective investigation was "an affront to every Bermudian." Noting that taxation and fiscal policy were a settled matter of internal self-government, I said that we would cooperate with the U.K. investigation as we had to do, but that independence must eventually "rightfully and righteously come."

Speaking against my remark from the other side of the aisle were Grant Gibbons, Bob Richards, and Patricia Gordon-Pamplin, respectively the Shadow Ministers for Education, Finance, and Works and Engineering. They took exception to my remarks on independence, which included noting the seven-figure annual cost associated with the Governor and Government House, and attacked me as an "imperial" Premier. A *Royal Gazette* editorial, "Premier's overreaction," soon followed, scolding me along the same lines and especially echoing Shadow Finance Minister Richards.

Flash-forward to late 2016 and early 2017, when Bob Richards, Deputy Premier and Finance Minister for the UBP's successor clone, the OBA, lashed out bitterly at U.K. meddling in Bermuda's financial regime. He said Bermuda might have to become independent to protect itself from unfair interference. Funnily enough, no *Royal Gazette* editorial criticized Deputy Premier Richards. The same sentiment that was an "overreaction" from a PLP Premier became perfectly okay and even a brave stand for Bermuda in the mouth of an OBA Deputy Premier. The truth is that my statement as Premier and Bob Richards's statement as Deputy Premier were both right.

To go back to November 2008, in the middle of that month we opened the new TCD building on North Street. Correia Construction completed the building four months ahead of schedule and on its $14 million budget. In my remarks at the opening ceremony I recognized the excellent work by Dennis Correia and his firm. With criticism of the PLP Government for awarding contracts to Correia Construction in mind, I said, "Maybe that has something to with why the Government likes to see you do work."

At the end of November we passed a bill for vehicle emissions testing to be contracted to Bermuda Emissions Control (BEC). As I've already mentioned, my cousin Donal Smith was one of the principals in BEC. In that regard the UBP's Wayne Furbert noted in the House that he was to some extent the originator of the bill because the Bermuda Government's work on emissions testing with Donal Smith "started with" him under a UBP administration.

As 2008 came to a close, tourism numbers as a whole continued to be disappointing. One bright spot, however, was an increase in visitors from the greater New York City metropolitan area, thanks to the success of our promotional deal with the New York Mets baseball team.

In the middle of December, I convened a summit of leaders of our international business sector to discuss what we could expect from Washington, D.C., and the incoming Obama administration in 2009, and what our response should be. In those discussions and in deliberations in Cabinet there was no need, and no one in Bermuda ever suggested there was, for us to consult the United Kingdom.

Yet any negotiations we might have with Washington about our financial regime would plainly fall under the heading of foreign relations, supposedly the exclusive purview of our colonial masters in London. Since the days of Henry Tucker it had been accepted that Bermuda Governments often had to engage directly with the U.S. government with no involvement or interference from the United Kingdom.

Little did I know how this Bermuda dogma would be turned upside down in 2009.

16. The Year of the Uighurs

E ARLY IN 2009, I ADDRESSED THAT SUMMER'S 400TH ANNIVERSARY of continuous settlement on Bermuda. "History belongs to all of us," I said, emphasizing we could not honestly celebrate the nation's origin without remembering slavery and racism.

For the UBP-OBA, inclusion has meant ignoring these evils in our past and their sequels in our present. A soon-to-be-unveiled statue of Sally Bassett, unjustly burned to death as a slave in 1729, was criticized for its size and location by people in the same league as Holocaust and Middle Passage deniers.

Bermudian artist Carlos Dowling's sculpture of Bassett at the stake was one-third larger than life size, because that is standard in sculpture of historical figures. Hamilton City Hall rejected the statue, so we put it on the grounds of the Cabinet Building, visible from Front Street. Dedicating it I said, "Little could Sally know that the Government that condemned and burned her would one day honor her."

The first public sculpture of a Black Bermudian was one at the eastern end of East Broadway of the late Johnny Barnes, erected in his lifetime by Hamilton's business community. White Bermudians sometimes voiced the wish that all Black Bermudians behaved like Johnny Barnes, who for many years showed up rain or shine on East Broadway, the entrance to Hamilton, smiling and waving to motorists as his statue depicted. The statue of Sally Bassett struck a different tone.

On January 20, 2009, I was in Washington for Barack Obama's inauguration as the first Black president of the United States. Tourism bought a $75,000 inauguration sponsorship. Although Shadow Tourism Minister Michael Dunkley scorned the sponsorship, the attendees were precisely the affluent demographic Bermuda wanted to attract.

The inauguration was a joyous moment for Black people everywhere, and I was proud to witness it. However, I had to do so from a secure location because security officials asked foreign leaders not to attend the swearing-in. This reflected a significant increase in threats of violence against Mr. Obama.

In Bermuda the Combined Opposition alleged corruption in a new building for the Hamilton Police Station and Bermuda magistrates' courts. Begun in 2007, construction was not yet complete.

The first allegation was that Government improperly advanced $800,000 to contractor Landmark/Lisgar Construction Limited for a performance bond. Landmark was a local business 61 percent owned by Bermudian Edmund Lee Matvey. Lisgar, Landmark's Canadian partner, was exiting the project, with Landmark/Lisgar Construction becoming LLC Ltd. The Combined Opposition questioned the performance bond, the financial arrangements in Landmark/Lisgar's divorce, and who owned the rest of LLC Ltd.

Echoed by the *Royal Gazette*, the *Mid-Ocean News* claimed a trust company held 39 percent of LLC for "a who's who of Cabinet Ministers and their relatives." But the trust company, established by a local law firm, had nothing to do with LLC. A week later, an apology to the law firm for erroneous reporting appeared in the *Mid-Ocean News* and the *Royal Gazette*.

The erroneous articles claimed corruption directly tainted Cabinet. The *Royal Gazette* wrote, "The *Mid-Ocean News* has learned . . . two . . . Cabinet Ministers have received payments . . . as consultants on the court project, despite a clear conflict of interest."

The "evidence" of corruption consisted of two checks, which were subsequently discovered in Ministry files only as Robert Horton, Works and Engineering Permanent Secretary, prepared answers to Parliamentary questions about the allegations. One check was ostensibly made out to me for $14,780, the other to Minister Burgess for $10,000.

How could the *Mid-Ocean News* and the *Royal Gazette* know about these checks before Robert Horton found them? Were they in cahoots with those trying to smear Minister Burgess and me? These questions have hung in the air ever since.

With the assistance of HSBC Bank of Bermuda, Minister Burgess and Robert Horton established that the checks had been altered. Their legitimate payees, two subcontractors, had received and cashed them in the normal course of business. Someone had taken the canceled checks, put my name and Minister Burgess's name on them, and reinserted them in Ministry files.

Governor Sir Richard Gozney visited Cabinet to express concern over the forged checks, promising an aggressive Police investigation. Subsequent events indicated no urgency in that investigation.

Even after the checks were proven false, the *Royal Gazette* described "allegedly false cheques" under the headline "Cheque 'doctoring' claim backed by construction boss." If the same situation had arisen with a UBP Premier and Minister, the newspaper would have accepted the falsity of the checks and not clung to a groundless "allegedly false."

In late February we announced Government would establish a Washington office like one recently opened in London. A Washington office would ensure that "we're in a position to communicate effectively with the Obama administration." My biggest priority was safeguarding our international business sector from President Obama's moves against offshore financial centers. This was a survival issue for Bermuda, especially since tourism had fallen back into the doldrums.

Late February also brought the budget for the new fiscal year. The UBP and a *Royal Gazette* editorial said we should implement severe austerity because of the Great Recession.

In hindsight, we in the PLP Government chose the correct path, making significant cuts while maintaining public expenditures that kept people working and primed our economic pump. Countries embracing austerity to the exclusion of all else did less well than those with a more balanced approach.

The UBP attacked expenditures for foreign consultants. Bermudianization aimed to make foreign expertise less necessary. But given our size, we had to look abroad in some instances. The analogy I drew was medical care. Our small population was likely to produce a good neurosurgeon every hundred years. That didn't mean a local allergist should do neurosurgery.

The UBP also failed to connect the dots between foreign consultants and productive developments. Shadow Health Minister Louise Jackson publicly recognized dramatic KEMH improvements, yet kept slamming the contract with Kurron, whose hospital management experts guided those improvements. At KEMH and elsewhere we were getting "value for money," as the Combined Opposition demanded.

A two-year renewal of GlobalHue's contract to manage Bermuda's $14 million tourism advertising budget was another Combined Opposition target. Both the UBP and the *Royal Gazette* repeatedly referred misleadingly to a $28 million contract for GlobalHue, which received a normal 10 percent annual fee of $1.4 million for creative and management services.

Auditor General Larry Dennis claimed GlobalHue endorsed overbilling of $1.8 million for the placement of Bermuda's television commercials by a media buyer. What happened departed from prior Bermuda Tourism practice, but it was not unheard of in the advertising industry.

Our budget was too small to buy slots on major outlets in the "up front" market, when big advertisers lock in commercial time. To put our commercials on CNN and other outlets our target demographics watched, GlobalHue paid a media buyer up front, so that it could cut deals on the fly for orphaned commercial time, at a discounted price, when another advertiser backed out of commitments. It looked like we had paid more in commissions than we should have, but in return we got commercial time we could not otherwise have afforded. Nonetheless, the uproar led to a decision that GlobalHue would no longer make such deals with a media buyer.

As the year wore on, there was criticism of GlobalHue's placing our ads with minority-interest publications and cable channels, even though most spending was with mainstream publications and channels. Some people considered these ad buys too Black for Bermuda.

Most of the criticism focused on renewing GlobalHue's contract without inviting other bids, even though prior agency Arnold Worldwide had its contract renewed that way. The two-year renewal recognized GlobalHue's sterling work through the "Bermuda—Feel the Love" campaign. The agency had helped achieve record tourist numbers in 2007, and it was not to blame for the Great Recession drop in arrivals.

Taking note of the same old misinformation about Don Coleman as my supposed "longtime friend," I cracked that I had known Shadow Tourism Minister Michael Dunkley, one of the chief GlobalHue critics, a great deal longer than I had known Don Coleman. The UBP refused to get the joke.

In addition to slamming GlobalHue, Michael Dunkley attacked the 2009 Bermuda International Love Festival at the Fairmont Southampton in February—and Wanda and me. The event cost Bermuda $150,000, and Wanda and I hosted it for 160 people all told, including 98 visitors from abroad, up from 72 in 2008. Rock Media, HSBC Bank of Bermuda, the PGA, JetBlue Airlines, Digicel, the Fairmont Southampton, and Tucker's Point Club all joined Government as sponsors because of the appeal to affluent travelers.

If 98 visitors each spent $2,000 in Bermuda—a very conservative estimate—we got the $150,000 back and more. The event also occurred in our "golf and spa season," when our hotels were hungry. Yet Senator Dunkley said he viewed the $150,000 cost "as just ludicrous." In a gratuitous slap at Wanda and me, he added, "A lot of these events have become something for the powers that be . . . to have some fun."

His comment exemplified the racist stereotype that Black people party rather than take work. Hosting the event was certainly enjoyable. However, it was still a job—tirelessly working the crowd to ensure they felt positively about Bermuda. That visitor numbers climbed 36 percent, despite the bad economy, indicated we could continue to build the event into a bright spot in an otherwise dead shoulder season.

During the festival weekend, Wanda and I had a room in the Fairmont Southampton because we were hosting Tourism guests until late each night. The first morning, a friendly hotel maid gave us a big smile as we left the room, and we stopped to chat. When I asked how she was doing that day, the maid said, "I'm fine, thanks. I want to tell you I'll never forget December 1, 2006."

"Why is that?"

She said, "That's the night you called out Grant Gibbons for being a racist dog and told him to stop disrespecting Mrs. Brown. A bunch of us cheered our heads off listening to the radio."

The Great Recession-induced drop in tourist arrivals persisted. To my dismay, I learned in March that a Tourism error had inflated arrival numbers since mid-2008. Expatriate workers returning to Bermuda and people visiting relatives had been mistakenly counted as tourists because of a change in an air passenger arrival form. I took responsibility for this and personally announced it to the public in tandem with steps to ensure the error never recurred.

My critics chorused I should give up my Ministerial portfolios. However, there were no obvious candidates to take them over. I felt that it was in Bermuda's best interest for me to keep serving as Tourism and Transport Minister as well as Premier.

One of the most consequential decisions in my Premiership also occurred in March—without criticism from the Combined Opposition. Butterfield Bank, Bermuda's second largest, had played too heavily in subprime mortgage-backed securities, the "toxic assets" that triggered the Great Recession. In the first quarter of 2009 the bank wrote down $37.5 million of bad investments and reported a net loss over $20 million.

The Bermuda Monetary Authority wisely ordered the bank to raise more capital. However, the bank's subprime exposure did not position it to launch a new share offering. Bermuda's financial services community feared Butterfield Bank might collapse, endangering the international business sector and local economy.

This situation became a top Cabinet priority. We decided Butterfield was too big to let fail. Early in March we took the unprecedented step for Bermuda of guaranteeing a $200 million share offering by the bank, promising to buy any or all of it if private investors did not do so by June. This reassured the market, and the offering succeeded.

I did not endorse the decision wholeheartedly because of reservations about Butterfield's financial strength, business plans, sense of responsibility as a Bermudian employer, and vulnerability to predatory investors. I also felt the direct benefit to Bermuda—the Finance Ministry could exercise warrants to buy a small ownership stake—was skimpy.

My reservations turned out to be well founded in terms of job losses and profiteering by outsiders. A year later the Carlyle Group, then the world's second-largest private equity firm and frequently described as an "asset stripper," became Butterfield's largest shareholder and determined its course until it exited early in 2017. It did much better than the average shareholder. Its preferential status included a $4 million annual fee for management advice. I regret Bermuda did not do better with this deal, especially because so many

Bermudian Butterfield employees have been made redundant since the Government saved the bank..

In effect the PLP Government, caricatured as concerned only with Black Bermudians, put up to 20 percent of the country's $1 billion annual budget on the line to bail out White establishment Bermuda for reckless financing. HSBC Bank of Bermuda had wisely avoided a dangerous level of subprime exposure.

Shadow Finance Minister Bob Richards said the share-offering guarantee was exactly what he would have done in a UBP administration, the only time to my knowledge that he supported a major PLP Government decision. He also assured Bermudians that despite our lack of bank deposit insurance, they need not fear losing any money they had in the bank: "I don't believe there was ever a danger of that."

The bank's subsequent major losses and recapitalizations showed the Shadow Finance Minister was certainly taking a rosy view of the bank's health. So was the *Royal Gazette*. In highlighting Richards's statements, the newspaper did not think it worth informing the public that his wife, Pauline, was on Butterfield's board. Compare that to the newspaper's habitually emphasizing HSBC Bank of Bermuda CEO Philip Butterfield was my brother and its attempts to distort every PLP Government contract during my Premiership as going to a "longtime friend" or relative of mine.

If Pauline Richards's remuneration as a Butterfield director was like that of most company directors, she received shares and share options. While praising the deal in Parliament and to the media, Bob Richards never disclosed that his wife was on the board.

The *Royal Gazette* editorialized that the PLP Government's action was "a sensible and prudent hedge" to sustain Butterfield Bank, but it gave little credit to my administration for our decision in the national interest. Instead the editorial ended by attacking the PLP Government's supposed "failure to prepare for a rainy day." Odd words, given that we were the ones propping up Butterfield, not the other way around.

Butterfield was a victim of its own decisions. The offering guarantee immediately lifted it from Standard and Poor's Credit Watch Negative to its Credit Watch Developing list.

My Cabinet and I knew a similar decision to help a Black-controlled entity would trigger hysterical outcries by the UBP and the *Royal Gazette*. Please hold that thought.

Tourism was now much the smaller of Bermuda's main economic sectors, but too big to let fail without every effort we could muster. In the last chapter I mentioned the law prohibiting cruise ship casinos from operating in port. Although conservative Bermudians opposed gambling, I thought it would be a good idea to let cruise ship casinos operate in port from 10 p.m. to 6 a.m. when there were no significant competing attractions on land. We tabled a bill in the House, but I halted debate mid-March because it seemed headed for defeat. With more time to consider the matter, some of the bill's PLP and UBP opponents might change their minds.

During this time I asked my brother Philip and U.S. Consul General Gregory Slayton to consider whether a bipartisan organization of business and community leaders could serve as a think tank on economic concerns. They both embraced the idea of the organization, which I suggested naming Bermuda First.

UBP Leader Kim Swan accepted my invitation to join the group, whose formation we announced in April. Don Kramer, a pioneer in our insurance and reinsurance sector, agreed to lead Bermuda First, and other prominent Bermudian business people, politicians, and community leaders served on its committees.

On April 1, on time and under budget, the Lamb-Foggo Urgent Care Centre opened at the east end of the Island. The first phase of FutureCare, our new health insurance plan for seniors, also began in April. Because of the poor economic climate, we budgeted only $10 million for the first phase, enrolling those seniors most in need. Affordable private insurance was available for those with greater means.

Instead of recognizing a phased introduction was prudent during the economic downturn, the UBP complained we were unfairly favoring some seniors over others. Shadow Health Minister Louise Jackson said we were "disenfranchising seniors" because we expected more affluent seniors to continue their existing health insurance for the time being. Apparently we were supposed to let impoverished seniors suffer rather than help them as soon as possible. That was not my idea of good government.

The experiment with American firm Sales Focus in our New York Tourism office ended unsuccessfully at this time. A *Royal Gazette* editorial said I had "destroyed" the office and put several hardworking Bermudians out of a job. The job losses were and are regrettable. However, change remained necessary and we kept trying to find a better way on Bermuda's behalf.

In mid-April, British Labour Prime Minister Gordon Brown warned the Overseas Territories to quickly meet OECD banking and tax transparency standards. He ignored the vast difference between a jurisdiction like Bermuda, soon to join the OECD's "white list" of countries in full compliance with the standards, and others near and distant to Britain's shores.

Also in mid-April, KEMH announced replacement of its 8-slice computerized tomography (CT) scanner with a 64-slice machine. It was trying to catch up with the Brown-Darrell Clinic's 64-slice scanner, in use for over a year.

On April 18 and 19, Trinidad and Tobago hosted the fifth Summit of the Americas held by the Organization of American States (OAS). Although Bermuda did not belong to the OAS, I took part in plenary sessions thanks to Prime Minister Patrick Manning of Trinidad and Tobago. Prime Minister Hubert Ingraham of the Bahamas also assisted me in attending meetings. I witnessed the odd moment when Venezuelan president Hugo Chávez went over to shake American President Barack Obama's hand. President Chávez kept calling President Obama "my brother," although the diplomatic look on the latter's face was hardly brotherly.

The hottest topic of discussion was the British heavy-handed action in suspending the Turks and Caicos Constitution and initiating long-drawn-out legal proceedings that have cost the Turks and Caicos people over $100 million and are still ongoing more than a decade later.

PLP MPs and Senators met in caucus Wednesday evenings during parliamentary sessions. On the last Wednesday in April, most of the caucus were present, when Wayne Perinchief and Randy Horton proposed a motion backed by former Premier Alex Scott. The three MPs wanted a discussion of the PLP leadership, followed by a vote—MPs only—on a leadership recommendation to be shared with PLP delegates. The motion failed, and Michael Scott then put a motion for a leadership discussion, but no vote, at the next week's Caucus.

Frustrated, Wayne Perinchief told the *Royal Gazette* a motion of no confidence was soon likely in the House. Randy Horton added, "We have a lot more than three people," although when push came to shove they had fewer than three—at least on the PLP side of the aisle.

As I told the press, I took this leadership challenge seriously. However, I also noted that its motivation was "more personal than political." I had dropped Wayne Perinchief and Randy Horton from my Cabinet, and I had defeated Alex Scott in a leadership vote. I saw no sign PLP delegates generally shared their disaffection.

The immediate sequel came Monday, May 4, in a meeting of the PLP's Central Committee, our MPs, and branch chairmen. The meeting ended with the Central Committee proclaiming support for me.

David Burt was PLP chairman, and my respect for him grew sharply that evening. He refused to be pulled to either side, giving everyone an opportunity to speak. Terry Lister, Randy Horton, Wayne Perinchief, and Alex Scott all had the chance to sway the party against me. They either said nothing or spoke so weakly that they might as well have kept their mouths shut. I said that if the party as a whole really wanted me to go, it only had to say so.

Following the meeting, reports claimed I asked Cabinet to sign "a loyalty oath." Deputy Premier and Finance Minister Paula Cox even referred to it that way on the radio some days later. This vocabulary signaled how passive-aggressively she was going to behave toward me in the second half of my Premiership.

I did not ask for a loyalty oath or any other document. Labour, Housing, and Home Affairs Minister David Burch circulated a statement of support, something often done in such instances. He did this in the same spirit in which Paula Cox and Cabinet Ministers expressed support for Premier Smith in 2003 and Premier Scott in 2006.

On Wednesday, May 6, the PLP Caucus took up Michael Scott's motion for a discussion of Party leadership. Over six hours, no one stepped forward to vie for leadership or offered an alternative agenda for the Party. The meeting ended with another affirmation of my leadership.

Given the *Royal Gazette*'s chronic bias against the PLP Government and my leadership, at this time I ordered the Cabinet, Tourism, and Transport communications officers to reduce their contact with the newspaper. International media associations, ignorant of the newspaper's history, cried censorship. The paper remained free to publish as it chose.

In chapter 13, I discussed the problems with ProActive, the original Berkeley construction contractor, and its 2004 replacement by Somers Construction. Premier Scott's Government had entered into a long arbitration proceeding with ProActive, seeking repayment of over $15 million. In fall 2008, arbitrators ruled for the Government, but ProActive was then bankrupt and defunct.

My Cabinet sought to recoup about half of what was owed via the $6.8 million performance bond underwritten for ProActive by BIU subsidiary UAH. The BIU argued it should not be liable, saying UAH received no opportunity to replace ProActive with its own management team. Having already spent a lot of taxpayers' money pursuing arbitration, the PLP Government now faced another expensive legal battle with the BIU.

Auditor General Larry Dennis's February special report on the Berkeley performance bond and GlobalHue's contract had predicted we would not ultimately force the BIU to pay because it might cripple the union. In May, Cabinet decided it was indeed against Bermuda's interest to cripple the BIU financially.

This difficult decision paralleled the one we had recently made on behalf of Butterfield Bank. The calculation came out the same for the BIU, which since its inception had been much more important to Bermuda's progress and well-being than Butterfield Bank. Bermuda had more than one bank, but the working people of Bermuda had only one labor union as their voice for economic justice. The BIU had done vital work to build a prosperous, equitable Bermuda, and its mission was not over. Personally I felt strongly about this and was determined that Bermuda's Government would not bankrupt, and therefore destroy, the country's foremost labor union. No way!

I therefore led Cabinet in deciding that the Government would forgive the $6.8 million performance bond in return for the BIU's instituting a 72-hour "cooling-off" period before any industrial action such as a strike or "work to rule." Over the long haul, this cooling-off period could be worth more than $6.8 million to Bermuda by preventing lost work days. For example, large portions of the international business and tourism sectors would grind to a halt in a bus and ferry strike. A cooling-off period would provide an important means and motivation to negotiate good compromises and avoid strikes.

This argument fell on deaf ears in the Combined Opposition. "The biggest debacle in this country's history," "the biggest raid on the Bermuda treasury in the history of this country," and similar hyperbole issued from the UBP. The *Royal Gazette* editorialized that the "moral hazard" in forgiving the performance bond for the BIU was somehow worse than guaranteeing a share offering for Butterfield Bank, that we should have tried to make the union pay the penalty in installments, and that the union had only issued a nonbinding statement of good intentions about the 72-hour cooling-off period. The reactions showed the Combined Opposition still had different rules for White and Black Bermuda.

The month of May also saw Parliament move National Heroes Day from the second Monday in October to the third Monday in June. Bermudians had shown they preferred a summer holiday.

In mid-May, U.S. Consul General Gregory Slayton and I announced our third annual delegation to Washington, D.C., on May 19 and 20. The *Royal Gazette* reported Consul General Slayton's view that Bermuda-U.S. relations had been "strengthened," without noting the credit he gave me for that.

Bermuda's relationship with the United States since World War II has reflected two things: the Cold War and our international business sector. Henry Tucker had founded Bermuda's modern financial regime in a triangular relationship with London and Wall Street. Tucker recognized that over the long term the more important partner for Bermuda was the United States, but he had no close ongoing contacts with American officials.

Premier John Swan put our financial regime on a firm footing with the United States through his signature achievement, the first Bermuda-U.S. tax treaty. He finished negotiating it in 1985 under an entrustment from the British government, while the U.S. Naval Air Station in Bermuda remained a valuable asset in the Cold War. In the process Premier Swan met President Ronald Reagan, Secretary of State George P. Schultz, Secretary of the Treasury James Baker, and National Security Advisor Robert McFarlane, although the negotiations were naturally conducted with State Department and Treasury undersecretaries and their staffs.

As Premier, I brought a unique set of relationships with members of Congress, especially in, but not limited to, the Congressional Black Caucus. The latter part of my Premiership fortunately coincided with Democratic control of the House of Representatives in 2009 and 2010, and most of my relationships in Congress were with Democrats. But not all of them: on this visit, for example, I had meetings with both Senator Max Baucus, Democrat of Montana, and Senator Susan Collins, Republican of Maine.

I had met then Senator Barack Obama at a Congressional Black Caucus dinner in 2008 and again at the Summit of the Americas in Trinidad and Tobago. In announcing the 2009 delegation with Consul General Slayton, I said I did not expect to meet President Obama, but hoped to talk with his staff.

Bermuda's delegation included Deputy Premier and Finance Minister Paula Cox, along with Finance and Tourism civil servants. Our schedule was packed with official meetings. Michael Douglas had generously agreed to contribute his star power as the guest of honor at a screening of *The Lion and the Mouse*, Bermudian Lucinda Spurling's documentary about U.S.-Bermuda relations. And the British Embassy was hosting a reception.

While we were in Washington, Congressman Charlie Rangel, then Chairman of the House Ways and Means Committee, which is centrally responsible for U.S. tax law, said Bermuda should not be seen as "a tax haven." From discussions with him and others in Congress, I told the media, I felt pretty sure that Massachusetts Democrat Richard Nea's bill to raise U.S. taxes paid by Bermuda's reinsurance sector was not likely to pass. However, the same conversations convinced me President Obama still wanted to reduce or eliminate tax advantages for U.S. companies domiciling themselves or subsidiaries in foreign jurisdictions and still considered Bermuda a problem spot.

On my first full day in Washington, I attended a breakfast meeting with Congressman G. K. Butterfield (Democrat, North Carolina) and other legislators. After that I had a midmorning meeting in the West Wing of the White House with Michael Strautmanis, Chief of Staff to Valerie Jarrett, President Obama's closest advisor.

The White House meeting was thanks to Arthur "Art" Collins, who had worked in President Obama's 2008 campaign and was a lobbyist in Washington. I had met Art fortuitously in fall 2008, and we had hired him to facilitate contacts with the Obama administration, such as the meeting with Michael Strautmanis. Tiny Bermuda wasn't on the priority list of Valerie Jarrett's Chief of Staff as a matter of course. Art Collins had also arranged a meeting for me the day before with Homeland Security Advisor John O. Brennan, who I hoped would carry my message about tax issues to President Obama.

My presentation to Michael Strautmanis, with Art Collins sitting in, hit the points my administration had developed since presidential candidate Obama started criticizing Bermuda. I highlighted the benefits our reinsurance sector provided to America's economy and consumers by making various kinds of insurance, such as homeowner's disaster coverage, more obtainable and affordable. I pointed out that if Bermuda lost its relative tax advantages, the sector would disperse to other foreign jurisdictions, leaving the United States with the same problem or worse because other jurisdictions were less transparent and responsible to deal with.

It was not really in America's long-term interest, I suggested, to risk destroying Bermuda's economy for this outcome. The long history of friendship and trade between our two countries and our close cooperation during the Cold War showed what a reliable international partner Bermuda was to America. Finally I said Bermuda looked forward to continuing to work with the United States to further shared interests.

Strautmanis responded in a positive but noncommittal way. And then he said, "The president is really concerned about Congress's refusal to cooperate on closing the Guantánamo Bay detention camp. We need places to send some of the people there who have not been associated with terrorist activity."

The title of Lucinda Spurling's *The Lion and the Mouse* captures the relationship of the United States and Bermuda. When a lion offers a mouse a chance to do him a favor, the mouse would be foolish not to consider it. Accordingly I said, "Maybe Bermuda can help."

Strautmanis said, "Thank you, that's good to hear."

The *Times* (London) later wrote that Art Collins suggested Michael Strautmanis's Guantánamo gambit. Art and I never discussed Guantánamo before this meeting. Walking out of the White House, I wondered if or when there might be a sequel to the conversation.

Two hours later I was on the golf course at Bethesda Country Club with John Lugar, then an executive at the company that found Bermuda's Washington office space. John is the oldest son of Richard "Dick" Lugar, Indiana's longest-serving senator and then the most senior Republican in the U.S. Senate (he left office in 2013).

A call from the White House, asking me to visit White House Senior Counsel Gregory Craig, ended the golf while John Lugar and I were on the front nine. About ninety minutes later I was sitting alone with Gregory Craig in his West Wing office. He explained that of seventeen innocent Uighur detainees still at Guantánamo (Albania gave five asylum in 2006), the United States hoped Bermuda would accept four as refugees. He said he could show me the confidential material documenting they had no involvement with terrorism. They could not be sent to their homeland, China, because the Chinese government considered them suspected terrorists. Rather than specific concerns about the men, this attitude reflected China's determination to quash unrest among its Uighur population.

White House Counsel Craig said further discussion would have to be secret, especially from the British, until the negotiations failed or the Uighurs arrived in Bermuda. I said I was willing to consider the issues and negotiate in secret.

I wondered if Britain was really in the dark or had an off-the-record understanding with America. Being officially in the dark gave Britain deniability in relation to China, which did not want the Uighurs to receive asylum. Or perhaps the Obama administration was prepared to upset the British, assuming we took the Uighurs, when the news broke. As junior partners in the War on Terror, the British would have to accept the situation.

Whether or not the British knew the Americans were discussing the Uighurs with me, it was in Bermuda's best interest to negotiate with the United States. Not doing so would have neglected Bermuda's fundamental security and economic survival.

Do not think for an instant that the United States was uninformed to start with, or misinformed by me, about Bermuda's status as a U.K. Overseas Territory. Given its resources and history with the British, including the naval installations on Bermuda, the United States well understood what I could do as Premier and what the British would have to accept afterward.

The confidential files convinced me the Uighurs were innocent men. I told Craig I had to consult the Cabinet Minister in charge of Immigration, but would otherwise keep the matter a secret. He accepted that, and the meeting ended.

The next day I told the Bermuda media my meetings at the White House had included one with "a high-level White House counsel, whom I am not at liberty to name." Aside from this oblique reference, I said nothing about the meeting to anyone until I could talk confidentially with Labour, Housing, and Home Affairs Minister David Burch, whose portfolio included immigration. Minister Burch said he would check the immigration law and get back to me.

In the meantime I turned to other matters, such as Tourism's initiatives for the rest of the year and early 2010. My critics said the initiatives were old hat because we were renewing efforts in the northeastern United States. However, that renewed effort did not repudiate other efforts to reach additional markets; it was a common-sense response to the economic downturn.

I was also looking for a chance to move the cruise ship casino bill. Because there had already been debate, I could bring it up for a snap vote whenever there was enough support in the House. I considered doing so when the House met on Friday, May 22, but backbench PLP MPs who were against gambling blocked me.

That weekend, three drive-by shooting incidents left four people injured and one dead. I called for increased policing in trouble spots and again asked the Governor about bringing in American experts on gang-related violence. The Governor responded, as usual, that outside expertise should come from the United Kingdom. A year or so later, British Conservative Prime Minister

David Cameron said American expertise was needed to reduce gang violence in Britain.

Between the shootings and my discussion with the Governor, my great friend Murray Brown, a part of my life since we were eight-year-old boys, died of a heart attack at age sixty-three on Monday, May 25. Only Wanda and other close family and friends knew how I was hurt by Murray's passing.

That night, Wanda and I were in our shared study when Murray's former wife, Andrea, called from the States to say their son, and my beloved godson, Adé, had found Murray dead at home on the Island. There was no flight Andrea could take to Bermuda until the next day, so Wanda and I went to get Adé and brought him home with us for the night.

You think politics is hard? Try hearing your best friend has suddenly died and then explaining to his teenage son that life will be okay.

That week GlobalHue issued a press release on the renewal of its contracts with Bermuda Tourism and the U.S. Navy. The press release addressed the agency's Bermudian critics by contrasting visitor numbers before and after we began to work with them. Even in 2008, during the Great Recession, visitor numbers exceeded the recent pre-GlobalHue average.

With the successful renovation of the Port Royal Golf Course in time for October's PGA Grand Slam of Golf, the Combined Opposition alleged corruption in the contract award and project accounting. This too became the subject of the Commission of Inquiry into Public Works during my administration, which I will discuss later.

At the end of May a *Royal Gazette* editorial, "Growing exodus," unwittingly made the case for accepting the four Uighur detainees as refugees—without consulting the British. The editorial began by noting that executives in Bermuda's reinsurance sector were saying they would take their business elsewhere if there were sufficiently adverse U.S. tax code changes.

The editorial said, "[I]t is absolutely critical that Bermuda . . . continue to make its case to the White House and to [U.S.] legislators of the importance of the Bermuda reinsurance market. . . . Visits like this month's by Premier Dr. Ewart Brown and Finance Minister Paula Cox must continue. . . . It is not an exaggeration to say that Bermuda desperately needs to retain the reinsurance sector, especially while tourism continues its free fall."

My sentiments exactly. The editorial recommended continuing efforts to get Bermuda onto the OECD "white list," as well as attention to labor and infrastructure issues. That got no argument from me either.

But then the editorial shifted focus to "And political stability matters too," code for "the PLP can't be trusted." PLP Governments as a whole were excellent stewards of Bermuda's international business sector. We knew how vital international business was and is to Bermuda.

The editorial continued, "That [the importance of political stability] is what is most worrying about the announcement on Tuesday that Accenture Ltd. is moving its domicile from Bermuda to Ireland." The editorial admitted Accenture Ltd., subsidiary of American consulting firm Accenture, had only a small presence in Bermuda, and its many contracts with foreign governments "attracted unneeded [foreign] political attention." Yet without naming any other companies, the editorial associated Accenture Ltd. with "the growing exodus of companies from Bermuda . . . [that] constitute billions of dollars in capital."

The supposed exodus showed that "there is no doubt . . . Bermuda is beginning to face 'brand' problems" because of alleged political instability. The editorial referred to a *Wall Street Journal* article, which quoted an Accenture spokesman who said, "There are continued questions about companies incorporated in Bermuda." According to the *Royal Gazette*, the Accenture spokesman elaborated by mentioning the prospect of U.S. tax code changes, bad publicity about Bermuda as a tax haven, and "the growing importance of the company's European business."

Thus according to Accenture the move stemmed from its European business agenda, along with the U.S. tax code issues my administration was addressing, but had nothing to do with political instability in Bermuda. That political instability existed only in the Combined Opposition's mind because the PLP held power.

The number of companies leaving Bermuda was insignificant. "[B]illions of dollars in capital" meant overseas capital under management, not billions of dollars in Bermuda's economy. However, I was determined to do all I could to sustain our international business sector and defend it from the threat of potential changes in U.S. legislation. If the United States eliminated the tax advantages of incorporating in Bermuda, we would indeed see a "growing exodus" of companies from Bermuda.

Put aside the groundless insinuations against the PLP Government, and the editorial captured the life-or-death stakes in Bermuda's relationship with the United States. The editorial nowhere mentioned the British or consulting them about Bermuda's relationship with the United States.

On Wednesday, June 10, Deputy Premier and Finance Minister Paula Cox and I announced Bermuda's inclusion on the OECD's "white list." This success was thanks to Minister Cox's tax treaty group in the Finance Ministry, whose twelfth Tax Information Exchange Agreement (TIEA) with another jurisdiction cleared the final hurdle for the white list. Prime Minister Gordon Brown wrote us about this achievement, abandoning the harsh tone of earlier in the year for warm congratulations.

The same day, Palau announced asylum for eleven Uighur detainees from Guantánamo Bay (only six accepted the offer). That was also when I concluded the arrangement with the United States to accept the four Uighurs whose files I saw in Washington. Labour, Housing, and Home Affairs Minister David Burch and I were satisfied that Bermuda was within its rights to do so without consulting the British. To signalize our agreement the United States and Bermuda exchanged notes, which in foreign relations parlance ranks below a formal treaty.

Later that day Minister Burch flew to Guantánamo to pick up the four Uighurs. When the return flight carrying Minister Burch, the Uighurs, and Art Collins was in the air, the United States informed the British embassy in Washington, and I called the Governor. I told him about giving refuge to four Chinese Muslims without mentioning Guantánamo.

Early June 11, the Governor called my home while I was feeding our dog Diamond. Wanda explained where I was, and the Governor said he would hold the line. When I got on the phone, he said he'd been informed about the Guantánamo connection by the British embassy in Washington. He asked me to cancel my press conference about the Uighurs later that morning and come straight to Government House. I said that I would get there as soon as possible, but that I could not cancel the press conference.

When I arrived at Government House around 10 a.m., the Governor was red-faced and angry. He complained about my not mentioning Guantánamo on the phone the night before. I said I didn't know I had to. The view I expressed to the Governor, and subsequently other British officials, was that I was on solid ground constitutionally.

After leaving Government House, I convened Cabinet and informed the Ministers about the Uighurs. After that I held the press conference and announced the Uighurs' arrival to the nation.

The *Royal Gazette* interviewed the Governor on Friday, June 12, and the next day reported, "Bermuda's relationship with Britain will not deteriorate because of the decision to let four Guantánamo Bay detainees seek asylum on the Island. Governor Sir Richard Gozney . . . assured the public that the U.K. is not reviewing the legal basis of relations with Bermuda or the [Bermuda] constitution. He did say he was 'disappointed' that Premier Ewart Brown did not consult him before the decision was made to allow the Uighurs to resettle here. . . . Sir Richard explained the U.K. would not be suspending the 1968 General Entrustment Agreement [covering Bermuda's freedom to negotiate on behalf of the British with advance consultation] . . . but will have an informal review."

The newspaper also quoted the Governor as saying, "As long as Bermuda keeps us in the picture we are happy for Bermuda to negotiate. We don't need to stay over Bermuda's shoulder. We need to know what's going on and then we're happy."

The Governor's restrained comments, which he must have discussed with the Foreign and Commonwealth Office in London, made me think again that perhaps the United States and the United Kingdom had a tacit understanding. It seemed Bermuda was going to receive a fairly mild British scolding.

The *Royal Gazette*'s first editorial reaction also struck a moderate tone with its "Hello, Uighurs" headline. However, the editorial said, "This newspaper does not yet have a position on yesterday's announcement that the Island will resettle four Uighurs previously held at Guantánamo Bay."

Was the newspaper waiting to confer with the UBP? The sequence of its positions seemed to say yes.

The UBP immediately condemned my bringing the Uighurs in without consulting the British. In the House on June 12, the UBP tabled the motion "That this Honourable House has no confidence in the Government led by Premier Ewart Brown." The newspaper soon editorialized to the same effect.

Meanwhile Britain's right-wing newspapers, notably the *Times*, *Daily Telegraph*, and *Daily Mail*, reported "anger" and "fury" at the Foreign and Commonwealth Office, and Conservative MP and Shadow Foreign Secretary William Hague expressed outrage. This apparently raised tension in London to the point where the Labour government had to make a bigger fuss. Of course, heightened criticism from Foreign Secretary David Miliband and others in London also appealed to China, given its opposition to asylum for the Uighurs.

The immediate reactions of Bermudians included confusion about who the Uighurs were and whether we were bringing terrorists to the Island. As we brought the four of them before the public and showed they were innocent men, polling found that most Bermudians were prepared to welcome them but disapproved of the lack of consultation.

The other members of the Cabinet and PLP Caucus, except for Minister Burch, were understandably upset about being kept in the dark. My chief PLP opponents, led by Wayne Perinchief, formed common cause with the UBP to end my leadership. On Saturday, June 13, the *Royal Gazette* published a photo of Wayne Perinchief at the House of Assembly the day before. He grinned like the cat who ate the canary, bursting with confidence that he could finally oust me.

The following Tuesday, the newspaper abandoned its lighthearted "Hello, Uighurs" tone and editorialized, "It's time to go, Dr. Brown." That day two Bermudian women, Janice Battersbee and Erica Rance-Cariah, respectively Black and White, led a lunchtime protest march on Parliament and the Cabinet Building. The two organizers wanted to convey the sense that both

Black and White Bermudians opposed my continuing as Premier. However, the 800 to 1,000 Bermudians on the Cabinet Office's Front Street site were overwhelmingly White. Education Minister El James joked, "It looks like Mount Everest out there, covered in snow."

The tenor of the protest was not a joke, however; it was one of White racist anger foaming at the mouth to shout down "niggers" in power. When Wanda and I arrived, we had flashbacks to scenes of violent White mobs surrounding civil rights protesters in the 1950s and 1960s. The crowd at the Cabinet Building looked like a lynch mob. Whatever most Black Bermudians thought about the Uighurs, the protest's blatant racism repelled them.

In anticipation of the protest, I had had a podium with a microphone and public address system put in front of the Sally Bassett Memorial. When I attempted to speak, the protesters drowned me out twice. I said if they didn't want me to speak, I would leave.

When the crowd quieted down, I said their protest showed democracy was alive in Bermuda. I said I would soon be leaving to meet the Governor and continued, "If there is someone who would like to speak on behalf of those who come here today, I'm prepared to delay my trip to Government House until I have heard you."

Janice Battersbee then spoke from the podium, reading a text Erica Rance-Cariah held for her. A self-described lifelong PLP supporter, Mrs. Battersbee had never been heard from politically in Bermuda until becoming the Black figurehead for White Bermudians' anger over the Uighurs and my leadership, and she has seldom been heard from since.

As Mrs. Battersbee began to read the speech, Wanda and I stepped around in front of her and listened attentively. The speech disparaged me, sought to diminish my accomplishments, and echoed every complaint White Bermuda had ever made against me. Wanda and I stood there respectfully until Mrs. Battersbee had finished, and I then left for Government House where the Governor again expressed his frustration.

At a press conference on Wednesday, the Governor raised his rhetorical level. Referring to the exchange of notes between Bermuda and the United States, he said, "Because it breaches [section 62 of] the [Bermuda] constitution, this exchange of notes . . . was in our view invalid. In other words, the Bermuda Government's action to solicit the arrival of the four Uighurs was unacceptable." The Governor had said the same thing to Cabinet the day before. Yet he also had told us, and he repeated at the press conference, that the Uighurs "cannot and should not go back" to Guantánamo Bay. In his remarks to the press, the Governor said, "I talked to the Bermuda Government yesterday, June 16, and suggested that they should now carefully consider their next steps."

All things considered, the next steps were to continue making the case for the Uighurs and wait for the uproar to subside. The logical implication of the Governor's acknowledgment that the Uighurs should not be sent to Guantánamo was that they would remain in Bermuda.

My case for the Uighurs was humanitarian. With 10,000 foreign residents already on the Island, I asked Bermudians to extend their hospitality to four innocent men released after seven years' unjust imprisonment. "Being small does not mean we cannot lead," I emphasized, noting the strong international support, apart from the United Kingdom and China, for taking in the Uighurs.

We had a precedent in UBP Premier David Gibbons's Government, which in 1980 brought to Bermuda five Vietnamese "boat people," refugees from the Communist takeover of South Vietnam. A ship with Bermudian registry had rescued a large number of Vietnamese boat people in the South China Sea and taken them to Hong Kong. The difference from the Uighurs was that the British knew about the boat people from the start.

The Americans tried to smooth the waters without annoying the British. During a press conference with the visiting Prime Minister of Italy, Silvio Berlusconi, President Obama stated, "I have to say, by the way, that Bermuda has done us a great service . . . and I'm grateful to them." He also made a brief phone call of thanks to me personally. Many members of the U.S. Congress, Democrats and Republicans in the House and Senate, expressed their support, and Secretary of State Hillary Clinton wrote me a very strong letter of support and gratitude.

I was between two countries. Britain castigated me. But I will forever be thankful to the Americans who defended me.

Speaking to international business sector executives at Bermuda's Insurance Day summit on June 16, I said there was no explicit quid pro quo with the United States: "I don't have a 'here's what we got list' . . . But what I do have is the supreme confidence that Bermuda's relationship with the United States . . . is better today than it was one week ago, one month ago, one year ago. That can only mean good things for the continued success of the country and the continued success of your companies."

Now, years later, I can still attest that there was no quid pro quo. However, I can also definitively note that the shrill buzz on Capitol Hill about the reduction or elimination of tax advantages for U.S. companies domiciling themselves or their subsidiaries in Bermuda ceased. I am grateful for that as long as it lasts.

In every forum in which I addressed the controversy, I expressed my continuing conviction that my administration had the constitutional and legal right to admit the four refugees without consulting the British. Minister Burch and I based that on section 25 of the Bermuda Immigration and Protection Act

1956, signed into law by Bermuda's then Governor, Lieutenant General Sir John Woodall.

Section 25 of the law is headed "Declaration of general principle regarding restriction on entry of persons into Bermuda, and subsequent residence, etc., therein." The section states that "it is unlawful for any person . . . to land in, or having landed, to remain or reside in, Bermuda, without in each case specific permission (with or without the imposition of conditions or limitations) being given by or on behalf of the Minister [responsible for immigration] . . . and such landing, remaining or residence shall be unlawful unless [the person] conforms to any requirements imposed by this Part: Provided that the Minister, in his discretion, may dispense with the requirements imposed by the foregoing provisions of this subsection." The entire law mentions no circumstances in which the British have a role to play.

Section 62 of the Bermuda Constitution, which the Governor claimed we breached by admitting the Uighurs, defines the "Governor's special responsibilities" as "(a) external affairs; (b) defence, including armed forces; (c) internal security; (d) the police." Yet the Constitution says nothing about immigration and in no way supersedes the Bermuda Immigration and Protection Act 1956. With regard to "(c) internal security," Section 62 of the Constitution gives the Governor a role in any limitations or conditions the Minister responsible for immigration might impose on people coming to live in Bermuda. But it does not give the Governor responsibility or authority over who enters the country. In settling the Uighurs in Bermuda, we were perfectly prepared to take the Governor's advice about limitations or conditions for internal security.

Another protest took place on Friday, June 19. Many fewer people took part, although the BPS inflated the crowd estimate to "up to 1,500." The protest featured no overt racism, but it was still predominantly White and could not escape the shadow cast by Tuesday's ugliness.

That afternoon the UBP's no-confidence motion came up in the House. Over the next fourteen hours, MPs in both parties vented about the Uighurs. For most of the time I was not in the House. For efficiency, during House debate I often worked in my office a short walk away. I listened on the radio so I could return to the floor whenever necessary.

One line of argument was the Uighurs were bad for tourism. We had received quite a few emails from people claiming they canceled visits because we let "terrorists" settle on the Island. No doubt some of these emails were genuine, whereas others were generated by my opponents. In either case, there was little reason to think the Uighurs would poison Bermuda's tourism industry over the long term. In hindsight their asylum has had zero effect.

In addition to forecasting grave damage to tourism, Shadow Finance Minister Bob Richards asserted the Uighurs were bad for our international business sector. He refused to accept that their arrival would help us with the sector's overriding concern, the threat of adverse America's tax code changes. Richards argued that granting the Uighurs asylum could force Bermuda to "choose between China and the United States" and that maybe we would be wise to choose China. This was ridiculous in view of geography and U.S. power for the foreseeable future. Yet others in the UBP parroted the argument.

PLP MPs and Cabinet Ministers were also upset. Seconded by backbencher Neletha Butterfield, Culture and Social Rehabilitation Minister Dale Butler called on me to apologize for keeping everyone in the dark. Wayne Perinchief and Randy Horton spoke at length in favor of the no-confidence motion. Deputy Premier Paula Cox spoke against the no-confidence motion, but encouraged PLP dissidents to seek a Special Delegates Conference on the party's leadership.

Thirteen hours into the debate, I spoke. I expressed sincere regret for the necessity of secrecy and the reaction it evoked. I also attacked the UBP and "its rabid newspaper," the *Royal Gazette*, for trying to use the Uighurs against me. I added, "I was performing an act of God that might not have been approved by the Queen, but I can assure you it was ordained by a higher power."

The PLP and UBP had MPs on three-line whips. (Whips are voting instructions, and MPs disobeying a three-line whip risk expulsion from their party.) Even before the debate began, there were signs of trouble for the no-confidence motion. Its wording—"That this Honourable House has no confidence in the Government led by Premier Ewart Brown"—suggested a yes vote would trigger dissolution of the PLP Government and a new election. UBP Leader Kim Swan and the PLP's Phil Perinchief insisted that if the motion succeeded, PLP MPs would be able to choose a new Party Leader and Premier. This was dubious.

When it finally came time to vote early Saturday morning, all the PLP MPs voted against the motion. No PLP MP was willing to risk expulsion from the Party or trust the UBP not to try to force a new election if the motion passed. Former UBP MP Wayne Furbert, sitting as an Independent, also voted no.

Most UBP MPs followed their party's three-line whip and voted for the motion, but two did not. Shadow Attorney General Mark Pettingill abstained on principle, later saying he felt the motion was really drafted by PLP rebels and he could not vote for it when none of them did. Subsequently he said he did not realize there was a three-line whip. Shadow Culture and Social Rehabilitation Minister Darius Tucker chose to go to the coffee room when it came time to vote. He later said the motion was doomed from the start and called me a "go getter" for addressing America's anti-tax haven drive by taking in the Uighurs. Neither MP was going to be a member of the UBP much longer.

The no-confidence motion failed 22 to 11. My PLP rivals muttered they weren't done yet, and the UBP, seriously wounded, faced an uncertain future.

After the vote, Dale Butler resigned from Cabinet. I accepted his resignation reluctantly, especially since he was number one on my list to replace me as Tourism Minister. Neletha Butterfield agreed to replace Dale as Culture and Social Rehabilitation Minister, and I named Walter Roban Minister without Portfolio.

Rev. Al Sharpton came to the Island to support the asylum, saying Bermuda had "set the tone for the world." A month later Minister Louis Farrakhan, who had a speaking engagement in Bermuda, said the decision was "right morally and wrong politically."

An expression of support that touched me deeply came from Dr. Clifford Maxwell, co-leader of the 1959 Theatre Boycott, which broke legal segregation in Bermuda. Dr. Maxwell caught my point of view when he told the *Royal Gazette*, "Sometimes you have to challenge things and say sorry afterwards." He also said White Bermudians were opposed to me because of guilty consciences about White racism and refusal to accept the fact that the majority of Bermuda's voters were Black: "They may think: are [Black Bermudians] going to treat us the way we treated them?"

On Monday, June 22, Neletha Butterfield and Walter Roban were sworn in as Cabinet Ministers, and we hosted a group of Chinese businesspeople. Two were from California's Chinese-American community, but the other two were prominent investors from China. The way China works, the latter two would not have come to Bermuda if there was really a policy to punish us over the Uighurs.

A third protest outside the Cabinet Building, again organized by Janice Battersbee and Erica Rance-Cariah, occurred on Friday, June 26. The BPS estimated up to 500 in attendance, again mostly White, although we thought the crowd was much smaller. To have legs, a political initiative must be for something with broad appeal, not just against something or someone.

In July a UBP survey revealed widespread discontent among the UBP's supporters with its "old faces," particularly Michael Dunkley and Grant Gibbons. No matter who was Party Leader, Senator Dunkley and Dr. Gibbons ran things, ensuring a White privilege agenda never changed.

Former UBP Leader Wayne Furbert said bluntly, "The UBP is dying." Later in the year he went public about how Senator Dunkley and Dr. Gibbons had undermined his attempts to extend the UBP's appeal to Black voters.

My frustration over the Uighur controversy got the better of me when the House met on July 10, its final sitting until Parliament reconvened in November. I had told PLP Whip Lovita Foggo I would not try to bring a vote on the cruise ship casino bill, and she had passed that on to our MPs. As the House began to take up the first items on the agenda, I saw that most of the bill's PLP opponents were not yet there. Seizing the chance to do something positive for Bermuda tourism, I moved the bill for a snap vote. Education Minister El James and Energy, Telecommunications, and E-Commerce Minister Terry Lister both voted yes with me. The bill's PLP opponents arrived in time, however, and it lost. Although some UBP MPs supported the bill, they weren't willing to vote yes so soon after the no-confidence motion.

As the session continued I received a phone call from Wanda, who said she was experiencing severe food poisoning symptoms. I rushed out of the House to make sure she was okay and then did not want to leave her in case she needed additional care. We were both listening on the radio when, as the House prepared to adjourn, Ministers James and Lister both spoke against my attempt to get the bill through. Joined by backbench PLP MPs Wayne Perinchief, who voted no, and Randy Horton, who was absent during the vote, they called for my resignation.

This forced me to sack El James and Terry Lister from Cabinet. I named Michael Scott to replace Terry Lister as Energy, Telecommunications, and E-Commerce Minister. Health Minister Nelson Bascome agreed to add the Education portfolio to his responsibilities.

Wayne Perinchief and Randy Horton clearly hoped the episode would end in my ouster. The PLP Central Committee was scheduled to meet Monday, July 13, to discuss the end of the Parliamentary session, and political Bermuda wondered what would happen that night.

Deputy Premier and Finance Minister Paula Cox thought the occasion was right not to challenge directly for leadership, but to convince me to resign in her favor. Shortly before the meeting she emailed me, "Now is your time to step aside. . . . I will give you a job in Washington. Don't fight it."

I thought that was cute.

The Central Committee meeting's four-hour discussion must have disappointed all five of them. The branch chairmen supported me, and there was no grassroots desire for a Special Delegates Conference on party leadership.

It was a long night. Wanda and I were both relieved, humbled, and grateful that my support throughout the party was so solid. At home, we looked forward to much-needed sleep. However, at 4 a.m. Tuesday morning we were awakened by a phone call saying Nelson Bascome had died of a heart attack in Washington, D.C., where he was attending a conference. His last stop on his way to the airport the week before had been at our home. His passing hit me hard, especially so soon after Murray Brown's death.

It was a severe loss for the country, recognized as such even by the Combined Opposition. The grief of Nelson's colleagues in the Health Ministry and people throughout Bermuda demonstrated the respect and affection he inspired. Nelson had been instrumental in establishing the Lamb-Foggo Urgent Care Centre. That week, less than four months after opening, it treated its thousandth patient. It was only one of Nelson's many contributions to Bermuda.

Julian Hall had then been seriously ill for some time. Eight months earlier, in December 2008, my administration had succeeded in reversing the UBP's 1984 law prohibiting practice by bankrupt lawyers. After the 1984 law, Julian had to practice law from Canada. Although he eventually stabilized his finances, he had to declare bankruptcy again in 2000, and I felt the first PLP administrations should already have undone the 1984 law. The UBP said the PLP's law inappropriately benefited a single lawyer. My considered and adamant view was that UBP should have been ashamed and apologized for their law's inappropriately penalizing a single lawyer for exercising his democratic rights.

On Monday, July 20, 2009, Julian died surrounded by family and friends. Throughout his career, Julian had worked for justice. He, too, made an enduring, positive impact on Bermuda. As is typical for Black public figures who buck the status quo, after his death even the *Royal Gazette* acknowledged his brilliance as a courtroom advocate and his devotion to his country. It reminded me of the famous line "The only good Indian is a dead Indian."

No one should know better than a physician that death comes for everyone. But as a person, I struggled to accept the loss of three of my closest friends in five months. Summing up how dear Murray, Nelson, and Julian were to us, Wanda said, "They all sat at our kitchen table." We were devastated. Wanda booked us on a European cruise so I could recuperate emotionally.

When we got home, Wanda printed Scriptures on pieces of paper she slipped into my briefcase. Each time I found one, it lifted my spirits. An excerpt from one of those Scriptures is the source of this book's title: "The Lord is my light and my salvation; whom shall I fear?" She also bought a beautiful crystal angel and placed it in my Cabinet office to symbolize the power of God watching over me.

For the time being I put off naming a new permanent Education Minister or Health Minister. Attorney General Senator Kim Wilson agreed to serve as acting Education Minister, and Walter Roban became acting Health Minister. Responding to more calls for me to relinquish the Tourism portfolio, I said that I would do so once a new hotel project broke ground.

It was always thought Bermuda's 400th anniversary celebrations would include a Royal Visit. In late July, the Governor said talk of this was "speculative." At the end of the month, the *Times* (London), *Daily Telegraph*, and *Vanity Fair* all reported, in the *Royal Gazette*'s words, "[T]he Queen has snubbed

Bermuda's 400th anniversary celebrations due to the Premier's decision to allow four former Guantánamo Bay prisoners to resettle in Bermuda."

This was wishful thinking, if not a deliberate attempt to prevent the Queen's visit. British monarchs set their foreign travel "on the advice" of government ministers, especially the prime minister. Talk of the Queen's "snubbing" any part of the British Commonwealth was disrespectful to her as a constitutional monarch.

Of course, Prime Minister Gordon Brown's Labour government might want to deny Bermuda a Royal Visit to punish me over the Uighurs. But I doubted even famously awkward Gordon Brown wanted this presented as the Queen's personal choice. The pro-Conservative Party character of the *Times* and *Daily Telegraph* indicated there was nothing to the story but right-wing mischief-making. Some in Bermuda were happy to take it seriously, however, and blame me in consequence.

El James had called on me to resign when Parliament adjourned. But I knew he didn't irrevocably oppose my leadership. Not long afterward, he said he would not rule out a return to Cabinet. In mid-August, we talked. I wanted to know not only that he was willing to serve in Cabinet again, but that he still wanted to help reform the Education Ministry and take the tough decisions this required. The result of our talk was that he again became Education Minister.

In late August, Bill and Hillary Clinton vacationed in Bermuda to celebrate his birthday. I believe at least one reason for coming to Bermuda was to support my decision on the Uighurs. In one of the oddities of political life, the former President of the United States and its current Secretary of State invited Wanda and me to join them for cocktails along with Governor Sir Richard Gozney and Lady Gozney, as well as Bermuda's new American Consul General, Grace Shelton. The Governor surely knew that Secretary of State Hillary Clinton had recently written to thank me for granting the Uighurs asylum. We all skated gracefully around that subject and enjoyed a pleasant chat.

Another oddity was that the Clintons cut short their visit because Hurricane Bill was expected to hit Bermuda. Fortunately, Hurricane Bill only struck a glancing blow. No one was hurt or killed, although the western end of the Island suffered property damage.

Walter Roban was proving a valuable Cabinet asset. At the beginning of September, I took "acting" off his job description and named him Health Minister.

Early that month I tried to reset the tone of public conversation in Bermuda. Speaking at the Trailblazer Awards honoring the organizers of the 1959 Theatre Boycott, I said in part, "I say to my White brothers: you can make a wonderful contribution to the move forward, if you will resist the temptation to speak negatively when you hear Black people speak pain. It's going to take a long time before the pain goes away and we can step forward free of that pain." Rolfe Commissiong, who organized the event, spoke brilliantly that night.

As in relation to the Sally Bassett Memorial, I was inviting White Bermudians to join an honest conversation about our history. We needed honesty about the past to bridge what divided us in the present. That was my unifying, inclusive message. The Combined Opposition's insistence on misrepresenting it as divisively "playing the race card" saddened but did not surprise me.

The day of the Trailblazer Awards, my administration announced the prevention of a hotel workers strike, thanks to our mediating between BIU President Chris Furbert and the Bermuda Hotel Association (BHA). The BHA said the continuing slump in tourism necessitated a wage freeze and even ruled out a cost of living increase. The BIU took counsel with us, and we averted a strike by suspending payroll tax deductions from hotel workers' wages.

Later that week, we revealed the line-up for the 2009 Bermuda Music Festival. It was star-studded, although with no acts as expensive as Beyoncé in 2008. The performers included Quincy Jones, Patti Austin, Erykah Badu, James Ingram, Wyclef Jean, John Legend, Michael McDonald, Kenny Rogers, and Naturally Seven.

September brought the UBP to the verge of collapse. MPs Shawn Crockwell, Donte Hunt, and Mark Pettingill, along with Senator Michael Fahy, threatened to leave the party unless Kim Swan resigned as leader, and four long-time MPs retired from politics to make way for new blood. They also wanted the party to change its name.

Two days later, the rebels resigned from the UBP. So did Wayne Scott and Sean Pitcher, respectively party chairman and former deputy party chairman. They joined Darius Tucker, who quit in late June, and Wayne Furbert as departures from the UBP within the previous twelve months. That left the UBP with 9 seats in the House.

Around the same time David Burt resigned as PLP chair for family and business reasons. I was sorry we were losing him for the immediate future. But I felt confident he would return to contribute to the PLP, and through it, to Bermuda.

On Friday, September 25, 2009, I was honored to deliver the address at Howard University's 142nd Opening Convocation. My beloved alma mater also conferred an honorary Doctor of Laws upon me that day.

In Washington I was able to meet U.S. Attorney General Eric Holder. It was a meeting I wouldn't have gotten before the Uighurs came to Bermuda. It gave me an opportunity to raise two issues. One, a long shot to be sure, was help with the U.S. Navy's toxic pollution at Morgan's Point. The other was waivers for Bermudians who were on the stop list for travel to the United States because of minor drug offenses.

The British were slowly accommodating themselves to the Uighurs' asylum. This movement required some diplomatic theater. The Americans cooperated by having Daniel Fried, State Department Special Envoy for the closure of the Guantánamo Bay detention facility, appear on British television in September to say the British government knew nothing about the Uighurs until they were in Bermuda. This was aimed at suspicions the Labour government was complicit in the transfer. In addition, Special Envoy Fried told the BBC he was "admonished by the British government in very clear terms."

Shortly thereafter, Buckingham Palace announced the Queen and the Duke of Edinburgh would visit Bermuda in late November. They would stay on the Island for two days to help commemorate our 400th anniversary and then proceed to Trinidad and Tobago for the 2009 Commonwealth Heads of Government meeting.

Thanks to the Combined Opposition, there was confusion in Bermuda about the Queen's visit. By the time the Uighurs arrived, the visit was already slated for November in tandem with the Commonwealth meeting. However, many Bermudians had the false idea, fueled by the *Royal Gazette*, that the Queen was supposed to come to Bermuda in July and that asylum for the Uighurs interfered.

For the record, the British government never drew any connection between the Uighurs and the Queen's visit. Again, however, pro-Conservative Party media in Britain were using the Uighurs to attack Gordon Brown's Labour government. Thus all the political theater.

I had to play my part in the theater piece. First I went to the Labour Party's annual conference in Brighton, England. Foreign Secretary David Miliband matter-of-factly said the Uighurs should not have been brought to Bermuda without consulting the Governor. But he didn't dwell on the matter, and we also discussed the Royal Visit and other Bermuda-related topics.

From there I went to London for a meeting with Overseas Territories Minister Chris Bryant, previously known as "Captain Underpants" because while an MP in 2003 he had posted a picture of himself wearing only underpants on an online dating site. He was also one of the British MPs caught up in the 2009 U.K. parliamentary expenses scandal.

In the presence of staff, Minister Bryant pointed his finger at me and said, "Don't do that again." I turned my back, as if to see where he was pointing. And then we moved on to arrangements for the upcoming Overseas Territories Consultative Council (OTCC) meetings.

Wanda and I attended a cocktail party that evening where Bryant was also present. When I introduced him to her, he said, "Did he tell you I had to put him in his place?" He seemed oblivious to the tone of Wanda's response, which conveyed her dismay at his inappropriate question and our disregard for whatever he thought my "place" was. Later Wanda and I shared a smile about his arrogant cluelessness.

On that visit I also met Shadow Foreign Secretary William Hague. Practically his first words were, "The best thing we Brits ever did is create the British Empire." There wasn't any place for the conversation to go after that, and I was out of his office in minutes.

A week later UBP MP Cole Simons attended the Conservative Party conference in Manchester, England, where he spoke to the Chinese ambassador to Great Britain. Ambassador Ying Fu warned that Bermuda's trade with China might suffer over the Uighurs. It was an empty threat. The Chinese turned to preventing other countries from accepting the Uighurs still at Guantánamo Bay, and they had some success in this.

From Bermuda's point of view, the irony of Simons thrusting himself into a foreign relations issue was palpable. People say that imitation is the sincerest form of flattery, so perhaps I should be flattered by his doing exactly what he and the UBP said I shouldn't have done.

As these events unfolded, another perspective on the Uighurs affair came from Lord Goldsmith, Prime Minister Tony Blair's attorney general. Lord Goldsmith criticized Gordon Brown for making it necessary for the Americans to deal directly with me. (Lord Goldsmith later became one of my lawyers, but at the time we didn't know each other.)

October 12 was the third anniversary of my resigning from Premier Scott's Cabinet to run for party leadership. Since winning that vote and becoming Premier, I had more than once reaffirmed my intention to serve only one four-year term as Party Leader. The 2009 PLP Delegates Conference would be the last I presided over as Party Leader and Premier. The clock was ticking on my self-appointed schedule, adding urgency to every day of my last year in office.

17. Delivering Change

O N OCTOBER 12, 2009, I PRESIDED AT THE OPENING of Bermuda's first residential drug treatment center. The creation of the center owed much to Nelson Bascome's wise leadership as Health Minister. Drawing on his experience as a drug treatment counselor, Nelson sought to move Bermuda from an excessive focus on punishing drug offenders to reducing harms in all areas, balancing strict law enforcement with effective prevention and treatment.

On the evening of October 14, I went on radio and television to talk about the continuing impact of the Great Recession and other issues as our 400th anniversary year closed. Although the recession was technically over, recovery for American consumers and the rest of the world was slow. We saw the effect of that in Bermuda's arrival numbers.

The reinsurance industry at the heart of our international business sector was relatively recession-proof but remained vulnerable to U.S. tax law changes. Fortunately, Bermuda–U.S. relations were at an all-time high.

Regarding overseas misperceptions of Bermuda as a tax haven, I gave credit to Finance Minister Paula Cox for the Tax Information Exchange Agreements (TIEAs) that put us on the OECD's "white list" and facilitated our selection as vice chair, along with Germany and China, of the OECD Global Forum Steering Group. Both outcomes testified to our being a responsible global financial center.

I also addressed Bermudian misperceptions, fostered by the Combined Opposition, that PLP Governments did not support our international business sector. The fact was my administration gave the sector everything it needed, while still expecting it to do right by Bermuda.

I explained that departures by Accenture and Tyco to Ireland and Switzerland respectively had nothing to do with supposed political instability in Bermuda. Six hundred international firms had established domiciles in Bermuda in 2009, showing our continuing appeal as a business headquarters.

The most controversial part of the speech discussed violent crime in Bermuda. Everyone knew I was pointing at Government House when I said,

"Constitutionally, we are hamstrung. We control the purse strings, but have little or no say in how the fight is managed." It was and is absurd that the BPS should be controlled by Governors with no understanding of Bermuda at street level.

With Parliament convening in early November, I invited public feedback on the draft Public Access to Information (PATI) bill. I underlined my administration's concern for Bermudians by noting our provision of free day care, plans to extend FutureCare, the residential drug treatment facility, services for the homeless, and support for small business development and job creation.

Finally I returned to our 400th anniversary. Looking ahead to the next four hundred years, I said, "Let us promise that day by day, year by year, with God as our witness and our guide, we will steadfastly move toward uniting as One People for One Bermuda—emboldened not by our differences, but by our common heritage and our shared hope for a prosperous future."

I hoped it would not take four hundred years to achieve a united Bermuda. But the immediate reaction to my speech was not encouraging. Governor Gozney said my administration had turned down frequent meetings on police issues, and Shadow Public Safety Minister Michael Dunkley accused me of "playing games in the fight against crime."

I responded that fighting violent crime was not a game and consultation without operational control was meaningless. I had been trying for years to raise awareness about the gang element in Bermuda. Governor Gozney refused requests to bring in U.S. experts, particularly those associated with falling street crime rates in New York City.

In most jurisdictions, elected governments have operational control of the police. Only if the Governor cedes day-to-day oversight to the Government can Bermudians exercise the basic right of citizens to hold elected officials responsible for law and order. Our model was not anti-British. We envisioned police operations would remain subject to the Governor's review, just as Scotland Yard answers jointly to the Mayor of London, the Home Office, and the Queen.

Opening October's PLP Delegates Conference, my last as Premier and Party Leader, I expressed satisfaction at the demise of the *Mid-Ocean News*, lead attack dog in falsely alleging corruption in PLP Governments, including my administration. Cutting Government advertising in sister paper the *Royal Gazette* had apparently hit owner Bermuda Press Holdings where it hurt.

During my Premiership, several friends and I thought of founding another newspaper to counterbalance the *Royal Gazette*. Concern about inadequate advertising support led us to purchase a majority stake in the online Bernews from editor-owner Patricia Burchall. During the time we held this stake, we boosted Bernews's capabilities but gave Burchall complete editorial freedom. A couple of years after I left office, my associates and I sold our stake back to Burchall.

As of October 2009 the Corporation of Hamilton had met in secret for two hundred years, subject to no public oversight, and it controlled port and wharfage fees that by any reasonable standard belonged to the country as a whole. As Hamilton grew over the years, especially after World War II, the Corporation boundaries never expanded, preserving power for a small group of mainly White property owners. Among other antidemocratic features, Hamilton and St. George's retained votes for nonresident property owners. Change was overdue.

Fearing reform action, the Corporation of Hamilton did two remarkable things in late October 2009. The first was flying the Bermuda flag rather than the Union Jack, which it had apparently flown without interruption since 1815. The second was opening a meeting of the Corporation to the public for the first time.

On November 2, we released the 233-page Mincy Report, "A Study of Employment, Earning, and Educational Gaps between Young Black Bermudian Males and their Same-Age Peers." The report compared young Black Bermudian males with young White Bermudian males and young Black Bermudian females, taking into account young Black Bermudian males' deficits in hard skills, represented by educational attainment, and soft skills, such as interpersonal communication and punctuality.

The Mincy Report showed:

- The under 50 percent of Black Bermudian males completing secondary school mostly achieved lower certifications, rarely qualifying for bachelor's programs.
- Young Black Bermudian males were more likely to be employed than White counterparts, but at very low wages.
- Young White Bermudian males were more likely to combine work with schooling.
- If Black Bermudian males had the same enrollment-to-population ratio as White Bermudian males, the unemployment rate of young Black males would be half that of young White males.
- Regardless of education, the average Black Bermudian male earned $5,600 a year less than the average White Bermudian male, with 29 percent of the gap attributable to race.
- Opportunities for Black Bermudian females in the corporate sector, along with cultural expectations, encouraged Black Bermudian families to direct their sons into construction, skilled trades, and hotel jobs. Because of the shift to service, administrative, and managerial

jobs, Black Bermudian males had much lower lifetime earnings than Black Bermudian females.

The report noted that nearly all young Black Bermudians attended public secondary schools, whereas nearly all young White Bermudians attended private secondary schools with vastly greater resources. For example, the ratio of guidance counselors to students was 1:35 in private schools and 1:200 in public schools. The report recommended programs with success helping disadvantaged young Black American males.

The same day, we released "Continuing Bermuda's Economic Miracle," prepared for Bermuda First by consultancy McKinsey and Company. The Bermuda First Report made a fascinating complement to the Mincy Report, and I had taken pains to see they reached the public together.

The Bermuda First Report captured the extent of Bermuda's modern economic miracle by noting that our $86,000 average income per capita was fourth in the world behind Luxembourg, Norway, and Qatar. It found that insurance represented 48 percent of Bermuda's economic output, with supporting goods and services another 20 percent and tourism 5 percent.

To grow the insurance sector, it recommended:

- Strengthen the Bermuda Monetary Authority.
- Extend corporate tax exemptions.
- Continue cultivating relationships with the United States, the United Kingdom, and OECD.
- Enhance promotion of Bermuda as a global business domicile.

To grow tourism:

- Decrease taxes on fractional resort and condo units.
- Consider legalizing gambling.
- Consider a tourism authority.
- Provide Hamilton attractions.
- Encourage Bermudian careers in hospitality.

To diversify the economy:

- Develop insurance-linked securities and new lines of insurance.
- Become an international arbitration center.
- Establish a risk-management institute with a leading business school.
- Become a center for managing intellectual property.
- Attract more hedge funds and wealth management services.

- Become a retirement haven for high net worth individuals.

And to improve socioeconomic foundations:

- Complete adoption of the Cambridge International Curriculum (CIC).
- Reduce crime.
- Continue developing affordable housing.
- Adopt green technology.
- Continue enhancing efficiency and transparency.

On Friday, November 6, 2009, Governor Gozney read the last Throne Speech of my Premiership. The speech implicitly connected the Bermuda First Report, the Mincy Report, and the 2007 Hopkins Report on education. The Bermuda First Report presented an agenda for maintaining high average income per capita. The Mincy Report and the Hopkins Report set templates for redressing historical inequities.

In the context of continuing trouble in the global economy and the close of our 400th anniversary year, the speech asked Bermudians to remember the personal qualities and teamwork needed to settle the Island. It was time, I wrote, "to reawaken these qualities . . . through a programme of national service."

I envisioned nonmilitary work in education, healthcare, and environmental renewal as well as service in the Regiment. I quoted Martin Luther King, Jr.: "Life's most persistent and urgent question is: what are you doing for others?" But I also emphasized the benefits of preparing for "the rigours of the working world" and becoming "assets to a broad range of employers."

I remained determined to advance education reform. Given the difficulties in that area, I quoted James Baldwin: "Not everything that is faced can be changed, but nothing can be changed until it is faced." I committed the Education Ministry to do "personalised assessment of at risk students," provide better career guidance, support the learning styles of boys, and "review the certification of teachers."

Teacher certification is a serious sticking point in advancing Bermuda's schools. Teachers rightly say they cannot solve all the social problems students bring to school. Moreover the Hopkins Report called for reform of the Education Ministry and better support for teachers as well as higher certification standards. All the same, I believe most of Bermuda's teachers could meet higher standards, just as my mother earned an education degree late in her teaching career. But realistically, some could not.

This situation should obviously concern teachers unions and naturally creates tension between unions and reform-minded administrators. But it is not difficult to envision protections for teachers nearing retirement age and ample opportunities for younger teachers to meet higher standards. Government-sponsored teacher retraining could be provided under union auspices.

Education reform becomes impossible, however, if a union refuses to accept a single incumbent teacher's ouster. So long as we refuse to face this problem, Bermuda's young people will underachieve, to their and the country's detriment.

The one concrete step forward on education the Throne Speech was able to mention was progress adopting the CIC. Given the many Bermudians of Portuguese heritage, I was happy to note this included Portuguese language instruction beginning in the 2010–2011 school year.

Following our successful introduction of free day care, I committed the Culture and Social Rehabilitation Ministry to identify ways to provide day care for special needs children. The Ministry was also charged with continuing the Mirrors Program and finding it a permanent home.

The Commission on Unity and Racial Equality (CURE), established by the last UBP Government, had failed to advance its remit of eliminating racism. The Throne Speech therefore announced a review of CURE and the assumption of its data collection function by the Department of Statistics.

The speech also committed the Government to a broad range of other initiatives from amending the Human Rights Act "to prevent discrimination against all classes of people" to environmental restoration, updated telecommunications legislation, a national health strategy, including better serving physically challenged Bermudians, expansion of FutureCare, a Visa Waiver Assistance program for those on the U.S. stop list for minor offenses, streamlining the Hotel Concessions Act and making tax concessions available to smaller hotels, joint marketing by Tourism and individual hotels, and seeking "a parliamentary conference, under . . . the Commonwealth Parliamentary Association," to modernize the Legislature.

It was a lengthy list typical of most Throne Speeches. But it was an action list, and for the next eleven months I measured my administration's work against it.

Governor Gozney added some words of his own in addition to declaring Parliament open. Mentioning "political tremors here in Bermuda" during 2009, obviously referring to the Uighurs, and our surviving the Great Recession relatively unscathed, he promised "to continue what your Constitution prescribes, that is to oversee those who provide the law and order, the security and the transparency, which underpin . . . this Island's high quality of life." In other words, the Governor was never going to cede managerial oversight of the BPS to the duly elected Government. It signaled that my last year as Premier was likely to be as embattled as the previous three.

Among other events in November 2009, Transport resolved a legal dispute with Bermuda Aviation Services (BAS). In 1997 the last UBP Government had awarded BAS an exclusive contract for private jet maintenance and services. The contract was in force when I became Transport Minister, and in 2003 we extended BAS's license until 2014.

Since 2003, Bermuda's private jet traffic had increased significantly. By 2007, complaints from private jet owners and operators indicated BAS was not providing exemplary service. Following legal advice that the Transport Ministry could waive BAS's exclusivity, in the summer of that year we granted a competing license to start-up Sovereign Flight Support.

BAS sued, and in December 2008 an arbitration panel of three lawyers ruled for it. We appealed, but in March 2009 Bermuda's Court of Appeal upheld the arbitration panel and ordered Government to pay BAS a little over $200,000 in legal costs and damages. The court decision triggered insinuations I was guilty of favoritism toward Sovereign. But when Sovereign's license for private jet support services expired in June 2009, we had not renewed it because of a material breach by the firm.

However, I still believed it was important to have a choice of providers of private jet support. This benefited our international business sector and luxury tourism. Transport therefore negotiated a payment of $2.75 million to BAS to reimburse some of its operating costs and cancel the remaining five years of its exclusive license window. Another firm stepped in to compete with BAS.

One of the most important decisions I took at the start of my last year in office was to appoint Zane DeSilva as Minister without Portfolio. From the start of Zane's Cabinet service, no one came to meetings better prepared.

The first month of the new session of Parliament brought two important healthcare votes. One was to permit the Health Ministry to begin formal planning for redeveloping KEMH over twenty-five years. The debate showcased the UBP's penchant for obstruction for its own sake. Referring to consulting outside experts about KEMH, UBP Shadow Health Minister Louise Jackson complained, "We've had three reports and all these costs. Why couldn't you get it right the first time?" Yet she admitted the process had resulted in sensible and realistic" plans. Former Premier Scott commented, "If we've satisfied the Opposition Member, then we must have satisfied most of Bermuda. This has to be a red-letter day."

The other vote, debated by the UBP at an even more feverish pitch, was to enable enrolling in our Health Insurance Plan (HIP) seniors who were not yet eligible for FutureCare because of its phased roll-out, but could no longer afford private health insurance. Bermuda's most affluent seniors could still comfortably afford insurance in the private market.

FutureCare had to be phased in gradually because of the Great Recession, and the new HIP provision was a sensible, compassionate response to the predatory actions of private insurers. However, echoed by the rest of the UBP, Shadow Health Minister Louise Jackson attacked FutureCare as "a total, total disaster for all" and asserted very affluent seniors were being left "out in the cold."

Shadow Education Minister Grant Gibbons said FutureCare was "unaffordable" and Government should "come clean" about FutureCare benefits. There was nothing to come clean about.

Shadow Works and Engineering Minister Patricia Gordon-Pamplin and Shadow Finance Minister Bob Richards criticized the Government for failing to anticipate the behavior of private insurers. Shadow Minister Gordon-Pamplin lamented that opening up HIP to more seniors was "a U-turn," and Shadow Minister Richards blamed us for describing the actions of private insurers in factual terms, which in his view was branding them as "scapegoats."

Health Minister Walter Roban answered these objections effectively. In my own comments, I stressed the leadership shown by the last UBP Government in which my aunt Gloria served. One of her final achievements in office was legislation introducing payroll deductions for employer-provided healthcare, which as I said was "revolutionary at the time." And I rebutted the notion that a country as prosperous as Bermuda could not afford decent health insurance for seniors.

The vote unanimously approved opening HIP to seniors who were not yet eligible for FutureCare and could not afford private insurance. UBP MPs did not want to vote against FutureCare or related legislation, fearing repercussions at the ballot box. But they could not restrain themselves from misrepresenting FutureCare and the new HIP provision.

With the Royal Visit approaching, I did not shy away from making a public comment about the desirability of independence. At my next call on Government House, a red-faced Governor Gozney berated me, more or less, "I hope we'll have none of that when the Queen is here! We cannot have Her Majesty made to be uncomfortable in Bermuda!"

I said, "Well, Governor, as I understand it, the Queen has met Idi Amin, Robert Mugabe, a few terrorists, and other assorted characters in her time. I think you can rely on her to be just fine meeting Ewart Brown. My mother and father raised me right."

On the eve of the Royal Visit, it was a pleasure to announce positive developments in tourism. Air arrivals were inching back up, and thanks to cruise ships, total visitor arrivals July to September had increased 12 percent compared to 2008. Our focused efforts in the northeastern United States were paying off: promotion with the Boston Red Sox had increased travel 40 percent on JetBlue's flights from Boston, and its passengers from New York City were up 28 percent. Visits to bermudatourism.com had increased 180 percent with an increase of 140 percent in Expedia bookings through the website. Aggressive hotel promotions had garnered bookings of approximately 46,000 room nights. Last but not least, we had secured WestJet as a discount carrier between Toronto and Bermuda with flights to begin spring 2010.

On the afternoon of Tuesday, November 24, Wanda and I together with Governor Sir Richard Gozney and Lady Gozney greeted Queen Elizabeth II and Prince Philip, the Duke of Edinburgh, on their arrival at L. F. Wade International Airport. The Governor, Lady Gozney, Wanda, and I then accompanied the Royal Party, including Foreign Secretary David Miliband, to King's Square in the center of St. George's. There the Queen received the Royal Salute from the Bermuda Regiment Guard of Honour. Welcoming dignitaries included Chief Justice Richard Ground, President of the Senate Carol Anne Bassett, Speaker of the House Stanley Lowe, the Cabinet, Government and Opposition MPs, Mayor Mariea Caisey, and the Corporation of St. George's.

On a brief walk from St. George's Town Hall to Ordnance Island, the Queen was cheered by and stopped to chat with schoolchildren, including members of the Boy Scouts, Girl Guides, and other organizations, as well as 1609 reenactors in historical costume and others. St. George's alderman Kenneth Bascome walked with the Queen to provide introductions. A motorcade then took the Royal Party to Government House, where the Queen hosted a reception.

At the Cabinet Office Wednesday morning, Prince Philip presented his Duke of Edinburgh's Awards to young Bermudians for self-development and volunteer projects. A horse-drawn carriage then took the Queen and Prince Philip to the Cathedral of the Most Holy Trinity for a Thanksgiving service celebrating our 400th anniversary. After, the Royal Party, seen off by Hamilton Mayor Charles Gosling, took a fast ferry to Dockyard, where a drumline from Sandys Middle School played everyone ashore.

While Prince Philip and Foreign Secretary Miliband visited the *Spirit of Bermuda* training sloop, the Queen toured the Clocktower with West End Development Corporation (Wedco) chairman Walter Lister. The Queen then watched Sandys Middle School students perform historically significant scenes and observed a cedar carving demonstration by former Premier Dr. David Saul.

After lunch at the Maritime Museum, which the Queen had opened on her 1975 visit to Bermuda, the Royal Party went to the Commissioner's House to unveil a mural depicting our 400 years of history by Bermudian artist Graham Foster. In midafternoon, a motorcade took the Royal Party to Government House along a route that enabled students of several public and private schools to cheer the Queen.

Wednesday's events concluded with a state dinner at the Tucker's Point Club, which Wanda and I hosted. Before the dinner we had the honor of a private audience with the Queen and Prince Philip. On behalf of Bermuda, we gave the Queen two blown glass sculptures, about a foot tall, of dancing Gombeys. Doubtless well informed by her staff of my love for golf, the Queen gave me a book about the game. Printed on Buckingham Palace's own press, the book was encased in a leather slipcase with "E II R" stamped on it in gold. An engraved card inside read, "*A History of Golf–The Royal and Ancient Game* by Robert Browning, M.A., LL.B. Presented by Her Majesty the Queen to the Premier of Bermuda 25 November 2009." The Queen gave Wanda a beautiful pillbox.

There were ten tables, with ten people at each table, including Bermudians, the Governor and Lady Gozney, and members of the Royal Party. Wanda and I sat at the head table with the Queen, the Duke of Edinburgh, Speaker of the House Stanley Lowe, and Senate President Carol Anne Bassett.

At the beginning of my short speech of welcome, ending in the Loyal Toast, I pointed out that the nine other tables each bore the name of one of Bermuda's nine parishes. I said, "We wanted you to know that as small as Bermuda is, it is not always easy for us to speak with one voice. Yet tonight we welcome you in unison, and offer our thanks and best wishes for continued prosperity on behalf of my wife and me, and the Government and people of Bermuda. Ladies and gentlemen: the Queen."

In reply, the Queen spoke of Bermuda's history over 400 years and her previous visits. She highlighted the role of Admiral Somers in the founding of Bermuda and recalled speaking with Sir Edward Richards on her 1975 visit, when he was Bermuda's first Premier, and with Dame Lois Browne-Evans on her 1994 visit.

Thursday morning I hosted an off-the-record breakfast at Camden House for Foreign Secretary Miliband. The afternoon before, the media arm of the Combined Opposition had tried to bait him into saying something about the Uighur controversy. Mr. Miliband replied, "Dr. Brown and I have been working very well together on a whole range of things, but I am not going to discuss what I will be saying through the media." In private, he spoke to me about the Uighurs as he had at the Labour Party Conference in September: "This too shall pass."

The breakfast provided an opportunity to introduce Mr. Miliband to some of Bermuda's leading business people, especially from our financial services and insurance sector. Among other topics, we addressed how helpful our reinsurance enterprises were to the British insurance market, including lowering costs for British consumers.

Shortly after 11 a.m. that morning, the Governor, Lady Gozney, Wanda, and I presided at a farewell ceremony for the Queen and the Duke of Edinburgh at L. F. Wade International Airport. From start to finish the Royal Visit had gone beautifully, including cooperative weather with lots of sunshine. Thousands of Bermudians turned out to cheer the Queen, and I was proud to represent the entire nation as I accompanied Her Majesty.

In December Canadian-born Dale Jackson replaced Jamahl Simmons as my executive aide. Previously Dale had been an officer in the Police and a guidance counselor for at-risk youth. Dale did an admirable job in his new role until the end of my Premiership.

That month the UBP attacked the cost overrun at Port Royal Golf Course, which had just successfully hosted Bermuda's third PGA Grand Slam of Golf. The players—U.S. Open winner Lucas Glover beat Masters winner Angel Cabrera, British Open winner Stewart Cink, and PGA winner Y. E. Yang—all praised the course, as did the PGA and other knowledgeable observers.

Minister without Portfolio Zane DeSilva, whose construction company was involved in the work, and Works and Engineering Minister Derrick Burgess effectively rebutted the criticism. Here let me note Minister DeSilva's accurate observation that during UBP Governments, the UBP and its media allies insisted UBP MPs and Cabinet Ministers whose companies won public contracts were competent, ethical business people, whereas during PLP Governments, the Combined Opposition alleged that any PLP MPs and Cabinet Ministers whose companies won public contracts were crooks. The partisan political rhetoric was plainly racist.

The UBP characteristically misrepresented the overrun, comparing the cost of $15.9 million to a 2008 budget placeholder figure of $7.7 million. That made the cost overrun appear to be 56 percent. But the final budget estimate before the Port Royal work began in 2009 was $13.6 million. Changes along the way included a $1 million concrete golf cart path. Take the cart path out of the picture, and the cost overrun was less than 10 percent. Include the cart path, and the overrun was about 17 percent.

By contrast, as Minister Burgess pointed out, when a UBP Government renovated the airport in the late 1980s, the final pre-start budget was $9 million and the ultimate cost was $26 million. Comparing the Port Royal and airport renovations on an apples-to-apples basis (over-budget cost to final cost estimate) gives cost overruns of 17 percent under the PLP and 177 percent under the UBP.

Minister Burgess said, "I am not criticising that [177 percent overrun]." Given the demands of the airport renovation in the late 1980s, he said, it was understandable that "you can start at $9 million and end up at $26 million." I don't believe the Combined Opposition ever treated a PLP Government project with the same honest understanding, one that put the interests of Bermuda ahead of party.

Among other topics of House debate in December were the bills for PATI and a Department of Internal Audit. Responding to reasonable concerns expressed by the public and MPs from all three parties—the PLP, the UBP, and the Bermuda Democratic Alliance (BDA), recently formed by UBP rebels—my administration agreed PATI should apply to all previous Governments. We also put the Internal Audit bill aside so that we could consider changes to it.

Echoing UBP Senator Michael Dunkley's claim that I was "playing games in the fight against crime" by asking the Governor to cede managerial oversight of the BPS, UBP Leader Kim Swan bizarrely asserted that there was a "sacrosanct rule followed by virtually all developed countries to keep police operations out of the hands of politicians." Our request for operational control was for Bermuda's police to report to the people's elected representatives, as they do in Canada, the United States, the United Kingdom, and every other developed democratic country.

In the middle of December the annual OTCC meetings were held in London. As usual, the OT heads of government met beforehand, with a gap in our ranks because of Britain's having suspended the government in Turks and Caicos. At the preliminary meeting in November in Anguilla, I had persuaded my fellow heads of government we should not let the British divide and conquer as usual. Instead we should insist on speaking to them with one voice in bilateral talks at the FCO in London with Labour government MP and new Overseas Territories Minister Chris Bryant. The other heads of government unanimously delegated me to lead the talks on our side.

Faced with our united front, the British agreed to deal with the OTs as a group. We discussed common concerns such as drug trade violence, climate change, and British control over our financial regimes. Bermuda's financial regime was the healthiest and most transparent in regard to international standards and regulations. But we in Bermuda—I mean the PLP, the international business community, and behind their anti-PLP rhetoric the UBP—shared the other OTs' view that British interference was heavy-handed and counterproductive.

The UBP hypocritically condemned my realistic approach to relations with the British government, as if I was endangering Bermuda's international business sector. The truth is that our international business community has no great reverence for Britain or British common law and respect for contract in the OTs. Our international business sector CEOs and other top executives also have no great emotional attachment to Bermuda.

The international business community locates itself for tax and regulatory purposes wherever is most convenient for making money. Nothing else matters.

Financial services CEOs and fund managers in Bermuda certainly have always valued the clarity and structure of British common law and civil procedure, but that goes with wanting the British, and even more so the Americans, to allow them to operate in relative freedom. That in turn means they want Bermuda to hold its own with London and Washington.

The Combined Opposition peddles the fantasy that our international business sector views PLP Government with trepidation over "political instability." The sector had no real concerns about that even during the Uighur crisis.

As I mentioned in chapter 15, the absurdity of the attacks on me as anti-British stood revealed in the OBA Government over the winter of 2016–2017. Finance Minister Bob Richards said Bermuda might have to declare independence rather than let the British regulate our financial regime. Imagine the backlash if a PLP Finance Minister had uttered such a statement.

Discussing drug crime at the 2009 OTCC meeting, I stressed the need for elected governments to be able to manage the police forces in their jurisdictions. In a phone interview with the *Royal Gazette*, I also spoke of the opportunity a small country has to intervene with at-risk youth in their early school years. Unfortunately, there was more enthusiasm in Parliament—in all parties—for punishment after the fact than for preventive intervention.

Following the OTCC meeting, I went to Copenhagen to read a statement on behalf of the OTs at the U.N. Climate Change Conference. Our island nations are all on the front line of climate change impacts such as rising sea levels.

The week before Christmas, the *Royal Gazette* headlined an article, "Breaking News! The story Government did not want you to see!" Based on a leaked memorandum, the article revealed my administration was negotiating to purchase the Swan Building on Victoria Street, Hamilton, owned by Sir John Swan, for under $25 million. Publicizing such negotiations serves no purpose except inflating the purchase price. The deal was always subject to parliamentary approval. My administration wasn't hiding anything. A public announcement was simply premature.

As head of Government, Premier Scott had sensibly said Bermuda should own its office space rather than pay rent in perpetuity. This arrangement would save money and be a good investment. Government was paying most of the rent to White UBP-connected landlords. It is not healthy for any political party to permanently command so much Government revenue. As a result, I wanted to follow Premier Scott's good example, and Works and Engineering Minister Burgess made this part of his agenda.

Finance Minister Cox almost single-handedly blocked the now public deal. The budget remained under pressure because of the Great Recession, but Bermuda's debt load was not out of proportion to our gross domestic product and the overall balance sheet was healthy.

The *Royal Gazette* quoted its source, "Even if it does make sense to buy a building at some point, you don't do it if you are in a recession." In fact, a recession is an excellent time to buy real estate because prices are lower and sellers are eager. The alternative is waiting until the economy recovers and prices increase. In hindsight the $25 million, with a modest 7 percent mortgage, would have been well spent.

I suspect Minister Cox opposed buying the building simply to dissociate herself from me. Bizarrely, she apparently thought this would diminish Combined Opposition attacks on her leadership. Shadow Finance Minister Bob Richards was bloviating that her handling of her responsibilities was "naive." This was not the case, and I always wished she were able to act more courageously on that basis. It would have been beneficial for her leadership, the PLP, and Bermuda.

As 2009 ended, the Bermuda government began to operate under a new General Entrustment letter from the British. The UBP's Trevor Moniz howled that Bermuda had "lost London's trust" over the Uighurs. The new letter was more detailed about consulting the British, but, practically speaking, nothing had changed.

The new year opened with more conflict between my administration and taxi owners and operators who kept their GPS units turned off. We were forced to levy fines because some owners refused to see GPS would not only benefit consumers but also help increase revenues and lower costs.

On January 12, 2010, a major earthquake hit Haiti. At least 220,000 people died, 300,000 were injured, and one and a half million were displaced from their homes. The PLP Government took the lead in organizing relief contributions from Bermuda, including funds raised through a telethon in March.

In the middle of January, Government House issued a statement about the faked checks planted in Works and Engineering files, saying that "there was no evidence of criminality which could be charged . . . in Bermuda." Because the faked checks were apparently produced in Canada, Minister Burgess and I announced we might seek redress there for the attack on the PLP Government through us.

On January 22 other Cabinet Ministers and I held a press conference on legislation to decrease gang-related crime. Attorney General Kim Wilson discussed amendments, modeled on recent British legislation, to enable the Police to act on antisocial behavior without public complaints. Attorney General Wilson also spoke about our Parental Responsibility Bill, under which parents would face civil penalties for having "failed to exercise reasonable care . . . and control" of their minor-age children. Acting Culture and Social Rehabilitation Minister Michael Scott reported that Paget Island could permanently house the Mirrors Program, perhaps including a partnership with Outward Bound. Minister Scott and Health Minister Walter Roban both discussed programs to intervene with at-risk youth. Labour, Home Affairs, and Housing Minister David Burch said six British officers were working with the Police on gang-related crime.

The balance of enforcement and prevention reflected the recent Throne Speech. But they needed public support. To parents I said, "Government cannot read a book to your child. Government cannot check . . . that your child does their homework. Government cannot teach your child respect for fair laws. . . . Only you can do that."

On January 30, the *Royal Gazette* published an article comparing budgets and final costs on six public works projects, three under UBP Governments and three under my PLP Government. According to the newspaper's numbers, the UBP projects had cost overruns of 177 percent (the late 1980s airport renovation), 94 percent (Westgate Correctional Facility), and 183 percent (Tynes Bay Waste Treatment Facility). Again according to the newspaper's numbers, the PLP projects had cost overruns of 16.9 percent (Port Royal Golf Course), 86 percent (Heritage Wharf pier), and 38 percent (Berkeley Institute).

On February 3, the newspaper published an op-ed by Grant Gibbons, complaining it had misrepresented the UBP's project management. Gibbons pointed out overruns should be calculated based on the final pre-construction budget estimate. Although he didn't spell this out, the formula for a percentage cost overrun is final cost minus final pre-construction budget, divided by final pre-construction budget, times 100. On this basis, Gibbons argued there was no overrun at Westgate and a 5.2 percent overrun at Tynes Bay. On the other hand, he argued that the overrun at the Berkeley Institute was 83 percent. He was silent on the airport, accepting the overrun there was indeed 177 percent.

Gibbons was also silent on applying his accounting principles to PLP projects. Calculated according to those principles, the Port Royal Golf Course overrun was under 10 percent (backing out the cost of the concrete cart path, which was not part of the original construction plan). Likewise, the Berkeley Institute overrun was 6.8 percent (using the *Royal Gazette*'s numbers and backing out the $27 million in additional work that was not part of the original construction plan) or 44 percent (using Gibbons's numbers).

As for Heritage Wharf, according to the Evans Commission (see chapter 18), the final pre-construction budget was $44 million and the final cost was $60 million, whereas the *Royal Gazette* reported the numbers as $35 million and $65 million respectively. The Commission's numbers yield a cost overrun of 36 percent, not 86 percent.

Another public project that deserves mention whenever cost overruns are discussed is CedarBridge Academy, the senior secondary school built by the last UBP Government. The *Royal Gazette*'s online archive (based on multiple searches) contains nothing about a budget overrun. I only learned a significant overrun had occurred when then Auditor General Larry Dennis defended his special audit of the Berkeley Institute project by saying he had uncovered CedarBridge's running $11 million over budget.

Given a final construction cost of $60 million, the cost overrun at Cedar-Bridge was 22 percent. And the work wasn't done right. Beginning under Jennifer Smith's PLP Government, Bermuda had to spend a considerable amount of money remediating mold contamination at CedarBridge. The *Royal Gazette* repeatedly hammered PLP Governments, including mine, over the Cedar-Bridge mold, ignoring the UBP mismanagement that created the problem. By contrast, there have been no major issues with the Berkeley Institute's new building.

Across these projects and the new airport terminal (see chapter 18), there is zero basis for the UBP/OBA to claim better stewardship of public money than the PLP.

At the end of the first week in February, I led a four-day trade delegation to India. The main objectives were opening the Indian market to our insurance sector and raising awareness of Bermuda as a tourism destination. I addressed the Confederation of Indian Industry and the Institute of Chartered Accountants of India, and met leading members of the Bollywood film industry, second only to Hollywood. During the trip Bermuda and India agreed on a TIEA. We also discussed Indian training for Bermudian civil servants and arrangements for Bermudians to attend the Whistling Woods Film Institute in Mumbai.

Also in February, we passed a bill establishing a Department of Internal Audit. As originally drafted, the bill protected the independence of the new department in the traditional way, by giving the Governor authority to appoint its director. However, my PLP colleagues and I acknowledged the validity of BDA and UBP MPs' concerns that more could be done to protect against political interference. The revised bill therefore stipulated that if an internal audit found irregularities or fraud, the department immediately had to inform the Auditor General. In revised form, the Internal Audit Act passed without fuss.

On February 6, 2010, the *Royal Gazette* began its article about this action, "A bill improving oversight of Government policies and programs was finally passed in the House of Assembly yesterday, two months after it had to be deferred following complaints."

Finally? Two months is a brief time for revising, reintroducing, and passing a bill of any kind in almost any legislature in the world. It is remarkably
fast for Bermuda. In addition, the paper gave no credit to my PLP Government
for recognizing that Bermuda's public sector needed better internal auditing.
No credit for engaging in open-minded debate with opposition parties. No
credit for agreeing the opposition parties raised valid points and incorporating
them in a revised bill. No credit for speedy action to increase transparency
and accountability in the national interest. Nothing but routine pro-UBP bias.
Was it any wonder I called the *Royal Gazette* part of the Combined Opposition?

February also saw Michael Dunkley renew criticism of the International
Love Festival as "a waste of valuable money." I renewed defense of the event
as a way to seed tourism during the worst time of the year for Bermuda's hotels, with the cost more than recouped in visitor spending. The sponsors (luxury Swiss watchmaker and jeweler Chopard, the PGA, Marquis Jet, Lindt,
Royal Caribbean and Norwegian Cruise lines, the Fairmont Hamilton Princess, and upscale publications *The Robb Report, Travel and Leisure, Veranda,
Departures,* and *Golf World*) obviously saw value in the event.

At this time my administration proposed granting over $500,000 in tax
concessions to the Grotto Bay Beach Resort. The UBP agreed without question, as always in such cases, unless the resort happened to be run by a PLP
supporter, like Coco Reef.

The Southlands–Morgan's Point land swap was still pending, and the
Combined Opposition revved up its noise machine to accuse me of blocking
the deal, echoing insurance magnate Brian Duperreault and his fellow Southlands owners. My administration was holding up the swap. As stewards of
Bermuda's interests, we needed to see the plans for Morgan's Point.

When the Duperreault group finally produced renderings and plans, including numbers of guest rooms and expatriate work permits, I was appalled.
They wanted to build the sort of concrete monstrosity we had imploded at the
Club Med site. Insensitive to the landscape, Bermudian traditions, and luxury
tourism trends, the plan was nothing but maximum guest rooms per square
foot.

I suggested to Brian Duperreault that he consult British developer Patrick
Ellis, a key person behind the Amanyara Resort in Turks and Caicos. Opened
in March 2009 by Indonesia's Aman group, Amanyara stands at the leading
edge of twenty-first century tourism, a beautiful, environmentally sensitive,
successful luxury resort. There is nothing like it in Bermuda.

Because of Michael Misick's legal troubles, the Combined Opposition
shouted, "Corruption!" The only connection was that I met Patrick Ellis and
learned about Amanyara through Michael Misick. I told Brian Duperreault the
Southlands–Morgan's Point swap could only occur if we negotiated like

grown-ups without appeals to the media. Fortunately, he agreed. In the meantime, he and his partners still needed a top hotel operator.

Two changes in my office occurred around this time. In February, young lawyer Liana Hall, one of Julian Hall's daughters, became administrative assistant, a job she performed admirably. In March, Jamahl Simmons fortunately came back into my administration to serve as press secretary for the rest of my tenure.

Parliament was then having its annual budget debates. Shadow Finance Minister Bob Richards, the *Royal Gazette*, and the rest of the Combined Opposition said the 2010 budget was imprudent given the effects of the Great Recession. Again, countries that maintained a reasonable amount of public spending fared far better than those that went all in for austerity.

The *Royal Gazette*'s "A bad Budget" editorial said modest increases in payroll taxes and international companies' fees were "bit[ing] . . . the hand that feeds us." The increases did not come close to tipping the scales against Bermuda as a domicile for international companies.

Deputy Premier and Finance Minister Cox regrettably responded to the shouts for austerity, "I am one aspect of the Government team. I am a cog in the wheel."

By tradition the Opposition decides when the House will debate parts of the budget, but is flexible if the Cabinet Minister concerned has a conflict. The UBP wanted to debate Tourism's budget on March 12. Well in advance, I informed the UBP I had to be in Dominica for a Caricom meeting on that day, and several times I requested rescheduling. The UBP insisted on March 12.

On March 8, at the last meeting of the House before I left for Dominica, we debated the Cabinet Office budget, and I used all but thirty seconds of the two hours allotted to the topic. In the spirit of that thirty-second lesson, when the Tourism budget was debated on March 12, Works and Engineering Minister Burgess used four hours and twenty minutes of the five hours allotted for debate before ceding the floor to the UBP.

Hardball tactics? Sure. But they were an appropriate response to the UBP's failure to respect the traditions of the House and be reasonably flexible in scheduling. UBP Governments often used up most of the time allotted for budget debates and left the PLP with little or no time to speak and ask questions.

The UBP mostly wanted to rehash everything to do with GlobalHue's contract as Tourism's advertising agency. Yet GlobalHue continued to perform well, with a freshened "Feel the Love" campaign that increasing numbers of visitors recalled favorably. A month and a half later, *AdWeek* named GlobalHue "Multi-Cultural Agency of the Decade," and the *New York Times* featured GlobalHue CEO Don Coleman in its Sunday "The Boss" column.

An innovation for the 2010 budget was a mega-fund for Tourism with contributions from Government and the hotel industry. This led to the first joint advertising by Government and individual hotels. Until then Tourism's ads were generic, and individual properties never advertised at all.

In March we tabled a Green Paper on gaming, which was drafted by leading gaming and leisure consultancy the Innovation Group. The Green Paper recommended against a lottery and Internet gambling and for casino(s) in Hamilton and perhaps elsewhere on the Island.

That month I asked Minister without Portfolio Zane DeSilva to take on responsibility for the Municipalities Reform Act. He immediately began to give the bill the push it needed, raising hackles inside the Corporation of Hamilton. Cabinet had decided reform of the Corporation of St. George's would follow.

In 2009 a bipartisan board reviewing parliamentary salaries had recommended raises for MPs, the House Speaker and Deputy Speaker, Senators, and half-time Cabinet Ministers. Given the economic climate, we postponed raises for MPs and Senators. But I felt we should provide overdue raises for the Speaker and Deputy Speaker, and put our only half-time Cabinet Minister, Finance Minister Cox, on full pay. She was doing a full-time job as Finance Minister, even though she was also full-time corporate counsel of ACE Limited, one of Bermuda's largest insurance firms.

The idea of half-time Cabinet Ministers was obsolete, a vestige of a bygone era. Bermuda had a modern developed economy, and all its Cabinet portfolios required full-time attention. Minister Cox said she would refuse to accept a salary increase (from $100,000 to $150,000). My critics said I moved the bill to undermine her chances of succeeding me as PLP Leader and Premier. This was nonsense. If Minister Cox did not want the additional salary, although I have no doubt she felt she deserved it, she could return it to Bermuda's general fund or donate it to charity. Either way she would shine. However, the bill failed to pass as too many MPs acted on short-term political interest rather than Bermuda's long-term needs.

Since his December 2008 resignation from the UBP, Wayne Furbert had been sitting on the Opposition side of the House as an Independent. On March 19, 2010, he crossed the aisle to join the PLP. The *Royal Gazette* reported antagonism to this move on the part of anonymous PLP MPs, who feared being eclipsed by him. However, it was a good development for the Party and Wayne. The PLP made sense for him as a political home as the UBP never did.

The next week we announced a new structure for the fifteenth Bermuda Music Festival. Instead of underwriting the entire festival, Tourism would provide an $800,000 sponsorship. We issued a request for proposals from producers interested in taking control of the festival.

My critics derided me. They were right that the costs had become disproportionate, and it is difficult to interest American tourists in performers they can see at home. On the other hand, the festival was one of a few events in our calendar with any appeal to tourists. Trying to boost that appeal was not a mistake; Bermuda needs new tourist draws. British colonial quaintness hasn't cut it for decades.

That was why I pushed casino gambling. The Combined Opposition portrayed my effort as a personal obsession rather than part of what tourism needed to grow—and avoid shrinking further!

Some PLP and UBP MPs sincerely objected to gambling. Others recognized Tourism needed it, but were unwilling to support the bill. The second group swelled after United We Stand, representing about 70 Protestant congregations, opposed casinos.

Leaders who hope to contribute in a lasting way must choose what parts of the future they try to advance, remembering two great truths: politics is the art of the possible, and it is always local. For me, countering racism always had priority. In addition my sense of what was locally possible in Bermuda included casinos, but not decriminalizing marijuana or allowing gay marriage.

Amending our Human Rights Act in 2010 bogged down as my administration sought to protect against discrimination without alienating most voters. Commentators suggested Dale Butler's hopes to become PLP Leader and Premier would founder because he was too left of center on gay rights. More recently, Marc Bean crashed out of PLP leadership and the House, largely because of his commitment to legalizing marijuana.

Those who say punitive drug laws or anti-LGBT discrimination may intertwine with racism have a point. But a democratic society can only progress as quickly as the majority is willing to go, and each step enables further steps.

Another aspect of LGBT rights deserves mention. I twice met at Camden with members of Bermuda's LGBT community, including sitting MPs. I finally told them I would not help them until they helped themselves, as Black civil rights activists had done, by declaring themselves publicly. I said, "If you want help, you've got to come out of the closet and put your blood, sweat, and tears on the line."

One of my long-standing concerns, preparing young Black Bermudians for tourism careers, required changing their attitudes to the hospitality industry. They needed to see entry-level jobs had dignity and could lead to good futures. With Cabinet support, during the December 2007 election I had committed the PLP Government to establish a new hospitality training program. This proposal hinged on getting the right person to run it. In early April 2010, I was delighted to announce Bermudian Karla Lacey as inaugural CEO of the Bermuda Hospitality Institute.

Early April 2010 also saw the beginning of our Visa Waiver Assistance program, as promised in the most recent Throne Speech. Rolfe Commissiong capably ran the program, which helped many Bermudians travel to the United States.

Another event in April illustrated a significant division within the PLP. At a caucus on the Municipalities Reform Act, the *Royal Gazette* reported, "About a third of [the] caucus was said to be against repealing the Municipalities Act 1923. . . ." In other words, if there were Black faces in high places, about a third of the caucus had no interest in reforming White-dominated business as usual. That was a recurring theme in PLP politics from the time I became an MP.

In mid-April my administration announced the hiring of an expatriate Assistant Police Commissioner with anti-gang expertise, firearms training and Tasers for Bermudian officers, and urban policing courses in Britain for three superintendents. The Governor remained unwilling to bring in American experts, but we forged a training-and-information link with the FBI. Thanks to Michael Bloomberg, then in his third term as New York mayor, and the Governor's acquiescence, Police Commissioner Michael DeSilva—he replaced retiring George Jackson—was consulting the New York Police Department's Gang Division.

Also under consideration was sending violent criminals to state prisons in the United States or joining Caribbean jurisdictions to create a high-security prison. It would be cheaper to send prisoners to American state prison systems, and some in Bermuda thought Westgate was not harsh enough. I believe a global comparison would show the harshest prison systems have the most recidivism. Although I doubted extra punishment was the answer, at the time I was willing to entertain the possibility that incarceration abroad and establishing a SWAT unit might ease our crime problem.

A few days after these announcements, I went to Britain with a Tourism team and hoteliers. We needed to remind British travel agents and media that Bermuda was under six hours away, about the same as Dubai, an increasingly popular destination for British tourists. Travel agents and media wanted to know about places and events to interest British travelers. We mentioned the Tucker's Point Club, site of the state dinner for the Queen, the PGA Grand Slam of Golf, Harbour Nights, and the Bermuda Music Festival.

While we were in Britain, Iceland's Eyjafyallajökull volcano erupted. Ash grounded air travel throughout Europe and the north Atlantic for several days, underlining Bermuda's dependence on air links.

British tourists were a minority of our visitors, and their numbers never climbed. But we had to sustain the stream as best we could. The limiting factor remained British Airways' exclusive hold on the Britain-Bermuda air route.

Without a discount carrier to replace Zoom, defunct since 2008, BA faced no pressure to lower exorbitant fares.

At the beginning of May, WestJet began to fly to Bermuda from Toronto. That soon increased the number of Canadian tourists.

In late March, I had agreed to Opposition Leader Kim Swan's request to postpone the debate on the Green Paper on gambling until after Easter. May 7 was the day we settled on, and the week before at Sandys Rotary Club, I said casinos would be "a win for job creation, . . . a win for tourism, . . . a win for construction, . . . a win for our tax base, . . . a win for our economy."

The Innovation Group's Green Paper estimated that one or more casinos could create 1,200 to 2,200 jobs and produce $83 million to $145 million in annual tax and fee revenue. Such projections must be taken with a grain of salt, but if we managed things well, casinos could contribute to employment and the national bottom line. Although there are social ills associated with gambling because some people become addicted, legal casinos would generate funds for counseling and other services.

The hoteliers were eager for casinos and afraid the UBP would desert them out of petty partisanship. Norman Mastalir, head of the Fairmont Hamilton Princess and Fairmont Southampton, said the Green Paper was "music to our ears."

Finance Minister Cox habitually waited until the end of debates in the House before expressing any views. On this occasion she was one of the first to speak, saying she opposed casinos "at this time." Both PLP and Opposition MPs echoed her. PLP MPs did so to curry favor with my likely successor. Opposition MPs acted to deny me an achievement they wanted for themselves. One MP after another said we should focus on violent crime and "economic dislocation" from the Great Recession. They ignored the possibility that more jobs and prosperity would help address these challenges.

Although Cabinet had approved the Green Paper, only Zane DeSilva joined me in speaking in favor of casinos. I understood the other Cabinet Ministers were looking ahead to Paula Cox's succeeding me as Premier. In the rest of the House, only PLP MPs Walter Lister and Michael Weeks, BDA MPs Shawn Crockwell and Mark Pettingill, and Independent MP Darius Tucker spoke for casinos.

The hoteliers' fears were realized, and the UBP deserted them. Deputy Opposition Leader Trevor Moniz said, "The [UBP] expects the Premier to focus his Government's attention on . . . gun violence and economic dislocation, and to drop his push for gaming." This ignored not only the jobs and revenue legalized gambling could bring, but the fact that I was the first Bermudian politician to address gang-related crime and never dropped the issue.

A *Royal Gazette* editorial said, "The gambling debate could not have come . . . at a better time for Ms. Cox . . . after her 'cog in the wheel' statement and her widely criticised Budget." The 2010 Budget was widely criticized only by the Combined Opposition, but the sentence probably captures how she saw things. The general political view was that she wanted to become PLP Leader and Premier without having to implement any controversial legislation. But it is impossible to lead progress without controversy and bucking the powers that be.

As if to illustrate that fact, the British threatened to revoke a 1999 entrustment, which had enabled Bermuda's Department of Civil Aviation to contract with the Russian Aviation Authority to oversee regulatory issues for commercial aircraft registered in Bermuda and leased by Russian airlines. Our winning the contract kick-started, and good management sustained, continued growth for the Bermuda Aircraft Register. Revenue for 2010 was on track to reach $16 million. The Aviation Working Group, a consortium of manufacturers, leasing companies, and financial institutions, said, "Bermuda registration has become a main element of aircraft leasing and financing."

Bermuda registration appealed to the airliner leasing industry because of our Category 1 status with the U.S. Federal Aviation Administration (FAA). This meant the FAA recognized us as meeting international safety standards, which was crucial for American leasing companies and lenders. There were also tax advantages for leasing companies, and Bermuda was an honest jurisdiction if airliners had to be repossessed.

A routine February 2009 audit by the International Civil Aviation Organization (ICAO) called for more technical staff. Aware of the problem, we had limited aircraft registration over the prior five months. In response to the audit, we created four temporary inspector positions, approved contracts for more positions, and adjusted our outsourcing. The ICAO accepted all our action plans, and the Bermuda Aircraft Registry remained in good standing.

The British felt our register competed too much with theirs. With the ICAO audit as a pretext, the British Department of Transportation complained in 2010 that "Bermuda is conducting a revenue-raising business" and said it "would find it hard to accept . . . the register in its current form at all."

Of course we were conducting a revenue-raising business. That is a fundamental reason for an aircraft register. Our register's strong market position resulted from hard work in successive PLP Governments. I was not going to let the British siphon off the millions of dollars it contributed to Bermuda's economy every year.

Saving the Bermuda Aircraft Register required meetings in Russia and the United Kingdom, reassuring the Russian Aviation Authority and Russian airlines and standing up to the British. We reached out to the register's other international customers, and I consulted the Bermudian law firms handling registrations. I also rebutted the UBP's reckless attacks, which ignored Bermuda's interests in order to stir up controversy, and corrected ill-informed reports in the Combined Opposition's media arm. True to form, the *Royal Gazette* only moderated its anti-PLP, pro-UBP reporting when Ian MacIntyre, recently retired White director of Bermuda's Department of Civil Aviation, confirmed what I was saying.

The British attack on our aircraft register was another example of how Bermuda is placed between the United States and the United Kingdom. We must sometimes stand up to, and even defy, the United Kingdom to protect our essential politico-economic relationships with the United States.

Louder protests surrounded my efforts to update Bermuda's media industry with a complaints council like those in the United Kingdom and other developed countries. The late Julian Hall had called for a media council as essential for journalistic responsibility in the House in February 1993. Over the following months and years, PLP and UBP legislators echoed Julian.

As chapter 16 relates, my administration proposed a self-regulating media council in the Throne Speech of February 1, 2008. A March 2008 *Royal Gazette* poll found 64 percent of Bermudians favored such a council. Although broadcast media operated under a statutory code of conduct for complaints about accuracy and fairness, print media did not. Leading members of Bermuda's media industry wrote me in December 2008 to propose that they form their own media council. I waited for them to follow up, but they did nothing.

On March 8, 2010, I told the House the Media Council Act 2010 was on the way, and on May 7 we tabled it. The *Royal Gazette* and the UBP immediately said the bill threatened press freedom. It did nothing of the kind, although the newspaper rallied international organizations to attack it.

The bill proposed a twelve-member council, six nominated by Government after consultation with the Opposition and five by the media. These nominations would be subject to approval by the Governor, who would select an executive director. Governor Gozney said these provisions protected against political bias, and I appreciated this unusual gesture of support for one of my initiatives.

After two and a half weeks of hysterical attacks, the *Royal Gazette* recognized crying wolf was ineffective. It said it would join other media outlets in a voluntary self-regulating council. I told the House the bill would remain on the order paper while we reviewed the media's proposal. In the second week of June, the media adopted a twenty-five-point code of practice. On July 20, I pulled the bill, mission accomplished. As the leading news outlet on the Island, the *Royal Gazette* could have prevented a bill from ever being tabled, simply by acting on the industry's December 2008 proposal.

The airport terminal needed replacement. In 2008 we had requested proposals from infrastructure firms with the idea of building a new terminal on adjacent brownfield land for a smooth transition. Late May 2010 we revealed the best proposal—from U.S.-based HNTB Corporation, which boasts several cutting-edge transportation projects—and a projected cost of $300 to $400 million.

That is a lot of money, and redeveloping KEMH was Bermuda's top in-frastructure priority. But the Great Recession meant borrowing costs were cheap, making it an excellent time to initiate public works for a jurisdiction with a healthy balance sheet like Bermuda. I expected no action before I left office, but I felt it was valuable to put the project on Bermuda's horizon.

With regard to the national balance sheet, during the summer Bermuda sold its first bonds on international capital markets. We raised $500 million. The UBP claimed we were taking on too much debt. However, our debt-to-GDP ratio remained very low compared to other developed countries and our balance sheet was healthy by any international standard.

I looked to the future with concern and hope in June as I initiated parlia-mentary debate and invited national discussion of marine biologist Anne F. Glasspool's "The Impact of Climate Change on Bermuda." Commissioned by the Bermuda National Trust, Dr. Glasspool's 190-page report catalogues the expected impact of human-induced global warming. Even a good case sce-nario, in which humanity halts the warming trend over coming decades, would challenge Bermuda. A worse, not worst, case scenario would drown much of Hamilton, St. George's, and other areas.

Hope remains, although the outlook is already grimmer than it was in 2010. Dr. Glasspool's report remains a valuable resource. In addition to de-scribing expected impacts, she identified a host of steps to sustain Bermuda and its ecosystem.

I led a delegation to Washington for the fourth and last time in June. The delegation included Deputy Premier and Finance Minister Paula Cox, Cabinet Secretary Marc Telemaque, and Financial Secretary Donald Scott. On Capitol Hill we met Congressman and House Majority Whip James Clyburn (South Carolina), Congressman G. K. Butterfield (North Carolina), Congressman and House Ways and Means Chairman Sander Levin (Michigan), Congressman and former House Ways and Mean Chairman Charles Rangel (New York), and Senator Richard Durbin (Illinois). There were also meetings with John Bren-nan, then President Obama's special assistant for Homeland Security and Counterterrorism; David Cohen, an assistant Treasury secretary with respon-sibility for thwarting terrorist financing; and Pentagon officials.

My agenda for the trip began with present challenges: the lingering pos-sibility of adverse U.S. tax law changes, fighting money laundering and terror-ist financing, and cleaning up Morgan's Point. The Americans could never open the Pandora's box of financial responsibility for toxic pollution at Mor-gan's Point, given their many military installations around the world. But it was worth reminding them of the mess they left behind. And we wound up doing well on our other priorities.

Having taken the Bermuda-U.S. relationship to new heights, I wanted to pass the baton smoothly to the next Premier, almost certain to be Paula Cox. Except for Sir John Swan, UBP Premiers never interacted effectively with the U.S. government. I saw the improved relationship as good for Bermuda and a strategic advantage for PLP Governments.

June also brought the annual Seniors Tea, one of the high points of the calendar for me as Premier. Wanda and I both loved celebrating Bermuda's seniors on the nation's behalf, and we greatly enjoyed our last such opportunity.

Although I visited schools throughout my Premiership, my visits as the 2009–2010 school year ended were especially joyful and poignant. Education was the one area where I had not been able to make significant progress for Bermuda except for adoption of the CIC. I remain frustrated by our school system's continuing problems. But the picture wasn't, and isn't, all bleak, thanks to many dedicated teachers and the growth potential and resilience of children.

Seeing the sixth Mirrors Program class graduate in June was also joyful. It was rewarding to know Mirrors was helping young Bermudian men and women avoid bad paths in life.

I regretted not being able to build support for national service options besides service in the Regiment. Influential members of the PLP and Civil Service had such an emotional attachment to the Regiment that they felt alternatives would demean it.

Just as I symbolically held a Cabinet meeting at Westgate Correctional Facility after becoming Premier, I wanted to make an official visit there before stepping down. I did so conscious of the fact that my two older sons, Kevin and Maurice, were incarcerated in the United States. The Westgate prisoners were Bermuda's sons. If we did not try to rehabilitate them, we consigned Bermuda to unending recidivism. At the start of the visit, I spoke to several corrections officers and senior prison officials. I then had a closed-to-the-press conversation with inmates.

The UBP condemned my visiting the prisoners. As a *Royal Gazette* headline put it, "Premier should have visited crime areas, spoken to prison officers, claims Senator Dunkley." I had spoken to prison officers, albeit not as a group, and I had visited every crime-ridden area of Bermuda multiple times during my political career. It is surely an understatement to say my understanding of these communities has always been deeper than Mr. Dunkley's.

I've discussed the Club Med site. Another problematical site was the old Golden Hind resort in Warwick. The developer's plan for the site included a new hotel, the Grand Atlantic, and low-cost housing. The hotel was not going to materialize, but in June the BHC finalized plans for the housing. We may have built a little more low-cost housing than the Island needed, but this project, Loughlands, and Southside fulfilled my administration's promise of decent housing for disadvantaged Bermudians.

At the beginning of July, the House's Public Accounts Committee, always chaired by an Opposition MP and then led by Shadow Finance Minister Bob Richards, held its first open meeting. I supported opening the meetings. With the participation of Auditor General Heathers Jacobs Matthews, Shadow Finance Minister Richards used the meeting to attack GlobalHue's contract renewal. The renewal broke no laws, but they opined there should be a law against renewing a contract of that size without competitive bidding. The argument hinged on GlobalHue's temporarily subcontracting with a media buyer, as I already discussed.

Shadow Finance Minister Richards bizarrely contended that because the renewal occurred during the Great Recession, my administration squandered an opportunity to get "the best advertising brains in the entire Madison Avenue" on Bermuda's account. In a Ministerial Statement in the House, I said his contention showed "that the Honourable Member does not find it plausible that the best advertising brains can be found in a firm like GlobalHue. That is tragic, and probably goes to the heart of many matters here."

My statement concluded, "I and others in the Government are often accused of playing the race card. What is hardly ever discussed is the fact there is no need to play the race card—it is already in play and so are its devastating effects. The Honourable Member Mr. Richards's comments are clear evidence of that."

My account of my last year in office would be incomplete if I did not mention the controversy over the fact that Customs officers always opened courier packages for Wanda and me and, somewhat less frequently, my Cabinet Ministers. The Finance Ministry, which included Customs, ordered that these packages only be opened in the presence of recipients or their representatives. A few Customs officers persisted in opening the packages on their own, finding such things as birthday cards for Wanda.

The Combined Opposition said I was putting myself above the law. But one member of the UBP seconded my request for "due respect" from Customs. Former Premier Sir John Swan told the media, "Premiers, like presidents, have privileged positions. . . . There should be a process that's understood by the Premier, the Collector of Customs, and the public."

I was not asking that Customs officers never open another package to Wanda, me, or Cabinet Ministers. No one is above the law. However, Customs officers had not previously opened a hundred percent of packages to Premiers and their spouses. Why open every single package to Wanda and me? Could it be because I was the only Premier to question the status quo in a fundamental way?

In late June, the pending Municipalities Reform Act 2010 triggered increased resistance. Mayor Charles Gosling sent Cabinet copies of a March Rotary speech, in which he claimed the Corporation of Hamilton was allied to the PLP Government and not part of the Opposition. He was apparently oblivious to the speech's expression of White privilege and condescension.

I ignored the letter, as did the rest of Cabinet except Senator Burch. He ripped up the speech and sent it back in its manila envelope, marked "Return to Sender!" He later said he did this because he felt disrespected and offended by the speech, something every self-respecting Black Bermudian understood perfectly.

For the past few months the Corporation of Hamilton had operated a website called SaveOurCityBermuda.org. Following Senator Burch's "Return to Sender!" the corporation hung "Help Save Our City" banners all over Hamilton. The question remained, was Hamilton owned by the undemocratic Corporation of Hamilton?

In July, Wanda and I vacationed in South Africa for the 2010 World Cup in football and to visit her beloved stepson from her first marriage, Kwame Calhoun, and his son, Caden. The trip fulfilled my long-standing ambition to see a World Cup final (Spain beat the Netherlands 1-0), but caused me to miss House debate. The UBP said this typified my poor attendance record in the House, although my 81.5 percent attendance in 2010 compared well with that of prior Premiers.

In my absence, Minister without Portfolio DeSilva brought up the Municipalities Reform Act at the July 7 PLP caucus. The Caucus declined to back the bill, and the *Royal Gazette* reported backbench MP and former Cabinet Minister Terry Lister was "particularly vocal" against it.

Some of those who spoke against reform missed the July 14 Caucus. However, there was a quorum, and the majority voted to support reform. In response, the Corporation of Hamilton flew its flag upside down, an internationally recognized signal of distress.

On Monday, July 19, Mayor Gosling came to my office to discuss the bill. Minister DeSilva, Cabinet Secretary Marc Telemaque, and Corporation of Hamilton COO Ed Benevides also attended.

The meeting lasted ten minutes. That was all it took for Mayor Gosling to display the Corporation's sense of entitlement by calling the bill a "takeover."

The PLP Government aimed to put Hamilton in the hands of all its residents and the Island's wharfage and port fees in the hands of all Bermudians rather than a coterie of White property owners. If this was a takeover, it was a just and democratic one. For generations the people of Hamilton had seen the Corporation of Hamilton hog wharfage and port fees—$7.5 million in 2010—for the Front Street district, giving the back of its hand to Back o' Town.

To maintain this injustice, the Municipalities Act 1923 allotted Hamilton residences one vote each, no matter how many adults lived there, and multiple votes to business owners with multiple properties in the city.

The House debated the Municipalities Reform Act 2010 on Friday evening, July 23. A group of mainly White protestors greeted the arrival of Minister DeSilva and his immediate family, who were going to sit in the visitors' gallery, by shouting abuse—"Traitor!" "Coward!" and worse—and thumping on their car.

Minister Zane De Silva opened the debate, "When the history of this country is written, the people of Bermuda should reflect on our actions today with pride, as we remove the last vestige of a system designed to preserve an unnatural imbalance in favor of the few. This Government is the party of universal adult suffrage and one man, one vote, each vote of equal value. This Government is the home of Dame Lois Browne-Evans, Dr. Barbara Ball, Freddie Wade, and Roosevelt Brown, and any vote or action that preserves this unjust system is an insult to their legacy."

He itemized the false claims and "manufactured hysteria" of the opponents of reform. Point by point, he showed how reform would make the Corporation of Hamilton worthy of present-day Bermuda.

I wasn't surprised to see that Zane De Silva had emerged as such an eloquent and effective leader. Zane grew up poor, has Black half-siblings, and was usually the only White student in his class and the only White player on his school and community sports teams—"the milk in the fly," he jokes. His identification with Bermuda's Black majority and the cause of social justice was fundamental to his own struggle for a better life, juggling jobs to make ends meet and eventually building one of Bermuda's most successful construction firms. Zane recognized Bermuda's racism in all its ugliness. He was as tireless in encouraging Black Bermudians to build their own futures through hard work as he was steadfast in opposing the White power structure. He had mentored several Black employees to the point where they started their own businesses.

It took me five years to convince Zane to run for the House as a PLP candidate because he knew the racist abuse he, his wife, Joanne, and their children, Zane, Jr., and Zara would suffer. But once he entered electoral politics in 2007, he never looked back.

UBP Leader Kim Swan proposed postponing the vote for six months, claiming more time for consideration was needed. When a copy of the motion was handed to me, I tore it in half, to PLP laughter, and said, "We've been talking about this since 2008."

Among those who spoke and voted in favor of the bill was Terry Lister. For eight hours of debate, UBP MPs posed a series of objections to the bill. Yet just as with its delaying-and-sabotaging tactics on PLP Government initiatives like single-seat constituencies and FutureCare, the UBP lacked the courage of its supposed convictions. None of its MPs wanted to go on the record as voting against Municipalities reform. Thus on July 23, 2010, the House passed the Municipalities Reform Act 2010 by voice vote with, to quote the Hansard transcript, "AYES and one audible NO."

Mayor Gosling admitted the racism of those who greeted Minister De-Silva with cries of "Traitor!" and "Coward!" But he attempted to minimize their actions by saying, "It is a shame that a few people really got carried away in the heat of the moment and went beyond the call of duty." His odd sense of "the call of duty" in defending an unjust system indicates why Minister Burch tore up his Rotary speech. Regarding the mob's behavior toward the DeSilvas, BDA MP Mark Pettingill told the media, "I was ashamed to be a White man in the community today."

On July 23, the House also passed the Public Access to Information Act 2010. The vote was unanimous.

That evening I gave my final speech in the House and said, "My regrets are personal, not political." I added, "The only guarantee of full, unbridled affection in this office is to do nothing and do it very well. . . . Cause one new idea to see the light of day and cedar beams will appear in your home." I also said, "The great work that remains undone is the psychological freedom of Independence. The veil of affluence and material comfort has numbed the senses of the people, and for that we are all to blame."

The three people most often mentioned as candidates to succeed me were Finance Minister Paula Cox and backbench MPs and former Cabinet Ministers Dale Butler and Terry Lister. In August, most PLP MPs backed Minister Cox to be the new Party Leader and Premier. She spoke about "turning the volume down" as head of Government. I doubted the wisdom of that, given the Combined Opposition, but leaders must have their own style.

Early in August, the National Medical Association (NMA) named me a Scroll of Merit recipient, along with U.S. First Lady Michelle Obama, honored for her campaign against childhood obesity, and U.S. Surgeon General Dr. Regina Benjamin, among others. In bestowing the awards, NMA executive director Kweisi Mfume, former five-term Democratic congressman from Maryland and past president of the NAACP, highlighted my career-long involvement in community medicine. Listening gratefully, I recalled my contentious relationship with the NMA as a student and thought of the extraordinary turns life can take.

A week or so later my press secretary, Jamahl Simmons, learned of an online death threat against me and asked the Police to investigate. The threat was made in connection with the upcoming Premier's Farewell Gala to raise money for the PLP. On bermudaisanotherworld.org, a members-only website with a history of hate speech against the PLP and me, "Buddha Bunny" had recently posted about the gala, "Point me to the grassy knoll"—a reference to John F. Kennedy's assassination—where "I'll have a better shot." "Shot" was struck through, followed by "view."

I hoped it was only a sick joke, although that was not a safe assumption. In its articles about it, the *Royal Gazette* highlighted bloggers who said the threat was likely not serious, replayed Shadow Public Safety Minister Michael Dunkley's claim that the bullet mailed to me on the eve of the December 2007 election was "a concocted story," and referred to an "alleged death threat."

As the second Premier of the OBA Government that won power in 2012, Mr. Dunkley apparently took a different view of an online threat against his life late in 2016. He did not describe the threat as "a concocted story," and the *Royal Gazette* never referred to it as "alleged." The contrast with my case is clear.

In August my administration strengthened Bermuda's link with the University of the West Indies (UWI). An agreement I signed with UWI Vice Chancellor Dr. Nigel Harris made Bermuda an associate contributing country, enabling Bermudians to pursue studies at a discounted rate. Nigel was an old Howard University friend, and I was delighted we could benefit Bermuda and UWI.

August also brought encouraging news for Tourism, with final April-June visitor numbers up 24.4 percent over 2009. And in late August we announced that the Department of Civil Aviation would open a London office. The office would grow the Bermuda Aircraft Register and help prevent another underhanded attack on it by the British.

On August 23 the *Royal Gazette* published "Continue the Big Conversation," an opinion piece I wrote to mark UNESCO's International Day of Remembrance of the Slave Trade and Its Abolition. The piece observed that the resistance to the Big Conversation of many Bermudians, Black and White, illustrated the continuing damage of post-slavery racism. I noted that a "society that accepts the notion that White skin is more relevant to economic opportunity and success than education and hard work will see . . . a perpetuation of . . . division and hatred."

The piece found reason for hope in the fact that significant numbers of White and Black Bermudians engaged sincerely in the Big Conversation. After I left office, the conversation unfortunately became muted.

On Monday, September 6, Labour Day, UBP Leader Kim Swan, BDA Leader Craig Cannonier, and I all spoke in praise of Bermuda's unions. Breaking stereotype as usual, I was the only one to offer constructive criticism, noting both the progress of unions under PLP Governments and their responsibility to help foster a better work ethic. I was repeating such statements throughout my political career, including three days before at the BIU's annual banquet.

In advance of Bermuda's fourth PGA Grand Slam of Golf in October, I said Tourism should consider whether to continue hosting it as the PGA wanted. Although the 2007, 2008, and 2009 Grand Slams brought lots of publicity and were worthwhile, none of them had a marquee name. We had missed out on Tiger Woods more than once, and we did not know if current Masters champion Phil Mickelson, golf's second biggest draw, was going to play in 2010. The other major winners of the year were Graeme McDowell (U.S. Open), Louis Oosthuizen (British Open), and Martin Kaymer (PGA Championship).

Mickelson soon bowed out because of a diagnosis of psoriatic arthritis. Three-time major winner Ernie Els (two U.S. Opens and the British Open) replaced Mickelson. Because of injury, Louis Oosthuizen also withdrew, replaced by past PGA champion David Toms.

It was an open question in my mind whether Bermuda should continue its partnership with the PGA or build on this experience to develop other events. The next Tourism Minister would have to resolve that issue. In the meantime I continued to work for the 2010 PGA Grand Slam's success.

In early September the final phase of construction on the Loughlands affordable housing complex finished. Around the same time I announced that Dame Jennifer Smith would chair the sixth African Diaspora Heritage Trail Conference in mid-October.

The Farewell Gala on September 11 through 13 included a beach party with DJs, a golf tournament, a black-tie dinner, a Sunday church service, and a Monday brunch cruise. The events were designed to fulfill the third of three pledges to the PLP I made on becoming Party Leader in October 2006. The first, paying off the mortgage on Alaska Hall, was accomplished in 2008. The second, having more PLP MPs than when I became Premier, was guaranteed by Wayne Furbert's joining the party. The third was a substantial contribution to the PLP campaign chest.

The black-tie dinner at the Fairmont Southampton was an emotional event. One of its highlights was a tribute to me on behalf of Wanda by her friends Star Jones and Lynn Whitfield. Pauletta Washington, Denzel Washington's wife, was also supposed to participate in the tribute, but extremely bad weather did not allow the plane she was on to land in Bermuda. However, actors Tichina Arnold, Duane Martin, and Tisha Campbell-Martin attended, along with Terrence J and Rocsi.

My speech closing the evening was one of profound thanks. Thanks to prior PLP leaders—Arnold Francis, Walter Robinson, Dame Lois Browne-Evans, Freddie Wade, Dame Jennifer Smith, and Alex Scott—for their many contributions to the Party and Bermuda. Thanks to the PLP Caucus, headquarters, and Central Committee. Thanks to the people of Warwick, who elected me to the House beginning in 1993. Thanks to friends and family, especially Wanda and my four sons, Kevin, Maurice, Trey, and Donovan.

Complete unanimity in politics is neither possible nor desirable, and I accordingly ended, "So to those who worked with me, thank you. To those who worked against me, thank you. To those who helped me grow as a person and a leader, thank you. To those who put their lives on hold, who sacrificed, struggled, laughed, and cried with me, thank you. To those who didn't understand and still don't, thank you. To those who think they should have been thanked but weren't mentioned, thank you and good night!"

No surprise, the Farewell Gala had its critics. They said the $500 a plate black-tie dinner, attended by a full house of 550 people, was not a success because some PLP MPs didn't come. They said the price was exorbitant, although the evening included entertainment by Gladys Knight and Bermudians Gene Steede, Toni Robinson, and McCartney Darrell. The UBP absurdly charged that the dinner was "pay to play" because individuals and companies that did business with the PLP Government bought tickets.

Wayne Furbert rebutted this charge with chapter-and-verse knowledge of UBP fundraising during his tenure as a UBP MP and stint as UBP Leader. As the Government and in Opposition, Wayne told the media, the UBP raised money the same way the PLP did. The only difference was higher prices. He cited UBP events where corporate and individual sponsorships cost "$5,000 and up."

All together the Farewell Gala netted about $250,000. It fulfilled my pledge to leave the PLP in sound financial shape.

Tuesday evening, September 14, a Hotel Owners Appreciation Dinner for me took place at the Fairmont Southampton. The hotel owners recognized I had always gone the extra mile for them. They gave me a beautiful sculpture of tanzanite, a blue gem crystal mined only in Tanzania. It was an emotional occasion for me, and I cried openly.

A few days later Bermuda "dodged a bullet," in Public Safety Minister David Burch's words, when Hurricane Igor veered away as it weakened slightly. It remained a Category 4 storm, and 93-mile-per-hour winds hit on Sunday, September 19. Fortunately, there were no fatalities or injuries, and property damage was relatively minor. I was proud of the good work of Minister Burch and the PLP Government departments responsible for disaster relief and recovery. In Governor Gozney's words, Bermuda "showed the world how [such] things should be done."

My remaining weeks in office mixed ceremonial events with work, including finalizing the Southlands–Morgan's Point swap. On September 22, we announced first steps to making the Sargasso Sea a marine protected area, an initiative featured in *Time*. Bermuda sits at the western edge of the Sargasso Sea and is its only landmass. The initiative formed part of a comprehensive plan for enhancing Bermuda's eco-tourism potential and sustainable maritime resource management.

On September 23, I hosted my last Open Thursday brown bag lunch with ordinary Bermudians. In response to a question about where I had failed as Premier, I expressed disappointment over education reform, which remains one of Bermuda's long-term challenges. Two days later the Bermuda Race Relations Initiative held its second annual Trail Blazers Award dinner. The honorees were my cousin Calvin Smith; Dr. Eva Hodgson, Arthur Hodgson's sister and a formidable, underappreciated fighter for racial justice; and the late Julian Hall. In my speech I emphasized that the path of progress was not easy, but expressed the conviction that "we can form one people out of two Bermudas, White and Black."

Attorney General Eric Holder of the United States visited Bermuda September 29 and 30 to show support before I stepped down, for which I am grateful. We discussed the Morgan's Point clean-up and our two countries' partnership against drug trafficking, money laundering, and terrorist financing. Joining us were Bermuda Attorney General Kim Wilson, Acting Governor David Arkley, and U.S. Consul General Grace Shelton.

After the four Uighurs received asylum, President Barack Obama no longer criticized Bermuda as a tax haven. Echoing this, Attorney General Holder told the media he would not characterize Bermuda as a tax haven. A *Royal Gazette* editorial said it was useful to have the statement "on the record," but refused to connect the dots with the Uighurs. Crediting me with safeguarding Bermuda's economic lifeblood was a bridge too far for the Combined Opposition's media arm.

With Toni Braxton headlining the roster of entertainers, the fifteenth Bermuda Music Festival went well on the first weekend in October. Rock Newman, Washington radio personality and former manager of heavyweight boxing champion Riddick Bowe, had stepped in to produce the festival.

During the first week of October the four Uighurs, who had become Port Royal groundskeepers, learned they were losing their jobs, which were never meant to be permanent. A *Royal Gazette* editorial, "Shameful treatment," slammed my administration for abandoning the Uighurs. Except we hadn't. Senator Burch was looking out for them. They had become so well known for their work ethic, they soon had good jobs in the private sector.

Late that same week Wanda and I traveled at our expense to the Commonwealth Games in Delhi, India. Minister of Environment and Sport Glenn Blakeney also attended the games. He stood in for Finance Minister Cox in signing the TIEA negotiated during my trade delegation to India.

Back at home, I opened Bermuda's second hosting of the Latin American Association for Risk Management's (ALARYS) annual conference on Monday,

October 11. During my administration, Bermuda's insurance sector made large strides in Latin America, a process I helped advance on official trips.

On Monday evening we held a media roundtable at the Berkeley Cafetorium. My staff resisted it, but I insisted on a last official encounter with the media. They naturally focused on controversies during my Premiership.

Over the following days, Bermuda's media assessed my leadership. A series of articles in the *Royal Gazette* found me lacking in almost every area. The most notable article was Matthew Taylor's "The Unsinkable Dr. Brown." It made much of the fact that, except for countering racism, I did not have a rigid template for Bermuda and worked to fix what I thought needed fixing without regard to ideology. Matthew Taylor seemed equally disappointed by my not sinking and his inability to pigeonhole me politically.

Bermuda's fourth PGA Grand Slam of Golf, October 18 through 20, was another success, despite the absence of a marquee competitor. Port Royal, which escaped significant damage from Hurricane Igor, once again provided a superb championship-worthy course. At age forty-one, Ernie Els showed he could still play competitive golf at a high level by winning the competition, a prelude to his fourth major win at the 2012 British Open.

During the pro-am tournament on Monday, October 18, I played in a threesome with Ernie Els and his good friend Brian Lara, one of the West Indies' greatest all-time cricketers. We enjoyed some impromptu cricket on the 16th hole with me bowling to Ernie Els. He connected on a few strokes with the bat and thanked me for not hurling too much pace.

On Thursday, October 21, it was a pleasure to announce that Park Hyatt was joining developer Carl Bazarian's plan for the old Club Med site. Everything finally seemed to be in place for breaking ground on a new hotel.

That same day Auditor General Heather Jacobs Matthews released her special report on the construction overrun for three TCD emissions testing centers. The centers were considered by the Evans Commission, which I discuss below. Here let me note that Governor Gozney immediately appealed to the public for information on any criminality associated with the centers. That was something he signally failed to do when the forged checks slandering Cabinet Minister Burgess and me were found, one of many such disparities connected with my Premiership.

On October 27, I gave my last speech as Premier and PLP Party Leader, addressing the PLP Delegates Conference. I proudly noted achievements hard and soft, you might say, from fast ferries to the Big Conversation to FutureCare. I also looked forward, warning that the Combined Opposition would continue to attack PLP Government in underhanded ways.

I had long since declared my intention to serve as Party Leader for one term only. Upon the expiration of my term, the PLP delegates elected Paula Cox Party Leader and Derrick Burgess Deputy Leader. On Friday, October 29,

2010, I also resigned as an MP. Governor Gozney swore in Paula Cox as Bermuda's tenth Premier, the fourth from the PLP.

I had entered the office of Premier promising change, and I had delivered. I felt proud, satisfied, and fortunate at being able to fulfill my lifelong dream of leading Bermuda forward on many fronts.

Part Four: The Battle Continues

18. Out of Office, Under Eternal Investigation

A FTER FOUR INTENSE YEARS AS PREMIER, I continued to pay attention to Bermuda politics as a PLP elder. But having passed the reins to Premier Cox and others, I was content to be on the sidelines.

On December 15, 2010, the PLP's Marc Bean easily won the by-election for my Warwick South Central seat in the House. Young, energetic, bright, and bold, Marc seemed on his way as a next-generation leader for the PLP.

In January 2011, poll numbers for the PLP and Premier Cox substantially topped the UBP, BDA, and all other politicians. Many senior PLP members thought she should call an election no later than the summer. She delayed. She said she didn't wish to "ambush" the Opposition, something I will never understand. UBP Premier John Swan's ambushing the PLP with two snap elections ensured his record tenure in office.

As Deputy Premier, Paula Cox spoke about "turning the volume down." As Premier, she turned it down so far no one could hear her. She apparently never realized that pleasing the Combined Opposition was a fool's errand.

January also saw UBP MP Maxwell Burgess, my immediate predecessor as Transport Minister, cross the aisle to the PLP. He had thrived under Premier Swan, the UBP's most progressive leader. However, he'd been increasingly marginalized by White UBP power brokers Michael Dunkley and Grant Gibbons. Maxwell spoke of joining the PLP as a homecoming.

In February the Combined Opposition gloated over the end of contracts with GlobalHue, Uncommon Results, Kurron, and Atlanta-based Ambling Consulting. The replacements lacked the energy and vision GlobalHue brought to marketing Bermuda tourism, Uncommon Results to Mirrors, Kurron to improving KEMH, and Ambling to hotel development issues. The Combined Opposition claimed all four vendors failed to provide value for money, and Premier Cox played to this view in announcing new procedures for public contracts. Her moves won praise from Governor Gozney, who repeatedly contrasted her administration favorably with mine.

Premier Cox's steps to tighten financial controls continued consistent PLP efforts to bring greater transparency and accountability to Bermuda's Government, unlike UBP administrations operating behind closed doors. Again, my administration furthered the positive trend through PATI and the creation of a Department of Internal Audit.

Assessing good governance and value for taxpayers' money requires apples-to-apples comparison of public contracts under UBP, PLP, and OBA administrations. Investigation of public contracts during my Premiership has evaded such an unbiased comparison.

From my administration onward, the Combined Opposition peddled the fantasy that Bermuda was on the verge of economic collapse because of too much debt. Debt had increased substantially, but our debt-to-GDP ratio remained enviable by international standards. From 1998 to 2012 the PLP Government kept Bermuda's balance sheet fundamentally sound. The OBA cried wolf about an "economic abyss," as the forces of wealth commonly do in imposing austerity on the less advantaged.

Bermuda's White establishment has always treated Government as a means to serve large business interests, and the UBP and OBA have governed accordingly. The PLP has always championed the idea that Government exists to serve all Bermudians.

I worried Premier Cox's administration was losing touch with that fundamental PLP principle and would eventually suffer with voters. The new budget went into austerity mode more than was necessary or wise at a time when public spending was vital to Bermuda's present and future well-being. In speeches and interviews, Premier Cox more often seemed to be placating the Combined Opposition than serving ordinary Bermudians.

In March 2011, Dr. Barbara Ball died just short of her eighty-seventh birthday. I described her extraordinary service to Bermuda as a physician and one of the PLP's early MPs. Most other White Bermudians ostracized her. And remember, her KEMH admitting privileges were revoked for a time because of her politics. That has always resonated with me because of the attacks on my medical business. Dr. Ball remains a beacon for all Bermudians committed to social justice.

At the end of March, Derrick Burgess, now Deputy Premier and Public Works Minister, and I announced a civil suit in our names in Ontario, Canada. The suit accused architect Sam Spagnuolo of Carruthers, Shaw and Partners of conspiring with Works and Engineering Chief Architect Lawrence Brady, brother-in-law of *Royal Gazette* editor Bill Zuill, in order to discredit the PLP Government with the faked checks purporting to show kickbacks to Minister Burgess and me. The BPS investigation indicated the fake check images reached Bermuda via Lawrence Brady's office computer.

The suit became controversial, as I'll discuss, but the big political story at this time was the death of the UBP. In April and May 2011 all but two of the party's remaining MPs joined with the BDA to create the One Bermuda Alliance (OBA), led by John Barritt.

This event fulfilled my prediction that the 2007 election spelled the end of the UBP as a viable party. PLP MP, and former UBP Leader, Wayne Furbert said the new party's formation followed a 2007 scenario prepared by the UBP's American political consultants, a charge the OBA denied.

In May, Premier Cox's administration named Dr. Roosevelt Brown, Dr. E. F. Gordon, and Sir Henry Tucker to be celebrated with Dame Lois Browne-Evans on National Heroes Day. I am of two minds about Henry Tucker's inclusion with three champions of social justice and the continuing fight against racism. He deserves praise for establishing Bermuda as a Switzerland of the Atlantic and taking modest steps to moderate racism and end legalized segregation. Yet he always worked to preserve White establishment power. He looked backward more than forward. Can a man who had the Bank of Bermuda call in people's mortgages to repress counter-racist politics be a hero for all Bermudians, now and in the future?

Politics involves compromise and never satisfies everyone on an issue. However, the PLP Government's elevation of Henry Tucker undoubtedly formed an element of Premier Cox's campaign to win UBP hearts and minds. The campaign was a nonstarter. She would have done better to concentrate on the majority of Bermudians who were the PLP's constituency. In ways large and small, she demotivated that majority before calling an election.

In June the new structure for the courts and the Hamilton police station opened as the Dame Lois Browne-Evans Building. The entrance lobby soon received a statue of Dame Lois seated in barrister's robes and powdered wig. The building's name and the statue paid fitting tribute to one of Bermuda's greatest figures. The same month, former UBP MP Darius Tucker joined the PLP.

I HAD NO WISH TO TAKE THE SPOTLIGHT off these events. However, in June 2011 husband-and-wife accountant-entrepreneurs David and Antoinette Bolden were on trial, charged with diverting $360,000 of their investors' money to their personal use. Shortly before the trial was to conclude, defense lawyer Saul Froomkin QC led David Bolden through allegations an unnamed member of my Cabinet tried to extort him and his wife on my behalf. David Bolden claimed this unnamed Cabinet Minister asked for 60 percent of the Boldens' commissions as Bermuda pension fund advisors, along with a board seat for Wanda and 10 percent stake in their wireless Internet venture.

The Combined Opposition had planted the presumption I was corrupt in many Bermudians' minds. David Bolden's effort to distract attention from his deeds and his wife's proved successful. The trial convicted them only of misleading the Bermuda Monetary Authority, and they received community service sentences of 200 hours each.

The idea that I would try to extort portions of the Boldens' pension fund commissions and Internet venture was absurd and insulting. Wanda's Wall Street securities registrations and New York Stock Exchange company directorships would have made it virtually impossible for her to be on the Boldens' board. Outside of running into them coincidentally a few times, she never had any meetings or encounters with either of them for business or personal reasons. The allegations were completely preposterous.

Neither the Boldens nor the Bermuda Police Service ever named the Cabinet Minister who supposedly attempted extortion on my behalf. But the BPS never closed the investigation of me. Instead the allegations furnished a pretext for an open-ended investigation, driven by innuendo and wishful thinking. The BPS also never announced an investigation of the allegedly corrupt unnamed Cabinet Minister.

In December, Auditor General Heather Jacobs Matthews submitted a special report, "On the Misuse of Public Funds," to the Speaker of the House. She asserted public funds were misused twice during my Premiership.

The first claim was that then Works and Engineering Minister Derrick Burgess had violated Government Financial Instructions in approving payments by the Bermuda Land Development Company (BLDC, a UBP-established quango overseeing the former U.S. base lands) for consulting work by the BLDC's chairman and deputy chairman.

The second claim had to do with the Ontario civil suit on the false checks. Auditor General Jacobs Matthews wrote indignantly about Government's paying around $30,000 in legal fees in the case. She insisted the case was a private matter for Minister Burgess and me and should not have involved Government because it was brought in our names.

The suit was in our names because Canadian law does not allow governments to pursue damages in civil suits. However, the contract for legal services with an Ontario law firm said the client was the Government of Bermuda. As far as I was concerned, that meant any damages the suit might win would go to Government.

The legal services contract gave me sole authority to direct the lawyers for two reasons. One was simply efficiency. The other was to protect confidential legal privilege until the suit was over. Citing legal privilege, Attorney General Kim Wilson denied the Auditor General some of the information she wanted on the suit. In her special report Auditor General Jacobs Matthews wrote, "In my opinion, to cover up an abuse of public funds behind the cloak of 'legal privilege' . . . is unacceptable and violates principles of good govern- ance and transparency." She demanded that those responsible be sanctioned and that Minister Burgess and I pay the Government the money it had spent.

The special report quoted the response of Premier Cox's administration: "The funding of the Ontario Action by Government was, in the judgment of the Government, an appropriate course to follow in the interest of the Gov- ernment, the Country and Bermuda's international reputation and . . . we con- sidered . . . this action to be for a Government purpose in that the personal action was the only means . . . [to] take action against those responsible for essentially attacking the Government via its Ministers. . . . The judgment to fund this matter was . . . made by the Government in good faith."

Auditor General Jacobs Matthews's report scorned these words, saying Government's funding of the legal action "shows complete disregard for the concept of good stewardship of public money." She added, "I cannot compre- hend how a personal legal matter could be . . . a legitimate Government matter to be funded out of the public purse." The Combined Opposition echoed the Auditor General loudly and often in late 2011 and early 2012.

Flash-forward to December 2014 when Auditor General Jacobs Mat- thews reported "On the Consolidated Fund of the Government of Bermuda for the Financial Years [Ending] March 31, 2010, March 31, 2011 and March 31, 2012," and the story changes. Appendix 11 of this report gives the state- ment of OBA Deputy Premier and Finance Minister Bob Richards to the House on the Ontario legal action. Having formed the Government, the OBA wanted the ability to defend its administration and support its Cabinet Minis- ters as my administration had done. The statement endorsed Government's paying for similar legal actions, the only difference being a promise to be clearer that potential damages would be paid to Government. It also endorsed the legal privilege position of my administration and Premier Cox's admin- istration.

Deputy Premier and Finance Minister Richards stated, "Mr. Speaker, it should be noted that the above mentioned position is consistent with the po- sition of the former administration. . . ."

Given her December 2011 special report's insistence that the Ontario le- gal action was "an abuse of public funds," basic decency suggests Auditor Gen- eral Jacobs Matthews should have acknowledged that three duly elected Governments, PLP and OBA, and their Attorneys General disagreed with her. All three administrations said there was no abuse of public funds and confi- dential legal privilege had to be maintained.

However, Auditor General Jacobs Matthews said nothing about this in her December 2014 special report. Somewhere along the way, it seems she abandoned impartiality and made it her mission to attack the PLP Government and me while never casting a critical eye on the OBA Government. To my knowledge, the *Royal Gazette* also said nothing about the OBA Government's endorsement of the PLP Government's position on the Ontario civil suit.

Let's go back to early 2012 and the response to Auditor General Jacobs Matthews's special report of December 2011 on the *alleged* misuse of public funds. On January 12, 2012, Police Commissioner Michael DeSilva told the media that U.S. law enforcement was assisting with investigations of corruption allegations against me that extended beyond those of David Bolden. Police Commissioner DeSilva spoke of "witnesses . . . who were not connected to the Bolden trial" and "activities that may have occurred in the United States." He refused to explain what those activities might be.

At the end of January, Governor Gozney, referring to the Auditor General's most recent report, called on the public to come forward with evidence of Government corruption. He cited David Bolden's unsubstantiated allegations as the sort of thing—"clear signs of suspected criminality"—that would trigger a BPS investigation. Governor Gozney stated, "Anyone who witnesses suspected criminality is urged to report to the Police, for example, any requests for bribes or any knowledge of backhanders." As I mentioned, he had previously appealed to the public for informaton on criminality in the last month of my tenure as Premier, following the Auditor General's special report on TCD's emissions testing centers. Contrast these pleas with his failure to ask for public information regarding the false checks in Works and Engineering files.

In February 2012 the anonymous group Concerned Bermudians sent the FCO and the MP chairing the OT committee a list of complaints against me, which they also posted online. Seeking a Commission of Inquiry into my conduct in office, the Concerned Bermudians tossed every negative thing they had heard or dreamed up against me into their document.

The Concerned Bermudians believed me guilty by association with former Turks and Caicos premier Michael Misick. I became friends with him because I admired his energy and innovation in almost single-handedly making Turks and Caicos the hottest upscale tourist destination in the Caribbean. Especially significant was how he ensured locals could move up the hospitality industry ladder. The young men and women check-in clerks I met on my first visits were succeeding as hotel managers a few years later. That never happened in Bermuda.

Among the other items in the Concerned Bermudians' screed were the allegations of "Son of the Soil" Harold Darrell and my selling property to the BHC. Harold Darrell bore a grudge against me because I terminated his contract to install televisions at the airport for nonperformance and against my brother Philip Butterfield because HSBC Bermuda refused him a loan. Again, a BPS investigation found nothing wrong with my sale of property to the BHC, and the BHC refused to sell the property back at the purchase-and-renovation cost because it was worth more than that. Contrary to the Concerned Bermudians, the property was mortgage-free when I sold it and not about to be repossessed. None of Harold Darrell's accusations, such as the supposed theft of Government-owned cedar beams for Gombey House, contains any truth.

The Concerned Bermudians insisted I was corrupt because I owned property in New York City, on Martha's Vineyard, and in Turks and Caicos. Except I don't own property in all these places. Wanda owned an apartment in New York before we were married in 2003, and after that she bought a second one. She bought a condo in Turks and Caicos in 2005, in which I later acquired a half interest. She first bought a house on Martha's Vineyard in 1990; she later sold that house, and in June 2010 she bought another house there.

Expressing racist and sexist bias, the Concerned Bermudians wrote, "It is our view that whilst his wife has worked previously, we find it difficult to believe that she was in a position financially to fund the purchase of the Martha's Vineyard property." Again, I am lucky to be married to a successful Black businesswoman with a sterling reputation on Wall Street. And I seriously doubt the Concerned Bermudians would have equally questioned the financial wherewithal of a White male former senior vice president of Lazard Frères.

The Concerned Bermudians also pointed to the $4 million bail bond required when my son Kevin was arrested, thinking I put up that sum in cash. Other family members and I put up around 10 percent of the total in cash with real estate and other property as collateral for the rest of the bond.

The Concerned Bermudians also alleged that $422,000 of the cost of Gombey House came from Bermuda taxpayers. Again, my original contractor was Bermuda Composite Construction (BCC). When BCC and I parted ways because of cost overruns and construction delays, Island Construction, whose principal owner, Zane DeSilva, also had a stake in BCC, took over. How monies flowed between BCC and Island Construction, and how they used their income from Government projects, had nothing to do with me or Gombey House.

My son Kevin's charitable fundraiser at the Playboy Mansion in Los Angeles was another target. Again, Wanda and I paid our own way to attend the fundraiser, the auctioned trips to Bermuda did not cost taxpayers a penny, and the celebrities and other well-heeled people in attendance were the demographic we—and later the OBA—wanted to attract as tourists.

The Concerned Bermudians repeated the Combined Opposition's false description of a 2002 campaign fundraising luncheon in Washington, D.C., as "pay to play." As chapter 14 details, it was not.

The Concerned Bermudians blamed me for things I was only indirectly involved in: the Bermuda cement concession, the lease for the Coco Reef Hotel (negotiated by my immediate predecessor as Tourism Minister), and construction of the Berkeley Institute's new secondary school building. I've discussed these insofar as I was involved as Cabinet Minister and Premier.

The Concerned Bermudians saw more guilty association in my faith-based tourism experiment with Andre Curtis (see chapter 15). Yet Auditor General Larry Dennis's audit of the experiment found nothing pointing to illegality on my part.

The rest of the Concerned Bermudians' ignorance, lies, and misunderstanding concerned TCD's emissions testing, GlobalHue, and Heritage Wharf. I discuss these below.

ON MARCH 22, 2012, AT THE UNIVERSITY COLLEGE of the Cayman Islands, I gave my first speech since leaving office at the 50-50 Caribbean Conference: "Surveying the Past, Mapping the Future." The title of my speech was "Is the U.K.– Overseas Territory relationship based on mutual interests? Bermuda and the Uighurs—A Case Study." I argued that the Uighurs controversy (see chapter 16) and other evidence show the relationship is based on a belief in British superiority on the part of the British and all too many OT citizens.

The speech mentioned that during my Premiership, Governor Gozney suggested abandoning the colonial plumed pith helmet and white military uniform he wore on ceremonial occasions such as opening Parliament. I insisted on the uniform. Why let the British mask their behavior as colonial overlords with ordinary business attire?

Without mentioning David Bolden's name, I described Governor Gozney's citing Bolden's unsupported allegations to solicit suspicions of official corruption. I pointed out the contrast with his actions regarding the false checks, incontrovertible physical evidence of wrongdoing.

Back in Bermuda, I shared with the media a response to the Concerned Bermudians that Courtenay Griffiths QC had sent to the FCO on my behalf and my letter to the FCO asserting Governor Gozney had "harmed the people of Bermuda and the Government of Bermuda." Based solely on innuendo, Governor Gozney's thinly veiled appeal for accusations against me displayed substantial bias and undermined representative democracy. The FCO expressed "full confidence" in Governor Gozney. But I was glad to begin setting the record straight about his partisanship.

Having parted ways with GlobalHue, the most effective advertising and marketing agency Bermuda ever had, Premier Cox's administration rolled out new tourism branding in August 2012. Tourism Minister Wayne Furbert announced "Bermuda—Feel the Love" was being replaced by "Bermuda—So Much More." A slogan with enormous positive emotional resonance and the distinctive tone of Bermuda's world-renowned friendliness, a phrase with a touch of magic, was out. A generic list header—so much more what?—was in.

The window for calling the election was closing. On November 11, 2012, Premier Cox called the election for December 17, almost five years to the day since I led the PLP to its third straight victory at the polls with a healthy margin of 8 House seats over the UBP. During the campaign period, the UBP consultant's document that Wayne Furbert had said scripted the creation of the OBA surfaced. It substantiated Wayne's description.

Premier Cox did not implement any major programs and she passed little significant legislation of her own that positively affected the lives of PLP members and supporters. In an effort to run away from my legacy, she also muted the accomplishments of the PLP Government during my administration. Combine that with her conciliatory tone toward the Combined Opposition, and it's no surprise she lost the attention of a significant number of Black Bermudians who previously voted PLP. They didn't vote for UBP clone the OBA. They simply didn't vote. Thanks largely to lower-than-normal Black turnout, the OBA won a razor-thin victory with a margin of only 2 House seats.

What really shocked political observers was that Premier Cox lost her seat in Devonshire North West, which had been Dame Lois Browne-Evans's constituency. In giving this PLP stronghold to the OBA, the public rendered a verdict against Premier Cox's leadership. The PLP soon elected Marc Bean Party Leader with Paula Cox's public support.

I endorsed the post-election call by *Royal Gazette* editor Bill Zuill for a Commission of Inquiry into public works under fourteen years of PLP Government provided it also examined fourteen years of UBP Government. I am confident PLP administrations including my own would fare well in such a comparison. My administration has received more scrutiny than those of all my predecessors and successors. Despite wishful thinking claims, that ongoing scrutiny has identified no illegality or malfeasance.

OBA MPs formed the Government promising they would not lapse ethically or as stewards of the public purse. Let's consider their performance and the Evans Commission on my administration.

The *Royal Gazette* cheered the OBA's victory and bent over backward to portray their administration positively. Bermuda's most famous American weekend visitor cheered, too. Billionaire Michael Bloomberg, who owned an estate on the Island and was in his last year as mayor of New York City, said in May 2013, "People love this new Government. And tourists will as well. It's like night and day down there with the new Government."

What effect tourists were supposed to notice from the change of Government remains a mystery. The OBA Government was still so new and had done so little that the "night and day" reference was thought to be only about skin color.

Ironically, the first scandal of the OBA Government was about to emerge, and it directly involved Premier Craig Cannonier. John Barritt had resigned his safe seat to ensure inaugural BDA Leader Craig Cannonier could also lead the OBA. In May 2013 Bermudians learned Premier Cannonier, business associate Steven DeCosta, Attorney General Mark Pettingill, and Tourism and Transport Minister Shawn Crockwell had flown to Washington in March for a five-hour meeting with an American real estate developer. The party traveled back and forth on the developer's Gulfstream 200 jet.

Recall that when members of my administration and I flew on GlobalHue's jet, the PLP Government reimbursed the company for the cost of commercial airline tickets. Premier Cannonier and his party not only failed to do likewise, they spent two nights at a Washington luxury hotel at the developer's expense. In the House on May 31, new PLP MP Rolfe Commissiong memorably dubbed this unethical boondoggle "Jetgate."

The episode shouted "pay to play," and these details were the tip of an iceberg. Although Attorney General Pettingill and Tourism and Transport Minister Crockwell surely regretted traveling and lodging secretly at a real estate developer's expense while on official business, Premier Cannonier conned them and the people of Bermuda. The Premier claimed he had never previously met the unnamed developer, whom he described in the House as "a wealthy individual from Maryland" with "extensive experience in the gaming industry."

In response to media questions, Economic Development Minister Grant Gibbons said the rest of the Cabinet was not informed about the trip. It beggars belief that Premier Cannonier's Cabinet did not know he was traveling to Washington with the Attorney General and Tourism and Transport Minister. No doubt that's why Community Development Minister Wayne Scott, Finance Minister Bob Richards, and Public Safety Minister Michael Dunkley either had no comment or referred the media to the Premier.

In July, the Bermudian media identified the developer as Nathan Landow. For almost a year that was about all Bermuda knew.

Thanks to PLP MPs' persistence, in May 2014 it was reported that Nathan Landow and his associates had donated $300,000 to the OBA's 2012 campaign via Steven DeCosta's Bermuda Political Action Club. The nation also learned that Premier Cannonier knew Nathan Landow before the March 2013 Washington meeting, and that Mr. Landow had once employed Steven DeCosta.

Nathan Landow and associates had in fact donated $350,000 to Steven DeCosta's OBA campaign slush fund. The figure dwarfed the campaign funds

I legitimately raised from affluent Black financial professionals at a 2002 luncheon the UBP, the *Royal Gazette*, and OBA falsely labeled "pay to play" (see chapter 14). So far as I can see from its online archives, the newspaper never used that phrase in connection with Jetgate.

Attorney General Pettingill and Tourism and Transport Minister Crockwell expressed dismay at the Jetgate revelations. They claimed only to have known Nathan Landow's name, which they had not divulged out of respect for the Premier. They also repeated statements from a year before that the meeting was a strictly informational discussion about foreign investment in Bermuda.

On May 19, 2014, Craig Cannonier resigned as Premier and was replaced the next day by Michael Dunkley, who had been Deputy Premier. On May 22, Mark Pettingill resigned as Attorney General from what was now Premier Dunkley's Cabinet. OBA chairman Thad Hollis also soon resigned over the slush fund, which had been kept secret from him.

Between the resignations of Premier Cannonier and Attorney General Pettingill, the *Royal Gazette* published an editorial titled "The politics of implausible deniability." The newspaper lamented the loss of Premier Cannonier's leadership and described his all-expenses-paid junket and deliberately misleading descriptions of it for an entire year as the actions of a "political neophyte."

Contrast that with how the *Royal Gazette* and the rest of the Combined Opposition have relentlessly attacked me for behavior that was never corrupt, dishonest, or illegal. Aspects of Jetgate were plainly corrupt and dishonest, if not illegal; yet those involved got a pass.

Craig Cannonier lived at Clifton, the official residence of the Bermuda Premier, at the government's expense until the end of September 2014—over four months after his resignation as Premier. Imagine the outrage if a PLP premier had done that.

Before Craig Cannonier left Clifton, former UBP Leader Kim Swan joined the PLP, emulating former UBP Chairman Gwyneth Rawlins, Jamahl Simmons, fellow UBP Leader Wayne Furbert, former UBP Transport Minister Maxwell Burgess, and Darius Tucker. It was a one-way street for senior Black politicians between the UBP/OBA and the PLP. No one ever went the other way, which obviously says a lot about the two sides of Bermuda's politics. Although I would not credit myself as a decisive factor in the decisions of the six politicians. I encouraged each of them in their moves to the PLP.

KEMH's new acute care wing opened in September. The Combined Opposition did its best to give the OBA credit, conveniently forgetting it was a PLP project. Although it was impossible to miss my brother Philip Butterfield in the *Royal Gazette*'s photo of officials and top administrators at the opening ceremony, the newspaper omitted mentioning him. It would never have treated a White Bermudian with a similar role in this way.

As chairman of the Bermuda Hospitals Charitable Trust, Philip had worked tirelessly with BHB chairman Herman Tucker, deputy chairman Wendell Hollis, and my PLP administration to make the new wing a model public-private partnership. Along the way, Philip raised almost $40 million in contributions for the construction of the new wing.

In October Auditor General Jacobs Matthews submitted a special report on the renovation of Port Royal Golf Course, mainly echoing UBP criticism (see chapter 17). Section 3 of her December report on "the Consolidated Fund of the Government of Bermuda for the Financial Years [Ending] March 31, 2010, March 31, 2011 and March 31, 2012" catalogued what she said were questionable public contracts, deviations from Financial Instructions, and other lapses of good governance during the three years.

Let's move ahead to 2016, although in due course we'll circle back to consider a few events of 2014 and 2015. On February 24, 2016, Premier Dunkley appointed a Commission of Inquiry to take the Auditor General's December 2012 report, especially Section 3, as the basis to "Inquire into any potential violation of law or regulations"; refer such matters as appropriate to the DPP, Police, and Civil Service and Government leaders; assess the Government's financial safeguards and accountability; recommend improvements; and "Consider any other matter which the Commission considers relevant to any of the foregoing."

Premier Dunkley named British judge Sir Anthony H. M. Evans to chair the panel and Bermudians John Barritt, Fiona Elizabeth Luck, and Kumi Bradshaw to complete it. Premier Dunkley was apparently blind to the optics, in current political jargon, of three White people and one Black person—Kumi Bradshaw, the most junior and least known of the four—judging a PLP Government.

Not quite a month later, on March 16, 2016, Shawn Crockwell resigned as Tourism and Transport Minister. He told the media, "I've lost faith in the Premier." Specifically, like the Black politicians who resigned from the UBP, he said Premier Dunkley and others calling the shots for the OBA were tone deaf, and worse, regarding racism.

"[I]t's not just the decisions that have been made but the manner . . . and the inability to communicate appropriately with the Black community in particular," Shawn Crockwell said. His OBA colleagues displayed "an inability to put aside political pride, listen, and make the required adjustments. . . . I . . . feel as if we are going backwards. . . . We have a majority Black electorate and they want to feel as if their Government is listening, has empathy, and is going to respond to what they are saying. . . . If you cannot gauge how the people are feeling, then you cannot lead them."

The straw that broke the camel's back for Shawn Crockwell was the OBA's Pathways to Status bill. The bill embodied the UBP/OBA's desire to create more White voters by giving Bermudian status to large numbers of expatriate workers, their spouses, and their children. Remember, in recent elections over half of White voters, almost exclusively UBP/OBA voters, were born outside Bermuda.

Premier Dunkley said of Pathways to Status, "How new Bermudians may vote plays no part in our policy-making process." Every honest observer knew it was the essence of decades-long policy-making, reflected, as the Mincy Report documents, in UBP work permit policies and the educational and employment experiences of Black Bermudian men.

Knowing that Pathways to Status constituted a White establishment effort to steal the country with imported voters, the recently formed People's Campaign for Equality, Jobs, and Justice mounted a protest over several days, including work stoppages. The People's Campaign is a diverse group of Bermudians including representatives of the church and labor union communities as well as members of the population at large. It is led by two fine gentlemen I am honored to call friends: Chris Furbert, president of the Bermuda Industrial Union, and Reverend Nicholas Tweed, pastor of the St. Paul A.M.E. Church. Reverend Tweed, whose father is Bermudian, was forced to go to court to reverse the OBA Government's decision to expel him from Bermuda. The nation is the richer for OBA's loss. Reverend Tweed has continually given Bermuda the benefit of his Christian teachings as well as his unswerving commitment to social justice and equality. Similarly Chris Furbert has dedicated his life to championing the rights of Bermuda's working men and women, at the same time that he approaches deliberations and negotiations on their behalf with courage, conviction, and an overwhelming commitment to doing what is right for all of Bermuda.

On Monday, March 14, members of the People's Campaign linked arms around Parliament for nine hours to prevent the OBA from holding a House session to ram the bill through. The peaceful blockade was an unprecedented, completely appropriate expression of the Bermuda majority's righteous anger and dismay.

In response Premier Dunkley offered window-dressing changes to the bill and named a "Consultative Immigration Reform Working Group." He also shifted Cabinet responsibility for Immigration from White to Black, moving the Immigration portfolio from Senator Michael Fahy to MP Patricia Gordon-Paplin. The bill stalled after that, as it should have.

When he resigned from Cabinet, Shawn Crockwell said he intended to remain in the OBA. However, on July 1, he also resigned from the party to sit in the House as an Independent. In doing so, he accused Attorney General

Trevor Moniz of "economic intimidation." Shawn Crockwell and fellow lawyer Mark Pettingill were forming a new firm focused significantly on labor law. Attorney General Moniz attempted to warn them off representing anyone in a dispute with Government. That was an economic death sentence because Government is Bermuda's largest employer.

Referring to my frequently noting that Bermuda's White establishment "came after" Black people who stood too tall, Shawn Crockwell said publicly, "When I was growing up, my uncles told me stories about how if you went up against the establishment, you could get your mortgage pulled. I used to think it was an exaggeration. I don't any more; I'm living it." He also described how the UBP had hijacked the BDA in creating the OBA. He said that as a BDA founder, "I was not just [in the OBA] to be window dressing. . . . But time and time again, that old UBP philosophy prevailed."

Again, the only significant UBP Government deviations from the UBP's White establishment philosophy occurred during Sir John Swan's tenure as Premier, primarily through his policies on education and Civil Service recruitment and promotion. These policies made him the most PLP-like of the UBP's leaders. In July 2016 Bermuda lost one of its leading citizens when his wife, Lady Jacqueline Swan, passed away. In her quiet way, Lady Jackie led many philanthropic efforts on the Island. She was a person of great grace, understated elegance, and fun.

Wanda and I enjoyed a positive relationship with the Swans when I was in office, and afterward the relationship ripened into a warm friendship. Such an across-the-aisle relationship is rare in Bermuda. For Wanda and me, it was unique, and we will always treasure it and our continuing friendship with Sir John. There was certainly not going to be anything of the sort with the leadership of the UBP's OBA clone.

IN MOST DEMOCRATIC COUNTRIES, A NATIONAL LEADER retired from service can expect to rest on his or her laurels and enjoy a well-earned rest. Unfortunately for me, the rancorous political climate of my country, driven largely by the continuing power of racism, has not granted me that privilege.

After I left office, my critics pinned their hopes to discredit my administration and me on the report on supposed "government corruption" issued by the Evans Commission, which first convened on April 4, 2016. Although it was supposed to report by September, the Commission did much of its work in fall 2016.

Chairman Evans revealed the fix was in and his panel could not be impartial when he declared on September 28, 2016, with testimony pending, that "straightforward fraud" had occurred in Port Royal Golf Course's reconstruction. This irrevocably tainted his Commission. No fraud had then been shown, and at this writing still has not been shown.

My lawyers advised me not to talk to the Commission. This was sound advice, as the Commission's February 2017 report revealed several BPS probes targeting me before it convened.

Here are the Commission's main findings on twelve contracts, one of them an OBA Government project, which it labeled A-L.

The Commission said contracts A (2008 renovation of Finance Ministry offices) and B (2007 construction of a maintenance and stores building) failed to comply with Financial Instructions. It criticized senior civil servants and Civil Service–Cabinet Minister interactions, but found "no evidence of possible criminal activity."

The Commission found an undeniable violation with contract C (2009 purchase of sand and rock for asphalt). It said Purchasing Officer Vic Ball, later an OBA Government Senator, failed to tell anyone his father owned half the company that won the bid. The Commission recommended a BPS investigation.

The Commission said contracts D (2008–2009 renovation of Department of Human Resources offices) and E (2008–2009 construction of the forensic laboratory at Marsh Folly and the central laboratory building at Southside) violated Financial Instructions. It criticized senior civil servants and Civil Service–Cabinet Minister interactions, but found "no evidence of possible criminal activity."

With respect to contracts A and E, the Commission questioned actions by Works and Engineering Minister Derrick Burgess. But it ultimately held those actions legitimately served PLP Government policy to empower Black contractors.

The Commission worked itself into a lather on contracts F (GlobalHue's two-year renewal), G (advisory services by Ambling Consulting), H (TCD's emissions testing centers), I (the Dame Lois Browne-Evans Building), J (Port Royal Golf Course renovation), and K (Heritage Wharf pier).

The Commission repeated the Combined Opposition's misrepresentation of GlobalHue's contract renewal by giving the contract value as $14 million per year. Again, $14 million was the Tourism Department advertising and marketing budget. GlobalHue received a standard 10 percent agency commission for creative and marketing services.

The Evans Commission agreed with Auditor General Jacobs Matthews that the two-year contract signed in spring 2009 should not be seen as a renewal of GlobalHue's original three-year contract in 2006. Why this should be so escapes me because the new contract plainly renewed the 2006 agreement with minor revisions.

Referring to Auditor General Larry Dennis's February 2009 report on GlobalHue, the Commission wrote, "There is no evidence that the criticisms of GlobalHue were brought to the notice of Cabinet when the 2009 Agreement was approved."

The GlobalHue renewal was signed in April. The entire Cabinet knew about the Auditor General's criticisms because they were headline news and constantly in the mouths of the Combined Opposition.

Auditor General Dennis's major complaint was GlobalHue's subcontracting with media buyer Cornerstone to place ads. Cornerstone's invoices were sketchy and, in the words of the Evans Commission, "showed that the margin [Cornerstone's commission] varied from a minimal level to as high as a 186 percent markup," against the industry average of 15 percent.

That sounds terrible. However, Cornerstone was snapping up orphaned commercial time for Bermuda at discounted rates.

Suppose the normal cost of a minute of commercial time is $1,000 and the markup is 15 percent. Then the total cost of buying the time is $1,150. But suppose the discounted cost of an orphaned minute is $700 and the markup is 30 percent. Then the total cost of buying the time is $910, a savings of $240. Consider, too, that this is all done on the fly and requires more effort and initiative.

Nothing Auditor General Dennis or the Evans Commission found indicates that taxpayers overpaid for the orphaned commercial time Cornerstone secured, or that any Government procedure or law was broken in renewing GlobalHue's contract. Yet the Commission said a BPS investigation should continue.

On contract G (advisory services from Ambling Consulting) the Commission reported the initial contract was not tendered, multiple agreements were executed but only one Cabinet approval sought, Financial Instructions were breached, and files at the relevant ministries contained "no coherent records of any services [Ambling] performed." The Commission said a BPS investigation should continue.

Ambling advised Bermuda in connection with Finance, Tourism, and Works and Engineering activities. One of its initial services was in connection with demolition and asbestos abatement at the Club Med site. Works and Engineering had secured demolition bids from four construction firms. Ambling suggested implosion as the best approach and found a reliable contractor who could do the job for almost 50 percent less than Works and Engineering's potential contractors.

As Marc Telemaque told the Commission, Ambling's most important work centered around discovering gross mismanagement and an urgent financial situation at Tucker's Point. It was only thanks to Ambling we learned

Tucker's Point might not make the next month's payroll. Ambling also prescribed the solution that kick-started negotiations with Rosewood Hotels and Resorts, operators of some of the world's most prestigious hotels, and satisfied HSBC as the lenders.

Echoing Auditor General Jacobs Matthews, the Commission criticized the awarding of contract H (TCD's emissions control centers) to Bermuda Emissions Control Limited (BECL) without open tender, emphasizing that BECL principal Donal Smith is my cousin. It charged then Transport Permanent Secretary Marc Telemaque with poor project management and Accountant General Joyce Hayward with failing to comply with Financial Instructions. It said a BPS investigation should continue.

In a country as small as Bermuda, there aren't six degrees of separation, but only one or two. Doing business with close or distant cousins is almost impossible to avoid. Again, Donal Smith was discussing an emissions testing contract with the UBP Government well before the PLP won the 1998 election and I became Transport Minister. Ignoring that would not have been fair or in the best traditions of Bermuda. The Evans Commission also ignored the fact that the OBA Government renewed BECL's contract to operate the emissions testing centers in 2014. If the original contract was so dubious, why did the Commission not question the OBA Government's renewal of it?

Marc Telemaque did a thorough job guiding the project. As he has noted publicly, the House approved every increase in the project's budget. And the cost overrun was much smaller than the Auditor General and Evans Commission said. The final pre-construction budget was around $14.2 million, meaning the cost overrun was around $1 million, not $10 million.

As chapter 16 explains, the 2007 contract for the Dame Lois Browne-Evans Building was redrawn in 2008 to reflect that the Bermudian construction company LLC was no longer working in partnership with a Canadian firm. The Commission found "no evidence of possible criminal activity" in the 2007 contract. However, it said the 2008 contract should have been submitted to Cabinet for approval, and that Cabinet should have been informed that LLC had two new investors, Winters Burgess and my brother Vincent Hollinsid. The Commission claimed that Works and Engineering Minister Derrick Burgess must have known about Winters Burgess and Vincent Hollinsid because Ministry consultant Julian Hall attended meetings where the investors' participation was discussed.

The Commission also wrote, "We have received no evidence suggesting that the then Premier was unaware either of the need for a new contract for this 'flagship' project or of the fact that two private individuals had become involved as principals and guarantors. We would find, on the evidence available to us, that he knew about them and who they were." Further, "Both the

Minister and the Premier failed to notify Cabinet and failed to ensure that Cabinet approval was obtained."

This is not a finding. It is a speculation.

The Commission said a BPS investigation should continue. However, it was "unable to agree, on the evidence before it, whether it should refer the then Premier for investigation in respect of this contract."

Minister Burgess has stated he was not really sure what, if any, blood relationship he had to Winters Burgess, but addressed him as "uncle." This is commonplace in Black communities throughout the Western Hemisphere. It indicates the impact of slavery and post-slavery racism, and Black people's resilience in reforming damaged and divided families. Unfortunately, Sir Anthony Evans was tone deaf when it came to racism.

Although I did not appear before the Commission, my lawyer, Jerome Lynch, QC, did so, submitting an affidavit on my behalf. When he pointed out that in addition to three of four Commission members, all the Commission's lawyers were White, Sir Anthony responded, "So what?" During his testimony, Derrick Burgess explained "so what" when he looked the Evans Commission in the eye and called them "a lynch mob."

Sir Anthony took grave exception to "an unnecessary and intemperate remark" of mine in the affidavit, which was that I did not trust the Bermuda Police Service. This book has shown multiple valid reasons for my distrusting the BPS.

I had no idea Vincent had invested in LLC—he and Winters Burgess did so by pledging second mortgages on their homes—until after it became a public controversy. At that point I also learned that Vincent's and my brother, Philip Butterfield, had no role in these financial arrangements, which were handled by HSBC Bermuda.

It is common practice in Bermuda for relatives to give each other plenty of space to pursue their business interests. Operating on a "need to know" basis is often the only way to avoid getting tangled in each other's lines. A less White-dominated Commission might have acknowledged this everyday reality in our country.

Auditor General Jacobs Matthews and the Evans Commission said contract J (Port Royal Golf Course) had a value of $7.7 million and the final cost was $24.5 million. But the final pre-construction budget was $13.6 million, making for a much smaller overrun (see chapter 17; $24.5 million includes operating costs and clubhouse work not part of the original work plan).

The Commission criticized the delegation of the project to Tourism and Transport, which had responsibility for Bermuda's public golf courses, rather than Works and Engineering; deplored PLP MP Zane DeSilva's service as a Port Royal Golf Course trustee while his Island Construction, which has worked on almost every golf course in Bermuda, was a contractor; charged sloppy accounting and breaches of Financial Instructions; and noted a $10,000 finder's fee to another Port Royal Golf Course trustee. There was apparently nothing illegal about the finder's fee, and the Commission did not go into detail about it.

Zane DeSilva worked hard and well as a Port Royal trustee to ensure the course was ready for the PGA Grand Slam of Golf. During the renovation, his brother and business partner, Allan, an expert in golf course excavation and landscaping, handled Island Construction's work without Zane's involvement in relevant business decisions. My critics have claimed equipment rental was overpriced, for example, when in fact it was competitively priced.

The Evans Commission said a BPS investigation should continue. When all the facts are understood, I am confident it will be shown the project gave value for taxpayers' money and Zane acted responsibly and ethically.

ACCORDING TO AUDITOR GENERAL JACOBS MATTHEWS and the Commission, contract K, the Heritage Wharf pier, had a value of $39 million and final cost of $60 million, mostly to mitigate potential harm to the animals in the nearby Dolphin Quest. However, the final pre-construction budget was $44 million, and the overrun was not unusual for a project of this scope in Bermuda or anywhere else.

The Commission held that delegation of the project to Tourism and Transport was "unclear, unsatisfactory, and inappropriately documented"; contract terms were not approved by Cabinet, which should have required better accounting and a performance bond; the contract award process "did not allow price competition to prevail"; and breaches of Financial Instructions and other management lapses occurred. The Commission said a BPS investigation should continue.

The oddest thing about the controversy over my administration's Heritage Wharf spending was that it had paid for itself in only three years of megacruise ship visits. Should we really not have rushed to get it done?

Valued at $250 million-plus for a new airport terminal, Contract L was the token OBA Government project the Commission considered in an effort to apply a veneer of even-handedness to the report. The OBA Government filed a formal objection against the Commission's examination, but it needn't have worried. The Commission concentrated on the "difference in perspective" between Accountant General Curtis Stovell and the Finance Ministry about a waiver to allow the OBA Government to make a sole source agreement with Canadian Commercial Corporation (CCC), a Canadian Crown corporation that secures business for Canadian companies. Accountant General

Stovell didn't think the waiver applied to CCC's preferred contractor, Aecon Group Incorporated, whereas Finance Minister Richards did.

The Commission asked if this sole source arrangement provided value for money, but did not press hard on the issue. It said Bermuda needed clearer Financial Instructions for public-private partnerships like the airport project. However, it found "no evidence of possible criminal activity" and gave the OBA Government a pass on its broad interpretation of Accountant General Stovell's limited waiver.

Earlier I explained why my administration moved some public works contracts to Tourism and Transport. The Evans Commission said such contracts should go through Works and Engineering, echoing the Combined Opposition. When the OBA came to power, however, it delegated the airport terminal project to the Finance Ministry.

In an April 2016 Public Accounts Committee meeting on Port Royal, OBA MP Cole Simons asked Zane DeSilva why the project had gone to Tourism. Zane said, "I would think it's the same reason why [Finance Minister] Bob Richards has taken over the airport, rather than leave it to the Ministry of Transport."

Simons challenged Zane, "Does anyone in Tourism build golf courses? Does anyone in Cabinet?"

Zane replied, "Has the Finance Minister built an airport?"

A double standard for the PLP compared to the UBP/OBA is nothing new in Bermuda. The remarkable thing about the airport terminal project is how the OBA Government misled Parliament and the people of Bermuda, and likely ensured the country will not receive value for money.

The evidence trail begins April 2014 when Aecon informed CCC about the project, saying the OBA Government's "intent is to privatize the airport operation." The companies soon signed an agreement naming Aecon as CCC's preferred contractor to build the airport and run it under a concessionary agreement, with Aecon paying CCC to secure the deal on its behalf.

At a press conference on November 10, 2014, CCC and Bermuda signed a memorandum of understanding (MOU) for a public-private partnership to build the airport terminal and operate it over the first thirty years of its existence. In the House later in the month, Finance Minister Richards said no decision had been made about the contractor to build and run the airport.

Evidence emerged right away that Minister Richards always knew Aecon was the preferred contractor and had the job locked down. Over the following months, the evidence, including Aecon-CCC emails, became inescapable.

The new terminal's construction was subject to an entrustment from the British government, which became so concerned about the procurement process, it paid for half of a report on it by global accounting firm Deloitte. The May 8, 2015, report identified many problems, including:

- The OBA Government did not make a full business case for a public-private partnership compared to open tender and public financing and "there is no robust evidence that a sole-source public-private partnership would offer more value for money than a competitive procurement strategy for a similar concession";
- The United Kingdom had questioned the lack of open tender in a CCC contract to build a new airport in the Cayman Islands, a project that collapsed under the scrutiny;
- Aecon was CCC's preferred contractor from the start;
- Aecon drafted the initial MOU;
- Aecon received "back channel" information from the OBA Government's financial advisor, the Canadian Imperial Bank of Commerce;
- Aecon was "heavily involved" in financial and technical feasibility studies for the terminal, meaning it could influence the studies to its advantage;
- Despite claims to the contrary by CCC and the OBA Government, "there was private sector appetite and bankability for airport deals"; and
- There was no contingency plan if the CCC-Bermuda plan collapsed.

A few days later Minister Richards engaged in one of many instances of double-talk about Aecon. He said that since he met representatives of CCC and Aecon in person for the first time together, "The notion that we were doing some sort of deal with Aecon before we met and dealt with CCC is nonsense."

That was not the issue. Minister Richards, who proclaimed the airport deal would be one of "total transparency," had said Aecon was not in place when he knew it was. I find it hard to interpret Minister Richards's statement in the House on November 21, 2014—"CCC will select a Canadian developer from its already preselected stable of Canadian firms"—as less than a lie. Aecon selected and paid CCC to represent it. If Minister Richards was not privy to the contractual arrangement between the two companies, there is no question he knew Aecon's role from the start. By the way, Michael Butt, head of one of Bermuda's biggest White-controlled construction companies, Somers Construction, sat on Aecon's board.

The British government said the procedural and ethical "gaps" Deloitte identified had to be addressed before Bermuda closed the deal. The OBA Government filled those gaps cosmetically, and the deal proceeded.

On August 24, 2015, the OBA Government and CCC finalized the Airport Development Agreement, which named Aecon as lead contractor. The agreement awarded Bermuda's biggest-ever public works contract without open tendering and competitive bidding.

When the agreement was tabled in the House December 16, 2015, Bermuda began to learn what a sweet deal Aecon was getting. In addition to tax and customs duty waivers, the OBA Government was guaranteeing Aecon's project income, subsidizing electricity costs, and paying all operating costs for the full thirty years of the concession. The medium for paying these costs would be a new quango, the Bermuda Airport Authority, which came into being February 2017.

In effect the OBA Government was privatizing thirty years of airport revenue—around $1 billion or more—and socializing the operating costs. To be fair, the Government was hampered by British insistence that no debt from the airport project go on Bermuda's books. Our completely manageable debt load was an affront to the Conservative government in Britain, which went all in for austerity. (In 2019 the U.N. reported on how the austerity immiserated much of Britain, and other reports linked it with a decrease in life expectancy.)

The OBA was also all for austerity. In a typical statement, Finance Minister Richards told the House on November 14, 2014, "We have a Government that is running a $260 million deficit. We have a Government which is in debt over $2 billion!"

The deficit and the debt were, and are, relatively modest compared to the size of Bermuda's economy. The austerity scolds like to compare a government to an individual or a household. All debts come due, but they come due differently for governments on the one hand and individuals and families on the other. And governments have responsibilities as well as options for dealing with debt that individuals and families don't.

It boils down to this: a government can help maintain an unjust distribution of wealth over generations or it can seek to spread national wealth more fairly. The UBP/OBA and the PLP stand on different sides of that divide.

THERE WAS ANOTHER WAY TO FINANCE THE AIRPORT and keep debt off Bermuda's books. The OBA Government could have established the Bermuda Airport Authority first, and the quango could have gone to the capital markets for financing and opened the project for competitive bidding. Bermuda would have retained full control of a vital public asset and its revenues.

This process might not have guaranteed a better result. But Deloitte's report documented that capital markets financing was available and that the OBA Government failed to exercise due diligence in exploring the approach. At the end of the day, the Government could still have gone with CCC-Aecon, and voters could have felt sure Bermuda got the best available deal.

Arguing for sole-source procurement, Finance Minister Richards said the request for proposals (RFP) process took too long and cost too much because consultants were needed to evaluate competing proposals. Repeating a UBP/OBA theme, he railed at the $10 million in consulting fees on KEMH's new acute care wing. He said the OBA Government would hire an independent contractor advisor to monitor costs and ensure value for money.

In the House in November 2014, PLP MP Walter Roban described the UBP/OBA's flip-flop on RFPs: "They dogged [the PLP Government] about the lack of RFPs. . . . RFPs were good then. But now RFPs are not so good." Of course, RFPs were going to be good again—for PLP Government—when the Evans Commission convened.

Walter reminded the House that independent international evaluators had rated KEMH's acute care wing project as "one of the best . . . of that size in a public-private partnership." And he pointed out that Minister Richards's independent contractor advisor was likely to be at least as expensive as the consultants on KEMH: "Do we really believe that they are going to be able to have an independent contractor advisor for less than $10 million on a $250 million-plus project? . . . It has got an odour to it and it is not an odour that smells like Chanel."

As time went on, increasing numbers of Bermudians became concerned about the project and its implications. It would temporarily produce a few hundred construction jobs for Bermudians, but what was going to happen to the airport's unionized staff? How much money was ultimately at risk? Was CCC-Aecon really the best solution? Were there danger signs in Aecon's falling out with Ecuador's government over a similar deal for the airport in Quito?

Nine years into its thirty-five-year concession to operate Quito International Airport, Aecon sold its 45.5 percent stake to a Colombian construction company and a Brazilian transportation firm and left the scene. Aecon would also be getting a huge stake in our new airport. Bermuda's right of review on a sale would not likely restrict Aecon significantly.

The People's Campaign and PLP MPs kept pressing for answers and proposing alternative project models. The OBA Government kept stonewalling.

In August 2016, the People's Campaign released a 71-page report on the airport deal. With emails and other evidence, the report documented how the OBA Government misrepresented the relationship between CCC and Aecon. It also mapped the negative aspects of the deal for Bermuda's present and future.

During a People's Campaign protest on December 2, 2016, the Bermuda Police Service pepper-sprayed peaceful demonstrators including senior citizens, attempting to enable the OBA Government to enter the House to push the deal along. That was a day of shame for the BPS and OBA. Imagine if the Police had pepper-sprayed and forcibly removed the mostly White anti-Uighurs demonstrators in 2009.

Even after this, the OBA Government withheld important information from the PLP. In January 2017, PLP MPs still awaited full disclosure of the airport deal terms.

To counter the negative publicity, Finance Minister Richards handpicked a panel to assess the deal in February. The panel predictably gave the deal a thumbs-up and refused to conclude that Minister Richards misrepresented Aecon's role in initiating it. The panel acknowledged "valid concerns on the process undertaken and the lack of clarity over the selection of CCC and Aecon." Yet with puzzling logic, it held that "some of the email correspondence which did not put leading players in a favorable light . . . could fairly lead to questions on transparency and process" only "when reviewed outside of the context of the deal." Finally, the panel did not say the CCC-Aecon deal was the best course or the most value for money, the standard my administration's projects have been held to, but only that it was a reasonable deal in the circumstances.

On the evidence available, the Evans Commission's finding "no signs of possible criminal activity" in the airport deal was the right call. But the commission encouraged criminal investigation of PLP projects on no greater grounds. I resent the double standard applied to PLP public works contracts and the OBA Government's. Beyond that, a major national asset was privatized in whole for thirty years and likely in part forever after Aecon's stake goes on the market, not because of objective economic and fiscal prudence, but because of politically biased economic views.

Since the Great Recession hit in 2008, history has shown that the countries that maintained spending to keep their national economies going and keep people employed have fared better, by a significant margin, than those that went all in for austerity, as the Combined Opposition demanded. The PLP responded appropriately and effectively to the global recession's impact on Bermuda. The OBA would have done well to follow our economic principles in the airport deal and thus maintain full Bermudian control of an essential and valuable national asset.

Another disappointing aspect of the airport deal is the terminal design. Builders of new passenger infrastructure around the world know design plays a crucial role in driving passenger satisfaction and volume. The OBA Government refused to consider the cutting-edge design by HNTB, which I mentioned earlier, and Aecon's generic design looks like dozens of midwestern

U.S. and Canadian terminals. It has no flair, nothing that evokes Bermuda visually and experientially.

The design process should have been open and reflective of public feedback. But the OBA–Aecon process remained tightly closed and opaque.

AS FAR AS MY ADMINISTRATION AND PLP GOVERNMENT in general are concerned, what does the Evans Commission's report amount to? The report documents instances of sloppiness and corner-cutting on the part of my administration and civil servants. It shows both PLP Cabinet Ministers and senior civil servants sometimes forgot or disregarded Financial Instructions. Such things occur in democratic governments everywhere. However, the report documents no instances of deliberate malfeasance, self-dealing, or other corruption by my Cabinet or me.

Did PLP Government see more breaches of Financial Instructions or other ethical lapses than UBP Government? To say one way or the other requires comparison of similar contracts in UBP and PLP administrations over a significant span of years. Again, I believe such a comparison would show the PLP, including my administration, advancing beyond the UBP in transparency, accountability, and good governance. UBP administrations didn't operate behind closed doors just to keep out drafts.

If the comparison extended to OBA Government, I suspect the public would see a decline in standards because of the OBA's aggressive use of anti-civil service, anti-labor union, anti-transparency quangos. For example, in June 2016 the OBA Government set up quangos for Bermuda's aircraft and shipping registries. It remains to be seen how these quangos affect Bermuda's income from the registries.

Curiously, Auditor General Heather Jacobs Matthews and her successor, Auditor General Heather Thomas, never questioned a single OBA Government action or expenditure. This was despite questionable matters such as Ministerial expenditures in connection with JetGate's "pay to play" campaign slush fund or the airport deal's being so plagued with ethical and fiduciary issues that the British government helped pay for a report documenting the great number and seriousness of those issues. It is impossible to imagine anything remotely similar happening on a PLP Government project without triggering a special audit and subsequent special report.

This kind of partiality in the Office of the Auditor General calls out for review. So do the shenanigans in Works and Engineering related to the forged checks, other attempts to undermine my administration's handling of public works, and the politically motivated BPS investigations of my administration and me. That many in Bermuda remain unwilling to acknowledge obvious discrepancies in the treatment of PLP and OBA Governments and the apparent UBP/OBA agenda of some civil servants should itself be a topic of national debate.

Regarding the OBA's former incarnation, the UBP, I am glad we made PATI retroactive "back to the *Sea Venture*," as I said when the bill passed. Public-spirited Bermudians should use PATI to cast light on both UBP and OBA Governments and redress the scrutiny deficit they have enjoyed compared to the PLP.

The Combined Opposition to my administration and to me plainly hoped the Evans Commission would find grounds for criminal indictments. On receiving the Commission's report in February 2017, the OBA Government must have been deeply disappointed that it merely echoed the overreaching allegations of Auditors General Dennis and Jacobs Matthews. It wasted taxpayers' money.

IT CAN HARDLY BE A COINCIDENCE THAT on February 14, 2017, the OBA Government filed a civil lawsuit in United States Federal District Court in Massachusetts against the Lahey Clinic, a partner for my Bermuda medical business since the late 1990s. Given the lawsuit's allegations of serious financial wrongdoing, it is telling that neither the federal government nor the state of Massachusetts chose to file criminal changes against the Lahey Clinic, one of the leading health care providers in the United States. Apparently the civil lawsuit was a last-ditch attempt by the OBA Government to tar and feather me by attacking Lahey on shaky grounds.

I'd been expecting a legal attack against my two clinics, Bermuda HealthCare Services (BHCS) and the Brown-Darrell Clinic. The first big warning sign came July 31, 2014, when BHCS's medical director, Dr. Mahesh Reddy, flew to visit family in the United States. A BPS officer questioned him about his travel plans in front of other passengers. In the words of a June 2017 ruling by Bermuda Chief Justice Ian Kawaley, the officer "invited [Dr. Reddy] to contact Detective Sergeant James Hoyte on his return to Bermuda."

Dr. Reddy consulted a lawyer on his return to Bermuda. The lawyer's efforts eventually led to a Police letter to the U.S. consul general in Bermuda saying there were "no concerns regarding Dr. Reddy's travel to any country."

However, on May 8, 2015, Dr. Reddy was again subjected to lengthy public questioning by a BPS officer at L. F. Wade International Airport. Following a protest from Dr. Reddy's lawyer, the Police apologized for "a failure to delete an "old enquiry that was closed," as Chief Justice Kawaley put it.

Was that "old enquiry" really closed? On January 3, 2016, Dr. Reddy was at JFK Airport in New York to fly to Bermuda. A U.S. Department of Homeland Security (DHS) officer interrogated Dr. Reddy in front of other departing passengers about an alleged scheme for unnecessary MRI and CT scans.

To quote again from Chief Justice Kawaley's ruling, which incorporated excerpts from an affidavit by Dr. Reddy, "The agent suggested that Dr. Brown ... had 'orchestrated the alleged fraud and instructed me [Dr. Reddy] to order unneeded diagnostic tests. ... The agent told me that I should provide testimony against Dr. Brown and that if I refused and returned to Bermuda, I would be arrested, jailed and prosecuted there, and then be deported back to my native country of India. The agent also told me there might be adverse consequences for my family in the U.S. if I did not provide testimony against Dr. Brown.'"

Here was the grotesque sequel to Police Commissioner Michael DeSilva's statement four years earlier that U.S. law enforcement was assisting with the investigation into alleged corruption. Dr. Reddy retained American legal counsel, who contacted the DHS officer in question and then met federal prosecutors on February 25 and April 8, 2016. The federal prosecutors asked, Chief Justice Kawaley wrote, about "over-utilisation of MRI and CT scans at BHCS and the Brown-Darrell Clinic, as well as [Dr. Reddy's] medical training and qualifications. [Dr. Reddy's] counsel supplied the prosecutors with documentation including documents relating to [his] medical qualifications. Since the ... April 8, 2016 meeting, no further information was requested of [Dr. Reddy] or his U.S. counsel by the Department of Justice."

The BPS didn't abandon high pressure intimidation. At 7 a.m. on May 19, 2016, a Police squadron led by expatriates Senior Investigator John Briggs (Britain) and Detective Sergeant Hoyte (Barbados) banged on the door of Dr. Reddy's home. Without a warrant, they arrested him, searched the house, and confiscated property including patient records.

Dr. Reddy did not go to the media about the incident, but I did. I said this was the latest politically motivated attempt to discredit me, my clinics never did scans without good medical reason, and the BPS and DPP should "put up or shut up and let us get on with the vital business of helping people with their healthcare needs."

On July 26, 2016, Dr. Reddy sued for wrongful arrest. Under British law, unless the police have compelling reasons, such as flight risk or someone's physical danger, an officer making a lawful summary arrest (without a warrant) must first have reasonable grounds for suspecting a person is guilty of an arrestable offence; have objectively reasonable grounds for suspicion; and consider other options, such as asking the person to report voluntarily for arrest and questioning.

Chief Justice Kawaley wrote that Dr. Reddy's suit hinged on the "third precondition for a valid arrest: validly exercising the discretion to deploy the summary arrest power. . . . Or, to put it more practically, was it necessary for a Police Officer to consider alternative options . . .? This aspect of the power of arrest has never seemingly been formally considered before by a Bermudian court."

The BPS twice tried to have Dr. Reddy's suit thrown out. Chief Justice Kawaley rejected both attempts, dismissing the second on January 24, 2017.

On Saturday afternoon, February 11, 2017, the Police raided BHCS and the Brown-Darrell Clinic. At BHCS they were admitted by one of the staff. However at Brown-Darrell, closed for the weekend, they broke a window rather than wait for someone to arrive to let them in. The Police had a warrant, and by presenting it to my lawyers could have entered without such tactics.

The Police spent around thirty-six hours on the premises of BHCS and the Brown-Darrell Clinic, illegally disabling security cameras in both locations. Thanks to staff watching from outside, we also know the Police spent more than twelve hours in my personal office at Brown-Darrell. They confiscated a large volume of patient records at both clinics.

After a nearly six-year investigation to that date, why the urgent need to search the offices on a weekend, three days before the suit against Lahey was filed?

The OBA Government's civil complaint against Lahey had desperation writ large on every page. Naming me a "non-party conspirator," the complaint claimed Lahey and I "concocted a scheme built upon bribery and greed and carried [it] out with complete disregard for Brown's position of public trust or for the physiological and psychological impact on patients"; Lahey paid me "bribes disguised as consulting fees"; I in turn "paid kickbacks . . . disguised as "commissions" . . . to local [referring] physicians"; and I "ensured that Lahey: received preferential treatment when bidding on healthcare contracts issued by the Bermudian Government; obtained privileged access to Bermudian patients . . .; and made millions of dollars reading and interpreting medically unnecessary MRI and CT scans performed at Brown's clinics."

Lahey and I made money—by delivering medically appropriate, top-quality care at reasonable cost. Lahey never received unfair advantage on Government contracts through me. There were never commissions or "kickbacks" for referrals.

Through a Massachusetts public relations firm, Attorney General Moniz issued a statement treating my guilt as a fact rather than an allegation. In Bermuda this statement would have placed him in contempt of court. Although the American legal system allows more leeway, Attorney General Moniz's comments effectively prejudiced any criminal action against me in Bermuda, denying me the constitutional right to being presumed innocent unless proven otherwise in court.

The Attorney General stated, "Bermudians . . . have been denied honest competition for healthcare services and forced to pay millions of dollars in increased healthcare costs. They have also been subject to the costs and health risks of medically unnecessary CT and MRI scans, which have nearly doubled in number since the start of Lahey's arrangement. Indeed, Bermuda is now among the highest in users of MRI and CT scans in the world and the cost of healthcare per person is also among the highest globally."

Bermuda had high healthcare costs per person before my clinics partnered with Lahey in 1996, two years before the PLP won an election to form the Government and ten years before I became Premier. Since 1996, Lahey has become the main tertiary care provider for patients from KEMH, which also sends patients to Massachusetts General Hospital and Brigham and Women's Hospital in Boston and Johns Hopkins Hospital in Baltimore. Lahey's fees are competitive with the other hospitals.

Responding to a motion by Lahey in the civil suit, a counter motion from the OBA Government's Massachusetts law firm said Lahey and I had "a secret pact." My relationship with Lahey was never a secret. The signs outside BHCS highlighted the expertise of "Lahey Physicians." Our letterhead said, "Affiliate of Lahey Hospital."

As for CT and MRI scan rates, Bermuda has one of the highest incidences of disease in the world. Bermuda is rampant with diabetes, heart disease, and prostate cancer, among other illnesses, and has a major problem with obesity. Bermuda also has one of the highest incomes per capita in the world. When I returned home in the early 1990s, I was appalled to find that healthcare available to the poorest residents of Los Angeles was out of reach for most Bermudians. Bermuda lacked mammography and specialists in rheumatology, neurology, and pulmonary medicine. Patients were having amputations when they needed vascular surgery. People were told nothing could be done for them, which meant Bermuda's insurance providers did not want to spend money for care to preserve life and limb.

As soon as I established BHCS, I wanted to forge a link with a top U.S. hospital like Lahey. That became possible when I met a Lahey doctor at an allergy conference in 1996. From the start the link with Lahey saved money, time, and worry for patients and improved care. Bringing Lahey specialists to Bermuda saved Bermudian insurers millions of dollars in reimbursable travel expenses. And thousands of patients who could not be treated adequately in Bermuda received world-class care at Lahey's facilities in Massachusetts—at competitive, reasonable costs.

BHCS and Brown-Darrell have always ordered and performed CT and MRI scans following American College of Radiology standards. We do scans for charges lower than those common in the United States. And we have cut the anxious wait for results from weeks for KEMH scans to one day for scans interpreted by Lahey's expert radiologists. With Lahey, my clinics raised the standard of healthcare in Bermuda. Honest competition forced KEMH to improve in relation to a higher standard. As Premier, I worked to help KEMH meet the challenge.

As for CT and MRI scans, the more prosperous a society, the more its people utilize advanced medical technology—if they have equitable access to it. CT and MRI scan rates have risen dramatically in every developed economy in the past decade.

Which healthcare provider has contributed the most to Bermuda's increased scan rates? BHCS and Brown-Darrell do about 2,400 CT and MRI scans a year. KEMH does about 22,000. That means my clinics do just under 10 percent of the scans, and KEMH does just over 90 percent—at higher fees than my clinics charge. I was always good at math, but it escapes me how my clinics' 9.8 percent can be more responsible for increased scan rates in Bermuda than KEMH's 90.2 percent. As I mentioned, when KEMH's MRI machine was out of commission in early 2016, BHCS picked up the slack and ensured hospital patients got the diagnostics they needed.

The OBA Government complaint against Lahey compared CT and MRI scans between Bermuda and the Cayman Islands because of their similar population levels. But Cayman has much lower average per capita income, and the wealth of a country, not the size of its population, drives its use of medical technology. Bermuda's use of CT and MRI scans is in the same range per thousand people as similar high-income countries, but far below that of the United States, with whom it shares more similar demographics in the Black community.

Given our extremely high rate of traffic injuries and the proportion of our population who are aging and sickly, Bermuda could justifiably have even higher CT and MRI scan rates. The OBA Government apparently wanted to eliminate my business and return Bermuda to the time when most of its Black population received substandard care, far below the level of its White population.

Good healthcare is expensive, and costs must be managed carefully. However, the cost of healthcare also contributes to the economy as an investment in productivity and wealth creation. Sick people aren't as efficient, productive, entrepreneurial, and innovative as healthy people.

Although Bermudian physicians such as the late Dr. John Stubbs occasionally brought British specialists to the Island to treat patients, these were ad hoc arrangements with individual doctors, not a formal link with a world-class medical center. Following the model of my clinics' link with Lahey, KEMH formed partnerships with Johns Hopkins Hospital, Boston's Partners

Healthcare System (Brigham & Women's Hospital, the Dana Farber Institute, Massachusetts General Hospital, and Spaulding Rehabilitation)—and the Lahey Clinic.

One of the best medical centers in the United States, Lahey noted that the OBA Government's civil suit made it "a pawn in an intense partisan political battle" in an election year, and that it delivers "the highest quality care . . . at a lower cost than other international healthcare providers." Together, the BPS and the OBA Government trampled on my patients' privacy rights in a desperate attempt to show results after years of investigation and discredit the PLP by association with me.

In July 2016 the BPS reported spending $2.2 million investigating me. The Evans Commission cost $1 million. And the OBA Government's legal and public relations fees for the Lahey suit, which Attorney General Moniz at first refused to disclose, were around $500,000 in spring 2017. In summer 2019 the total cost of investigating my medical business and me was around $7 million—for a politically driven vendetta!

The civil complaint against Lahey may have violated U.S. law. To quote from my lawyers' letters of March 9, 2017, to Commissioner DeSilva and Attorney General Moniz, it is "difficult to believe that the Complaint could have been prepared without the benefit of material and information gathered during the course of the ongoing criminal investigation into our client." Any material the BPS obtained through American law enforcement required the consent of the U.S. government and a U.S. court order for use in a civil case. There is no indication of either to date.

The Bermuda Constitution prohibits communication about criminal investigations between the Office of the Attorney General and the Police/DPP. The Constitution explicitly bars the Attorney General from involvement in criminal investigations or prosecutions. If information in the civil complaint against Lahey came from Police files, Attorney General Moniz violated the Constitution and abused the powers of his office for partisan political advantage.

A week after my lawyers' letters, Independent MP and former OBA Tourism and Transport Minister Shawn Crockwell said the Evans Commission reported "nothing new." He added that its nearly all-White membership "heightened . . . tension . . . and . . . polarization in our community along racial lines." Referring to the civil servants the Commission criticized, leaving "dark clouds hanging over their heads," he concluded, "Enough is enough. If someone has evidence, bring it and lay it. One has to question whether this was a political exercise."

That same day, former OBA Attorney General Mark Pettingill resigned from the OBA and said he would sit in the House as an Independent until the next election. Echoing Shawn Crockwell's statements on resigning from the OBA a year earlier, Mark Pettingill said the OBA had become "UBP-centric."

At the end of March, a *Royal Gazette* poll showed 55 percent of Bermudians agreed the investigations of the PLP and me were "politically motivated." In May, ten present and former MPs, including some I'd been at odds with politically, joined me in a "friend of the court" brief on the OBA Government suit against Lahey. The other signers were former Premier Alex Scott, former UBP Opposition Leader and current PLP member Kim Swan, Independent MPs Shawn Crockwell and Mark Pettingill, and PLP MPs David Burt, Zane DeSilva, Wayne Furbert (another former UBP Leader), Walter Roban, Michael Scott, and Kim Wilson. I am forever grateful to each of the signers for standing tall and publicly avowing what we all knew to be true. As former Health Ministers, Wayne Furbert, Walter Roban, Michael Scott, and Kim Wilson hand firsthand knowledge of Lahey's role in providing great medical care for Bermudians.

The friend of the court brief addressed the OBA Government's claim that Lahey and I had "a secret pact," which I "affirmatively concealed." The brief stated that in July 1998, when Wayne Furbert was UBP Health Minister, "the [UBP] Government at the time was aware of and had no issue with Dr. Brown's relationship with Lahey" and "the public at large" also knew about it.

Mark Pettingill attested to its long being public knowledge because that was how he knew to ask for my help in getting a family member treated at Lahey. Shawn Crockwell and Mark Pettingill's new law firm was representing a patient whose medical records were seized in the Police raids. However, they gained no legal or financial advantage from signing the brief.

On June 23, 2017, Chief Justice Ian Kawaley ruled completely in favor of Dr. Reddy. Chief Justice Kawaley threw out Dr. Reddy's arrest and ordered the property confiscated at his house returned.

One of Chief Justice Kawaley's remarks is particularly telling. He wrote, "Bermuda has a free enterprise economy and making what may appear to Police Officers to be eye-watering amounts of money through professional activities and investing it overseas is not a crime."

The belief that I am corrupt divides pretty much along party lines in Bermuda. It also accords with a belief in White superiority—in Black and White minds. Again, my own mother and my aunt Gloria believed the White person's ice is colder. The most insidious, deeply rooted impact of slavery and post-slavery racism is many Black people's belief that they really are inferior in some way. If significant numbers of Black Bermudians did not harbor such beliefs and fears, parties like the UBP and OBA could never win an election.

THE OBA GOVERNMENT ADOPTED A TOURISM AGENDA with event-based marketing and casino gambling. On December 2, 2014, it giddily announced Bermuda as the venue for the America's Cup in June 2017. Its Casino Gaming Act 2014, authorizing up to three casino licenses, passed the House and Senate respectively on December 13 and 17, 2014, without opposition, including from the PLP.

The Combined Opposition repeatedly said the PLP spent too much on tourism events, although it quieted down about the PGA Grand Slam of Golf when its success became obvious. In hindsight, the combined investment was modest compared to the OBA's roll of the dice on the America's Cup.

The OBA Government and its supporters maintained a steady drumbeat of self-congratulation on the America's Cup. Yet the television coverage had disappointing ratings and showed little of Bermuda because the cameras were almost exclusively on the racing boats in the water. Although the big hotels were pretty well booked, they had many empty rooms because the America's Cup teams took whole floors. The actual number of tourists who came to Bermuda for the races was much lower than the OBA forecast. After all, the global luxury tourism market includes many more recreational golfers than sailors.

The lopsided victory by Emirates Team New Zealand took the America's Cup to Auckland and left Bermuda high and dry. The *Royal Gazette* might write hopefully about hosting another big yacht race, but there is nothing in the same league as the America's Cup.

The OBA Government said in summer 2017 it had spent $77 million on the America's Cup. I suspect the total price tag ultimately reached over $100 million. Four-time America's Cup winner Dennis Conner rated the event "an economic disaster for Bermuda."

Bermuda tourism still needs exciting new hotels. The Morgan's Point developers, led by insurance/reinsurance magnate Brian Duperreault, blamed me for their inability to build a hotel. In March 2016, five and a half years after I left office, Morgan's Point still had no hotel, and OBA Finance Minister Bob Richards gave them a loan guarantee of up to $165 million. America's Cup expectation finally got ground broken at Morgan's Point, but the work soon halted despite the loan guarantee. Eventually the project collapsed, leaving Bermuda's taxpayers on the hook for the $165 million guarantee plus interest. As I write, it is now fall 2019, nine years since I left office, and there is still no hotel on Morgan's Point.

On the eve of the 2017 America's Cup, Premier Dunkley faced a no-confidence vote brought by new PLP Leader David Burt, succeeding Marc Bean on his retirement from politics the previous November. (PLP candidate Neville Tyrrell won the by-election to replace Marc Bean in my old House seat.) The resignations of Shawn Crockwell and Mark Pettingill had erased the OBA's two-seat majority in the House, and on June 8 Premier Dunkley called an election for July 18.

Tragically, Shawn Crockwell was found dead at his home on June 10. Had he lived, I believe he would eventually have followed the other progressive Black members of the UBP/OBA—Gwyneth Rawlins, Jamahl Simmons, Wayne Furbert, Maxwell Burgess, Darius Tucker, and Kim Swan—and joined the PLP. Shawn's death saddened me greatly because of my genuine affection for him in spite of our political differences.

The next day was the eighth anniversary of the Uighurs' finding asylum in Bermuda, and I granted the *Royal Gazette*'s request for an interview, which it published on June 14. The interview ran with a companion article, "After eight years, secrecy still shrouds the case," reporting the scant results of the newspaper's PATI request for Bermuda Government documentation on the Uighurs.

An eighth anniversary is not usually considered special, and I can only think the *Royal Gazette* requested the interview hoping it might help the OBA. The headline and tone of the companion article suggested dark secrets kept from the public. However, the small number of documents in Government files did not mean the public was denied important facts. As I explained in the interview, there was little documentation—a handful of Department of Immigration records—because David Burch, the Minister responsible for immigration, and I spoke directly to the U.S. officials involved and committed little to paper. We did this to preserve secrecy and prevent leaks until the Uighurs reached Bermuda. At that point I openly declared what had happened and why the Uighurs received asylum.

I had no qualms about the interview's timing. I was confident most Bermudians had accepted the Uighurs as law-abiding, hard-working residents and would not punish the PLP by not voting or voting for the OBA. I also remained proud of giving four innocent men a measure of justice after years of wrongful imprisonment. I told the newspaper it remained up to the British government to complete the loop of justice for the Uighurs and grant them passports, so they could travel freely and were no longer officially stateless. The British finally came through in August 2018.

AS THE RETURNS CAME IN ON THE JULY 18, 2017, general election, a landslide victory for the PLP—24 House seats to the OBA's 12—became apparent. I felt enormous pride and satisfaction. Over the previous eight months, David Burt had led from the front on the floor of the House, and the PLP collectively bested the OBA Government in debate on a consistent basis. During the campaign David also led from the front, proving his mettle as a parliamentary leader in the most fundamental way by winning a general election, something neither of his predecesssors Paula Cox nor Michael Dunkley has achieved.

It was gratifying to see the resounding victories of David Burch (his first win of a House seat), Derrick Burgess, Zane DeSilva, Walter Roban, Michael Scott, Kim Wilson, Wayne Caines, Rolfe Commissiong, and Jamahl Simmons. They all worked in my administration. I was proud to see the light of the PLP torch shine vibrantly.

The most remarkable constituency result was PLP candidate Christopher Famous's large win over OBA Deputy Premier and Finance Minister Bob Richards, who immediately announced his retirement from politics. Bermuda had grown sick and tired of Finance Minister Richards's unnecessarily harsh austerity policies, which savaged the middle class on down, leaving the rich unscathed. Public dissatisfaction with his airport terminal deal also contributed significantly to his defeat.

OBA Premier Michael Dunkley and OBA Cabinet Ministers Grant Gibbons, Patricia Gordon-Pamplin, and Trevor Moniz retained their safe White-voter-dominated seats, as did first OBA Premier Craig Cannonier. Acknowledging his party's crushing loss, Premier Dunkley voiced the OBA claim that its policies and Finance Minister Richards had brought Bermuda "out of the economic abyss."

The *Royal Gazette*, returning to its Combined Opposition role after four-and-one-half years as OBA Government cheerleader, echoed him in an editorial, "The people have spoken": "It is not too often that a political party can leave the public purse in such a state of disrepair and then return to government at the first time of asking."

No objective observer would say Bermuda fell into an economic abyss under PLP Government, and I challenge the Combined Opposition to find a leading economist of international stature who believes it did. Bermuda has suffered economically since the Great Recession, but it has fared far better than most of the world. Most of the damage its people have experienced resulted from OBA austerity policies.

Bermuda's international business sector has chugged along, thanks to good relations with the United States. At the end of 2013, the OBA Government got the USA–Bermuda Tax Convention Amendment Act 2013 through the House and Senate. No surprise, as the bill had complete bipartisan support.

On March 18, 2018, U.S. District Judge Indira Talwani dismissed the Lahey lawsuit. In the words of Attorney General and Legal Affairs Minister Kathy Lightbourne Simmons, "[T]he result is what I had anticipated from the beginning."

The election of a PLP Government in 2017 brightened Bermuda's immediate future. Yet the road ahead remains full of pitfalls from the past. Progress to full racial equality continues to be opposed and undermined by a White economic power structure. Legitimate points of difference will always arise between rival political parties. But Bermuda cannot meet its long-term challenges, while the Combined Opposition demonizes the PLP and refuses to acknowledge that it can govern the country responsibly. In this regard, although the *Royal Gazette* made Black Bermudian Dexter Smith its editor in 2015, its editorial slant still follows the regressive agenda of its White owners.

To thrive in the future, Bermuda cannot forget the past. Racism remains the fundamental fact of Bermuda's political life, and Bermudians must find common ground to address it. I hope and pray we will.

Epilogue: "To Thine Own Self Be True"

T HE LONGER I LIVE, THE MORE I CHERISH my mother's frequent quotation of Shakespeare's famous lines, "To thine own self be true, / And it must follow, as the night the day,/ Thou canst not then be false to any man." I hear the words themselves and the lilt in my mother's voice as she said them, and I am glad to have grown up in the household she and my father led together with their fundamental integrity and upright character triumphing over their inevitable human imperfections.

I draw on the strength and grace of their joint example every day. It motivates my efforts to help Kevin and Maurice get their lives on track and to help Trey and Donovan build on their good starts in life. It complements the equally extraordinary strength and grace I find in my marriage to Wanda. And it inspires me to continue to be a voice for progressive change in Bermuda.

I count myself lucky to have been able to give back to Bermuda in the spirit of my parents; my maternal aunt Gloria and her husband, Dr. Bert McPhee; and other beloved family elders. A host of initiatives that the Combined Opposition scorned and fought to undermine at every turn—from fast ferries to Mirrors and FutureCare—have become indispensable parts of Bermuda's societal and material infrastructure, and I believe history will judge them positively.

This book has shown that my relationships with my two older sons started out complicated, but I am grateful for the mutual affection, respect, and concern we now share. Kevin will hopefully complete his sentence in a California prison soon. In the meantime I enjoy my relationship with his children, Caleb and Kira. Caleb was on a football scholarship at Hampton University and Kira was starting her first year at Spelman College as I finished this book. They are fine young people with great futures.

Maurice completed his sentence in California at a halfway house in Louisiana in 2015. Maurice and I have agreed that as he approaches forty years of age, he is too old to be guided by me and must do things his way. I will support him in any way I can, but I will no longer try to be the architect of his course in life. He has recently brought me great delight by giving me a beautiful granddaughter, Kesi.

Trey and Donovan are both in California and doing well. Trey, who graduated from Howard University in 2011, is working for an artificial intelligence company and is thrilled with that new endeavor. Donovan, who graduated from Howard in 2013, is a young social media and marketing executive and building a music career on the side. It gives me great joy to see them progressing on their chosen paths and to have their love and support.

My marriage to Wanda was truly a case of third time lucky. Despite all the vicious, baseless attacks on our reputations, our bond of love and respect remains solid as a rock. Without her constant support and her daily gifts of affection, insight, humor, and joy, my life would be impoverished. She is amazing!

It is a privilege and pleasure to be part of the Henton clan through Wanda. Life brings losses to every family over time. Her sister Shirley Henton Larkin, "Tiny" to family and friends, died without warning of an aneurysm at age sixty-four on Wanda's birthday, December 6, 2012. It was a crippling blow to the woman I love. Wanda tells me that I carried her through that horrible time.

Little did we know that almost a year to the day later, and equally unexpectedly, Wanda would be faced with losing the bedrock of her life and a man I had come to cherish, her father, Mack. On December 2, 2013, we were called to rush to Louisiana. Mack had experienced a serious reaction to medication after a brief stomach disorder. It was fortunate that we got there in time for Wanda to be at her father's bedside as he passed away early the next morning, December 3, at the age of ninety-four.

This blow so soon after the death of her sister Tiny knocked Wanda down emotionally as low as I ever saw her. All I could do was show her some semblance of the love, support, and total commitment she has given me through the years. I refused to leave her side for many days until she was ready to again go out by herself.

Wanda and I came through that experience determined to carry on some of the traditions of Mack and Van Henton. While we can never fill their shoes and be the beacon they were to their offspring and succeeding generations, we do all we can to lessen the vacuum they left. With the help of nephew Reginald and brother-in-law Burnell, Deloris's husband, we maintain the family homestead in Alexandria, Louisiana. Every Thanksgiving and Christmas we go there to be the last stop for the kids, grandkids, great-grandkids, and now great-great-grandkids. As Mack and Van did for so many years, we tell our stories and hear theirs. I sit in Mack's chair—not as a former Premier but as Uncle Ewart. I love it!

I cannot finish this book without highlighting my own extended family and their astounding support throughout my various ordeals. My sister, Emelita, who still lives in Los Angeles, has been a pillar of strength. She and her husband, Gary Johnson, are very close to Wanda and me. Emelita's daughter, Kimberly, and her son, Kyle, have been sources of great pride to all of us. Kimberly now works as a clinical psychologist in the Washington, D.C., area, while Kyle is a computer whiz who works for the rich and famous in Los Angeles.

My brothers, Philip Butterfield and Vincent Hollinsid, add immeasurably to our family. For people who never came together until the 1990s, Emelita, Phil, Vincent, and I have a miraculous chemistry. Unfortunately, Vincent lost both of his sons to accidents, as I mentioned, but he was Bermuda's best fire chief and after modernizing the Island's fire and rescue service is enjoying an active retirement. Phil, whose business and philanthropic contributions to Bermuda I have mentioned several times, without ever capturing them all; his wife, Roz; and their daughters, Vernée and Charlene, have been sweet and kind at every twist and turn of our shared journey. Charlene has followed her father into the business world and is an analyst at Standard and Poor's, and Vernée recently completed a Ph.D. in educational psychology and works in that field.

How did this miracle happen? How did Emelita, Phil, Vincent, and I end up as such a close-knit and fearless group? You would have had to know our father, D. A., to understand fully. What we have done and continue to do today is directly related to his uncanny blend of charm, wit, and persistence. I credit my father for my willingness to fight relentlessly for what I think is right. He used to tell me, "You're very lucky. Your mother represents the tea and crumpets set, and I represent the streets." Every passing day shows me how right he was, and how both my parents' legacies have made me who I am.

I credit the Bible's teachings for giving me the determination to say no to those who would destroy me. I end with the Scripture (Psalms 27) I quoted in the epigraph: "The Lord is my light and my salvation; whom shall I fear? The Lord is the strength of my life; of whom shall I be afraid? When the wicked, even mine enemies and foes, came upon me to eat up my flesh, they stumbled and fell."

The words of the Bible and Shakespeare's "To thine own self be true"— these are the words I have always tried to live by, and I will continue to do so to the end of my days. This book is my testament to that effort, and I hope it will also serve Bermudians as a guide to our country's true history through perilous, yet ultimately positive events.

Acknowledgments

I could not have written this book without the help of many people. My siblings Emelita Johnson, Philip Butterfield, and Vincent Hollinsid, my cousins LaVerne Furbert and Calvin Smith, and my uncle Dr. Bert McPhee all shared their recollections and perspectives with me. They each enriched my understanding of our extended family's experiences in Bermuda over the generations, and their wholehearted support and encouragement sustained me in my writing.

My sons Kevin Brown, Maurice Pitt, Trey Brown, and Donovan Brown also generously shared their recollections and unvarnished perspectives. They gave me fresh insights into my relationships with each of them. I will always be grateful for their positive interest and encouragement as I worked on the book.

Several friends, colleagues, and associates also gave me the benefit of their recollections and perspectives. Thanks to Derrick Burgess, Wayne Caines, Zane DeSilva, Wendell Hollis, Jim Howes, Jamahl Simmons, Kim Swan, Marc Telemaque, and Dennis Wainwright for the information and insights they contributed. Gary Phillips and LaVerne Furbert read the manuscript and gave me valuable feedback on it, as did Wendell Hollis and Marc Telemaque. I am grateful to all of them for their efforts on the book's behalf.

Michelle Dismont-Frazzoni of the Bermuda Department of Communications, Dexter Smith and Akil J. Simmons of the *Royal Gazette*, Howard University librarian Lopez D. Matthews, and Kimberley Jackson of the Mirrors Program greatly assisted me in identifying and assembling the book's illustrations, as did my sister, Emelita, LaVerne Furbert, Kelley McKinney, Jamahl Simmons, Joe Simons, and Lovette Brangman. Shernette Wolffe, Clerk to the Legislature in the Bermuda Parliament, helped me document key events in the House of Assembly. I am grateful to all of them.

Dr. Mahesh Reddy, my dear friend and the medical director of my clinics, has contributed immeasurably to the growth of the clinics, allowing me the time to serve in Bermuda as a Member of Parliament, Cabinet Minister, Deputy Premier, and Premier. Thanks to all the management and staff of Bermuda HealthCare Services, the Brown-Darrell Clinic, and the Bermuda Urology Clinic for all they do. Thanks to the clinics' patients for their loyalty, support, and prayers over the years.

For giving me the unbridled innocence of my youth, I will always be indebted to Flatts Village.

Jamaica, particularly St. Jago High School and Spanish Town, gave me the medicine and spirituality to cure my wayward adolescent ways and teach me id control, which substantially shaped me as a person.

Howard University—my beloved Howard!—gave me the freedom to be a young BLACK man and taught me well beyond the instruction needed for my bachelor's and medical degrees. Thanks to a great university for enhancing my intelligence, validating my Blackness, strengthening my resolve, and maturing me as a man.

Thanks to the communities of my adult life, where family and close friends abound, providing bastions of love, goodwill, and unwavering support: Martha's Vineyard, Massachusetts; Turks and Caicos; Los Angeles, California; and Alexandria, Louisiana.

Thanks to Hilary Hinzmann for his expert editorial services throughout the book's development. At Rivertowns Books, editor and publisher Karl Weber also provided insightful editing. In addition Karl personally designed the book's interior layout and astutely shepherded the book into print. I am also grateful to Alice Levine for her copy editing and to Glenn Blakeney for his contributions to the book's marketing and publicity.

In this book as in everything since our marriage, my wife, Wanda Henton Brown, has been my indispensable partner. Whenever the process bogged down for one reason or another, Wanda urged me to carry on. Time and again she suggested effective solutions to roadblocks along the way, and she gave me unerring feedback on every aspect of the manuscript. To say this book would not exist without her daily help and support would be an understatement. Thank you, Wanda, for being the wind beneath my wings.

Finally, where I would I be without Bermuda's Progressive Labour Party (PLP)? Thank you, PLP, for the love, patience, confidence, and support throughout the years. Thank you for being the anchor that has held me steadfast "in spite of it all." Without you, I "never would have made it. I'm stronger, wiser, and better, much better. When I look back over all you have brought me through, I can see that God, through you, was the one I held onto."

I humbly thank you, PLP, for the opportunity to serve as a Member of Parliament from 1993 to 2010 and as Party Leader from 2006 to 2010. I give special thanks to the late PLP Party Leader, L. Frederick Wade, JP, MP, for bringing me home at the right time to enter politics; to my Warwick constituency; and to my esteemed predecessors: Dame Jennifer Smith, DBE, JP, DHumL, and Honourable W. Alex Scott, CBE, JP. I also specially thank and acknowledge our PLP Party Leader and Bermuda's current premier, Honourable E. David Burt, JP, MP.

My eternal gratitude is extended to all the people of Bermuda for the honour of serving as Premier from 2006 to 2010.

Ewart F. Brown, M.D.
September, 2019

Terms, Abbreviations, and Acronyms

BEC	Bermuda Emissions Control
BFS	Bermuda Fire Service
BHB	Bermuda Hospitals Board
BHC	Bermuda Housing Corporation
BHCS	Bermuda HealthCare Services
BIU	Bermuda Industrial Union (formerly Bermuda Workers Assocation, BWA)
BLDC	Bermuda Land Development Company
BPS	Bermuda Police Service, the Police
BPSU	Bermuda Public Services Union
BTOA	Bermuda Taxi Operators Association
BUT	Bermuda Union of Teachers
BWA	Bermuda Workers Association
Caricom	Caribbean Community
DPP	Director of Public Prosecutions
FCO	Foreign and Commonwealth Office, UK; also Foreign Office (FO)
HIAB	Health Insurance Association of Bermuda
ICAO	International Civil Aviation Organization
KEMH	King Edward VII Memorial Hospital
MP	Member of Parliament
MWI	Mid-Atlantic Wellness Institute (formerly St. Brendan's Hospital)
OAS	Organization of American States
OBA	One Bermuda Alliance
OECD	Organization for Economic Cooperation and Development
OT	Overseas Territory, UK

OTCC	Overseas Territory Consultative Council
PATI	Public Access to Information Act 2010
PLP	Progressive Labour Party
TCD	Transport Control Department
TIEA	Tax Information Exchange Agreement
UAH	Union Asset Holdings
UBP	United Bermuda Party
Wedco	West End Development Corporation

Index

About the Author

EWART FREDERICK BROWN WAS BORN IN BERMUDA IN 1946. He attended primary and secondary schools in Bermuda before going to Jamaica, where he was an outstanding student-athlete at St. Jago High School in Spanish Town. In 1966 he represented Bermuda at the Commonwealth Games in Kingston, Jamaica, where he ran the 440 yard sprint and mile relay.

Brown attended Howard University in Washington, D.C., where he served as president of the Howard University Student Association and captained the track team. After graduating from Howard with a B.Sc. degree in chemistry, he received his M.D. from Howard University College of Medicine. He also earned an M.P.H., with an emphasis on child health, maternal family population control, and international health from the University of California at Los Angeles. He is a certified Diplomate of the American Board of Family Practice and the American Board of Quality Assurance and Utilization Review Physicians.

Dr. Brown has served as a trustee of both Howard University and Charles R. Drew University of Medicine and Science; assistant professor in the Department of Family Practice at Charles R. Drew University of Medicine and Science; director, Marcus Garvey School in Los Angeles, California; and vice president of the Union of American Physicians and Dentists (California Federation).

He is a former member of the California State Commission on Maternal, Child and Adolescent Health, a former director of Marina Hills Hospital in Los Angeles, and a founding commissioner of the Board of Prevention Commissioners for South Central Los Angeles Regional Center for Persons with Developmental Disabilities. He was also a founder and chairman of the board of directors of Western Park Hospital in Los Angeles.

After working as a physician in Los Angeles for many years, he returned home to Bermuda, where he served as a Member of Parliament from 1993 to 2010, Deputy Premier from 2003 to 2006, and Premier from 2006 to 2010.

Dr. Brown is the recipient of many awards including the Physicians Recognition Award from the American Medical Association; the Grassroots Health Award from the Sons of Watts, California; the Community Leadership Award of the Dubois Academic Institute; the Pacesetter Award of the NAACP; the Humanitarian of the Year Award from Marcus Garvey School in Los Angeles; the Scroll Award of the Union of American Physicians and Dentists; and the Scroll of Merit Award from the National Medical Association. He received an Honorary Doctorate of Laws from Howard University in 2009, when he also delivered the 142nd Opening Convocation Address.

He is married to Wanda Henton Brown, and he has four sons: Kevin, Maurice, Ewart III, and Donovan; and three grandchildren: Caleb, Kira, and Kesi.